W9-CIK-511

NEW ANALYSES OF WORKER WELL-BEING

RESEARCH IN LABOR ECONOMICS

Series Editor: Solomon W. Polachek

IZA Co-Editor: Konstantinos Tatsiramos

Volume 28: Work Earnings and Other Aspects of the Employment Relation
Edited by Solomon W. Polachek and Konstantinos Tatsiramos

Volume 29: Ethnicity and Labor Market Outcomes
Edited by Amelie F. Constant, Konstantinos Tatsiramos and Klaus F. Zimmermann

Volume 30: Jobs, Training, and Worker Well-Being
Edited by Solomon W. Polachek and Konstantinos Tatsiramos

Volume 31: Child Labor and the Transition Between School and Work
Edited by Randall K. Q. Akee, Eric V. Edmonds and Konstantinos Tatsiramos

Volume 32: Who Loses in the Downturn? Economic Crisis, Employment and Income Distribution
Edited by Herwig Immervoll, Andreas Peichl and Konstantinos Tatsiramos

Volume 33: Research in Labor Economics
Edited by Solomon W. Polachek and Konstantinos Tatsiramos

Volume 34: Informal Employment in Emerging and Transition Economies
Edited by Hartmut Lehmann and Konstantinos Tatsiramos

Volume 35: 35th Anniversary Retrospective
Edited by Solomon W. Polachek and Konstantinos Tatsiramos

Volume 36: Research in Labor Economics
Edited by Solomon W. Polachek and Konstantinos Tatsiramos

Volume 37: Labor Market Issues in China
Edited by Corrado Giulietti, Konstantinos Tatsiramos and Klaus F. Zimmermann

RESEARCH IN LABOR ECONOMICS VOLUME 38

NEW ANALYSES OF WORKER WELL-BEING

EDITED BY

SOLOMON W. POLACHEK
Department of Economics, State University of New York at Binghamton and IZA

KONSTANTINOS TATSIRAMOS
School of Economics, University of Leicester and IZA

United Kingdom – North America – Japan
India – Malaysia – China

Emerald Group Publishing Limited
Howard House, Wagon Lane, Bingley BD16 1WA, UK

First edition 2013

British Library Cataloguing in Publication Data
A catalogue record for this book is available from the British Library

ISBN: 978-1-78350-056-7
ISSN: 0147-9121 (Series)

CONTENTS

LIST OF CONTRIBUTORS

Ernesto Aguayo-Tellez	Facultad de Economia, Universidad Autónoma de Nuevo León, Monterrey, Mexico
Jim Airola	Department of Economics, Santa Clara University, Santa Clara; Monterey Institute of International Studies, Monterey, CA, USA
Laura Arranz-Aperte	Autonoma University of Madrid, Spain; Hanken School of Economics and BA, Helsinki, Finland
Timothy J. Bartik	W.E. Upjohn Institute for Employment Research, Kalamazoo, MI, USA
Kenneth A. Couch	Department of Economics, University of Connecticut, Storrs, CT, USA
Nikolaos Georgantzis	Agriculture Policy and Development, University of Reading, Reading, UK; Economics Department, Universitat Jaume I – Laboratorio de Economía Experimental, Castellón, Spain
Marco Guerrazzi	Department of Economics, University of Genoa, Genoa, Italy
Howard M. Iams	Social Security Administration, Office of Research, Evaluation, and Statistics, Washington, DC, USA
Chinhui Juhn	Department of Economics, University of Houston, Houston, TX, USA

Marta Lachowska W.E. Upjohn Institute for Employment Research, Kalamazoo, MI, USA; Swedish Institute for Social Research (SOFI), Stockholm University, Stockholm, Sweden

Gayle L. Reznik Social Security Administration, Office of Retirement Policy, Washington, DC, USA

Núria Rodríguez-Planas IZA, Bonn, Germany and IAE-CSIC, Barcelona, Spain

John G. Sessions Department of Economics, University of Bath, Bath, UK

Christopher R. Tamborini Social Security Administration, Office of Retirement Policy, Washington, DC, USA

Nikolaos Theodoropoulos Department of Economics, University of Cyprus, Nicosia, Cyprus

Efi Vasileiou LEMMA University of Panthéon-Assas (Paris 2), Paris, France; Economics Department, Universitat Jaume I – Laboratorio de Economía Experimental, Castellón, Spain

Carolina Villegas-Sanchez Department of Economics, ESADE-Universitat Ramon Llul, Barcelona, Spain

EDITORIAL ADVISORY BOARD

PREFACE

In no economy do all employees earn the same salary. Indeed pay variation is the norm rather than the exception. Some pay variation stems from innate worker heterogeneity, some from differential human capital investment, some from imperfect information, some from industry and occupation specific demand shocks, and some from asymmetric technological change; but there are many other reasons, as well. The ideal level of wage dispersion in any economy is a hotly debated topic. On the one hand, greater wage variation increases incentives to take risk often leading to hard work, innovation, and economic growth. On the other hand, too wide an earnings dispersion possibly instills resentment, perhaps leading workers to decrease cooperation, thus lowering output and stymying growth. At the extreme, too wide a dispersion could lead to political instability and even revolution. This volume contains eight articles, each dealing with an aspect of remuneration. Of these, one articles deals with competition, women's wages and employment, one articles deals with incentives to invest in human capital, four deal with compensation schemes, and finally two with unemployment and earnings.

One component of wage dispersion is the gender wage gap. Clearly government policy can affect what women earn relative to men. Most academic analyses concentrate on equal pay legislation. Few, if any, examine how broader government policies, such as those relating to international trade, affect pay for women. In the first article, Ernesto Aguayo-Tellez, Jim Airola, Chinhui Juhn, and Carolina Villegas-Sanchez examine the effects of NAFTA on the gender wage gap. They argue three forces are at work: First, greater competition, brought about by a free-trade policy, could force efficiency, which decreases a firm's ability to pay men higher wages than equally competent women. Second, industrial shifts might favor women. Third, tariff reductions possibly encourage technology upgrades, again favoring women workers. To test these hypotheses, Aguayo-Tellez, Airola, Juhn, and Villegas-Sanchez decompose the overall increase in female employment and wage bill shares into between and within industry components. They then link these changes to tariff changes across sectors. From this analysis, they find women's relative wages in Mexico increased, employment shifted favoring women, and more women were hired in skilled blue-collar jobs. Thus, NAFTA benefited Mexican women relative to men, and probably narrowed the overall wage distribution in Mexico.

Earnings dispersion is currently rising in the United States and elsewhere. One reason is the rising proportion of students dropping out of high school. A higher dropout rate widens earnings variance nationwide and exacerbates concerns about poverty. Motivating an individual to do better in high school has important ramifications. It raises a person's chances of going to college and succeeding better in the labor market. However, determining the factors that prompt an individual to do better in school has been elusive. In November 2005, anonymous donors promised to pay between 65 and 100 percent of college tuition for any Kalamazoo, Michigan public school student who got into college and maintained a 2.0 average. Obviously, admission to more demanding colleges required students to have better academic performance. In the next article, Timothy J. Bartik and Marta Lachowska report on school performance outcomes emanating from this "Kalamazoo Promise" quasi-experiment. Using difference-in-differences regression techniques, they compare the change in secondary school student outcomes across time. They find significant increases in student performance and a lower number of days students spend in suspension. The results are most notable for African Americans.

Analyzing the impact of earnings dispersion nationwide is difficult because nations are widely heterogeneous and change is slow. However, investigating dispersion on a micro-level can be more manageable and still lead to global implications. In the next article, Laura Arranz-Aperte analyzes how wage dispersion affects worker productivity using plant data for Finland. She postulates two possible effects: First, higher wage dispersion motivates workers to put out more effort in hopes they will be rewarded adequately, thus raising output. Alternatively, too high a wage dispersion reduces comradery, thus decreasing worker cooperation, which results in lower plant productivity. To test the relative strengths of these hypotheses, Arranz-Aperte utilizes 1990–2002 Finnish matched employer–employee data. She finds a significant positive relationship between intra-firm wage dispersion and output (sales per capita). This validates incentive based approaches to enhance productivity rather than fairness-type arguments.

Another method of inducing greater employee productivity is for a firm to steepen the slope of the tenure-wage profile. In the next article, John G. Sessions and Nikolaos Theodoropoulos derived a two-period efficiency wage model in which firms face a trade-off between the level of monitoring and the wage-tenure gradient. Using two cross-sections of matched employer–employee British data with an instrument that exploits variations in monitoring costs across establishments, they find that steeper tenure compensation schemes require less monitoring, thus providing evidence that firms increase output by deferring pay. They conclude that agency considerations are an important driver of the wage-tenure profile.

Sometimes firms are forced to pay more because markets must compensate workers in dangerous jobs. However, a large number of studies have had great difficulties detecting compensating wage differentials. In the next article, Nikolaos Georgantzis and Efi Vasileiou take another approach. Instead of looking simply at monetary aspects, they examine job satisfaction. Holding wage constant, one can conclude that job attributes other than safety cause utility to be equalized, should job satisfaction be comparable between safe and dangerous jobs. Georgantzis and Vasileiou test this proposition. They use a switching regression technique adjusted for selectivity applied to a unique data set on 3,030 workers from France, Greece, the United Kingdom, and the Netherlands. They find that overall job satisfaction is not affected by the wage differential for dangerous jobs. Thus they argue that job attributes other than money might be important in understanding compensating differentials.

Obviously getting workers to be more productive is crucial to becoming a more competitive firm. In a purely theoretical article, Marco Guerrazzi derives a game-theoretic model in a two firm economy. Each firm competes for labor by increasing its wage offers to screen for high-quality workers. He derives three theorems. First, each firm increases its wage offer to follow its competitor. Second, this dynamic leads to a stable equilibrium. Finally, high unemployment equilibria lead to greater levels of effort.

Some unemployment is voluntary. Clearly receiving a wage offer below one's reservation wage induces a person to remain unemployed because one could have accepted, but did not. Crucial to this decision is how one sets his or her reservation wage. In the next article, Núria Rodríguez-Planas examines how employees might signal high productivity by setting reservation wages sufficiently high to lead to longer unemployment spells. In short, she argues that because high productivity workers know they are more likely to be recalled than low-productivity laid-off workers, they so signal their productivity through higher reservation wages. As such they remain unemployed longer. To test this hypothesis, Rodríguez-Planas uses the 1988–2006 Displaced Workers Supplement of the Current Population Survey. She compares the post-displacement earnings of laid-off workers, some of whom may be recalled by their old employer, to workers who lose their jobs due to a plant closure, and therefore cannot be recalled. She finds that for white-collar workers, post-displacement earnings fall less rapidly with layoffs than for plant closings, thus supporting her thesis that high productivity workers signal their productivity through their unemployment duration.

Long-term unemployment can be costly, but these costs are difficult to measure because of endogeneity. If lower quality workers are more prone to layoffs, then lower subsequent wages might be caused by innate lower quality, rather than layoff. Similarly, if poor health induces separations, then poor health might be a cause instead of an effect of job separation. Isolating the effects of long-term unemployment is important to understanding its effects on individuals and the economy. In the next article, Kenneth A. Couch, Gayle L. Reznik, Christopher R. Tamborini, and Howard M. Iams use the 1984 Survey of Income and Program Participation (SIPP) data linked to social security longitudinal earnings, disability, and mortality data to get at the costs of long-term unemployment. They examine changes in earnings, disability benefits, and mortality through the year 2000 for men who experienced prolonged joblessness lasting as long as three years around the time of the 1980–1982 recession, compared to changes for men who were employed during that time period. To get at endogeneity, they contrast these effects for involuntary and voluntary joblessness, as well as for those with and without preexisting health problems. Noteworthy is the magnitude of losses facing the long-term unemployed.

As with past volumes, we aim to focus on important issues and to maintain the highest levels of scholarship. We encourage readers who have prepared manuscripts that meet these stringent standards to submit them to Research in Labor Economics (RLE) via the IZA web site (http://rle.iza.org) for possible inclusion in future volumes. For insightful editorial advice, we thank Joan Brownell Anderson, Rodney J. Andrews, Keith A. Bender, David J. Berri, Petri Böckerman, Sylvie Démurger, Donghun Cho, Polona Domadenik, Robert Fairlie, Shuaizhang Feng, Alfonso Flores-Lagunes, Gaia Garino, John T. Gilles, Xiaodong Gong, Oecon Ola Honningdal Grytten, Björn Gustafsson, Luojia Hu, Mohamed Jellal, Peter Kuhn, Marc P. B. Klemp, Fidan Ana Kurtulus, Håkan Locking, Mauro Mastrogiacomo, Pierre-Carl Michaud, Dongshu Ou, Matloob Piracha, Nancy Qian, Ray Rees, Francois Rycx, Martin Salm, Pia Sophia Schober, Håkan Selin, Judith Scott-Clayton, Xinzheng Shi, Steven Stillman, James X. Sullivan, Laura Turner, Raymundo M. Campos Vazquez, Le Wang, Yaohui Zhao, Jeffrey Zax, Junfu Zhang, Zhong Zhao, and Thomas Zwick.

Solomon W. Polachek
Konstantinos Tatsiramos
Editors

DID TRADE LIBERALIZATION HELP WOMEN? THE CASE OF MEXICO IN THE 1990s

Ernesto Aguayo-Tellez, Jim Airola, Chinhui Juhn and Carolina Villegas-Sanchez

ABSTRACT

With the signing of the North American Free Trade Agreement (NAFTA) in 1994, Mexico entered a bilateral free trade agreement which not only lowered its own tariffs on imports but also lowered tariffs on its exports to the United States. We find that women's relative wage increased, particularly during the period of liberalization. Both between and within-industry shifts also favored female workers. With regards to between-industry shifts, tariff reductions expanded sectors that were initially female intensive. With regards to within-industry shifts, we find a positive association between reductions in export tariffs (U.S. tariffs on Mexican goods) and hiring of women in skilled blue-collar occupations. Finally, we find suggestive evidence that household bargaining power shifted in favor of women. Expenditures shifted from goods associated with male preference, such as men's clothing and tobacco and alcohol,

New Analyses of Worker Well-Being
Research in Labor Economics, Volume 38, 1–35

ISSN: 0147-9121/doi:10.1108/S0147-9121(2013)0000038001

to those associated with female preference such as women's clothing and education.

Keywords: Trade; gender; inequality

JEL classifications: D3; F15; J16

INTRODUCTION

Gender equality, along with ending hunger and poverty, is one of the eight stated goals in the U.N. Millennium Development Goals Report (UN, 2009). Given that many developing countries have adopted trade reforms, an important question is whether trade liberalization policies will further or hinder the goal of gender equality. Furthermore, equity concerns aside, the effect of liberalization policies on gender outcomes may be of interest from the point of view of economic growth since there is now growing evidence that empowering women promotes education and better children's outcomes (Duflo, 2000; Qian, 2008; Thomas, 1990). Quoting from a recent paper by Duflo (2012), "empowerment [of women] can, in other words, accelerate development."

In this paper, we examine the impact of tariff reductions associated with the signing of the North American Free Trade Agreement (NAFTA) on gender outcomes in Mexico. Relative to the existing literature, our paper makes the following contributions. While most papers focus on the gender wage gap, our paper also examines employment as well as wage changes.[1] Using the labor demand approach taken to study U.S. wage inequality (Berman, Bound, & Griliches, 1994; Katz & Murphy, 1992), we decompose the overall increase in female employment and wage bill shares into "between" and "within" industry components, and link these changes to tariff changes across sectors. Finally, ours is the first paper we are aware of that examines household expenditure patterns to assess changes in women's well-being as well as income.

What are some possible theoretical links between trade liberalization policies and gender outcomes? If men and women are imperfect substitutes in production, the labor demand framework that has been used for skill demand can be applied to discuss and quantify relative demand for female workers.[2] In this framework, industries utilize male and female workers in different intensities, and trade liberalization, by affecting the relative size of industries, will generate demand shifts by gender. For this to be an important channel, we should observe substantial labor reallocation toward those sectors that are female-intensive.[3]

Another channel through which trade liberalization policies can affect gender outcomes is through technology. In an effort to explain rising wag inequality within industries as result of trade liberalization, recent theoretical papers in trade have built models with product differentiation, increasing returns, and heterogeneity across firms (Melitz, 2003; Yeaple, 2005). In these models, tariff reductions encourage the more productive firms to enter the export sector. Verhoogen (2008) and Bustos (2011) show that these exporting firms also upgrade quality and technology, thereby increasing the demand for skilled workers. While most of the focus in the literature has been on the impact of technology on skill demand, technology upgrading may also complement female workers by being complementary with cognitive skills and reducing the demand for physical skills.[4] Juhn, Ujhelyi, and Villegas-Sanchez (2012) consider a model where men and women differ in terms of their capacity to perform physically demanding tasks. In their model, the introduction of new technology lowers the need for physical skills thereby benefiting women. They find that firms which upgraded technology also shifted toward hiring more female workers in blue-collar jobs, but not white-collar jobs. To the extent that exports and technology upgrading is an important channel, we should observe shifts toward female labor *within* sectors, and this type of activity should be concentrated in sectors with larger export tariff reductions.

A third channel is through the reduction of discrimination brought about by foreign competition. Building on the insight of Becker (1957), Black and Brainerd (2002) report that U.S. industries which were subject to more competition through trade experienced greater reductions in the gender wage gap.[5] A recent paper by Ederington, Minier, and Troske (2010) find that trade liberalization in Colombia increased employment of women relative to men in blue-collar occupations – a change the authors attribute to increased product market competition and reductions in employer discrimination. This channel suggests that we should observe a systematic relationship between reductions in import tariffs and female wages and hiring. We examine each of these channels in our empirical work.

To summarize our findings, we find that trade liberalization policies improved women's labor market outcomes in Mexico. First, relative wages of women increased even as employment rates increased, and this pattern is particularly pronounced during the trade liberalization period, 1990–2000. In contrast to studies conducted in the United States (Berman et al., 1994) and Mexico in an earlier period (Hanson & Harrison, 1999; Revenga, 1997), we find evidence of substantial labor reallocation across industries, shifting employment toward initially female-intensive sectors. Between-industry shifts, usually thought to be consistent with trade-based explanations, account for up to 40% of the increase in wage bill share of women from 1990 to 2000. Comparing across industries, we find that tariff reductions were positively related to industry growth and concentrated in initially female-intensive industries. We also find evidence that within-industry shifts favored women. Using establishment-level data for the manufacturing sector, we find that larger declines in export tariffs (U.S. tariffs on Mexican goods) are associated with larger increases in wage bill shares of women in skilled blue-collar occupations. This result suggests that the exports and technology channel emphasized in the recent trade literature may be important for explaining gender outcomes as well as skill premiums. We find a much weaker relationship between reductions in *import* tariffs and female wage bill shares, however, suggesting that reductions in discrimination brought about by trade liberalization played a relatively minor role in the Mexican case.

Women's relative earnings increased but are they necessarily better off? We find that household expenditures shifted from goods associated with male preference, such as men's clothing and tobacco and alcohol, to those associated with female preference such as education and women's clothing, suggesting that women's bargaining power within the household improved along with their relative earnings. We recognize, however, that these findings are only suggestive, and many other factors could also potentially explain the aggregate spending patterns we highlight here.

This paper is organized as follows. The second section briefly describes the trade liberalization policies behind the signing of NAFTA. The third section examines aggregate changes in relative wages and employment of women. The fourth section examines between and within industry shifts and their associations with tariff changes. The fifth section reports the results on household expenditure patterns. The sixth section concludes.

MEXICO'S TRADE LIBERALIZATION UNDER NAFTA

Mexico implemented unilateral tariff reductions in the 1980s to join the GATT in 1986. By 1987, the highest tariff was reduced to 20% and the tariff structure was simplified to include only 5 different rates: 0%, 5%, 10%, 15%, 20%. Starting in 1990, Mexico's opening strategy switched to pursuing bilateral free trade agreements, with the most important being the North American Free Trade Agreement (NAFTA) with United States and Canada which took effect in 1994. NAFTA reduced tariff rates with the United States from a maximum of 20% to zero in 15 years and many of the reductions to zero took immediate effect (Zabludovsky, 2005). One question is whether NAFTA had any effect given that tariff rates were already low following GATT. There are at least two reasons why NAFTA had a strong impact on trade. First, as Fig. 1 shows, tariff rates rose again after 1987. Fig. 1 shows the trend in average effective tariff rate calculated by taking a weighted average of nominal tariff rates using initial import shares as weights. The figure shows that while the average effective tariff rate did indeed fall in 1987 following GATT, it rose again in the late 1980s and early 1990s.[6] The increase was due to the fact that the Mexican government increased tariffs on goods assigned to the lowest category, 0–5%, with the stated purpose of reducing disparity of rates across sectors. The second reason is that NAFTA differed from GATT in the bilateral nature of the agreement. As illustrated in Table 1, not only did Mexican tariff rates on imported goods fall, U.S. tariff rates on Mexican exports fell as well. Columns (1) and (2) of Table 1 show Mexican import tariffs in 1993 before NAFTA as well as the change in tariffs from 1993 to 2000. Columns (3) and (4) report U.S. tariff levels in

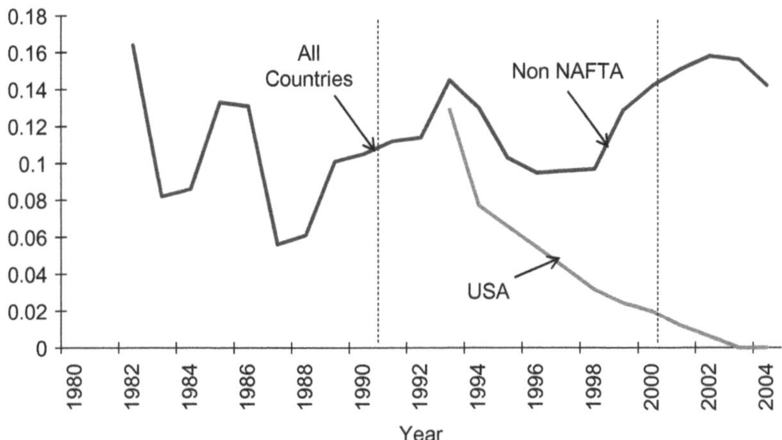

Fig. 1. Effective Tariffs, 1980–2004. *Source*: Zabludovsky (2005), Table 1. Own calculations based on tariff schedules published and by Ministry of the Economy, (SECOFI).

Table 1. Tariff Rates Pre- and Post-NAFTA.

Industry	Mexico		United States	
	1993 Rate % (1)	Change 1993–2000 (2)	1993 Rate % (3)	Change 1993–2000 (4)
Agriculture	4.5	−3.8	4.1	−3.6
Livestock	4.5	−3.2	0	0
Fish	0	0	0	0
Oil and gas	10	−7	0.5	−0.5
Minerals	6.1	−5.9	0.3	−0.3
Food	12.4	−9.1	3.6	−2
Beverage and tobacco	18.9	−14.4	3.7	−3.2
Textiles and fabrics	12.9	−10	13.2	−13.1
Textile mill products	19.3	−14.4	6.1	−6
Clothing	20	−17.1	13.2	−12.9
Leather	9.3	−7.6	11.6	−8.8
Wood	17.5	−14.4	1.2	−1.1
Paper	8.3	−6.2	0	0
Printed matters	9	−8.1	0	0
Petroleum and coal products	1.9	−1.4	1.5	−1.1
Chemicals	9.4	−7.8	1.8	−1.6
Plastics and rubber	15.2	−11.5	1.2	−1
Nonmetallic mineral products	14.9	−12.5	4.7	−1.8
Primary metal	8.8	−6.5	3.2	−2.6
Fabricated metal	13.8	−12.1	0.5	−0.5
Machinery, except electrical	14.6	−13.9	0	0
Computers and electronics	12.8	−12	1.7	−1.7
Electrical equip & appliances	14	−10.9	0.2	−0.2
Transportation equip	11.4	−8.9	1.3	−1.3
Furniture	16.1	−11.9	0	0
Miscellaneous	15.3	−14	0.8	−0.8

Source: Mexican tariff data, *Fracciones Arancelarias y Plazos de Desgravacion, Tratado de Libre Comericio de America del Norte*, 1994. U.S. tariff data, from Romalis (2002). For both the U.S. tariff data we begin with eight-digit harmonized tariff system categories and aggregate up three-digit SCIAN97 (NAICS) categories using initial import and export shares as weights. Details of the data construction are in the data appendix.

1993 and the change from 1993 to 2000.[7] The table illustrates the bilateral nature of the agreement where reductions in Mexican tariffs were accompanied by corresponding reduction in U.S. tariffs. "Textiles" and "clothing" are especially notable in that NAFTA abolished relatively high tariffs in these industries on both sides of the border.[8] Since more than 80% of the trade occurs with the United States, the decline in

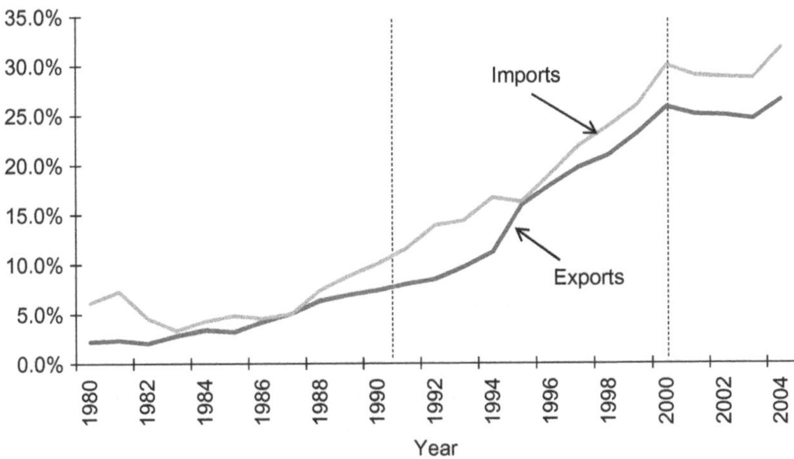

Fig. 2. Non-oil Exports and Imports as Share of GDP, 1980–2004. *Source*: www.inegi.gob.mx

effective tariffs resulted in dramatic increases in trade flows. Fig. 2 shows the trends in exports and imports as fractions of GDP. The figure shows that while the unilateral tariff reductions had some impact in the 1980s, trade flows accelerated in the 1990s. Interestingly, trade flows appear to have stagnated again in the 2000s mostly likely due to a recession in the United States and China's entry into the WTO.

CHANGES IN WOMEN'S RELATIVE WAGE AND EMPLOYMENT BEFORE AND AFTER NAFTA

Women's Relative Wage

Fig. 3 documents changes in relative wage of women during the period 1984–2004. We use multiple rounds of a representative household survey, Household Income and Expenditure Surveys (ENIGH) and the 10% samples of the Mexican Population Census of 1990 and 2000 available from the census IPUMS. Our wage sample consists of men and women who are 15–64 years old, who reported working full-time (30 hours or more), and who either did not have self-employment earnings or reported that they were not self-employed. Additionally, since we are calculating means in Fig. 3, we are wary of outlier observations and proceed by deleting the top and bottom 1% of observations by gender.[9] Details of the data construction and sample selection statements are in the data appendix.

Fig. 3(a) graphs the mean female–male wage ratio. Using multiple rounds of the ENIGH household survey, we estimate annual rates of change in the female–male wage ratio for three separate periods, 1984–1989, 1989–2000, 2000–2004, by regressing the female–male wage ratio on a linear spline with break points in 1989 and 2000. In Fig. 3(a), we graph the predicted value as well as the actual female–male mean wage. We estimate an annual rate of decline of 1.1 percentage points in 1984–1989, an increase of .4 percentage points annually during 1989–2000, and a decline of .5 percentage points annually during 2000–2004. All but the last estimate is statistically significant.[10] The Census data indicate that female-male wage ratio increased approximately 2.7 percentage points from 1990 to 2000. Note that Fig. 2 showed accelerated increase in trade flows during 1990–2000 in comparison to either before or after. Similarly, in Fig. 3(a), we estimate a rising trend in the female–male wage ratio during the 1990–2000 period, and declining trends in periods before and after.

One concern is that women's education levels may have increased relative to men and this may be driving the above changes in relative wages. Fig. 3(b) addresses this issue by calculating mean wage ratios holding

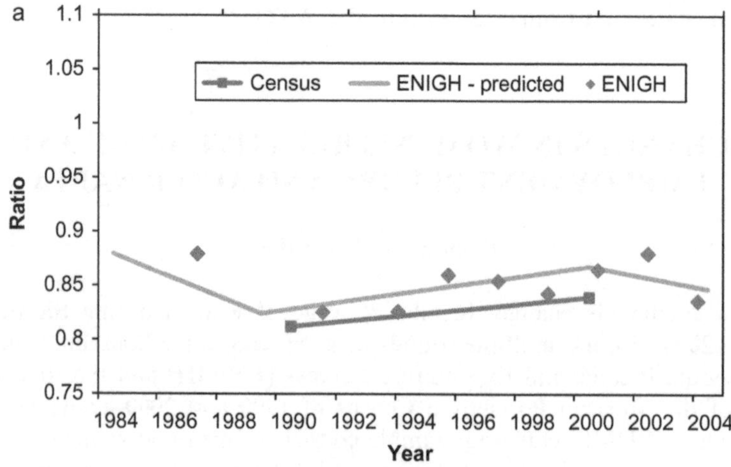

Fig. 3a. Female/Male Mean Weekly Wage Ratio.

the composition of workers fixed across age and education categories.[11] Fig. 3(b) illustrates that correcting for compositional changes makes little difference. In Fig. 3(c) we examine whether deleting self-employed workers substantially biases our results. We include self-employed workers in Fig. 3(c) and find similar trends. Finally, in Fig. 3(d) we examine the most inclusive sample by including self-employed workers and part-time workers. We report hourly wages by dividing weekly wage by hours worked per week. We find that women are paid slightly better than men on an hourly basis (the ratio is often greater than 1) and moreover, both in the

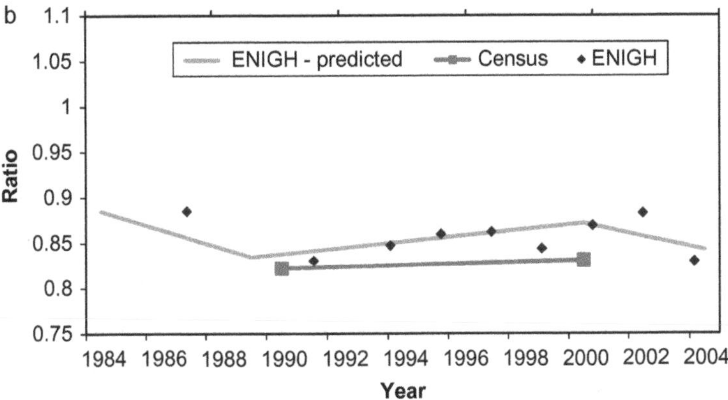

Fig. 3b. Female/Male Mean Weekly Wage Ratio Composition Fixed.

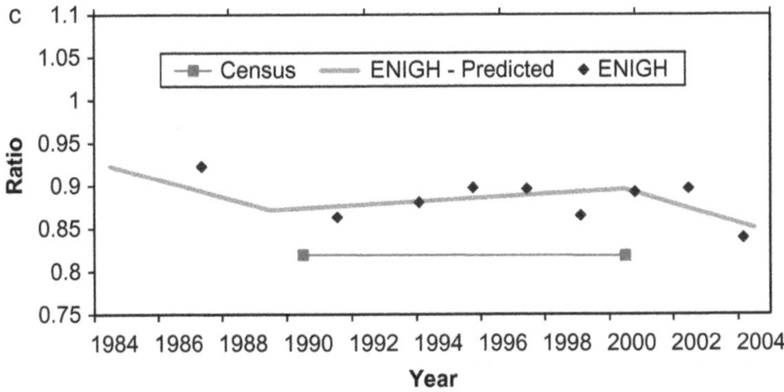

Fig. 3c. Female/Male Mean Weekly Wage Ratio Including Self-Employed.

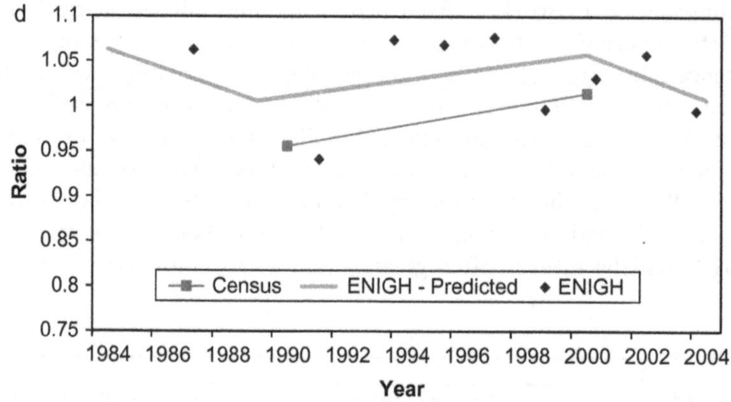

Fig. 3d. Female/Male Mean Hourly Wage Ratio Including Self-Employed.

ENIGH and the census, hourly wages of women increased relative to wages of men during the 1990s. This suggests that we may be slightly understating wage gains of women by focusing on full-time wage and salary workers. The basic message we take away from Fig. 3 is that women's relative wage increased slightly and certainly did not decrease during the period of trade liberalization, 1990–2000.

Employment and Female Share of the Labor Force

We next examine changes in employment to population ratios of women and men as well as changes in the female share of the labor force. Table 2 reports the employment to population ratios of women (top panel) and men (bottom panel) who are 15–64 years old. Employment rates (especially of women) are much lower in Mexico than the rates observed in developed countries. For example, the ratio for comparable women in the United States during this period would be .60 and higher, while in Mexico the rate is still only .44 in 2004. Employment rates did rise rapidly for women, however, over the entire period, while employment of men increased much more modestly. Over the 1990s, the employment–population ratio of women increased 12.3 percentage points (ENIGH) and 13.4 percentage points (census) in the two surveys.

Table 2. Employment-Population Ratios of Men and Women.

	Year								
	1984	1989/90	1992	1994	1996	1998	2000	2002	2004
Employment–Population Ratio 15–64 Year Old Women									
ENIGH									
<12	0.255	0.263	0.29	0.337	0.375	0.394	0.387	0.412	0.395
≥12	0.421	0.498	0.502	0.53	0.562	0.562	0.525	0.559	0.58
All	0.267	0.289	0.315	0.363	0.402	0.419	0.412	0.44	0.441
Census									
<12		0.166					0.294		
≥12		0.478					0.541		
All		0.211					0.348		
Employment–Population Ratio 15–64 Year Old Men									
ENIGH									
<12	0.791	0.795	0.817	0.827	0.817	0.842	0.846	0.832	0.816
≥12	0.658	0.763	0.77	0.798	0.802	0.8	0.819	0.779	0.82
All	0.774	0.79	0.809	0.821	0.814	0.832	0.84	0.819	0.817
Census									
<12		0.727					0.774		
≥12		0.762					0.816		
All		0.733					0.784		

Source: ENIGH 1984–2004, Census 1990, 2000. Sample includes 15- to 64-year-old males and females. Employment is defined as those with positive hours of work during the survey week.

Table 3 describes the changes in female share of the labor force. Top panel reports shares based on the ENIGH while the bottom panel refers to data from the census. Panel A reports female share of total hours worked. Panel B reports labor shares in efficiency units.[12] Focusing on the census-based results in the bottom panel, the table shows that both measures of female labor share increased by approximately 5 percentage points with the change in hours shares being slightly larger.

The decline in the female/male wage ratio from 1984 to 1989 is consistent with the increase in the relative supply of women where rapid entry of women led to a decline in own wage. Over the period, 1989–2000, relative wage of women increased even as their labor share increased. Taken together, the evidence on the gender wage gap and relative supplies suggest that relative demand for women must have increased. In the special case of

Table 3. Female Labor as a Share of Total Labor.

ENIGH – Female Labor as a Share of Total Labor

	Year								
	1984	1989	1992	1994	1996	1998	2000	2002	2004
A. Hours									
<12 Years	0.215	0.238	0.247	0.269	0.293	0.3	0.303	0.31	0.312
≥12 Years	0.232	0.273	0.275	0.301	0.316	0.321	0.316	0.349	0.387
All	0.217	0.244	0.252	0.274	0.298	0.304	0.306	0.319	0.333
B. Efficiency Units									
<12 Years	0.195	0.223	0.229	0.251	0.27	0.278	0.289	0.295	0.291
≥12 Years	0.177	0.211	0.219	0.24	0.262	0.261	0.247	0.285	0.321
All	0.19	0.219	0.225	0.246	0.266	0.271	0.27	0.29	0.306
C. Wage Bill Shares									
<12 Years	0.209	0.221	0.23	0.249	0.266	0.282	0.285	0.292	0.279
≥12 Years	0.174	0.211	0.223	0.233	0.267	0.254	0.241	0.311	0.327
All	0.201	0.218	0.227	0.242	0.266	0.27	0.265	0.301	0.303

Sample includes 15- to 64-year-old males and females. The table reports the female shares of total labor measured in hours, in efficiency units of labor, and in wage bill shares. To calculate shares in efficiency units, we weight hours by the group specific average wage, fixed over years. With wage bill shares, average wages by group vary by year.

Census – Female Labor as a Share of Total Labor

	A. Hours		B. Efficiency Units		C. Wage Bill Shares	
	1990	2000	1990	2000	1990	2000
<12 Years	0.215	0.254	0.207	0.238	0.212	0.232
≥12 Years	0.28	0.356	0.23	0.301	0.228	0.309
All	0.226	0.281	0.215	0.267	0.217	0.27

Sample includes 15- to 64-year-old males and females. The table reports the female shares of total labor measured in hours, in efficiency units of labor, and in wage bill shares. To calculate shares in efficiency units, we weight hours by the group specific average wage, fixed over years. With wage bill shares, average wages by group vary by year.

Cobb-Douglas production where the elasticity of substitution between male and female labor equals one, we can interpret changes in female wage bill share as an increase in relative demand for female labor (see Autor & Katz, 1999). Wage bill shares are reported in Panel C and the table shows that wage bill shares of women also increased by approximately 5 percentage points.[13] The evidence on the last period, 2000–2004, is mixed. On the one hand, relative wage declined. Table 3 shows, however, that women's labor share increased most rapidly over this period and taken together, wage bill share also increased. Interestingly, the increase in wage bill share since the year 2000 was entirely due to educated women, those with at least 12 years of schooling. Wage bill shares of women with less than 12 years of schooling actually declined 2000–2004.

WOMEN'S LABOR MARKET OUTCOMES AND TRADE LIBERALIZATION

Between-Industry Shifts in Female Wage Bill Share

Table 4 reports labor shares across broad industry classes using census data. The most significant change reported in the table is the declining share of agricultural employment throughout the period. Agriculture's share fell from 12.5% in 1990 to 7.7% in 2000. As indicated in column (3) female labor share in agriculture in 1990 was only 2.9%. Since predominantly men work in agriculture in Mexico, we would expect this to negatively impact men relative to women. Somewhat surprisingly, the manufacturing sector also decreased modestly. Instead, several services sectors registered large growth, such as professional services, education, hotel and restaurants, and other services.

Table 5 disaggregates the manufacturing sector further and shows that while manufacturing employment was flat overall, there have been winners and losers within manufacturing. Female-intensive sectors (based on initial female share in 1990) such as "clothing" and "computers and electronics" grew while predominantly male-intensive sectors such as "petroleum and coal products," "chemicals" and "primary metal" declined. "Transportation equipment" which includes car assembly, on the other hand, grew over this period.

One method of summarizing these changes is to calculate within and between-industry changes in employment and wage bill shares of female workers. Between-industry changes in women's wage bill share would be consistent with trade-based explanations. For example, tariff reductions associated with NAFTA may have increased the relative size of textiles and clothing sectors which more intensively utilizes female labor. These types of changes would be captured by between-industry shifts and we view gauging

Table 4. Industrial Distribution (Census).

Industry (SCIAN97)	Year		
	1990	2000	Female Share in 1990 (%)
Agriculture	12.5	7.7	2.9
Fishing	2.5	1.8	3.6
Oil and gas	1.3	0.8	9
Electricity and water	1	0.7	9.7
Construction	5.8	7.9	1.8
Light manufacturing	7.2	7	25.7
Medium manufacturing	4.9	4.1	14.4
Heavy manufacturing	6.6	7.1	14.4
Wholesale	2.2	1.6	13.8
Retail	13.8	14.6	28.4
Transportation and storage	9.1	8.9	4.4
Communications	1.2	1.2	25.5
Financial services	2.2	1.5	29.1
Real estate services	0.4	0.6	24.3
Professional services	3.3	4.8	21.5
Education	7.7	8.1	46.9
Health services	5.3	5.1	48.4
Recreation services	0.7	0.8	21.1
Hotels and restaurants	3.6	4.5	35.4
Other services	3.3	5.2	62
Government	5.5	6.1	21.8
Total	100	100	21.7

Source: Mexican Census IPUMS, 1990 and 2000. The table reports shares of labor in efficiency units.

the importance of between-industry shifts as the first step toward assessing the role of trade liberalization policies.

We decompose the change in the female share into two components according to the following formula:

$$\Delta\text{Female\_share}_t = \sum_i \frac{E^f_{it-1}}{E_{it-1}} * \left(\Delta \frac{E_{it}}{E_t}\right) + \sum_i \left(\Delta \frac{E^f_{it}}{E_{it}}\right) * \frac{E_{it}}{E_t} \qquad (1)$$

The term (E^f_{it-1}/E_{it-1}) is the share of women in industry i and $\Delta(E_{it}/E_t)$ is total employment growth of industry i. The first term corresponds to the "between" component and captures the extent to which growth in female share was due to differential growth across industries. The second term reflects within-industry changes in female share. We use

Table 5. Industrial Distribution: Manufacturing (Census).

Industry	Year		Female Share in 1990 (%)
	1990	2000	
Food	16.4	15.3	19.3
Beverages and tobacco	4.8	3.8	7.7
Textiles and fabrics	3.5	2.5	12.7
Textile mill products	0.9	1.4	30.3
Clothing	8.2	11.9	55.6
Leather	5.1	3.8	21.3
Wood	1.4	1.6	5.9
Paper	1.8	1.9	11.3
Printing	4.7	2.6	19.2
Petroleum and coal products	2.8	1.7	10.2
Chemicals	5.7	4.6	20.3
Plastic and rubber	2.6	2.5	17.7
Nonmetallic mineral products	6.8	7.4	8.5
Primary metal	3.7	2.6	6.4
Fabricated metal	7	7.1	14.1
Machinery, except electrical	2.7	2.1	7.6
Computers and electronics	2.7	4.5	30.2
Electrical equip & appliances	4.1	3.4	32
Transportation equipment	5.9	8.4	12.9
Furniture	6.3	6.9	5.1
Miscellaneous	2.7	4	25.1
Total	100	100	18.7

Source: Mexican Census IPUMS, 1990 and 2000. The table reports shares of labor in efficiency units.

69 industry classifications which we can consistently match across the 1990 and 2000 census.

The top panel of Table 6 reports changes in employment shares (in efficiency units) as well as changes in wage bill shares for all sectors. We distinguish four different groups, less educated (<12 years of schooling) males and females, and more educated (≥12 years of schooling) males and females. We also report all women's wage bill share in the last row. The table shows that the wage bill share of women increased 5.3 percentage points overall between 1990 and 2000. Between-industry shifts account for 40% (2.1/5.25) of the total change. Between-industry shifts account for a smaller (32%) but still substantial share of the change in employment share suggesting that employment shifts across industries were important.

Table 6. Change in Share of Workers by Education and Gender, 1990–2000.

Group	Employment Share			Wage Bill Share		
	Between	Within	Total	Between	Within	Total
Change in Share of Workers by Education and Gender, 1990–2000, All Sectors						
Men <12	−2.39	−8.59	−10.98	−4.15	−10.38	−14.53
Women <12	1.42	−2.22	−0.8	1.05	−3.68	−2.63
Men ≥12	0.73	5.04	5.77	2.04	7.23	9.28
Women ≥12	0.24	5.78	6.01	1.05	6.83	7.88
Women	1.66	3.55	5.21	2.10	3.15	5.25
Change in Share of Workers by Education and Gender, 1990–2000, Tradables Only						
Men <12	−4.02	−7.07	−11.09	−4.85	−8.44	−13.29
Women <12	2.18	0.92	3.1	1.63	0.27	1.9
Men ≥12	1.53	3.85	5.38	2.76	5.44	8.2
Women ≥12	0.31	2.31	2.62	0.46	2.73	3.19
Women	2.49	3.22	5.71	2.09	2.6	5.09
Change in Share of Workers by Education and Gender, 1990–2000, Manufacturing Only						
Men <12	−2	−7.83	−9.83	−2.57	−8.94	−11.51
Women <12	1.99	0.07	2.06	1.08	−0.71	0.37
Men ≥12	−0.12	4.42	4.3	1.17	6.13	7.3
Women ≥12	0.12	3.34	3.46	0.33	3.52	3.84
Women	2.11	3.41	5.53	1.40	2.10	4.21

Source: Mexican Census IPUMS 1990 and 2000. The panel is based on 69 industries, the middle panel is based on 28 industries, and the bottom panel is based on 21 industries. Employment shares are reported in efficiency units.

The middle and bottom panels of Table 3 show similar results for the 29 industries in the tradables sector (including agriculture) and for 21 industries in the manufacturing sector. Taken together, approximately between one-third and up to 40% of the rise in female wage bill share can be attributed to between-industry shifts. These results stand in sharp contrast to Attanasio, Goldberg, and Pavcnik (2004) who find stable employment patterns across industries in Colombia and also Revenga (1997) and Hanson and Harrison (1999) who examine an earlier period in Mexico. These authors conclude that trade liberalization impacted industry wage premiums rather than reallocated labor across sectors. Our finding here is that labor reallocation is an important part of the story in Mexico during the 1990s. It is also important to keep in mind that the lack of detail in our industry categories is likely to underestimate the true shift in employment across industries thus giving us a lower bound of the importance of between-industry shifts.

Can these between-industry shifts be linked to trade liberalization policies? Note that the "between-industry" shift consists of the following expression from Eq. (1):

$$\text{Between} = \sum_i \frac{E^f_{it-1}}{E_{it-1}} * \left(\Delta \frac{E_{it}}{E_t}\right).$$

The first term, (E^f_{it-1}/E_{it-1}), refers to female share in the industry in the initial period, while the second term, $\Delta(E_{it}/E_t)$, refers to industry growth. We show below that trade liberalization (tariff reductions) is positively related to increase in industry share $\Delta(E_{it}/E_t)$ and also initial female share (E^f_{it-1}/E_{it-1}).

Fig. 4 relates the change in total industry wage bill share, $\Delta(E_{it}/E_t)$ from 1990 to 2000 to the change in industry level tariff rates from 1993 to 2000 for the 29 industries in the tradables sector.[14] As illustrated in Fig. 4, larger tariff reductions are positively related to industry growth.[15] It is interesting to note that this is contrary to the predictions of the standard Heckscher-Ohlin (HO) trade model, which would predict contraction among sectors that experienced a decline in their output price (due to tariff reductions). We find that tariff reductions from 1993 to 2000 are *positively* related to industry growth. Although it is not clear why Mexico would have protected industries in which it has a comparative advantage, the coincident reduction in tariffs by the United States likely had a large effect especially in the

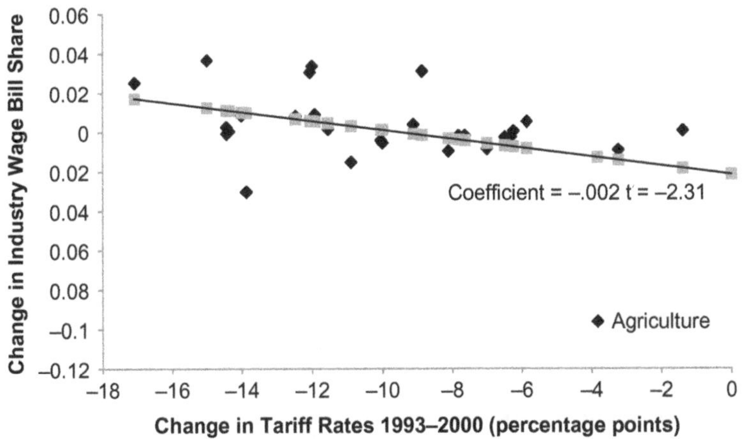

Fig. 4. Industry Growth and Tariff Changes.

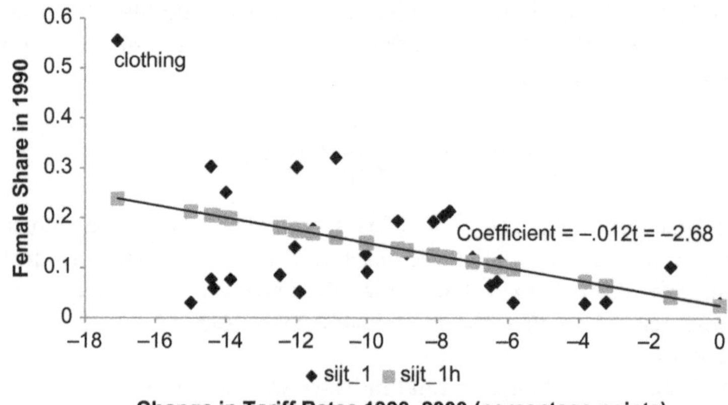

Fig. 5. Female Share in 1990 and Tariff Changes.

most impacted industries such as textiles and clothing. In addition, recent papers have pointed out that trade liberalization not only reduces output prices but also the prices of imported intermediate products. Tariff reductions could lead to the expansion of domestic firms by reducing cost of existing imports as well as by allowing firms to increase scope and expand to new product varieties (Amiti & Konings, 2007; Goldberg, Khandelwal, Pavcnik, & Topalova, 2010).

The next question is whether tariff changes were concentrated in initially female-intensive industries. In Fig. 5, we graph initial female share in the industry in 1990 against tariff changes. The figure shows that the largest declines in tariffs were concentrated in initially female-intensive industries, with "clothing" playing an important role in terms of both female share and tariff declines.[16]

Within-Industry Shifts in Female Wage Bill Share

While Table 6 showed that up to 40% of the increase in female wage bill share was due to between-industry shifts, the table also showed that majority of the increase occurred within industries. In this section, we examine what may account for the rise in female wage bill share *within* industries. To examine this question, we use establishment level data, Encuesta Nacional de Empleo, Salarios, Tecnologia y Capacitacion (ENESTyC).

ENESTyC is a survey of establishments in the manufacturing sector and was carried out in 1992, 1998, and 2001. We use the 1992 and 2001 samples in our analysis which refer to the years 1991 and 2000. Table 7 provides a summary of the main variables.[17]

To investigate the link between within-industry shifts in female wage bill share and trade liberalization policies, we consider the following regression at the establishment level:

$$\text{Female\_Share}_{jit} = \alpha + \beta_{T1}\text{Tariff}_{it} + \beta_X X_{jit} + + \eta_t + \lambda_i + \varepsilon_{jit} \quad (2)$$

where $\text{Female\_Share}_{jit}$ represents the female wage bill share in establishment j in industry i in year t, Tariff_{it} refers to industry tariff levels in 1991 and 2000, X_{jit} refer to various establishment-level controls, and η_t and λ_i refer to year and industry fixed effects. Our first specification is estimation of Eq. (2) via OLS. While all tariffs are expected to be eventually reduced to zero under NAFTA, not all industry tariffs had been reduced to zero by 2000, and one concern is that the actual timing of the changes may be endogenous and subject to more political pressures and contemporaneous industry performance. We therefore use initial tariff levels in 1991 interacted with 2000 year dummy as an instrument for Tariff_{it} and report the IV results as our second specification. Finally we also report the reduced form regression with the initial tariff levels in 1991 interacted with 2000 year dummy directly included as a regressor as

Table 7. Summary Statistics – Establishment Survey (ENESTyC).

Variable	1991			2000		
	N	Mean	Std.	N	Mean	Std.
Log (capital/value added)	4151	−0.38	1.41	5272	−0.52	1.68
Log value added	4151	10.61	1.7	5272	10.31	1.96
R&D/Income	4238	0.01	0.02	4848	0	0.01
Share of white-collar workers	4238	0.29	0.17	5654	0.28	0.19
Foreign ownership (≥10%)	4238	0.23	0.42	5037	0.24	0.43
Exports > 0	4238	0.43	0.5	5570	0.55	0.5
Foreign exporter	4238	0.17	0.38	4975	0.21	0.5
Share of foreign-owned assets	4238	0.19	0.37	5037	0.21	0.39
Exports as share of sales	4238	0.2	0.36	5570	0.22	0.34
Export share*foreign share	4238	0.09	0.27	4975	0.12	0.29
Maquila	4238	0.09	0.29	5654	0.1	0.3

Source: Encuesta Nacional de Empleo, Salarios, Tecnologia y Capacitacion (ENESTyC) survey 1991 and 2001. The table reports means for establishments with more than 15 employees.

our final specification. More specifically, we estimate the following equation via OLS:

$$\text{Female\_Share}_{jit} = \alpha + \beta_{T1}\text{Init\_Tariff}_i{*}\text{2000\_Dummy} + \beta_X X_{jit} + \eta_t + \lambda_i + \varepsilon_{jit} \tag{3}$$

In the above specification, the coefficient β_{T1} compares female wage bill shares in 2000 across industries with different initial tariff levels, controlling for industry fixed effects, λ_i. Since industries with higher initial tariff levels experienced larger declines, we expect the sign of β_{T1} to be positive. Unlike the previous sections where we were limited to three-digit industry classifications, we have more detailed industry information, six-digit level of the Mexican Classification of Activities and Products system (CMAP), available in the establishment level data. Tariff data, both Mexican tariffs on imports (import tariffs), as well U.S. tariffs on Mexican exports (export tariffs), were merged at the CMAP level.[18]

The ENESTyC oversampled small firms in the 2001 survey but we were unable to obtain clear details of the oversampling. Since the sampling design for larger firms, those with 100 employees or more, were consistent across the surveys, we restricted our analysis to these larger firms to ensure comparability across the two years. We are aware that this selection on firm size comes at a cost, however, since the results in this section apply only to larger firms and have less to say about the impact of trade reforms on smaller firms. We also excluded maquiladoras and firms who earned more than 50% of their income from maquiladora activity from our main analysis. Since maquiladoras were not subject to import duties or tariffs even before the trade liberalization, it is likely that these firms were not as impacted. We report results including maquiladora firms in the appendix and we do indeed find that our results are weaker, although most of the coefficients have the same sign. Additional controls in the regression include age of firm, age squared, log(capital/value added), log(value added), R&D expenditures as share of total income, share of white-collar workers, and foreign dummy which is equal to one if at least 10% of assets is foreign-owned.

Table 8 reports the results of all three specifications, with panel A referring to our OLS specification, panel B referring to tariffs instrumented with initial tariffs and panel C referring to the reduced form regression with initial tariffs. Column (1) reports the results for overall female wage bill share, while columns (2)–(5) examine various subcategories such as white-collar (column 2), blue-collar (column 3), "specialized blue-collar" (column 4), and "general blue-collar" (column 5). In panel A and panel B,

Table 8. Female Wage Bill Share and Export Tariffs – Establishment Data.

	All	White-Collar	Blue-Collar	Specialized Blue-Collar	General Blue-Collar
	(1)	(2)	(3)	(4)	(5)
A. OLS					
U.S. tariff	−0.195	−0.288*	−0.029	−0.318	0.199
	(0.150)	(0.170)	(0.180)	(0.220)	(0.220)
Industry FE	Yes	Yes	Yes	Yes	Yes
Year FE	Yes	Yes	Yes	Yes	Yes
Number of obs.	5059	5044	5027	4166	4761
R Squared	0.575	0.339	0.581	0.427	0.529
B. Instrumental Variables: U.S. Tariff 1991 × 2000 Dummy Used as Instrument					
U.S. tariff	−0.276	−0.304	−0.228	−0.498**	0.084
	(0.190)	(0.20)	(0.210)	(0.220)	(0.240)
Industry FE	Yes	Yes	Yes	Yes	Yes
Year FE	Yes	Yes	Yes	Yes	Yes
Number of obs.	5049	5034	5017	4157	4751
R Squared	0.575	0.339	0.581	0.427	0.529
C. Reduced Form: Regressor is 1991 U.S. Tariff Interacted with 2000 Dummy					
1991 U.S. tariff	0.208	0.229	0.172	0.377**	−0.063
× 2000	(0.130)	(0.140)	(0.160)	(0.180)	(0.190)
Industry FE	Yes	Yes	Yes	Yes	Yes
Year FE	Yes	Yes	Yes	Yes	Yes
Number of obs.	5049	5034	5017	4157	4751
R Squared	0.575	0.339	0.582	0.428	0.529

Source: ENESTyC. Standard errors in parentheses; **significant 5% level; *significant at 10% level. The dependent variable for column (1) is female wage bill share, for column (2) female wage bill share in white-collar jobs, for column (3) female wage bill share in blue-collar jobs, for column (4) female wage bill share in specialized blue-collar jobs, and for column (5) female wage bill share in general blue collar jobs. For details on sample selection, see text. Additional controls in the regression include age of firm, age squared, log(capital/value added), log(value added), R&D expenditures as share of total income, share of white-collar workers, dummy for at least 10% of capital that is foreign

a negative coefficient indicates that export tariff reductions lead to increases in female wage bill share. While the coefficients are generally negative, most of the coefficients are not significant at the 5% level. The one exception is female wage bill share in "specialized blue-collar" category in the IV specification reported in panel B. We obtain similar results using the reduced form specification in panel C, where the positive coefficient indicates that industries with initially higher tariff levels in 1991 (presumably those which experienced the largest tariff reductions under NAFTA) witnessed the largest increases in female wage bill share. For both the IV and the reduced form specifications, the estimated effects suggest that reduction in export tariffs led to increases in female wage bill share in the skilled blue-collar category.

What is the channel which links reductions in export tariffs to increases in female wage bill share? Recent papers have emphasized productivity differences between exporting and non-exporting firms (Bernard & Bradford Jensen, 1999; Bustos, 2011; Verhoogen, 2008). In particular, Bustos (2011) shows that in the aftermath of the regional free trade agreement between Argentina and Brazil, the MERCOSUR, the number of exporting firms increased. In a paper that builds on a model of firm heterogeneity and worker heterogeneity along gender and skill dimensions, Juhn, Ujhelyi, and Villegas-Sanchez (2012) find that reductions in export tariffs increased the number of exporting firms and these firms adopted technology which appears to be more complementary with female blue-collar workers. While we show only the reduced relationship between tariffs and female wage bill share in Table 8, our results are broadly consistent with this technology-based explanation.

Table 9. Import Tariffs and Female Wage Bill Share.

	All	White-Collar	Blue-Collar	Specialized Blue-Collar	General Blue-Collar
	(1)	(2)	(3)	(4)	(5)
1991 Mexican tariff	0.085	0.106	0.105	0.081	0.039
× 2000	(0.060)	(0.060)	(0.070)	(0.10)	(0.090)
Industry FE	Yes	Yes	Yes	Yes	Yes
Year FE	Yes	Yes	Yes	Yes	Yes
Number of obs.	4636	4623	4605	3805	4362
R Squared	0.553	0.332	0.564	0.393	0.511

Source: ENESTyC. Standard errors in parentheses; ***significant at 1% level; **significant 5% level; *significant at 10% level. The dependent variable for column (1) is female wage bill share, for column (2) female wage bill share in white-collar jobs, for column (3) female wage bill share in blue-collar jobs, for column (4) female wage bill share in specialized blue-collar jobs, and for column (5) female wage bill share in general blue collar jobs. For details on sample selection, see text. Additional controls in the regression include age of firm, age squared, log(capital/value added), log(value added), R&D expenditures as share of total income, share of white-collar workers, dummy for at least 10% of capital that is foreign.

Finally, another channel is the role of competition and discrimination. Table 9 addresses this issue by using the same specification as in panel C of Table 8 but using Mexican tariffs (import tariffs) as the independent variable. A recent paper by Ederington et al. (2010) finds that reductions of import tariffs increased employment of women relative to men in blue-collar occupations in Colombia – a change the authors attribute to increased product market competition and reductions in employer discrimination. While the coefficients are positive, Table 9 shows that in the case of Mexico, the relationship between import tariffs and female share is much weaker. These results suggest that increased competition and reductions in discriminatory hiring practices were likely to be of secondary importance in Mexico.

HOUSEHOLD EXPENDITURES AND SHIFTS IN HOUSEHOLD BARGAINING

We have shown that during the period of trade liberalization women's wage remained stable while they worked more (at least in the non-household sector). This brings us to the question of whether women's well-being improved as a result. Recent papers on household bargaining have rejected the common preference model of the household. Using a policy change in Britain where child allowance was transferred from the husband to the wife as a natural experiment, Lundberg, Pollack, and Wales (1997) show that an exogenous shock to wife's income altered household expenditures toward "women's clothing" and "children's clothing" at the expense of "men's clothing" and "tobacco and alcohol." The exogenous shift in relative incomes altered the bargaining position of the wife and shifted household expenditures toward goods reflecting her preferences. Bobonis (2009) also finds that cash transfers to the wife in the Mexican Progressa program shifted expenditures toward children's goods. In this section, we examine changes in household expenditure patterns to see if bargaining position of married women increased to reflect the increase in their relative earnings.

We use two rounds of the Mexican Household Income and Expenditure Survey (ENIGH), 1992 and 2000. Our sample consists of married households with children where the husband and the wife are between 18 and 54 years old. Different households are interviewed in each round, thus we are unable to follow the same household over time. Households report total expenditures as well as expenditures in various categories covering the third quarter of the year previous to the survey. We deflate expenditures by the national consumer price index published by the Bank of Mexico with 2000 as the base year. We divide by total expenditures to obtain shares and run the following OLS regression:

$$\text{Share}^k_{it} = \alpha + \beta_1 \text{Kids\_Young}_{it} + \beta_2 \text{Kids\_Old}_{it} + \beta_3 \text{Kids}_{it} + \beta_4 \text{Totexp}_{it} + \delta_t + u_{it} \quad (4)$$

where Share^k_{it} refers to expenditure share of good k in total expenditures for household i in year t. We also control for total expenditures, number of

Table 10. Expenditure Shares 1992 and 2000–Married Couples with Children.

	1992	2000	2000 Dummy with Controls
	(1)	(2)	(3)
Total expenditures (2000 pesos)	4683.4	4470.3	
Male clothing	0.0263	0.0244	−0.0014**
			(0.0006)
Female clothing	0.0112	0.0141	0.0035**
			(0.0004)
Child clothing (only young children)	0.0117	0.0039	−0.0038**
			(0.0011)
Education	0.0678	0.077	0.0061**
			(0.0019)
Alcohol and tobacco	0.0112	0.0058	−0.0049**
			(0.0005)
Child clothing/male clothing (with older children)			−0.3629**
			(0.0466)
Child clothing/male clothing (only young children)			−0.0228
			(0.0973)
Female clothing/male clothing			0.1562**
			(0.0369)

Source: ENIGH, 1992 and 2000. Sample includes married households with children where the husband and the wife are between 18 and 54 years old. We divide each expenditure category by total expenditures to obtain shares. Columns (1) and (2) report mean shares for 1992 and 2000, respectively. Column (3) reports coefficients on the 2000 dummy for the respective expenditure category. Additional controls in the regression include total expenditures, number of children aged less than 3, number of children aged 3–5 and total number of children. Standard errors in parentheses; **significant at 5% level; *significant at the 10% level.

children younger than 3, number of children aged 3–5 and total number of children. The year dummies in the above regression indicate whether expenditure share of good *k* increased in 2000 relative to 1992.

Results are reported in Table 10. The coefficients on the 2000 year dummy indicate that expenditures on male clothing fell over time while expenditures on female clothing increased. The survey only reports expenditures on "infant and toddler clothing." Expenditures in this category fell over time. "Education" expenditures which are typically associated with female preference increased while "alcohol and tobacco," associated with male preference, fell over time. The bottom three rows investigate the change in the ratio of expenditures. Children's clothing fell relative to male clothing if we include families with older children where clothing may be handed down from older siblings. When we look at families with young children only, we find no significant change in the ratio of children's to male clothing. The ratio of female to male clothing, however, increased from 1992 to 2000. The table offers suggestive evidence that women's bargaining power within the household improved along with their relative earnings over the 1990s. Household expenditures shifted from goods associated with male preference, such as men's clothing and tobacco and alcohol, to those associated with female preference such as education and women's clothing. We note, however, the necessary caveat that these findings are only suggestive, and many other factors could also potentially explain the aggregate spending patterns we highlight here.

CONCLUSION

Some view rising wage and income inequality in Latin America as an unacceptable consequence of following more efficient market-oriented policies. The impact of trade liberalization and foreign direct investment on domestic wage structure, therefore, is of central policy concern. The evidence in this paper suggests that rather than immiserizing women, trade liberalization improved women's labor market outcomes. Particularly during the reform period, 1990–2000, the gender wage ratio increased while employment of women increased. This suggests that the relative demand for women must have increased over this period. We find that both between and within-industry shifts favored female workers. With regards to between-industry shifts, we find that tariff reductions expanded industries which were initially female intensive. With regards to within-industry shifts, we find that declines in export tariffs are positively associated with increased hiring of women in skilled blue-collar occupations. This suggests that the exports and technology channel emphasized by recent papers to explain skill premiums (Bustos, 2011; Verhoogen, 2008; Yeaple, 2005) may be as important for explaining gender outcomes. Finally, changes in household expenditure patterns are consistent with increases in household bargaining power for women following the rise in their earnings. Expenditures shifted from male-oriented goods such as male clothing and tobacco and alcohol to female-oriented goods such as women's clothing and children's education.

NOTES

1. Papers that examine the gender wage gap include Brown, Pagan, and Rodriguez-Oreggia (1999) that decomposes the gap into the component due to differences in characteristics between men and women and the component due to discrimination. Pagan and Ullibarri (2000) find that the gender gap is larger for older workers, larger in smaller firms, large in the informal sector, and larger at the border. Sanchez and Pagan (2001) find a large earnings gap between female and male-owned micro-enterprises which is partly explained by lower levels of education and experience of female owners although surprisingly, not much is explained by differences in sectoral composition of female and male-owned businesses. Oostendorp (2004) presents cross-country analysis relating the gender gap to measures of trade and FDI. The paper finds that trade and FDI inflows reduce the gender gap among low skilled occupations while results are mixed for high skilled occupations. A recent volume (Bussolo & De Hoyos, 2009) also examines the link between trade liberalization and poverty through the channel of women's labor market outcomes.

2. See, for example, Katz and Murphy (1992), Bound and Johnson (1992), Berman et al. (1994). Acemoglu, Autor, and Lyle (2004) use WWII mobilization rates across states to isolate exogenous shifts in female labor supply. They find that the wage effects of increases in female labor supply are more negative for women than for men suggesting that men and women are imperfect substitutes. They estimate the elasticity of substitution to be in the 3.2–4.2 range. This would indicate that men and women are close although far from perfect substitutes.

3. Alternatively, one may assume that men and women are perfect substitutes in production but women have lower levels of skill. This is the assumption, for example, in Bussolo et al. (2009). There is little evidence, however, that trade liberalization raised relative wages and employment of less skilled workers.

4. Galor and Weil (1996) and Welch (2000) explore the notion that women have advantage in cognitive vs. physical skills and that advances in technology increase the relative demand for women over time. Using U.S. data, Weinberg (2000) shows that female employment growth is positively related to computer use across industries and occupations. Also using U.S. data and Dictionary of Occupation Titles

(DOT), Rendall (2010) shows that occupations that are more "brain" intensive have expanded over time, favoring female workers.

5. Artecona and Cunningham (2002) employ the same methods for Mexico but do not find a significant relationship between tariff changes and reductions in the gender wage gap across industries.

6. Feliciano (2001) documents the decline in tariffs following GATT but also notes the rise in rates after 1987 although she does not discuss explicitly the reasons for the increase.

7. The Mexican tariff data are from the volume published by Ministry of the Economy (formerly SeCOFI), Fracciones Arancelarias y Plazos de Desgravacion, Tratado de Libre Comercio de America del Norte (1994). The U.S. tariff data are from John Romalis, as described in Feenstra, Romalis, and Schott (2002). For both Mexican and U.S. tariffs, we begin with eight-digit harmonized tariff system categories and aggregate up to three-digit SCIAN97 (NAICS) categories using initial import and export shares. Details of the construction of the tariff data are in the data appendix.

8. The correlation of Mexican and U.S. tariffs changes reported in the table is approximately 0.3.

9. We experimented with various alternative cutoffs and other measures such as medians and log wage differences and found similar trends in relative wages.

10. We define our regressors as s1 = min(year-1984, 5), s2 = max(0, min(year-1989, 11)), and s3 = max(0, year-2000) and graph the predicted values from the regression.

11. In order to hold composition across education and age constant, we first calculated average wages by single-year age and education categories and aggregated over these groups using a fixed distribution across all years.

12. To calculate shares in efficiency units, we weight hours by the group specific average wage which is fixed over years. In addition to men and women, we define 10 five-year age groups and five education groups.

13. In calculating wage bill shares, we also allow group specific wages to vary by year. More specifically, we define 10 five-year age groups and five education groups. We use our wage sample to calculate average wage of group *j* in year *t* in the following manner: $W_{jt} = \sum_{i \in j} \text{Wageinc}_{it} / \sum_{i \in j} \text{Hours}_{it}$ and use our quantity sample to sum total hours by group *j* in year *t* as $H_{jt} = \sum_{i \in j} \text{Hours}_{it}$. Wage bill share of women in year *t* is calculated as follows: $WB_t^f = \sum_j (W_{jt}^f * H_{jt}^f) / \sum_j (W_{jt} * H_{jt})$.

14. These are the industries for which we are able to match both across census years and also to the tariff data using the Sistema de Clasificacion Industrial de America del Norte 1997 (SCIAN97). We do not utilize establishment level data from the Encuesta Nacional de Empleo, Salarios, Tecnologia y Capacitacion (ENESTyC) in this section for two reasons. First, the ENESTyC includes only manufacturing firms and we would lose the agricultural sector. Second, the ENESTyC oversampled small firms in 2000 but we do not have clear details of the oversampling. While we believe the household data gives us a more complete overview of the entire economy and the tradables sector, we have also investigated within and between demand shifts among a sample of firms we were able to match across the 1992 and 2001 surveys. Among these 941 firms, we find that the wage bill share of women increased 3.5 percentage points from 1991 to 2000, and between industry shifts accounted for 1.3 percentage points, or approximately 37 percent of the total change.

15. Fig. 4 also shows that the agricultural sector is an outlier which may be due to the fact that tariff changes in agriculture were slowly implemented with the last of the reductions scheduled to go into effect in 2008. In preparation, however, the government implemented land reforms and began to dismantle price supports and subsidies which resulted in a steep decline in agricultural employment well before the tariff reductions. Running the regression without agriculture results in a coefficient equal to −.001 with *t*-stat of −1.86.

16. The relationship is still negative although somewhat weaker without the "clothing" industry. If we exclude "clothing," the regression coefficient is reduced to −.007 with *t*-stat of −1.79.

17. We would like to thank INEGI officials for granting on-site access to the establishment level data used in this study under the commitment of complying with the confidentiality requirements set by the Mexican laws and in particular, to Maria Luisa Meza Leon, Lizi Ivette Gonzalez Jimenez, and Gabriel Romero Velasco.

18. We thank Leonardo Iacovone for providing us with the tariff data. Tariff data were available originally at the eight-digit harmonized system (HS) classification and was matched to the Mexican CMAP class classification as explained in Iacovone and Javorcik (2010).

REFERENCES

Acemoglu, D., Autor, D., & Lyle, D. (2004). Women, war, and wages: The effect of female labor supply on the wage structure at midcentury. *Journal of Political Economy*, *112*(3): 495–551.

Amiti, M., & Konings, J. (2007). Trade liberalization, intermediate inputs, and productivity: Evidence from Indonesia. *American Economic Review*, *97*(5), 1611–1638.

Artecona, R., & Cunningham, W. (2002). *Effects of trade liberalization on the gender wage gap in Mexico*. Working Paper, The World Bank.

Attanasio, O., Goldberg, P., & Pavcnik, N. (2004). Trade reforms and wage inequality in Colombia. *Journal of Development Economics*, *74*, 331–366.

Autor, D., & Katz, L. (1999). Changes in the wage structure and earnings inequality. O. Ashenfelter and D. Card (Eds.), *Handbook of Labor Economics* (*Vol. 3A*). New York, NY: North-Holland.

Becker, G. (1957). *The economics of discrimination*. Chicago, IL: The University of Chicago Press.

Berman, E., Bound, J., & Griliches, Z. (1994). Changes in the demand for skilled labor within U.S. manufacturing: Evidence from the annual survey of manufacturers. *Quarterly Journal of Economics*, *109*, 367–398.

Bernard, A., & Bradford Jensen, J. (1999). Exceptional exporter performance: Cause, effect, or both? *Journal of International Economics*, *47*(1). 1–25.

Black, S., & Brainerd, E. (2002). Importing equality? The impact of globalization on gender discrimination. NBER Working Paper 9110.

Bobonis, G. (2009). Is allocation of resources within the household efficient? New evidence from a randomized experiment. *Journal of Political Economy*, *117*. 453–503.

Bound, J., & Johnson, G. (1992). Changes in the structure of wages in the 1980s: An evaluation of alternative explanations. *American Economic Review*, *82*, 271–392.

Brown, C., Pagan, J., & Rodriguez-Oreggia, E. (1999). Occupational attainment and gender earnings differentials in Mexico. *Industrial and Labor Relations Review*, *53*(1), 123–135.

Bussolo, M., De Hoyos, R. (2009). Introduction and overview. In M. Bussolo & R. De Hoyoy (Eds.), *Gender Aspects of the trade and Poverty Nexus*. Washington, DC: World Bank Press.

Bustos, P. (2011), The impact of trade on technology and skill upgrading: Evidence from Argentina. Working paper.

Duflo, E. (2000). *Grandmothers and granddaughters: Old age pension and intra-household allocation in South Africa*. NBER Working Paper, No. 8061.

Duflo, E. (2012). Women's empowerment and economic development. *Journal of Economic Literature*, *50*(4), 1051–1079.

Ederington, J., Minier, J., & Troske, K. (2010). Where the girls are: Trade and labor market segregation in Colombia. Working Paper.

Feenstra, R., Romalis, J., & Schott, P. (2002). *U.S. imports, exports, and tariff data, 1989–2001*. NBER Working Paper, No. 9387.

Feliciano, Z. (2001). Workers and trade liberalization: The impact of trade reforms in Mexico on wages and employment. *Industrial and Labor Relations Review*, *55*(1), 95–115.

Galor, O., & Weil, D. N. (1996). The gender gap, fertility, and growth. *American Economic Review*, *86*(3), 374–387.

Goldberg, P., Khandelwal, A., Pavcnik, N., & Topalova, P. (2010). Imported intermediate inputs and domestic product growth: Evidence from India. *Quarterly Journal of Economics*, *125*(4), 1727–1767.

Hanson, G., & Harrison, A. (1999). Trade and wage inequality in Mexico. *Industrial Labor Relations Review*, *52*(2), 271–288.

Iacovone, L., & Javorcik, B. (2010). Multi-product exporters: Product churning, uncertainty and export discoveries. *The Economic Journal*, *120*, 481–499.

Juhn, C., Ujhelyi, G., & Villegas-Sanchez, C. (2012). *Men, women, and machines: How trade impacts gender inequality*. NBER Working Paper 18106.

Katz, L., & Murphy, K. M. (1992). Changes in relative wages, 1963–1987: Supply and demand factors. *Quarterly Journal of Economics*, *107*(1), 35–78.

Lundberg, S., Pollak, R., & Wales, T. (1997). Do husbands and wives pool resources? Evidence from the UK child beneft. *Journal of Human Resources*, *32*, 463–479.

Melitz, M. (2003). The impact of trade on intra-industry reallocations and aggregate industry productivity. *Econometrica*, *71*(6), 1695–1725.

Oostendorp, R. (2004). *Globalization and the gender wage gap*. Working Paper, Free University, Amsterdam.

Pagan, J. A., & Ullibarri, M. (2000). Group heterogeneity and the gender earnings gap in Mexico. *Economia Mexicana. Nueva Epoca*, *IX*(1).

Qian, N. (2008). Missing women and the price of tea in China: The effect of sex-specific earnings on sex imbalance. *Quarterly Journal of Economics*, *123*(3), 1251–1285.

Rendall, M. (2010). *Brain versus brawn: The realization of women's comparative advantage*. Working Paper, University of Zurich.

Revenga, A. L. (1997). Employment and wage effects of trade liberalization: The case of mexican manufacturing. *Journal of Labor Economics*, *15*(3), S20–S43.

Sanchez, S. M., & Pagan, J. A. (2001). Explaining gender differences in earnings in the micro-enterprise sector. In M. Correia & E. Katz (Eds.), *The Economics of Gender in Mexico: Work, Family, State and Market*. Washington, DC: The World Bank.

Thomas, D. (1990). Intra-household resource allocation: An inferential approach. *Journal of Human Resources*, *35*, 635–654.

United Nations. (2009). *UN millennium development goals report 2009*. New York, NY: United Nations.

Verhoogen, E. (2008). Trade, quality upgrading, and wage inequality in the Mexican manufacturing sector. *Quarterly Journal of Economics*, *123*(2), 489–530.

Weinberg, B. (2000). Computer use and the demand for female workers. *Industrial and Labor Relations Review*, *53*(2), 290–307.

Welch, F. (2000). Growth in women's relative wages and in inequality among men: One phenomenon or two? *American Economic Review*, *90*(2), 444–449.

Yeaple, S. (2005). A simple model of firm heterogeneity, international trade, and wages. *Journal of International Economics*, *65*(1), 1–20.

Zabludovsky, J. (2005). El Tlcan y La Politica de Comercio Exterior en Mexico: Una Agenda Inconclusa. *Informacion Comercial Espanola*, *821*, 59–70.

DATA APPENDIX

Household Surveys (Census, ENIGH)

We use data from nine rounds of the Household Income and Expenditure Surveys (ENIGH), a nationally representative survey which spans the period 1984–2004. We also use data from the 10% samples of the Mexican Population Census of 1990 and 2000 available from the Census IPUMS. Unlike the ENIGH, statistical inferences using the larger Census samples are significant at the two-digit industry level (92 categories) and at the state level (32 states). Table A.1 provides summary statistics of the data.

ENIGH and census databases present slightly different results for female employment to population and female share of total labor. These differences result for several reasons. First, the census is conducted in February while ENIGH is conducted from August to November. Second, the census interviews only one person per household, usually the mother or any adult present at home at the time of the interview. In the ENIGH, every member of the household is interviewed, resulting in more accurate data collection. Third, the census asks whether the individual worked last week, while the ENIGH asks whether the individual worked last month. If the respondent worked, the census asks about the total number of hours worked, while the ENIGH asks about the number of hours worked by job (around 15% of all workers report having two jobs).

While the ENIGH is one of the best sources of earnings information in Mexico, the samples are relatively small (25,471 workers in 2000). The census, with a much larger size (581,107 workers in 2000), has the advantage of allowing us to make inferences at the three digit industry classification level. An alternative source of employment information is the National Survey of Urban Employment (ENEU). However, this survey covered only urban areas until 2004, which limits its usefulness for examining longer run changes.

For calculating wages, we construct a wage sample consisting of men and women who are 15–64 years old, who worked at least 30 hours during the survey week and reported no self-employment income. Wages are reported wage and salary earnings last month converted to a weekly wage by dividing by 4.33. Earnings were deflated by the national consumer price index published by the Bank of Mexico with 2000 as the base year.

For reporting quantities of labor by education and by industry, we construct a sample of 15–64 year olds who report positive hours during

Table A.1. Summary Statistics.

Individuals ages 15 and over	Summary Statistics (ENIGH)								
	Year								
	1984	1989	1992	1994	1996	1998	2000	2002	2004
Number of observations	12,841	32,491	28,483	34,623	37,677	28,140	25,471	43,617	57,077
% worker	51.24	52.87	55.07	58.05	59.74	61.53	61.34	61.89	61.73
Men	77.37	78.96	80.89	82.15	81.45	83.32	83.99	81.94	81.69
Women	26.72	28.88	31.48	36.29	40.19	41.94	41.22	44.03	44.14
% fulltime	80.47	82.63	80.32	78.09	77.08	76.55	78.98	77.10	81.98
Education	5.4	6.25	6.44	6.61	6.96	7.07	7.53	7.68	8.07
Men	5.9	6.73	6.84	6.97	7.39	7.48	7.95	8.07	8.32
Women	4.93	5.81	6.06	6.28	6.58	6.7	7.16	7.33	7.84
Average hourly wage	17.98	17.52	18.42	20.52	14.15	15.01	17.35	17.88	17.56
Men	18.37	18.23	19.1	21.41	14.65	15.62	18.26	18.21	18.07
Women	16.8	15.51	16.64	18.27	12.99	13.57	15.28	17.19	16.48

Summary Statistics (Census)

Individuals Aged 15 to 64	Year	
	1990	2000
Number of observations	458,411	590,898
Urban share (%)	74.2	77.25
% Workers	47.54	55.61
Men	74.74	78.07
Women	22.28	34.99
% Fulltime	86.01	83.53
Education	6.69	7.9
Men	7.01	8.14
Working men	6.88	8.16
Women	6.4	7.68
Working women	8.76	9.02
Average hourly wage	21.44	18.25
Men	22.26	18.75
Women	19.16	17.14

the survey week, including the self-employed. We report hours-weighted employment shares and employment shares in efficiency units of labor. To calculate efficiency units of labor, we first calculate average wages (fixed across all years) by two gender, 10 age and 6 education categories. We weight hours by these average wages to calculate efficiency units of labor.

All our calculations are weighted by the household weights to make the sample nationally representative.

Data on Tariffs, Exports, and Imports

We match industry classifications available in the 1990 and 2000 Census samples to the Sistema de Clasificacion Industrial de America del Norte 1997 (SCIAN97 and also called the NAICS in the United States). Tariff, export, and import data for 1993–2000 were obtained from the Ministry of the Economy (formerly SECOFI), international trade statistics (www.economia.gob.mx). Tariffs, exports and imports are reported in "fracciones arancelarias" which is a classification system for products. There are more than 34,000 products. For tariff schedules we used the book *Fracciones Arancelarias y Plazos de Desgravación, Tratado de Libre Comercio de América del Norte* (1994), published by the Ministry of Economy. The book publishes each product with the 1993 tariff rates (0%, 5%, 10%, 15%, 20%) along with a code, A, B, C, D, or B6 that describes the rate at which the tariff is reduced to zero. For example, Code A corresponds to a tariff which is reduced to zero in 1994. We aggregated products and tariff schedules up to the SCIAN97 industry codes using the 1993 import shares as weights. U.S. tariff data come from John Romalis (http://faculty.chicagobooth.edu/john.romalis/more/) with the description and documentation available in the NBER Working paper 9387. We aggregate the six-digit harmonized tariff schedules available in the Romalis data up to the 3-digit SCIAN97 categories using the 1993 shares of Mexican exports to the United States. These matched tariff data are available from the authors upon request.

Establishment Surveys (ENESTyC)

The establishment-level data come from Encuesta Nacional de Empleo, Salarios, Tecnologia y Capacitacion (ENESTyC). The samples in ENESTyC are representative cross sections of establishments in the manufacturing sector for the years 1992, 1998, and 2001. We use the 1992 and 2001 samples in our analysis which refer to the years 1991 and 2000. We drop micro establishments (those with 15 employees or less) from the analysis since these smaller establishments were oversampled in 2001 but we do not have clear details of the oversampling. "Value added" is defined as the value of output minus materials. We deflate output by the producer price index (PPI) at the industry level and materials by the materials price index (MPI) provided by the Central Bank of Mexico. Wage bills are deflated by the consumer price index (CPI). "Capital" is value of total assets deflated by PPI. "R&D Share" refers to share of income devoted to research and

Table A.2. Female Wage Bill Share and Export Tariffs – Establishment Data Including Maquiladoras.

	All (1)	White-Collar (2)	Blue-Collar (3)	Specialized Blue-Collar (4)	General Blue-Collar (5)
A. OLS					
U.S. tariff	0.175	−0.095	0.071	−0.15	0.446
	(0.270)	(0.170)	(0.210)	(0.180)	(0.360)
Industry FE	Yes	Yes	Yes	Yes	Yes
Year FE	Yes	Yes	Yes	Yes	Yes
Number of obs.	6051	6031	5267	4355	5697
R Squared	0.613	0.35	0.598	0.45	0.554
B. Instrumental Variables: U.S. Tariff 1991 × 2000 Dummy used as Instrument					
U.S. tariff	0.092	−0.091	−0.113	−0.306	0.299
	(0.310)	(0.220)	(0.240)	(0.180)	(0.370)
Industry FE	Yes	Yes	Yes	Yes	Yes
Year FE	Yes	Yes	Yes	Yes	Yes
Number of obs.	6040	6020	5257	4346	5686
R Squared	0.613	0.349	0.598	0.45	0.553
C. Reduced Form: Regressor is 1991 U.S. Tariff Interacted with 2000 Dummy					
1991 U.S. tariff ×2000	−0.071	0.071	0.085	0.233	−0.231
	(0.250)	(0.170)	(0.180)	(0.150)	(0.30)
Industry FE	Yes	Yes	Yes	Yes	Yes
Year FE	Yes	Yes	Yes	Yes	Yes
Number of obs.	6,040	6,020	5,257	4,346	5686
R Squared	0.613	0.349	0.598	0.451	0.553

Source: ENESTyC. Standard errors in parentheses; **significant 5 percent level; *significant at 10 percent level. The dependent variable for column (1) is female wage bill share, for column (2) female wage bill share in white-collar jobs, for column (3) female wage bill share in blue-collar jobs, for column (4) female wage bill share in specialized blue-collar jobs, and for column (5) female wage bill share in general blue collar jobs. For details on sample selection, see text. Additional controls in the regression include age of firm, age squared, log(Capital/Value Added), log(Value Added), R&D expenditures as share of total income, share of white-collar workers, dummy for at least 10 percent of capital that is foreign.

development. To construct female wage bill share, we first aggregate wage bills of workers in different white and blue collar categories, supervisors, clerical workers, special production workers, and general production workers, all of which are reported separately by gender. Some categories have missing values in which case we replace with zeros before adding. The wage bill shares refer to basic salary for full time workers and exclude payment for extra hours or contributions to social security. We also exclude part time workers, hourly employees, and subcontractors from wage bill calculations. "Foreign" refers to establishments where 10% or more of the assets are foreign-owned. "Exporter" refers to establishments with positive exports. "Foreign exporter" refers to establishments which fulfill both conditions (Table A.2).

THE SHORT-TERM EFFECTS OF THE KALAMAZOO PROMISE SCHOLARSHIP ON STUDENT OUTCOMES

Timothy J. Bartik and Marta Lachowska

ABSTRACT

In order to study whether college scholarships can be an effective tool in raising students' performance in secondary school, we use one aspect of the Kalamazoo Promise that resembles a quasi-experiment. The surprise announcement of the scholarship created a large change in expected college tuition costs that varied across different groups of students based on past enrollment decisions. This variation is arguably exogenous to unobserved student characteristics. We estimate the effects of this change by a set of "difference-in-differences" regressions where we compare the change in student outcomes in secondary school across time for different student "length of enrollment" groups. We also control for student fixed effects. We find positive effects of the Kalamazoo Promise on Promise-eligible students large enough to be deemed important – about a 9 percent increase in the probability of earning any credits and one less

New Analyses of Worker Well-Being
Research in Labor Economics, Volume 38, 37–76

ISSN: 0147-9121/doi:10.1108/S0147-9121(2013)0000038002

suspension day per year. We also find large increases in GPA among African American students.

Keywords: Academic output; educational incentives; universal scholarship; natural experiment

JEL classifications: I21; I22

INTRODUCTION

The Kalamazoo Promise provides an unusual model for revitalizing an urban school district and its community. Announced on November 10, 2005, the Kalamazoo Promise provides large college scholarship benefits to graduates of Kalamazoo Public Schools (KPS), a midsized school district (numbering a little over 12,000 students) with a racially and economically diverse student population. Anonymous donors promised to pay up to 100 percent of college tuition for any KPS graduate attending a public college or university in Michigan. Tuition subsidies start at 65 percent of college tuition for students enrolling in KPS from ninth grade on, and gradually increase to 100 percent for students attending since kindergarten. The scholarship does not require any minimum high school grade point average (GPA) or financial need. Students must simply get into college and maintain a 2.0 college GPA. In sum, the Kalamazoo Promise is unusual among scholarship programs in its universality and generosity.

The Promise, as it is called, has attracted much attention and many imitators. In 2008, *The Economist* ran a piece on the scholarship, "Rescuing Kalamazoo: A Promising Future" (The Economist, 2008). In part because of the Promise, in 2010, President Obama gave the commencement address to the graduating class of Kalamazoo Central High School. At least 24 areas around the country have started or are trying to start Promise-style programs, with private or public funding.[1]

The tuition subsidies of the Promise provide incentives for higher academic output. Students who otherwise might choose to attend the state university located in Kalamazoo, Western Michigan University (WMU), may use the tuition subsidy to attend higher-ranked state universities such as Michigan State University or the University of Michigan. Students who otherwise would have attended the local community college may use the subsidy to attend WMU.[2] Students who without the Promise might not have attended college may use the subsidy to go to a community college.

Admission to and graduation from more demanding colleges requires students to have better academic performance. Despite the Promise's incentives for better academic performance, the magnitude of student responses to such incentives is doubtful, for several reasons. Many students may view the Promise's benefits as too uncertain and too delayed. Even if students want to respond to the Promise by improving their academic performance, students may not know how academic performance can best be improved. Therefore, there is a need for rigorous research to determine the magnitude of positive benefits of Promise-style programs, or indeed, whether there are discernible benefits.[3]

Our paper estimates the effects of the Kalamazoo Promise on student achievement and behavior. We use one aspect of the Promise that bears resemblance to a "quasi-experiment." The surprise 2005 announcement of the Kalamazoo Promise created a large change in college tuition costs that varied across different groups of students based on prior enrollment decisions. The morning after the Promise was announced, some KPS students found themselves to be eligible for a 100 percent tuition subsidy, others for a smaller tuition subsidy, while still others could expect to receive no scholarship. The tuition subsidy depended upon how long the student had been enrolled in KPS. That enrollment decision, however, had been made without knowledge of the Promise. This variation across student groups in the surprise change in college tuition costs is arguably exogenous to unobserved student characteristics. Therefore, it is plausible to argue that changes in student achievement and behavior that are statistically linked to such exogenous tuition changes can be interpreted as program effects. We estimate this effect by estimating a difference-in-differences regression where we compare the change in student outcomes across time for different "length of enrollment" groups. This procedure controls for unobserved differences between students who started their enrollment in KPS at different grades. We also control for student fixed effects. As we will explain, this accounting for student fixed effects controls for changes in group composition that are due to differential out-migration of different groups from the district after the Promise.

Our analysis finds that the Kalamazoo Promise has statistically and substantively significant effects on improving student achievement levels and behavior. For the overall sample, we estimate a decrease in the number of days spent in suspension by one or two days per school year, which is large compared to sample means and standard deviations. For the overall sample, we do not find effects on high school GPA. We speculate that when confronted with incentives generated by the Promise, students are more likely to react along a margin that they perceive that they can control, such as improving their behavior. On the other hand, for African American students, we estimate a dramatic increase in GPA, ranging from about 0.17 of a standard deviation to about 0.60. For these students, whose baseline achievement and behavior indicators lag behind those of white students, the decrease in the number of days spent in suspension appears to spill over into a higher GPA. We speculate that this could be due to the number of days in suspension exceeding a "tipping point" beyond which GPA increases by virtue of students being present in the classroom for some critical number of days. Finally, the estimated positive effects of the Promise are only apparent when the analysis controls for student "fixed effects" – that is, when it actually considers differences in behavior of the same student before and after the Promise announcement.

The remainder of the paper is organized as follows. The following section discusses related previous research literature. The next section provides further background information on the KPS district and the Kalamazoo Promise. We then describe the data we use, our econometric models, and our results. The final section offers conclusions.

RELATED LITERATURE

Research relevant to this paper includes studies of how college costs or other financial incentives affect student achievement and behavior. Other relevant research focuses on how the Promise has affected students, the school district, and the Kalamazoo area.

The Kalamazoo Promise offers a generous college tuition subsidy with minimal requirements. As described in the previous section, the Kalamazoo Promise may relax the financial constraints of going to a more selective college. This creates incentives for greater academic effort. However, the Promise's incentives may be somewhat similar to the incentives created by many states' merit aid programs for college. As described by Dynarski (2004), these state merit aid programs, which have become increasingly prevalent, often have modest high school achievement requirements.[4] The Promise is at an extreme in terms of its broad eligibility. However, qualifying for many of these state merit aid programs is not unduly difficult. It is unclear to what degree these differences between the Promise and state merit aid programs will matter for student behavior and achievement. Therefore, it is of interest to see how these somewhat different college tuition subsidies affect high school behavior and achievement. These previous studies provide a context for considering our Promise estimates.

Among state merit aid programs, Georgia HOPE (Helping Outstanding Pupils Educationally) is the largest program and has been much studied. Georgia HOPE increases college enrollment and shifts college choices toward eligible in-state colleges (see e.g., Dynarski, 2002, 2004; Cornwell, Mustard, & Sridhar, 2006). Of more relevance for the current paper, Georgia HOPE increases academic performance in high school (Henry & Rubenstein, 2002), especially among African American students. However, Georgia HOPE may also have some unintended consequences. For example, Georgia HOPE has led to decreased course loads in college and increased course withdrawals (see Cornwell, Lee, & Mustard, 2005), which may reflect the program's requirement that recipients maintain a minimum college GPA.

Researchers have also studied other state merit-based scholarships. For example, Kane finds increased college enrollment resulting from both the D.C. Tuition Assistance Grant program (Kane, 2006) and California's Cal Grant program (Kane, 2003). Pallais (2007) finds that the Tennessee Education Lottery Scholarship (TELS) affected students' college choices. Of particular relevance for our paper, Pallais also finds that TELS improves student achievement in high school. Scott-Clayton (2010) studies the effects of West Virginia's merit aid program (called the West Virginia Promise) and finds an increase in the effort students put forth in college as well as a higher likelihood of completing a bachelor's degree within four years. Interestingly, the particular design of the West Virginia Promise prompts Scott-Clayton to conclude that the observed impacts are not solely due to a reduced cost-of-college effect, but also to an incentive effect.

Some recent studies have looked at how student achievement and behavior are affected by financial incentives. Kremer, Miguel, and Thornton (2009) study the effects of a merit-based randomized scholarship program for girls in primary schools in Kenya and find that the scholarships substantially increased performance. Another important study finding is that this scholarship has positive spillover benefits for nonscholarship students. For example, the program is estimated to increase academic achievement for boys, who are ineligible for this scholarship, and for girls with low odds of being scholarship winners.[5] As we will explain later, the possibility of spillover effects means we must be careful in interpreting our estimates as representing the total effects of the Kalamazoo Promise.

Other research has examined the effects of financial incentives in developed economies. This research often finds effects mainly for women or high-ability groups. Angrist and Lavy (2009) look at the effects of a cash rewards experiment on teenagers graduating from Israeli high schools and find strong effects among high-ability women. Angrist, Lang, and Oreopoulos (2009) study the effects of merit-based scholarships on first-year undergraduates at a large Canadian university. They too find strong effects for women. In a similar study, Leuven, Oosterbeek, and van der Klaauw (2010) conduct a randomized experiment among first-year undergraduates in the Netherlands. The experiment provides a cash reward for those students who completed all of their first-year requirements by the start of the next academic year. They find that rewards matter only for high-ability groups.

The aforementioned studies deal with incentives related to academic output – performance on tests, grades, or fulfilling certain requirements. Standard agency theory suggests that if we want to incentivize a student to exert effort, and we do not observe the resultant effort perfectly, the optimal contract should be conditional on output. Jackson (2010) studies a program in Texas that paid students cash for attaining certain grades on Advanced Placement tests in high school. Using differences in the timing of the adoption of this program, Jackson finds effects on measures of achievement, as predicted by contract theory. However, the prediction of a simple agency model fails if students do not understand the mapping between educational inputs and outputs. Fryer (2011) has studied this issue in experiments on what incentives work best in urban schools. Based on randomized experiments in New York City, Dallas, Chicago, and Washington, DC, Fryer concludes that incentives tied to output (e.g., being paid to do well on a test) are not as effective as those tied to inputs (e.g., being paid to read a book).[6]

In the case of the Promise, as mentioned above, the program provides some incentive for students to improve high school behavior and achievement in order to be admitted to and succeed at more selective postsecondary institutions. However, as Fryer's (2011) work underlines, students may not fully understand what behavior needs to change or how to alter it. In addition, from the perspective of the students, the tuition subsidies of the Promise might be too delayed and too uncertain.[7] For example, Levitt, List, Neckermann, and Sadoff (2012) argue that financial incentives are less potent if they are handed out with a delay.

A skeptic could also argue that the Promise may reduce the incentive for students to work hard to obtain merit-based scholarships. A theoretical argument could also be made that the Promise does not provide additional incentives for low-income students to work hard, because the Promise may simply replace need-based aid. However, we doubt whether these potential negative incentive effects of the Promise are large for most students. Most students do not have a good understanding of how our current system of need-based and merit-based scholarships will affect their college costs.[8] The Promise makes a much more simple "promise" of tuition assistance. This simple "promise" is more likely to be understood by students than the current scholarship system. However, it remains an open question whether even this simple tuition assistance offer is sufficient to make large changes in behavior and academic achievement.

Although there have been no in-depth studies of whether the Promise has changed student behavior, other aspects of the Kalamazoo Promise program have been analyzed (see e.g., Miller-Adams, 2009). Bartik, Eberts, and Huang (2010) find a dramatic post-Promise increase in enrollment. Furthermore, after decades of shrinking enrollment among white students, the Promise has led to a stabilization of KPS's racial makeup. These enrollment effects are due to a one-year increase in the entry rate to KPS, in the year after the Promise, accompanied by a permanent decrease in the exit rate, with these patterns occurring for all ethnic groups. These entry rate and exit rate effects are consistent with the Promise making KPS significantly more attractive to students. Bartik, Eberts, and Huang also find evidence that since the establishment of the Promise, KPS test scores have increased somewhat faster than in similar Michigan school districts.

These results are further corroborated by Miller (2010), who also looks at whether the effects of the scholarship have been capitalized by the real estate market. Using a difference-in-differences design, Miller (2010) does not find positive effects of the Promise on housing prices, but does find that the Promise has had positive effects on student culture – for example, by improving school safety.

Andrews et al. (2010) use a difference-in-differences method to study the effects of the Kalamazoo Promise on college choice. Using proprietary data from the ACT Student Profile Questionnaire, they estimate the effect of the Promise on the test takers' intended college choice set. Using other public high schools in the state of Michigan as a control group, the authors find large effects of the Promise on college choice, especially for students who are economically disadvantaged. The Promise increases student interest in all Michigan public colleges and universities, with particularly strong effects on student interest in the flagship schools – the University of Michigan and Michigan State University. Therefore, this study provides some evidence that the Promise increases student interest in more selective universities, admission to which will require higher student achievement during high school. This paper also suggests that the response might be concentrated among marginal students.

BACKGROUND INFORMATION ON THE KALAMAZOO PUBLIC SCHOOL SYSTEM AND THE KALAMAZOO PROMISE

Kalamazoo Public Schools is a midsized, predominantly urban school system. As Figs. 1 and 2 show, before the Kalamazoo Promise, enrollment had been declining for many years. This partially reflects relatively modest economic growth in Michigan and Kalamazoo. In addition, it reflects Kalamazoo's status as a district centered in a core city (although also including some nearby suburban and rural areas) that has more economic problems than its surrounding metropolitan areas. For example, family poverty rates as of the 2000 census were 13.6 percent in the city of Kalamazoo and 6.5 percent in all of Kalamazoo County.

Even before the Promise, the Kalamazoo school district had many low-income students and many students from diverse ethnic backgrounds. Fig. 3 shows trends in the number of black, Hispanic, and non-Hispanic white students in the district. As can be seen in the figure, in the years before the Promise, although KPS retained a considerable percentage of white students (as well as students who did not qualify for free and reduced

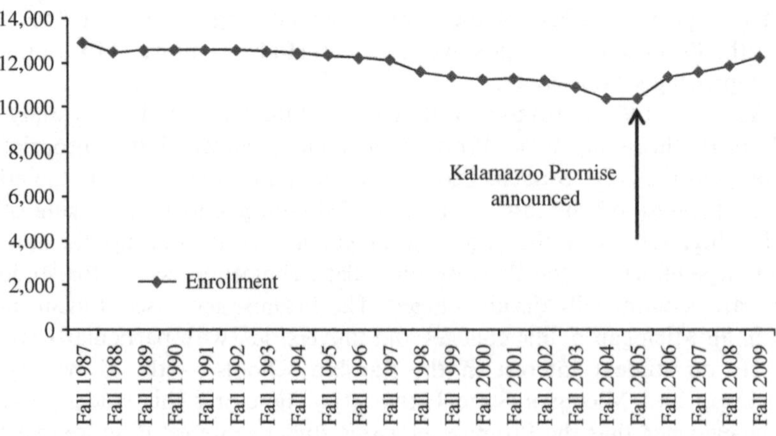

Fig. 1. KPS Enrollment, by Year. *Source*: Bartik et al. (2010).

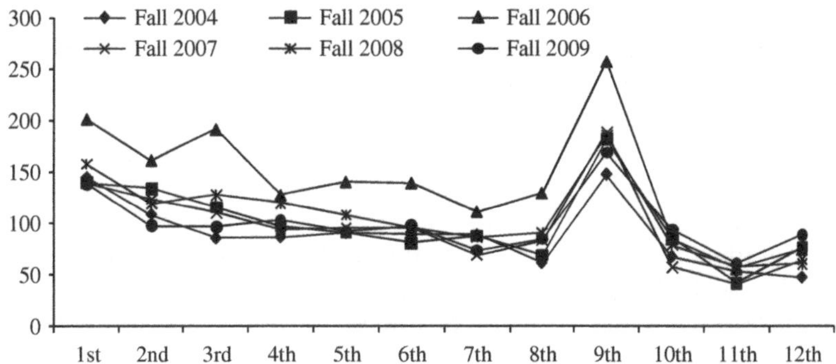

Fig. 2. New Student Entrants to KPS in Fall of Recent School Years, Grades 1–12. *Source*: Bartik et al. (2010).

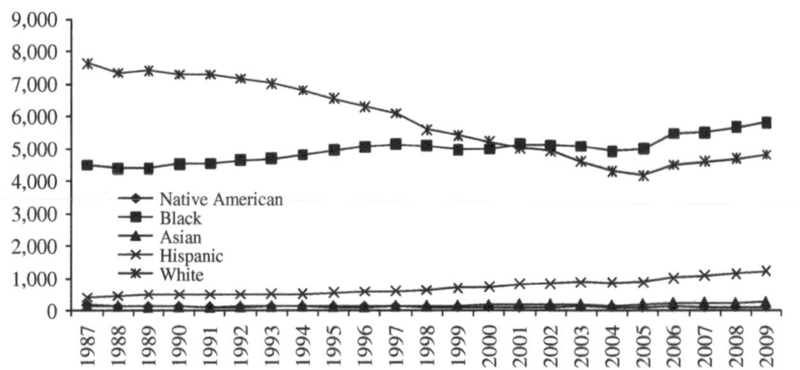

Fig. 3. Number of KPS Students in Various Ethnic Groups, 1987–2009. *Source*: Bartik et al. (2010).

price lunches, not shown), the percentage of such students was clearly falling. Since the advent of the Kalamazoo Promise, enrollment in KPS has been on the rise. Furthermore, enrollment seems to be up proportionately for all ethnic groups, so the ethnic percentages have stabilized. These patterns are consistent with a Promise effect.

The Kalamazoo Promise

According to information provided by the school district, the anonymous donors believe that the Promise's purposes are threefold: (1) to promote local economic and community development, in part by attracting parents and businesses to the Kalamazoo area; (2) to boost educational achievement and attainment; and (3) to help increase confidence in KPS.

The Kalamazoo Promise is available to all students who graduate from KPS, reside in the district, and have been KPS students for four years or longer.[9] The scholarship covers up to 100 percent of all tuition and mandatory fees for up to four years and must be used within 10 years of high school graduation. The benefit is graduated based on the length of attendance in the KPS system. Fig. 4 traces the relation between grade-level enrollment in KPS and the expected fraction of tuition and fees covered if the student graduates from KPS.

Between grades 3 and 9, there is a 5 percent decrement in the generosity of the scholarship for each additional year of postponing enrollment in KPS. The biggest discrete drop-off in generosity occurs between enrolling in ninth grade (65 percent) and tenth grade or later (0 percent). A student entering KPS in grade 10 or afterward is ineligible for Promise tuition benefits.

The requirement of the scholarship is that enrollment and residency must be continuous. For example, suppose a student started in KPS in kindergarten. If that student stays in KPS until graduation, she is eligible for a 100 percent Promise tuition subsidy. If that student instead switches to another district in fifth grade and later reenrolls in KPS in

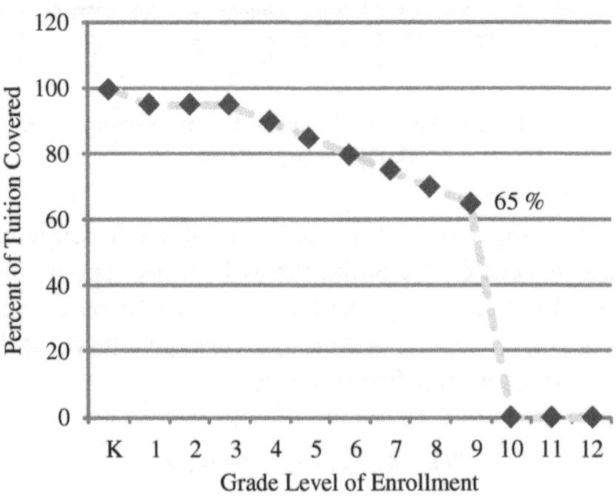

Fig. 4. Generosity of the Kalamazoo Promise Scholarship, by Grade of Enrollment.

ninth grade, she will only be eligible for a 65 percent Promise tuition subsidy.

Other than date of continuous enrollment, no other aspect of a student's K-12 experience or family background directly affects eligibility. Students do not have to demonstrate financial need, maintain any minimum GPA in high school, or take any particular mix of courses. However, students obviously need to be admitted to a college to receive Promise benefits.

The scholarship applies to students who are admitted to and enrolled at any public university or community college in the state of Michigan. The students must be full-time (taking 12 credit hours per semester at a minimum) and maintain a 2.0 GPA in college. Students who fall below a 2.0 GPA can become eligible again for the Promise if they continue attending college on their own dime (or their family's) and then succeed in increasing their cumulative GPA above the 2.0 college GPA requirement.

Students are eligible for Promise benefits for up to 130 credits of undergraduate college or university education. As stated above, this eligibility extends for up to 10 years after high school graduation. The Promise's benefits can be applied to certificate programs at community colleges, not just programs leading to an associate or bachelor's degree.

To gain an appreciation of the value of the Kalamazoo Promise, we calculate a "back-of-the-envelope" estimate of the discounted present value of the scholarship. Our calculations use information about the enrollment decisions of the first cohort of Kalamazoo Promise recipients. About 45 percent of new enrollees in 2006 attended a community college (almost all of them attended the local Kalamazoo Valley Community College, KVCC). The remainder, 181 students, enrolled in public universities, of which the majority enrolled at WMU (101 students), followed by Michigan State University (37) and the University of Michigan (17). We assume that these college-going probabilities remain constant over time and across different tuition subsidy groups.[10] In Table 1, we calculate a present value of the Promise for different subsidy groups. Our calculations indicate that for someone eligible for a 100 percent tuition subsidy, the present value averages $27,413, while for someone who is eligible for a 65 percent subsidy, the present value averages $17,818. We also computed the present value of the 100 percent tuition subsidy version of the Promise at the most expensive college, the University of Michigan, and the present value of one of the cheaper options, KVCC. The present value of four years' tuition at the University of Michigan equals $55,545, whereas the cost of KVCC for two years is $4,731.

Table 1. Present Value of the Kalamazoo Promise for Graduates of KPS.

Tuition Subsidy Group (%)	Present Value (1) ($)	Present Value (2) ($)
0	0	0
65	17,818	21,839
70	19,189	23,519
75	20,560	25,199
80	21,930	26,879
85	23,301	28,559
90	24,671	30,237
95	26,042	31,919
100	27,413	33,599
Present value of Kalamazoo Valley Community College (KVCC) ($)	4,731	
Present value of University of Michigan ($)	55,545	

Source: Tuition costs for community college are based on the 2011–2012 tuition costs for KVCC: http://www.michigancc.net/data/tuition (accessed August 17, 2012). Tuition costs for four-year universities are based on Michigan State Notes: http://www.senate.michigan.gov/sfa/Publications/Notes/2011Notes/NotesSum11bb2.pdf (accessed August 17, 2012).

Note: We assume a 4.7 percent discount rate (we use this number from a study of parents' discount rate for investing in children's health – a proxy for quality; see Agee and Crocker, 1996); a 7 percent annual increase in tuition costs for four-year universities; and a 4 percent increase for community colleges. In column (1), we fix the probability of going to a community college at 0.45 and to a four-year university at 0.55. We base these percentages on enrollment numbers in 2006–2007 of the first cohort of Kalamazoo Promise recipients. In column (2), we change the probability of going to a community college to 0.3 and to a four-year university to 0.7. We assume the tuition cost of community colleges to be equal to $2,385 per year (15 credits). Within the universe of four-year universities, we assume that 13 percent attend the University of Michigan at an annual cost of $13,437; 21 percent attend Michigan State University at $12,769; and 66 percent attend Western Michigan University at $10,140. The last two rows show the discounted present value of a 100 percent tuition subsidy of going to KVCC for two years and of four years at the University of Michigan.

Take-Up of the Kalamazoo Promise and Variation in Eligibility

The Kalamazoo Promise has been widely used among KPS graduates. As Table 2 shows, in the various graduation years, 80–90 percent of KPS graduates have been eligible for at least some Promise benefits. Of those eligible, between 82 and 85 percent at some point have used Promise benefits.

There is wide variation in the Promise subsidy across KPS students. As shown in Table 3, among KPS graduates, the largest group is made up of

Table 2. Trends in Kalamazoo Promise Scholarship Use.

	2006	2007	2008	2009
KPS graduates	518	579	550	535
Eligible for Promise	410	502	476	474
Percentage of graduates eligible	79	87	87	89
Have used Promise	347	419	406	389
Percentage of eligible students who have used Promise at any time	85	83	85	82

Source: Kalamazoo Promise.

Table 3. Promise Eligibility Summary.

Class	0%	65%	70%	75%	80%	85%	90%	95%	100%	Grand total	% eligible	100%
2006	108	45	25	17	18	16	9	40	238	518	79	46
2007	77	57	39	30	24	21	16	38	277	579	87	48
2008	74	50	15	19	16	8	23	48	297	550	87	54
2009	61	43	15	24	17	24	23	60	268	535	89	50
2010	75	74	7	23	22	17	24	59	248	549	86	45
Grand total	395	263	102	113	97	86	95	245	1328	2731	86	49

Source: Kalamazoo Promise.

those eligible for a 100 percent tuition subsidy (attended KPS since kindergarten). However, there are also large numbers ineligible for a subsidy (last entered KPS after ninth grade), eligible for a 65 percent tuition subsidy (entered KPS at ninth grade), and eligible for a 95 percent subsidy (entered KPS at first, second, or third grade).[11]

DATA AND METHODS

Data

Our data come from KPS administrative records. In our analysis, we focus on students in grades 9–12. We chose this focus for several reasons. First, it allows the analysis to include some students who end up being ineligible for the Promise because they entered after ninth grade. Obviously, all students in earlier grades are potentially eligible for at least a 65 percent tuition subsidy. Second, for high school students as opposed to younger students, the tuition subsidy benefits of the Kalamazoo Promise are closer in time. Third, high school students are more likely than students in earlier grades to believe that their achievement and behavior in school will affect their admission prospects at more selective colleges.

Our regression sample consists of ninth- through twelfth-graders from the school years 2003–2004 to 2007–2008. Our "window of observation" thus consists of two pre-Promise years, the year the Promise scholarship was announced, and two post-Promise school years. Because our enrollment data go back to 1997–1998, we consistently track enrollment histories for everyone since sixth grade. Our data set is an unbalanced panel – students are in the panel for various lengths of time, depending upon what grade they started in and how long they stayed in KPS. We have data on student characteristics, GPAs, and disciplinary actions. The disciplinary data consist of information on days of suspension and detention.

We use our data to calculate for each student what his or her Promise subsidy would have been had the Promise been in effect for that year and had the student continued attending KPS until graduation. We call this the student's "virtual Promise benefit." Our hypothesis is that for every time period, students are forward-looking and adjust their behavior as a function of the expected generosity of the Promise, given that they maintain a continuous enrollment in KPS, graduate, and enter a public college or university in Michigan. Our interest lies in estimating how the variation in this perceived future tuition subsidy *at the time of observation* affects achievement and behavior. Throughout our analysis, we therefore focus on these virtual Promise benefits (as opposed to the levels of tuition subsidy at the time of graduation), since they capture a shock to the expectations of the student following the announcement of the scholarship.

For school years 2003–2004 and 2004–2005, these "virtual Promise benefits" are virtual in the sense that the student was unaware of them, as the Promise was not announced until November 2005. Therefore, we would assume that any effect of this simulated Promise benefit in those years reflects effects that are associated with the grade level in which the student entered KPS, rather than the effect of a Promise benefit of which the student had no knowledge.

Including 2003–2004 as an additional control year allows us to see whether there are different trends for Promise-eligible versus ineligible groups during the pre-Promise years. If there are differences in pre-Promise trends between these groups, then there is reason to question whether any post-Promise differences between these groups are actually caused by the Promise.

On November 10, 2005, students became aware of the potential Promise benefits that would accrue to them given their enrollment in KPS to date. This allows some effect of Promise benefits on student achievement and behavior after that date. However, it would be reasonable to assume that there might be some lag time before students fully understood and acted on the incentives of the Promise. By November 2005, students had already made certain decisions about that academic year, such as what courses to enroll in for the fall of 2005. The school year 2006–2007 is a full post-Promise year. By fall 2006, students may have more fully understood what the Promise might mean for their future. Including the 2007–2008 school year adds a second full post-Promise year to help confirm effects estimated for the 2006–2007 year.

Restricting the analysis to these five years limits the extent to which other changes in KPS's policies and practices might differentially affect "length of enrollment" groups, which may differ in unobserved characteristics. Furthermore, in controlling for student fixed effects, we must restrict our attention to years close to the Promise to have students whose high school careers comprise the years both before and after the advent of the Promise.

By comparing changes in the behavior and achievement of Promise-eligible versus Promise-ineligible students, we are likely understating the overall effects of the Promise. It is plausible that even Promise-ineligible students are positively affected by the Promise. If Promise-eligible students improve their achievement and behavior, Promise-ineligible students will be positively affected by peer effects. In addition, the Promise triggered efforts by the school district to increase overall academic standards and college focus among all students. Because of the Promise, teachers and parents may have increased their educational expectations. Higher expectations may have spilled over into benefits for all students, whether Promise-eligible or ineligible. Our comparison of changes from before and after the Promise for Promise-eligible versus ineligible students will only capture the narrow effects of the Promise's monetary offer. This comparison will not fully capture the Promise's effects on overall school climate, through changes in attitudes and actions of administrators, teachers, and parents.

In our sample, we excluded students who moved into the school district at ninth grade after the Promise was announced. These students' families might well have moved into the district because of the Promise. Including such students might lead to Promise-related differences between different groups of students. We do include data for students who moved in at tenth grade or higher grades after the Promise announcement. These students were ineligible for the Promise, so the Promise's monetary benefits are unlikely to be directly motivating them. We also explore how estimates vary if we exclude all such in-migrants.

No data are available on post-KPS academic achievement or behavior for students who left the district. Therefore, we cannot include academic outcomes and behavior for student out-migrants after they leave KPS. There may be differences because of the Promise in the types of students leaving the district. Fully controlling for these differences is impossible in the absence of data on post-out-migration behavior and achievement. As a partial control, and as we will explain further below, our model includes controls for student fixed effects. These student fixed effects use each student as a control for that student's own behavioral and academic achievement tendencies. This minimizes statistical problems due to differences in unobserved characteristics among out-migrants from the district before and after the Promise announcement.

However, we do include achievement and behavior data while in the KPS district for students who end up leaving the district before graduating. These students end up not receiving the Promise. However, if they were potentially Promise-eligible at the time of their enrollment in the district, they are counted as Promise-eligible in our estimates. This definition of Promise eligibility is chosen by us because the decision to leave the district is endogenous, and if we defined the Promise eligibility variable based on students' decision to leave the district, our policy variable would depend on a choice of the student taken with full awareness of the existence of the scholarship (i.e., conditioning on an outcome). Indeed, part of the Promise effect may be due to inducing students to pass more credits, and behave better, and therefore to be less likely to drop out of school. We therefore chose to define the Promise eligibility variable in a way that is less subject to students' endogenous choices. However, this means that our estimates should be interpreted as "intention to treat" estimates and hence are likely to understate the Promise's effects on student achievement and behavior, relative to hypothetical effects on students who knew for certain that they would remain in the district.

We analyze a wide variety of dependent variables reflecting possible student responses to the Promise. The dependent variables include measures of whether students were suspended and days suspended from school, as well as whether students received in-school detention. We also look at various academic achievement measures, such as credits earned and GPA.[12,13]

Student behavior, such as suspensions or detentions, may be more straightforwardly and immediately affected by student choices than the academic achievement measures. Academic achievement could be argued to be the ultimate "bottom-line" measure of whether the program has been effective in improving student outcomes. However, policymakers may also care about whether the program affects "soft skills," which may be reflected in student behavior. Furthermore, student behavior should eventually have effects on academic achievement. For all these reasons, both student behavior and academic achievement are of interest and are examined in this paper.

Table 4 presents descriptive statistics for the sample. We pooled the years together into "before" (2003–2004 and 2004–2005) and "after" (2005–2006 through 2007–2008) periods. We also separated whether the student is eligible for any or no future tuition subsidy ("Benefit > 0" and "No benefit"). We report the sample means, the standard deviations (although not for proportions), and the number of observations (i.e., the number of student-year cells).

As can be seen from the demographic data, the student population of KPS over this time is certainly diverse. Many disadvantaged students are included, as well as many racial minorities, but there are also many white students and nondisadvantaged students. We notice several demographic differences between the groups that were eligible for some future tuition subsidy and those that were not. Before the announcement of the Promise, the recent enrollees – entitled to no future tuition subsidy – were more likely to be African American and beneficiaries of free and reduced-price lunches. These differences may in part reflect differential out-migration behavior as well as our exclusion of post-Promise ninth-grade in-migrants.

For our dependent variables on student behavior and achievement, low baseline levels of behavior and achievement leave plenty of room for improvement, whether because of the Promise or other influences. Prior to the Promise, over 20 percent of students received an out-of-school suspension each year. Average GPA levels were low, at around 2.0 (a C average). Average credits earned were around six credits out of the eight credits per year normally available under the district's block scheduling program.[14] Although these numbers are low, they do not appear to be unusual for urban school districts.[15]

Table 4 emphasizes the need to include careful controls to uncover the true effects of the Promise, as well as possible contradictory results for different variables. For example, a simple post-Promise announcement comparison of GPA and credits earned between Promise-eligible and ineligible

Table 4. Summary Statistics: Means (Standard Deviations in Parentheses), Before and After the Promise, by Eligibility for the Promise (No Benefit Versus 65 Percent or More).

	Before (2003/2004–2004/2005)		After (2005/2006–2007/2008)	
	No benefit	Benefit > 0	No benefit	Benefit > 0
Variable				
Demographic characteristics				
Female	0.50	0.48	0.55	0.48
Free/Reduced price lunch	0.60	0.49	0.53	0.54
White	0.36	0.45	0.38	0.40
Black	0.51	0.46	0.52	0.50
Hispanic	0.10	0.07	0.06	0.08
Outcome variables				
Suspended (0/1)	0.20	0.22	0.15	0.23
Days suspended	1.12	1.73	0.89	2.13
	(3.39)	(9.50)	(3.64)	(8.32)
In detention (0/1)	0.07	0.09	0.08	0.12
Credits earned (0/1)	0.87	0.96	0.88	0.93
Credits earned	4.62	6.12	5.25	5.77
	(3.23)	(2.63)	(3.31)	(2.77)
GPA	1.57	2.15	1.78	2.05
	(1.22)	(1.21)	(1.27)	(1.25)
Grade				
Grade 9	0.19	0.40	0.06	0.36
Grade 10	0.30	0.25	0.28	0.24
Grade 11	0.25	0.19	0.30	0.21
Grade 12	0.26	0.17	0.36	0.18
Benefit				
Benefit = 0	1.00	0.00	1.00	0.00
Benefit = 65	0.00	0.15	0.00	0.09
Benefit = 70	0.00	0.06	0.00	0.04
Benefit = 75	0.00	0.06	0.00	0.06
Benefit = 80+	0.00	0.73	0.00	0.80
Number of observations	786	5,226	724	7,693

Source: Kalamazoo Public Schools.
Note: "Days suspended" is days of out-of-school suspension during the school year. GPA average is computed on the four-point scale ($A = 4.0$, $B = 3.0$, $C = 2.0$, $D = 1.0$, $F = 0$). The number of observations is the number of student-year cells used in computing the above statistics. Standard deviations for continuous variables are in parentheses below the sample mean.

students suggests somewhat greater academic achievement by Promise-eligible students. However, the post-Promise behavior of Promise-eligible students, compared to ineligible students, is actually somewhat worse.

In addition, although academic achievement was somewhat higher post-Promise for Promise-eligible students, the trends appear worse when we look at pre-Promise data. Even prior to the Promise, students whose enrollment decisions would have made them eligible for the Promise had higher academic achievement. If anything, it appears as if the academic gap between eligible students and ineligible students has narrowed from before the Promise to after the Promise. For behavior, the trend from before and after the Promise announcement shows some worsening of behavior in the Promise-eligible group relative to the ineligible group.

These patterns suggest that it will be difficult to find Promise effects by making simple comparisons of group differences in levels or trends of achievement or behavior. A variety of factors, such as differential out-migration, may confuse such comparisons. This justifies a more careful effort to fully control for unobserved influences on student achievement and behavior, which we do using student fixed effects.

As the table shows, the data include a wide variety of grade levels, from ninth through twelfth. We might expect that different grades would have their own characteristic patterns of GPA, credits earned, and behavior. Therefore, it is important to control for grade differences. All of our statistical analysis includes controls for grade effects.

Table 4 shows that some ninth-graders are not eligible for the Promise. In those cases, the student had enrolled after the state's fall census date for schools, and according to conversations with the administrators of the scholarship, the enrollment of such a student counts as if the student had enrolled in tenth grade. Finally, we see a decline in the fraction of students eligible for 65 percent or more of the future tuition subsidy. This happens because we drop all of the new students entering ninth grade after November 10, 2005.

As the data show, the overwhelming majority of students who are eligible for any benefit are eligible for a benefit of 80 percent or more of college tuition.[16] This suggests that it will be difficult to make fine distinctions for students receiving subsidies for different tuition subsidy groups. In addition, it is unclear whether the difference between a 65 percent subsidy and greater subsidies is salient for most high school students. Our empirical work therefore focuses on differences in academic achievement and behavior between Promise-eligible and ineligible students, before and after the Promise for the same students.[17]

METHODS

We measure the effects on student behavior and achievement of the Promise's monetary offer by comparing differences, from before and after the Promise, for Promise-eligible versus ineligible students. This comparison controls for fixed effects for the year of the observation, for the grade, and for the student. Our key focus is on estimating the effect of the interaction between the year of the observation and the student's Promise-eligibility status. If we see a clear change or trend in this variable after the Promise, with no sign of a clear trend before the Promise, we regard this as good evidence of a Promise effect. We summarize this model in Eq. (1):

$$y_{it}=\sum_t \delta_t T_t+\varphi I\{Benefit>0\}_i+\sum_t \gamma_t(T_t\times I\{Benefit>0\}_i)+x'_{it}\beta+F_i+G_{it}+u_{it} \quad (1)$$

where y_{it} is a dependent variable showing student i's achievement or behavior at year t (GPA, credits earned, suspensions, detentions). The fixed effect T controls for the way the outcome variable of interest varies by year, where the t subscript indexes the year. The indicator function $I\{Benefit > 0\}$ equals 1 if the student i would be eligible for any tuition subsidy from the Promise scholarship (65 percent or more), given that he or she continues attending KPS until graduation. The interaction between the year effect and the Promise eligibility allows for unrestricted variation by year in how Promise eligibility is related to student achievement or behavior. The fixed effect F_i holds constant any fixed student characteristics, observed or unobserved, that influence student achievement or behavior.[18] x_{it} are time-varying student characteristics, such as free and reduced-price lunch status, which might influence academic achievement or behavior. (Time-invariant student characteristics, such as gender or race, are captured by the fixed effect for each student.) The grade effect (G_{it}) controls for effects of a given grade (ninth through twelfth) on average academic achievement or behavior. u_{it} is the disturbance term.[19]

The model is estimated via a regression in all cases. In some cases, y_{it} is a discrete zero-one variable (whether any credits earned that year, whether any suspensions that year, whether any detentions that year). In those cases, the model estimated is a linear probability model.

The model is estimated using data over all students in the sample for which descriptive statistics are provided in Table 4. This includes any student in KPS high schools at any point in the five years 2003–2004 through 2007–2008, except for those who moved in after the Promise was announced and were eligible for the Promise (e.g., moved in at the beginning of ninth grade). However, because of the inclusion of student fixed effects, students with only one annual observation must be dropped from the estimation using student fixed effects.

Our preferred model includes student fixed effects. As with virtually any educational policy analysis, it is impossible in principle to exclude student fixed effects on student educational achievement and behavior. Prior research suggests that such student effects may be large. However, here the relevant issue is whether we need to control for student effects, e.g., to condition on these effects and thereby treat them as fixed, in order to get unbiased estimates of Promise effects. We will need to control for student effects as fixed effects if such student fixed effects are correlated with the $T \times I\{Benefit > 0\}$ interaction terms. The student fixed effects will be correlated with year dummy multiplied by Promise eligibility interaction terms when there is differential migration of different Promise eligibility groups into or out of the KPS district after the Promise. For example, we could imagine that some families with "better students" – in part, "better" for reasons that are unobserved – may be less likely to move students with zero eligibility out of KPS because of the Promise. This might occur if such students also have younger siblings who *are* eligible for the Promise.

In our regressions, we choose the "zero eligibility" category and the immediate year preceding the announcement of the Promise (2004–2005) as our omitted reference categories. Our interest is the time pattern of effects of Promise eligibility by year versus those omitted reference categories. The assumption is that, after controlling for student fixed effects and all the other fixed effects, if there is no clear time trend prior to the Promise announcement in the effects of Promise eligibility, but there are clear effects on the level and trend of student achievement and behavior after the Promise announcement, then this provides reasonable evidence of a true Promise effect. In other words, it seems implausible to us that such a pattern of Promise eligibility effects over time would be due to time trends in the disturbance term that just happen to be correlated with the year multiplied by Promise eligibility interaction terms in a way that produces this pattern. More formally, we are assuming that controlling for student fixed effects, year fixed effects, Promise eligibility fixed effects, and grade fixed effects, the disturbance term is either exogenous to the year multiplied by Promise eligibility interaction term or, more weakly, is not correlated in a way that will produce this pattern. However, if we see an effect on the post-Promise trend in some outcome but, at the same time, a trend is also evident in pre-Promise data, we deem that post-Promise trend to not provide convincing evidence of a true Promise effect. To see whether student fixed effects make a difference, we also estimate a model without student fixed effects. Such models add in controls for observable characteristics of the students that do not vary over time, such as gender and race.[20]

As stated earlier, our data set is an unbalanced panel, where we observe new students entering as well as established students leaving the school district. There is little concern that, before the announcement of the Promise, this in- and out-migration would be systematic with respect to anticipation of a universal scholarship. However, in the post-Promise years, students have an incentive to enroll in KPS. Because this post-Promise sorting is endogenous, we exclude all the new students who enrolled in ninth grade after November 10, 2005 (as these students are entitled to have 65 percent of the tuition covered if they stay enrolled). We allow for new entrants in grades 10–12, as they are entitled to zero coverage and have no financial incentive to enroll in KPS because of the Promise. Nevertheless, in order to be prudent about maintaining the exogenous nature of how the Promise assigns the different levels of generosity, we conduct a robustness check by excluding these observations. This turns out not to matter much for our main results, though for some results it leads the point estimates to lose some precision.

RESULTS

Main Results

Table 5 shows results for academic achievement-dependent variables, and Table 6 shows results for behavioral-dependent variables. The omitted dummies are the immediate pre-Promise year of 2004–2005 and the zero benefit category.

We do not report coefficients on other controls. In the specifications without student fixed effects, these other variables include controls for gender and race/ethnic group (white, black, Hispanic). Such non-time varying controls are dropped from the fixed-effect specifications. Both fixed-effect specifications and non-fixed specifications include controls for year of the observation by itself and by grade level. In addition, all specifications include control for free and reduced-price lunch status, which varies over time. Finally, all specifications include a dummy that indicates whether

Table 5. Estimated Effect of the Kalamazoo Promise on Academic Achievement.

	(1)	(2)	(3)	(4)	(5)	(6)
	OLS	FE	OLS	FE	OLS	FE
Variable	GPA	GPA	Credits earned	Credits earned	Credits earned (0/1)	Credits earned (0/1)
Interaction terms: γ_t						
2003–2004 × Benefit > 0	0.0779	−0.0675	0.812***	0.172	0.0492**	−0.00978
	(0.964)	(−0.913)	(3.707)	(0.681)	(2.099)	(−0.331)
2004–2005 × Benefit > 0	–	–	–	–	–	–
2005–2006 × Benefit > 0	0.0450	0.0584	−0.239	−0.284	0.00243	−0.00987
	(0.496)	(0.750)	(−0.955)	(−1.083)	(0.0998)	(−0.436)
2006–2007 × Benefit > 0	−0.159	0.133	−0.437	−0.0830	−0.00278	0.0331
	(−1.428)	(1.315)	(−1.418)	(−0.246)	(−0.0880)	(0.949)
2007–2008 × Benefit > 0	−0.330**	0.205	−0.466	0.587	−0.000759	0.0879*
	(−2.526)	(1.274)	(−1.278)	(1.293)	(−0.0197)	(1.819)
Constant	2.042***	2.075***	4.637***	5.514***	0.860***	0.879***
	(18.87)	(102.7)	(20.36)	(83.44)	(40.18)	(111.8)
Observations (NT)	14,429	14,429	14,429	14,429	14,429	14,429
Observations (N)		6,618		6,618		6,618
R-squared	0.298	0.019	0.196	0.044	0.059	0.077
F-test	4.906	0.550	0.278	2.448	0.0163	2.514
p-value	0.00743	0.577	0.758	0.0865	0.984	0.0810
Effect size 2005–2006	0.0354	0.0459	−0.0861	−0.103	0.0103	−0.0418
Effect size 2006–2007	−0.125	0.104	−0.158	−0.0300	−0.0118	0.140
Effect size 2007–2008	−0.259	0.161	−0.168	0.212	−0.00322	0.373

Source: Kalamazoo Public Schools.

Note: Robust *t*-statistics in parentheses. ***$p < 0.01$; **$p < 0.05$; *$p < 0.1$. Regressions include the following controls: female, free and reduced-price lunch, white, black, Hispanic, grade level (9–12), indicator for whether the student is new enrollee, an indicator for whether the student has had a change in the eligibility level over time, and a full set of interactions between school years (2003–2004, 2005–2006, 2006–2007, and 2007–2008) and Promise eligibility dummy (Benefit > 0). For the regressors of interest, the benchmark category is the school year 2004–2005 and eligibility level equals to zero. Hence, for the positive eligibility level, the estimate is the difference in the outcome variable over time (from 2004–2005 to 2007–2008) relative to the same change in the zero eligibility group (control). The *F*-test and *p*-value show test statistics from a joint test of significance for the interaction terms γ_t for the years 2005–2006, 2006–2007, and 2007–2008. The effect size is calculated by dividing the coefficient from each regression by the standard deviation of dependent variable in the control year (school year 2004–2005). Universe: Students enrolled in KPS in grades 9–12 during school years 2003–2004 through 2007–2008 subject to sample restrictions; see the text for details.

Table 6. Estimated Effect of the Kalamazoo Promise on Student Behavior.

Variables	(1) OLS Suspended (0/1)	(2) FE Suspended (0/1)	(3) OLS Days suspended	(4) FE Days suspended	(5) OLS In detention (0/1)	(6) FE In detention (0/1)	(7) OLS Days in detention	(8) FE Days in detention
Interaction terms: γ_t								
2003–2004 × Benefit > 0	0.00894	0.00950	−0.134	−0.0117	0.0259	−0.00258	0.0613	0.0825
	(0.313)	(0.226)	(−0.396)	(−0.0277)	(1.342)	(−0.0917)	(1.026)	(0.873)
2004–2005 × Benefit > 0	–	–	–	–	–	–	–	–
2005–2006 × Benefit > 0	0.00786	−0.00969	0.369	−0.357	−0.00712	−0.0157	0.0466	−0.0411
	(0.260)	(−0.253)	(0.914)	(−0.796)	(−0.298)	(−0.521)	(0.593)	(−0.370)
2006–2007 × Benefit > 0	0.0249	−0.0215	−0.115	−1.296**	0.0542**	0.00936	0.0933	−0.0671
	(0.693)	(−0.427)	(−0.235)	(−2.396)	(2.147)	(0.252)	(1.218)	(−0.588)
2007–2008 × Benefit > 0	0.0378	−0.0579	−0.502	−1.796***	−0.00185	−0.0207	−0.0687	−0.179
	(1.034)	(−0.924)	(−1.036)	(−2.833)	(−0.0675)	(−0.468)	(−0.938)	(−1.379)
Constant	0.207***	0.210***	1.772***	1.521***	0.122***	0.106***	0.245***	0.197***
	(6.876)	(18.09)	(5.040)	(4.218)	(5.798)	(11.38)	(4.470)	(4.888)
Observations (NT)	14,429	14,429	14,429	14,429	14,429	14,429	14,429	14,429
Observations (N)		6,618		6,618		6,618		6,618
R-squared	0.149	0.056	0.047	0.023	0.090	0.042	0.056	0.037
F-test	0.411	0.431	2.018	3.319	4.394	0.491	3.834	1.019
p-value	0.663	0.650	0.133	0.0363	0.0124	0.612	0.0217	0.361
Effect size 2005–2006	0.0187	−0.0230	0.0310	−0.0301	−0.0231	−0.0509	0.0426	−0.0376
Effect size 2006–2007	0.0593	−0.0510	−0.00965	−0.109	0.176	0.0304	0.0853	−0.0613
Effect size 2007–2008	0.0899	−0.138	−0.0423	−0.151	−0.00602	−0.0671	−0.0628	−0.164

Source: Kalamazoo Public Schools.
Note: Robust *t*-statistics in parentheses. ***$p < 0.01$; **$p < 0.05$. Other details are same as in Table 5 footnote. Universe: Students enrolled in KPS in grades 9–12 during school years 2003–2004 through 2007–2008 subject to sample restrictions, see the text for details.

there is variation in the student's expected benefit across time after the school year 2005–2006 within students and any new enrollees post 2005–2006. Such variation could occur if a student moved out of the district and then back in, as the Promise benefit is based on length of continuous enrollment.

Our focus is on the estimated effects of the Promise benefit categories interacted with the dummy for the year 2005–2006 (the year of the announcement) and for 2006–2007 and 2007–2008, the post-Promise years. These interacted effects are relative to the effect for the zero-benefit category in the school year 2004–2005. For the fixed-effect regressions, these estimated effects also control for the student's performance or behavior in other years. In other words, we look at whether students in the various Promise benefit categories differentially changed in the years following the announcement relative to their own history, and then compare these findings to what happened to students in the zero-benefit category.

As the tables show, in the regressions without fixed effects, Promise eligibility frequently has the unexpected sign, and it is sometimes statistically significant and negative. For example, without student fixed effects, students entitled to any Promise tuition subsidy are estimated to have a statistically significantly reduced GPA. In contrast, results are more often of the expected sign and statistically significant when we control for student fixed effects. For example, the GPA effects switch to being of the expected sign in the fixed effect (FE) specification.

Although results are more often of the "expected sign" in the FE specifications, estimates are sometimes imprecise. Estimated effects in the FE specifications on GPA, number of credits earned, the zero-one dummy for whether suspended, and the detention variables are all of the expected sign (e.g., positive effects on GPA and credits earned, negative effects on the behavioral variables). However, these estimates are imprecise enough that we cannot rule out a wide range of effects.

However, some of the FE estimates are of the expected sign and statistically significant. In these FE specifications, we find statistically significant positive effects (at a 10 percent level) of Promise eligibility in 2007–2008 on whether a student earned any credits at all during the year. We also find statistically significant negative effects (at a 5 percent level or more) of Promise eligibility in 2006–2007 and 2007–2008 on the number of days a student was suspended from school during the year.

The bottom rows of Tables 5 and 6 provide another way of ascertaining the size of the estimated effects of the Kalamazoo Promise benefits on student achievement and behavior in the years following the Promise. As is often done in educational research, we compute the "effect size" of this policy for the dependent variables that are continuous. This simply rescales the estimated effects by the standard deviation of these variables across individual students in some control group, which in this case is taken to be the standard deviation across individual students in the pre-Promise year of 2004–2005. For GPA, the estimated effect sizes in the fixed-effects model are about 0.05σ–0.16σ in magnitude, which represent effect sizes that are typical of many educational interventions.[21]

The average number of days of out-of-school suspension declined for Promise beneficiaries in 2006–2007, compared to nonbeneficiaries, by a little over one day per school year. This is averaged across all students, including the approximately 80 percent of all students who received no out-of-school suspensions, and is large compared to the average number of days suspended over all students (which is about two days). We see that this effect is even more pronounced in the school year 2007–2008, with a decline of about two days.

As Tables 5 and 6 show, results differ considerably when controlling for individual student fixed effects. This implies that individual student fixed effects and their trends over time must be correlated with the interactions between year dummies and benefit categories.[22] These differential time trends are consistent with the absence of controls for fixed effects leading to the "wrong" sign for Promise benefits in the post-Promise year. Because fixed effects are the same for all students who remain in the sample over time, these trends reflect differences in the students moving into or out of KPS during that period. For the zero benefit group, this out-migration and in-migration has tended to lead to higher student fixed effects of the students that remain, whereas for the students in the positive benefit categories this is not as true. The causes of this differential migration form an interesting topic that we hope to explore in future research.

Multiyear difference-in-differences analysis can be represented in a graph and enables detection of existing pre-intervention group multiplied by time trends. The idea is that if our estimation procedure is sound, we would not see any significant effects for Promise-eligible groups versus non-Promise-eligible groups in the years preceding the announcement of the Promise. This is a type of falsification test for our model.

The various panels of Figs. 5 and 6 plot the difference-in-differences point estimates from the fixed-effects regressions, along with 90 percent confidence intervals, across the pre- and post-Promise years. Recall that 2005–2006 was only a partial Promise year, as the Promise was announced in November 2005. We might expect effects in this first Promise year to be smaller, as it may take some time for students, parents, and teachers to make much of a substantial adjustment to the incentives provided by the Promise. In general, the effects are statistically insignificant for 2005–2006.

Panel A of Fig. 5 shows the difference-in-differences point estimates for GPA from column (1) in Table 5. It is clear from the plot that the estimate seems driven by a preexisting trend. In addition, the post-Promise point calculation is estimated imprecisely. Therefore, it is hard to argue that there is any convincing evidence of a causal effect of the Promise on GPA.

As a robustness check we have also grouped students based on whether they are eligible for a 65 percent tuition subsidy or a subsidy that is 80 percent or more. The findings for GPA are very similar to the trend displayed in Panel A of Fig. 5.

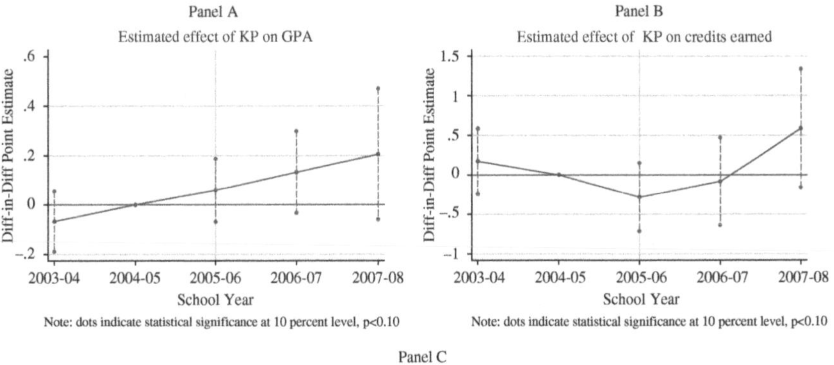

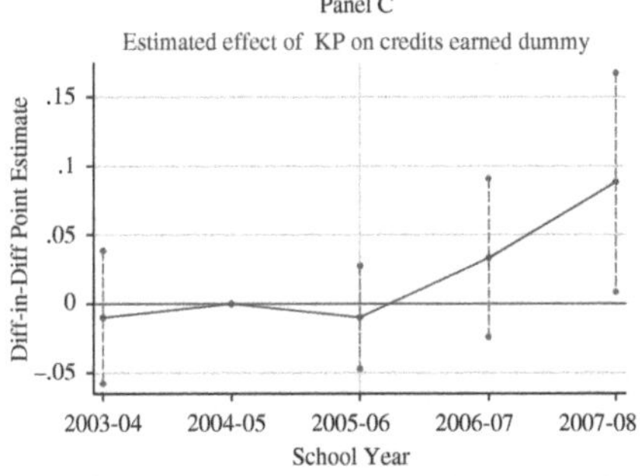

Fig. 5. Estimated Effect (Fixed Effects) of the Kalamazoo Promise (KP) on Academic Achievement. *Note*: The Kalamazoo Promise was announced on November 10, 2005 (school year 2005–2006). Panels A–C use the same specification as fixed-effects regressions in Table 5. Dots around estimates indicate statistical significance at the 10 percent level, $p < 0.10$.

Turning to Panels B and C, which plot the effect on credits earned and whether the student earned any credits (i.e., the point estimates from columns (4) and (6) in Table 5), we observe that following 2005–2006, any preexisting group multiplied by year trend appears to have been reversed. The point estimate in the school year 2007–2008 suggests that the probability of earning any credits is about 8.8 percent higher for students eligible for some future tuition subsidy. This latter point estimate is significant at the 5 percent level.

Fig. 6 plots the point estimates from Table 6. The results are clear: there are no statistically significant differences in the pre-Promise effects. In addition, the point estimates in 2003–2004 in Panel A through Panel D are

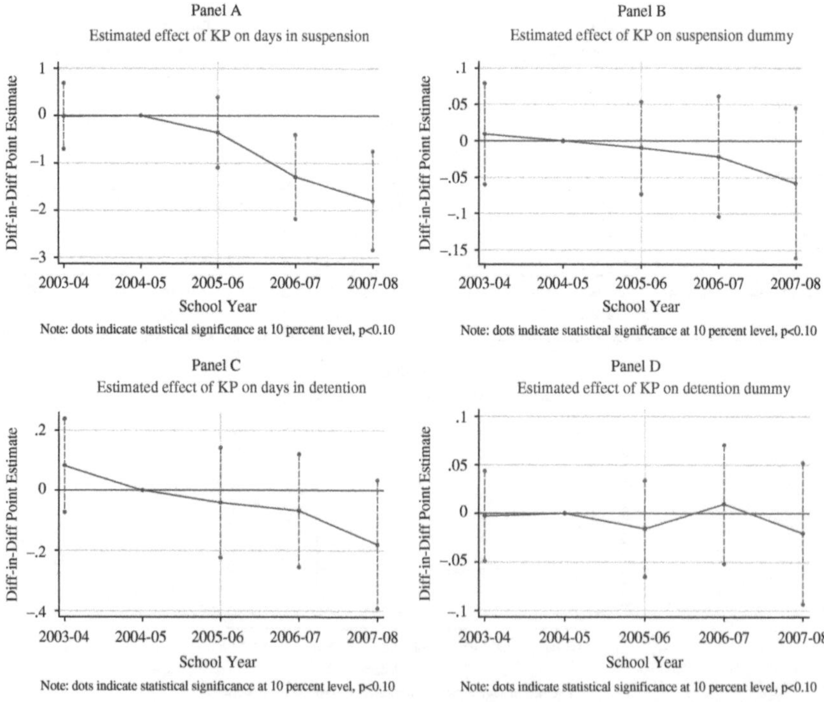

Fig. 6. Estimated Effect (Fixed Effects) of the Kalamazoo Promise (KP) on Student Behavior. *Note*: The Kalamazoo Promise was announced on November 10, 2005 (school year 2005–2006). Panels A–D use the same specification as fixed-effects regressions in Table 6. Dots around estimates indicate statistical significance at the 10 percent level, $p < 0.10$.

approximately zero. Following the Promise, days spent in suspension decrease during the school year 2005–2006 and continue to decrease.

Table 4 shows that the distribution of days spent in suspension and detention is quite skewed – as most students are not suspended or detained, there is a large cluster of zeros. In order to determine whether the effect on total days suspended or in detention is driven by the extensive margin, we also plot the point estimates of the effect of the Promise on the probability of being suspended or assigned detention. The point estimate on the probability of being suspended is imprecise but also suggests a decrease; see Panel B of Fig. 6. This implies that the overall effect on days suspended is at least in part due to effects on the likelihood of being suspended.[23]

For detention, the pattern is different; the probability of being assigned detention at school appears not to have been affected. Hence, it is likely that the overall effect on days spent in detention is driven by the intensive margin.

Robustness Checks

Figure 7 shows some robustness checks: it shows the point estimates for probability of earning any credits and days spent in suspension for a reduced sample. We focus on these two outcome variables, as (1) we deem them not to display pre-Promise trends and (2) the post-Promise point estimates were significantly different from zero, at least at the 10 percent significance level.

This restricted sample drops all the students who entered tenth–twelfth grade in KPS after the Promise was announced in November 2005. (We already excluded ninth-graders who came after the Promise, as they would be eligible for Promise benefits, which might differentially affect in-migration. However, we previously included tenth- through twelfth-graders who came after the Promise announcement, as they are ineligible for Promise benefits.) This reduced sample also excludes those who had a change in their benefit (for example, dropped out and reenrolled) in 2005–2006 or later. In sum, 1,037 observations are dropped. Who are the students in this zero eligibility group? They consist of the following groups:

- Students who enrolled in KPS in 2005 in their ninth-grade year after the state fall count date or did not stay throughout the whole school year. Thus, the first year "countable" toward the Promise for them was when they were tenth-graders, and that makes them ineligible.
- Students who enrolled as tenth-graders in 2005 – these students will not get any benefit, even if they came before November 10, because they were not in KPS as ninth-graders.

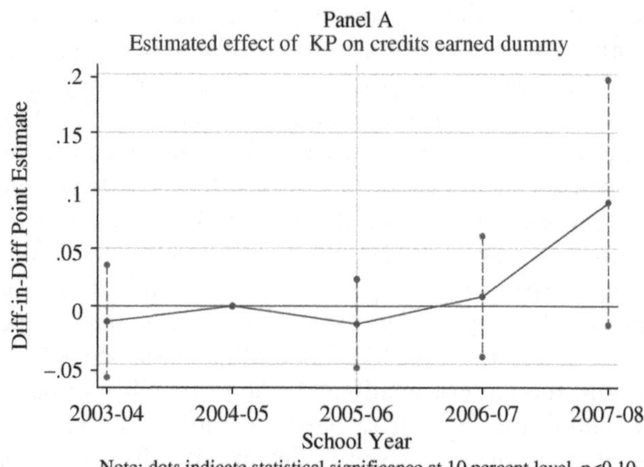

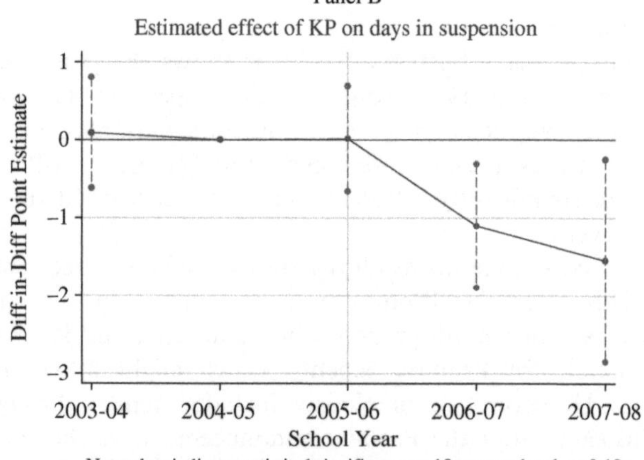

Fig. 7. Estimated Effect (Fixed Effects) of the Kalamazoo Promise (KP) on Outcomes – Robustness Checks for Selected Results. *Note*: The Kalamazoo Promise was announced on November 10, 2005 (school year 2005–2006). In both specifications we drop all the new enrollees since and including 2005–2006 and all of those who changed their eligibility level after and including 2005–2006. This sample consists of 13,392 observations.

The main effects of moving to this reduced sample are twofold. First, the estimated effects of the Promise on the dummy for credits earned lose some precision; it is now only statistically different from zero at a 16.4 percent level. Second, the effect is still positive and of important size: a 9 percentage point increase in the probability of earning credits.

The lower panel for Fig. 7 shows the effect on days spent in suspension. This effect is still statistically different from zero, though the point estimates are a bit smaller in absolute magnitude: in 2007–2008, the decrease in days spent in suspension is 1.55.

We also considered specifications in which we dropped all newly enrolled ninth-graders for all years. We wanted to make sure that our baseline results were not driven by our decision to only drop newly enrolled ninth-graders after the Promise announcement. We found that dropping all newly enrolled ninth-graders for all years did not significantly change any of our results.

Analysis by Subsamples

Previous research studying the effects of educational interventions often finds heterogeneous responses for boys and girls and by race/ethnicity. The economically and racially diverse nature of KPS allows us to analyze student outcomes by race.[24] Specifically, in Fig. 8 we focus on African American students and impose the same sample restrictions as used in the robustness analysis in Fig. 7. This subsample consists of 6,385 observations – 5,808 eligible for any tuition subsidy and 577 observations not eligible for anything.

The results for African American students are striking. For black students, unlike for the entire sample, there do not appear to be clear group multiplied by pre-Promise trends in GPA. Panel A suggests that following the Promise, GPA has increased and continues to improve for these Promise-eligible black students. There does not appear to be a clear pre-Promise effect in the school year 2003–2004. The results are also very big in magnitude; for example, in the school year 2007–2008 there was an increase of 0.70 in GPA. The GPA effects traced in Fig. 8 translate to a 0.174σ increase in the school year 2005–2006, followed by a 0.280σ increase in 2006–2007, and an enormous 0.63σ increase in 2007–2008. One might wonder why these difference-in-differences point estimates keep trending up following the Promise, as opposed to observing a one-time increase in GPA. We would expect to find such a continuing increase if following the Promise there are synergies cross-mapping into higher performance – for example, higher effort and performance in one school year could lead to still higher performance the next school year.

Panels C and D show the impact on days spent in suspension or detention. On average, the point estimate for black students implies a decrease of two days of suspension in the first full post-Promise year and a three-day decrease in 2007–2008. Note that the effect on the number of days spent in detention is not precisely estimated.

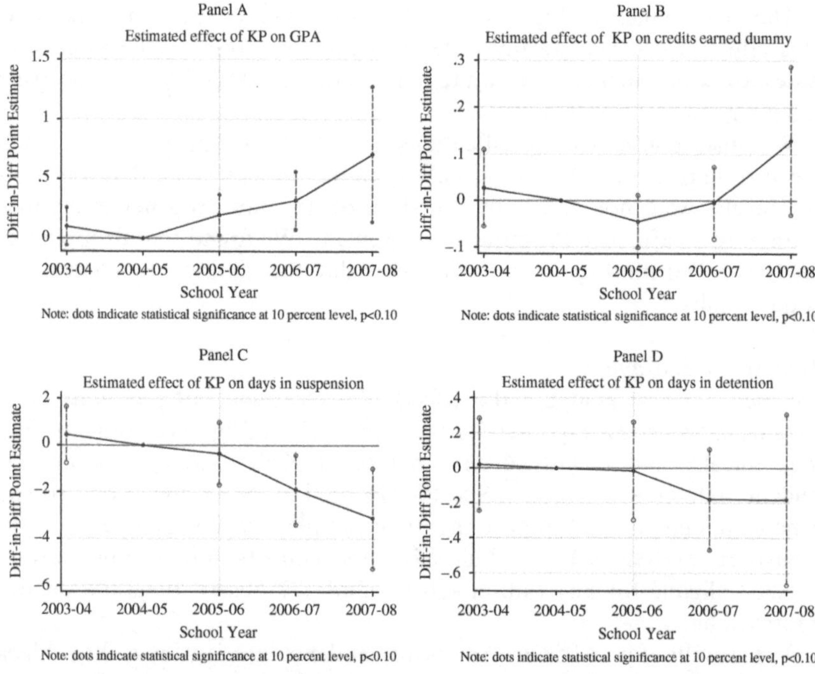

Fig. 8. Estimated Effect (Fixed Effects) of the Kalamazoo Promise (KP) on Outcomes – Selected Results for the Subsample of African American Students Only. *Note*: The Kalamazoo Promise was announced on November 10, 2005 (school year 2005–2006). This specification includes only African American students. Additionally, we drop all the new enrollees since 2005–2006 (including that year) and all of those who changed their eligibility level after and including 2005–2006. This sample consists of 6,385 observations.

For African American students there is a contemporaneous change in the effect the Promise has on days spent in suspension and GPA that we do not observe for the overall sample. On average, these students have a lower GPA and more days spent in suspension than their white counterparts. We can only speculate whether this decrease in the days spent in suspension might have shifted past some "tipping point" beyond which more presence in the classroom leads to higher grades, while leaving the white students unaffected.

Discussion

Overall, we believe that the results suggest that the Kalamazoo Promise did have some differential effects on student achievement and behavior even in the first full post-Promise year, which is 2006–2007. These differential effects on Promise-eligible students are most convincing for increasing the probability of earning any credits and for reducing out-of-school suspensions – and, mainly for the African American students, for an increase in GPA. There is less convincing evidence that the Promise may have increased GPA in the full sample.

Our results relate directly to the body of work trying to understand the incentives in urban education. In his work on incentivizing students in urban schools, Fryer (2011) concludes that, in general, paying for inputs tends to give better results than conditioning rewards on student output. These findings are consistent with students not fully understanding the education production mapping between inputs and achievement. Specifically, Fryer finds that rewarding works best when the students perceive that they can exert control over the input.

Our findings indirectly support Fryer's notion. It is possible that students simply do not know what inputs map directly into a higher GPA, but they understand that the opportunities given by the Promise are dependent on displaying better behavior in school. Thus, the relevant margin along which the students react could be that of altering their behavior so that fewer days are spent in out-of-school suspension.

If this hypothesis is correct, our findings suggest that Promise-style policies, and other policies focused on making higher education more affordable, may be usefully supplemented by helping students better understand how their behavior affects their future. Subsidies for higher education may make a greater difference in student achievement and behavior if students understand the link between their behavior and work habits and their GPA, and the link between their GPA and the future rewards offered by the Promise.

CONCLUSION

This paper uses the large change in expected college tuition costs induced by the surprise announcement of the Kalamazoo Promise's tuition subsidies to estimate the Promise's effects on student achievement and behavior. The structure of the Kalamazoo Promise benefit formula creates a quasi-experiment for evaluating the impact of the scholarship on Promise-eligible students. We find positive effects for credits earned and a decrease in days spent in suspension.

Our results suggest that universal scholarships can be effective in incentivizing students to exert effort by improving their behavior at school. Our results lead us to speculate about ways to strengthen the effects of Promise-type tuition scholarships and other policies to make postsecondary education more affordable. If students in urban school districts do not completely understand their education production function, the incentives provided by a universal scholarship such as the Kalamazoo Promise might lead them to react by improving their behavior but not necessarily by taking actions (such as doing more homework) that would directly lead to a higher GPA. One possible future role for school policies could be to help students better understand the link between their student work effort and achievement and future returns to education.

As mentioned before, our paper focuses on short-run effects of the Kalamazoo Promise. Promise-caused trends may have increased further in subsequent years. In addition, our paper, by its very necessity, can only examine individual effects of the Kalamazoo Promise. Promise effects that stem from changes in the school district's atmosphere or morale or from better peer effects cannot be estimated by our methodology. Certainly, school administrators and the Kalamazoo community have been trying both to help more students access the Promise and to change attitudes of students toward their futures. We hope in future work to analyze these subsequent effects.

NOTES

1. See http://www.upjohn.org/promise/promisescholarships.html for a list of such programs (accessed August 17, 2012).

2. For empirical evidence of such a shift in the choice set of colleges in the years following the adoption of the Promise, see Andrews, DesJardins, and Ranchhod (2010).

3. As we will briefly mention below, a skeptic could even argue that the Promise might reduce incentives for academic performance for some students by reducing the need to depend on merit scholarships for college tuition. We disagree with this skeptical argument, because we doubt whether most students understand how their behavior and decisions translate into eligibility for merit scholarships.

4. Dynarski (2004) compares the eligibility requirements of several state merit aid scholarships: the majority of such programs require a high school GPA of between 2.5 and 3.0; some additionally require ACT or SAT scores of a certain level, or demonstration of financial need, or both. Similar to the Kalamazoo Promise, most of these scholarships require maintaining a certain minimum GPA while in college.

5. Sharma (2010) studies the impact of a randomized cash rewards program among Nepalese eighth-graders and finds that the financial impact of these incentives equaled about a 0.09 standard deviation gain in aggregate scores. A related strand of research looks at vouchers. Angrist, Bettinger, Bloom, King, and Kremer (2002) and Angrist, Bettinger, and Kremer (2006) study the randomly distributed vouchers in Colombia that partially covered the cost of private secondary school for students who maintained satisfactory academic progress. The authors find that, three years after the lotteries, the winners of the vouchers were more likely to have finished eighth grade and to have scored higher on achievement tests.

6. Fryer (2011) is, however, cautious in interpreting his findings as a panacea and points out the need to understand the relationship between inputs in the education production function. If there are important complementarities between various inputs, then conditioning rewards on one input may prove ineffective.

7. The anonymous donors have stated their intention for the program to continue indefinitely and have guaranteed that if the program ever ends, all students enrolled in KPS at that time would receive the scholarship. However, we cannot rule out that students are still uncertain about receiving the Promise.

8. Such informational asymmetries in the context of federal need-based scholarships have been studied by Avery and Kane (2004), who find that qualified students often believed that they were not qualified for aid, and who report that students from disadvantaged families were deterred by the complexity of applying for financial aid. Complexities associated with applying for federal Pell Grants have been the focus of work by Dynarski and Scott-Clayton (2006) and of the experiment conducted by Bettinger, Long, Oreopoulos, and Sanbonmatsu (2011). Both papers advocate simplification of the Free Application for Federal Student Aid (FAFSA) application procedure.

9. This information comes from the Kalamazoo Promise Web site: http://kalamazoopromise.com/uploaded/Promise%20Senior%20Information%20Brochure.pdf (accessed August 17, 2012).

10. In fact, the Kalamazoo Promise has altered these probabilities. Our aim with this calculation is for illustrative purposes only. In column 2 of Table 1, we lower the probability of going to a community college to 0.30, as mentioned in the table note. Since the likelihood of attending a four-year college correlates with family background, such weights might better reflect the preferences of high-income families. This reweighting increases the present value of the scholarship, holding other parameters constant. For an in-depth study of how the Kalamazoo Promise altered the college choice set across time and different income groups, see Andrews et al. (2010).

11. Anecdotally, we know that many of those who enter KPS at ninth grade have previously been students who attended private or charter schools from kindergarten through eighth grade. Many private and charter schools in the Kalamazoo

area do not include high school, perhaps because of the larger costs per student that are characteristic of high school. We therefore might expect some differences in academic performance between students entering at ninth grade and students entering at other grade levels.

12. We also did some estimates of effects on enrollment in Advanced Placement (AP) classes, but we do not find any significant effects, so these results are not presented in this paper. AP enrollment in the District in this time period is relatively small, generally less than 10 percent for most benefit groups either before or after the Promise.

13. Standardized achievement measures are not included because the state-required tests changed timing and format in the fall of 2005, just about the time when the Kalamazoo Promise was announced. Thus, we cannot control for pre-Promise trends in these achievement tests. As our empirical results on other variables will show, controlling for pre-Promise trends is important.

14. The district during this period used a four multiplied by four block schedule. Each student normally took four courses a semester. Each course was counted as if it were equivalent to a full year of a course under the previous six-period day. Students who are behind may participate in a credit-recovery system. Under this system, they can take course modules using a computer system, which allows these students, if they pass the exams, to accumulate more credits per year than the normal eight per school year. We top-coded the maximum number of credits earned at 12. This procedure affects 59 observations. It is also possible for students to fail all courses and earn zero credits in a given school year. This does necessarily imply dropping out, as we observe that about half of the students with zero credits earned in one school year come back for the following school year. About 7 percent of students report earning zero credits.

15. The mean pre-Promise GPA in our sample is 2.07, averaged over both eligible and ineligible students. In Chicago Public Schools, the average ninth-grade GPA is around 1.7 or 1.8 (Lesnick, George, Smithgall, & Gwynne, 2010, calculated using information on page 23 and in Table 3 on page 13). The six credits earned in our pre-Promise sample is 75 percent of the normal course load of KPS. Chicago Public Schools reports pass rates for first-year high school students that have varied over the years from 74 percent to 80 percent (Miller, Allensworth, & Kochinek, 2002).

16. We cannot for all students tell whether their subsidy is 80 percent or some percentage greater than that, because our enrollment data only go back to 1997–1998.

17. We also did some examination of differential effects for different subsidy percentages, but did not find anything of interest.

18. Because we include a fixed effect for unobserved student characteristics, it might seem that we do not need to include the Promise eligibility variable by itself, as it is captured by the student fixed effects. However, some students' eligibility for the Promise changes because they move out of the District and then move in again, and Promise eligibility is based on the most recent date of continuous enrollment. We do include as a control a dummy variable for whether the student's Promise eligibility changed over time. In addition, as we will discuss later, we see how robust our results are to excluding such students from the estimation.

19. We cluster the standard errors on the individual student to take into account effects that are correlated across years for the same individual. In our application, one might worry that the appropriate cluster is not the individual student but rather a more aggregate group, such as a school. Including individual fixed effects in the regression controls for some of the within-group error correlation, but this might not suffice, depending at which level one assumes the "between"-group correlation not to be problematic for inference (this level is usually unknown). This potential problem of grouped structure is referred to as the Moulton problem (Moulton, 1986, 1990) and has recently received much attention in applications using difference-in-difference methods (see e.g., Bertrand, Duflo, & Mullainathan, 2004; Angrist & Pischke, 2009 for a textbook treatment). Bertrand et al. (2004) recommend clustering the standard errors on the level of aggregation where a policy change takes place. Donald and Lang (2007) suggest conducting the analysis on data aggregated to the group level and use a t-distribution for inference. In our case, with only six schools, and with a majority of students concentrated in only two, this approach becomes problematic. Conley and Taber (2011) focus on a case with few policy changes (as in our case) and a large number of comparison groups. This case is difficult to implement in our setting as, again, we have a small number of control clusters. Given these data limitations, we try to infer how sensitive our standard errors are to clustering at the class-school level. As expected, this typically inflates the standard errors, but usually not to the point where all the difference-in-difference coefficients of a given model lose their precision. To illustrate this, in our preferred fixed effects specification using days spent in suspension as the outcome variable, the cluster-robust standard error on the coefficient on the interaction term for the year 2006–2007 (coefficient equals −1.296) equals 0.577, whereas when clustering on the individual student it equals 0.541. However, the cluster-robust coefficient for the interaction term on the year 2007–2008 (equal to −1.796) loses its precision (the standard error increases from 0.634 to 1.13). Given the small number of more aggregate clusters, we choose to report the individual-cluster-robust standard errors in the tables. The results using the school-grade-cluster-robust results are available from the authors.

20. The models without student fixed effects account for random effects that are correlated across years for the same student in calculating standard errors and t-statistics.

21. Bloom, Hill, and Lipsey (2008) discuss magnitude of effect sizes across different grades. It is known that learning gains are typically greatest between kindergarten and first grade, ranging sometimes in effect sizes larger than one standard deviation. The learning gains in later grades are typically much smaller. This in turn implies that an effect size of an intervention of 0.1σ in high school is a more pronounced impact than a 0.1σ in kindergarten.

22. In an appendix, available upon request, we present some figures showing trends in average fixed effects over time for different benefit categories.

23. We do not model the analogous effect along the intensive margin because of the usual issues with regressions conditioning on the positive value of the outcome variable (see Angrist & Pischke, 2009 Chapter 3). In order to get an idea of how much of this effect is due to the intensive margin, we conduct the following back-of-the-envelope calculation. When differentiating the equation

$E(y|x)=E(y|x,y > 0)Pr(y > 0|x)$ with respect to x, we obtain that the overall average effect of a variable x on y is a weighted average of the intensive and extensive margins: $(\partial E(y|x)/\partial x) = (\partial E(y|x, y>0)/\partial x)Pr(y>0|x) + (\partial Pr(y>0|x)/\partial x)E(y|x, y>0)$. Plugging in sample means and regression effects from columns 2 and 4 of Table 6, for the school year 2007–2008, we can back out the conditional effect on suspension equal to a reduction of less than six days of suspension.

24. We also conducted separate regressions for boys but did not find the response different from the rest of the sample, i.e., from girls.

ACKNOWLEDGMENTS

We thank the following persons and groups for their comments and suggestions: Susan Dynarski, Douglas Harris, Susan Houseman, Caroline Hoxby, Brian Jacob, Lars Lefgren, the participants at various conferences where we have presented this paper (PromiseNet, AEFP, MEA, SOLE, APPAM, and the NBER Economics of Education Program Meeting), two anonymous referees, and Solomon Polachek. We have benefited from our discussions with Michael Rice. We thank Ben Jones and Allison Colosky for their editorial assistance. Wei-Jang Huang has provided outstanding research assistance. All errors are our own.

REFERENCES

Agee, M. D., & Crocker, T. D. (1996). Parents' discount rates for child quality. *Southern Economic Journal, 63*(1), 36–50.

Andrews, R. J., DesJardins, S., & Ranchhod, V. (2010). The effects of the Kalamazoo Promise on college choice. *Economics of Education Review, 29*(5), 722–737.

Angrist, J., Bettinger, E., Bloom, E., King, E., & Kremer, M. R. (2002). Vouchers for private schooling in Colombia: Evidence from a randomized natural experiment. *American Economic Review, 92*(5), 1535–1558.

Angrist, J., Bettinger, E., & Kremer, M. R. (2006). Long-term educational consequences of secondary school vouchers: Evidence from administrative records in Colombia. *American Economic Review, 96*(3), 847–862.

Angrist, J., Lang, D., & Oreopoulos, P. (2009). Incentives and services for college achievement: Evidence from a randomized trial. American Economic Journal. *Applied Economics, 1*(1), 136–163.

Angrist, J., & Lavy, V. (2009). The effects of high stakes high school achievement awards: Evidence from a randomized trial. *American Economic Review, 99*(4), 1384–1414.

Angrist, J., & Pischke, J.-S. (2009). *Mostly harmless econometrics – an empiricist's companion.* Princeton, NJ: Princeton University Press.

Avery, C., & Kane, T. J. (2004). Student perceptions of college opportunities: The Boston COACH program. In C. M. Hoxby (Ed.), *College choices: The economics of where to go, when to go, and how to pay for it* (pp. 355–394). Chicago, IL: University of Chicago Press.

Bartik, T. J., Eberts, R. W., & Huang, W.-J. (2010). *The Kalamazoo Promise, and enrollment and achievement trends in Kalamazoo Public Schools.* Kalamazoo, MI: W.E. Upjohn Institute for Employment Research.

Bertrand, M., Duflo, E., & Mullainathan, S. (2004). How much should we trust differences-in-differences estimates? *Quarterly Journal of Economics*, *119*(1), 249–275.

Bettinger, E. P., Long, B. T., Oreopoulos, P., & Sanbonmatsu, S. (2011). *The role of simplification and information in college decisions: Results from the H&R block FAFSA experiment.* NBER Working Paper No. 15361. National Bureau of Economic Research, Cambridge, MA.

Bloom, H. S., Hill, C. A., & Lipsey, M. W. (2008). *Performance trajectories and performance gaps as achievement effect – size benchmarks for educational interventions.* MDRC Working Papers on Research Methodology. MDRC, New York, NY.

Conley, T. G., & Taber, C. R. (2011). Inference with 'difference in differences' with a small number of policy changes. *Review of Economics and Statistics*, *91*(1), 113–125.

Cornwell, C. M., Lee, K. H., & Mustard, D. B. (2005). Student responses to merit scholarship retention rules. *Journal of Human Resources*, *40*(4), 895–917.

Cornwell, C. M., Mustard, D. B., & Sridhar, D. J. (2006). The enrollment effects of merit-based financial aid: Evidence from Georgia's HOPE program. *Journal of Labor Economics*, *24*(4), 761–786.

Donald, S. G., & Lang, K. (2007). Inference with difference-in-differences and other panel data. *Review of Economics and Statistics*, *89*(2), 221–233.

Dynarski, S. (2002). The behavioral and distributional implications of aid for college. *American Economic Review*, *92*(2), 279–285.

Dynarski, S. (2004). The new merit aid. In H. Caroline (Ed.), *College choices: The economics of where to go, when to go, and how to pay for it* (pp. 63–100). Chicago, IL: University of Chicago Press.

Dynarski, S. M., & Scott-Clayton, J. E. (2006). *The cost of complexity in federal student aid: Lessons from optimal tax theory and behavioral economics.* NBER Working Paper No. 12227. National Bureau of Economic Research, Cambridge, MA.

Fryer, R. G. (2011). Financial incentives and student achievement: Evidence from randomized trials. *Quarterly Journal of Economics*, *126*(4), 1755–1798.

Henry, G. T., & Rubenstein, R. (2002). Paying for grades: Impact of merit-based financial aid on educational quality. *Journal of Policy Analysis and Management*, *21*(1), 93–109.

Jackson, C. K. (2010). A little now for a lot later: A look at a Texas advanced placement incentive program. *Journal of Human Resources*, *45*(3), 591–639.

Kane, T. J. (2003). *A quasi-experimental estimate of the impact of financial aid on college-going.* NBER Working Paper No. 9703. National Bureau of Economic Research, Cambridge, MA.

Kane, T. J. (2006). Evaluating the impact of the D.C. Tuition Assistance Grant Program. *Journal of Human Resources*, *42*(3), 555–582.

Kremer, M. R., Miguel, E., & Thornton, R. (2009). Incentives to learn. *Review of Economics and Statistics*, *91*(3), 437–456.

Lesnick, J., George, R. M., Smithgall, C., & Gwynne, J. (2010). *Reading on grade level in third grade: How is it related to high school performance and college enrollment?* Chicago, IL: Chapin Hall at the University of Chicago.

Leuven, E., Oosterbeek, H., & van der Klaauw, B. (2010). The effect of financial rewards on students' achievement: Evidence from a randomized experiment. *Journal of the European Economic Association*, *8*(6), 1243–1265.

Levitt, S. D., List, J. A., Neckermann, S., & Sadoff, S. (2012). *The behavioralist goes to school: Leveraging behavioral economics to improve educational performance*. NBER Working Paper No. 18165. National Bureau of Economic Research, Cambridge, MA.

Miller, A. (2010). *College scholarships as a tool for community development? Evidence from the Kalamazoo Promise*. Working Paper. Princeton University Press, Princeton, NJ.

Miller, S. R., Allensworth, E. M., & Kochinek, J. R. (2002). *Student performance: Course taking, test scores, and outcomes*. Chicago, IL: Consortium on Chicago School Research.

Miller-Adams, M. (2009). *The power of a promise: Education and economic renewal in Kalamazoo*. Kalamazoo, MI: W.E. Upjohn Institute for Employment Research.

Moulton, B. R. (1986). Random group effects and the precision of regression estimates. *Journal of Econometrics*, *32*(3), 385–397.

Moulton, B. R. (1990). An illustration of a pitfall in estimating the effects of aggregate variables on micro unit. *Review of Economics and Statistics*, *72*(2), 334–338.

Pallais, A. (2007). Taking a chance on college: Is the Tennessee education lottery scholarship program a winner?. *Journal of Human Resources*, *44*(1), 199–222.

Scott-Clayton, J. E. (2010). On money and motivation: A quasi-experimental analysis of financial incentives for college achievement. *Journal of Human Resources*, *46*(3), 614–646.

Sharma, D. (2010). *The impact of financial incentives on academic achievement and household behavior: Evidence from a randomized trial in Nepa*l. Unpublished Paper. Ohio State University, Columbus, OH. Available at http://dx.doi.org/10.2139/ssrn.1681186. Accessed on August 19, 2012.

The Economist. (2008). Rescuing Kalamazoo: A promising future. *Economist*, February 7. Retrieved from http://www.economist.com/node/10650702. Accessed on March 1, 2012.

THE IMPACT OF WAGE DISPERSION ON LABOR PRODUCTIVITY: EVIDENCE FROM FINNISH WORKERS

Laura Arranz-Aperte

ABSTRACT

Using an extensive data set on Finnish workers during the years 1990–2002, we analyze the relation between dispersion of wages within plants and labor productivity. We find a positive and significant relation between dispersion of wages within plant and average sales per worker. This relation is quadratic when dispersion is conditioned on workers' observable characteristics. We also find positive and significant relation between unconditional dispersion of wages within plant and value added per hours worked, while we find a non-significant relation between conditional wage dispersion and valued added per hours worked. Results indicate that the incentive effect of wage dispersion dominates fairness or sabotage considerations.

Keywords: Fairness; tournaments; wage dispersion; labor productivity

JEL classifications: M52; J31; L25

New Analyses of Worker Well-Being
Research in Labor Economics, Volume 38, 77–103

ISSN: 0147-9121/doi:10.1108/S0147-9121(2013)0000038003

INTRODUCTION

Relative wages are key determinants of workers' effort, as workers compare their wages, both with peers in the same job position and with other employees within the firm (typically top managers and direct supervisors). Thus, their perception of their relative wage is an important determinant of their effort provision. Still, there is no agreement in the literature about which type of effect wage dispersion has on workers' productivity. While tournament theories – Lazear and Rosen (1981) and Lazear (1989) – argue that wage dispersion creates the right incentives, fair wage models – Akerlof and Yellen (1990), Levine (1991), and Milgrom and Roberts (1990) – argue for a degree of wage compression within firm, emphasizing the importance of fairness and cooperation within the workforce, and the avoidance of unproductive rent seeking. As relative wages are key determinant of worker's effort, it is a relevant empirical issue to determine the impact of wage dispersion on performance.

In this paper, we analyze the effect of within-plant wage dispersion on labor productivity in the Finnish manufacturing sector, during the period 1990–2002. We study two measures of dispersion: conditional wage dispersion and unconditional wage dispersion. Conditional wage dispersion measures differences in pay among "observationally equal" workers. This measure is relevant in the test of Lazear and Rosen's (1981) tournament model. In a tournament model setup, a pay spread as incentive for being promoted is only effective for those who compete for a superior job, which means workers with similar observable characteristics. As indicator for conditional wage dispersion, we use the standard errors (SEs) of (log) wage regressions, run for each plant and year separately. Unconditional wage dispersion refers to the dispersion of wages among all workers within plant, regardless of their individual characteristics. We use the coefficient of variation (CV) of (log) wages as measure of unconditional wage dispersion. Unconditional wage dispersion is relevant in the study of the relation across work groups, as discussed by Akerlof and Yellen (1990). They argue that workers are more productive when wages are compressed between different job categories. Conditional wage dispersion is not relevant for the fair wage model designed by Akerlof and Yellen (1990) as the model predicts that similar workers are paid the same wage, and workers compare their wage rate with the wage rate of other job categories.

Our sample contains information on all Finnish plants and firms in the paper, machinery manufacturing, and manufacturing of electronic products industries. These three sectors are representative of the Finnish economy during the period 1990–2002. The paper industry and the machinery manufacturing industry are economic sectors that have traditionally been at the core of the Finnish economy, while the manufacturing of electronic products industry is associated with the rapid growth of technological and telecommunication sectors (firms that produce electronic and telecommunications equipment, such as Nokia, are included in this sector). This industry represents and industry that emerged from the economic crisis that hit Finland in the mid-1990s and was the motor of the rapid recovery, turning Finland into a major producer of technology. Even when these three industries are representative of the Finnish economy, we have run additional sensitivity analysis to rule out the possibility that our results are driven by industry-specific factors.

Regression results indicate that there is a positive and significant relation between within-plant conditional wage dispersion and sales per person. This relation is also positive (albeit non-significant) when value added per hours worked is used as dependent variable. We also find evidence of a quadratic relation when sales per person is the independent variable, the coefficient of conditional dispersion squared being negative and significant. This is what tournament models predict. In tournaments, dispersion of wages among similar workers enhances productivity, as wage dispersion provides incentives for workers to exert effort for a wage prize. But while a certain degree of dispersion enhances productivity, too much of it can induce workers to engage in unproductive predatory practices, being the relation between wage dispersion and productivity not linear, but quadratic.

Our results suggest that the incentive effect of wage dispersion predicted by tournament models dominates fairness and sabotage considerations. We find that a 10% increase in conditional wage dispersion leads to a 0.13% increase in sales per worker, and a 0.07% increase in plant value added. However, this positive effect should be rather limited, taking into account the scarce significance found when plants value added per hours worked is the dependent variable. There is currently consensus in the literature on the use of value added per plant as a proxy for workers' productivity. Some studies (such as Simmons & Berri, 2011) are able to use individual output, in settings where this measure is directly observable (usually sport competitions and top management performance). Although the use of individual productivity (rather than a plant average) would be preferable, this measure is unobservable for workers in firms and plants where team work is essential for firm output. Studies using large linked employer–employees data sets (as those of Braakmann, 2008; Heyman, 2005; Hunnes, 2009; Lallemand, Plasman, & Ryck, 2004; Winter-Ebmer & Zweimüller, 1999) use different proxies for performance, such as value added, aggregated both at plant and firm level, sales, gross production, and so on. In this essay, we include an extensive variety of measures of performance, to take into account differences in definitions and measurement errors. This way, we find a positive and significant relation between conditional wage dispersion and productivity, when we measure productivity by sales per person, firm-level return on assets, value added per worker at firm level, and firm return to assets, while this relation is positive (albeit not significant) when productivity is measured by value added hours worked plant, and firm total factor productivity. Although significance levels vary depending on the definition of performance used, we do not find a negative relation between different measures of dispersion and firm productivity in any case. This non-negativity does not necessarily imply causality (as endogeneity cannot totally be accounted for), but it provides partial support to fair wage models of dispersion.

Fair wage effort models, as designed by Akerlof and Yellen (1990), receive no support from our data. While fair wage effort models predict a negative and linear relation between unconditional wage dispersion and labor productivity, we find a positive and significant relation. A 10% increase in within-plant (log) wage dispersion leads to 0.26% increase in sales per worker. We also find a positive and significant relation when value added is used as dependent variable (although the relation turns non-significant when we use lagged values of dispersion to partially control for endogeneity). This positive relation is robust to different definitions of wage dispersion, like Gini index, standard deviation and relative mean deviation, and CV of (log) wages.

This paper contributes to the existing empirical literature in several ways. First, we analyze the concepts of conditional and unconditional wage dispersion separately, and stress the different meaning of both terms. Unconditional wage dispersion is key in fair wage models, while dispersion of wage conditioned on observable characteristics is relevant in tournaments. Previous studies concentrate on one or the other measure, but do not take both simultaneously into account.

We also explore the quadratic relation between conditional wage dispersion and labor productivity, which is the type of relation stated in the tournament models of wage dispersion (those models argue that a certain degree of wage dispersion is positive, but too much dispersion can turn out to be negative, when workers engage in predatory competitive practices). The inclusion and test of a quadratic test improves the test of tournament models, and provides evidence of inflexion points in the relation between wage dispersion and productivity of labor.

Regarding methodology, we make use of the advantages of a linked employer–employee panel data set. We use individual level data to create the dispersion measures, and then plant level outcomes, like value added per worker or sales per worker in the plant performance analysis. For example, Winter-Ebmer and Zweimüller (1999), in lack of direct observation of firm output or value added, use employment growth and standardized wages as indicators for firm performance. On the other hand, Lallemand et al. (2004) use a linked employer–employee data set, but they use a cross section for the year 1995. We also take advantage of the time dimension of the panel in different ways. For example, we use lagged values of dispersion and different dimensions of plant growth in the analysis to address plausible endogeneity problems. We also use panel data techniques that allow controlling for firm effects, to reduce the problems with standard errors (SEs) due to within-firm heterogeneity.

The data set that we use provides detailed information on firm, plant, and individual characteristics. The panel covers a relatively long period of time, 1990–2002. This research benefits from this high-quality data in many aspects: the dispersion measures include a sufficiently high number of individuals per plant; the time dimension of the panel allows to control for firm effects, to include lags, leads and yearly changes in the variables of interest, and to study the evolution of dispersion and productivity over a relatively large time span; besides detailed information on plant and firm allows to introduce many control variables and test for robustness of the results.

The remainder of the paper is organized as follows. In the second section, we present a review of the literature. We describe the data in the third section. Section fourth contains the methodology. Results are presented in the fifth section and the sixth section concludes.

RELATED LITERATURE

There is no consensus in the theoretical literature on the effect of wage dispersion on individual productivity. While tournament models state that wage dispersion creates the right incentives, fair wage models argue for a degree of wage compression within the firm, emphasizing the importance of fairness and cooperation within the workforce.

In their seminal work, Lazear and Rosen (1981) argue that wage dispersion creates the right incentives, as wages based on rank induce the same efficient allocation of resources as incentives based on individual output levels. In a subsequent paper, Lazear (1989) proposes a model where the initial incentive effect of wage rewards based on relative comparison might be offset by sabotage behavior of some worker when the reward (the wage spread) is relatively high. As a result, some wage compression might be efficient within certain relevant groups in this model.

On the other hand, fair wage models argue for a degree of wage compression within firm, emphasizing the importance of fairness and cooperation within the workforce. Akerlof and Yellen (1990) state that workers proportionately withdraw effort as their actual wage falls short of their fair wage; Milgrom and Roberts (1990) add to the advantages of a cohesive wage structure the avoidance of rent seeking activities. In a related paper, Levine (1991) suggests that firms pay efficiency wages to the low end of the distribution to increase group cohesiveness.

Empirical studies relating wage disparities and firm performance yield mixed results. Numerous studies test this relation using data from sport competitions. Those studies use team sport outcomes as measure of productivity and relate those outcomes to the relative pay of different individual athletes. For example, Frick, Prinz, and Winkelmann (2003) relate pay inequalities to team performance in North American Major Leagues, finding that results differ significantly depending of the league. In a subsequent paper, Mondello and Maxcy (2009) use data from the American National Football League to find that more compressed pay structures improve on-field performance, while neither Burger and Walkers (2008) nor Simmons and Berri (2011) find support for fair wage theories using use data from baseball labor market. It is nevertheless questionable whether results from professional teams can be extrapolated to the whole population of workers. Another branch of studies are those that use linked employer–employee databases for a test of the relation between dispersion of pay and productivity. Winter-Ebmer and Zweimüller (1999) provide the definition of wage dispersion as the SE of wage regression of each plant of firm in the data. This definition has been used in a test of the relation between wage dispersion and productivity in countries such as Austria (the cited Winter-Ebmer & Zweimüller, 1999), Belgium (Lallemand et al., 2004; Mahy et al., 2011b), Germany (Braakmann, 2008; Jirjahn & Kraft, 2007), Sweden (Heyman, 2005), Denmark (Grund & Westergaard-Nielsen, 2008), Norway (Hunnes, 2009), or Portugal (Martins, 2008). Results of these studies differ depending on the country analyzed, the definition of productivity (sales, value added per worker, gross production, etc.), and the methodology used. While several of these studies (Heyman, 2005; Lallemand et al., 2004; Winter-Ebmer & Zweimüller, 1999) find evidence of a positive relation, others, such as Grund and Westergaard-Nielsen (2008), Mahy, Rycx, and Volral (2011a, 2011b), and Braakmann (2008), find evidence of a hump-shaped relation. Among the empirical studies that suggest that wage compression is associated with higher productivity, we find Martins (2008) and Jirjahn and Kraft (2007). Among those finding no relation or mixed evidence, we can cite Hunnes (2009), Frick et al. (2003), and Charnes and Kuhn (2005).

Additional studies using different measures of dispersion also bring inconclusive results. For example, Cowherd and Levine (1992) analyze the pay gap between top management and lower level employee, and Pfeffer and Langton (1993) use the dispersion of wages within academic departments, finding both studies that higher compression leads to higher productivity; Kawaguchi (2007) reaches the opposite conclusion using women participation to measure wage dispersion and Hibbs and Locking (2000) use the aggregate wage dispersion of the Swedish economy in the later part of last century to find that productive efficiency was affected positively by wages dispersion trends associated with Phase I solidarity policy but was impaired by dispersion trends under Phase II policy; Leonard (1990) finds not significant relationship when he uses the unconditional standard deviation of pay.

In Finland, wage inequality has been studied by Uusitalo and Vartiainen (2009), Asplund (2004), and Piekkola (2002). Uusitalo and Vartiainen (2009) study wage structure and wage dynamics of Finnish manufacturing employees during the years 1980–2002. They find that wage differences have not increased but the differences across firms are increasing, and this is only partly accounted for by sorting between firms. They find that the overall cross-section variance of salaries has changed very little. This is true for the distribution of final salaries but almost true even for salary residuals. Differences between salaries of firms started to increase at the end of the 1980s and this process accelerated after the deep slump of the 1990s.

Asplund (2004) contrasts the traditional belief that increased inequality enhances economic efficiency with more recent literature. She concludes that recent empirical evidence has challenged the traditional views that increasing inequality has a positive impact on economic growth, and that redistribution through education has a negative effect on growth.

Piekkola (2002) studies the changes in wage dispersion, and relates those to returns to human capital at the plant level. He uses data for the entire private sector during the years 1987–1998. He concludes that the major change within this period has been an increase in wage dispersion between plants, while the education premium has risen mainly within plants.

He explains wage dispersion by changes in human capital compensations in existing plants/firms. He finds a rise in individual heterogeneity. He also finds no major increase in within-plant dispersion.

This paper departs from previous studies of Finnish data in that we concentrate in pay differences across different groups within plants, and relate those differences to productivity of the plant labor force, contrasting different existing economic models about the benefits of dispersion for the productivity of Finnish labor.

THE DATA

We use a linked employer–employee data set of Finnish workers that covers the years 1990–2002 and contains information on individuals, plants, and firms. Information on individuals is obtained from Finnish Linked Employer Employee Data (FLEED) data; information on plants is obtained from Business Register and Manufacture Census; and information on firms is obtained from Business Register, Financial Statements statistics, and Information and Communication Technologies (ICT) survey.

We use the data set on individuals to obtain the dispersion measures. The plant level data set is used in the study of productivity and some variables from the firm level data set are included in the sensitivity analysis. In Table 1, we present a definition of the variables used in this study, and the source of the data. The source of the data refers to the dataset from which each variable originally comes from.

To obtain a measure of conditional wage dispersion, one needs to have enough observations per plant. For this reason, we include only plants with more than 20 employees in this study. Plants where less than 10 workers are observed are also dropped from the analysis. All monetary variables are deflated using 1990 consumer price index.

The data cover years 1990–2002, and these include all plants and firms in three key economic sectors. These sectors correspond to Statistics Finland definition: wood, pulp, paper, and paper products (tol 20 and 21); machinery, equipment, office, and electrical machineries (tol 29–31); and radio, television, communication, instruments, and so on (tol 32 and 33). They will be hereafter named as (1) paper industry, (2) machinery manufacturing, and (3) manufacturing of electronic products.

These sectors are examples of three industries with different progress during the period 1990–2002. This was a period of extraordinary

Table 1. Definition of the Variables.

Variable	Definition	Source of Data
Wage	Yearly earnings	Individual
SE	Standard error of (log) wage regression	Individual
SE^2	Standard error squared	Individual
CV	Coefficient of variation of (log) wages	Individual
CV^2	Coefficient of variation squared	Individual
Gini	Gini coefficient of (log) wages	Individual
SD	Standard deviation of (log) wages	Individual
RMD	Relative mean deviation of (log) wages	Individual
Value added	Value added/hours work per plant	Plant
Sales	Sales per person	Plant
Plant age	Year of entry of the plant (8 categories)	Plant
Plant capital	Capital stock estimated by POM/hours worked	Plant
Size	Size class according to employment (3 categories)	Plant
Education	Average (per plant) years of schooling	Plant
Age	Average age of personnel	Plant
Women	Proportion of female workers	Plant
Seniority	Average tenure in months	Plant
Sector	Industry classification (3 categories)	Firm
ROA-Firm	Return on assets	Firm
TFP-Firm	Total factor productivity	Firm
VA-Firm	Value added per person (firm value added/ employees)	Firm
Change in sales	Change of sales from the previous year, %	Plant
Change in wages	Change of the wage sum from the previous year, %	Plant
Change in employment	Change of employment from the previous year, %	Plant

macroeconomic turbulence in Finland. It can be divided in three different intervals: (1) the economic crisis (years 1990–1994), with unemployment rates increasing by 4–5% every year; (2) the years of economic recovery, 1995–1999, associated with the expansion and growth of technological and communication industries; and (3) the period of normalization of economic growth, years 1999–2002, with unemployment stuck at 9%. The key of the recovery is often associated with rapid boom of technological and telecommunication sectors. As a result, Finland became a major producer of technology. This skill-biased technological change should have increased wage inequality according to the theory in two ways: more educated versus less educated workers and inter-industry wage differences.

From the three industries in this study, the paper industry can be considered a core industry in the Finnish economy. It was very important at the beginning of the 1990s, and has remained so despite the macroeconomic turbulence. The machinery manufacturing is an example of an old-line manufacturing that loses importance after the economic crisis of the mid-1990s. The electronic industry represents an industry that emerged from crisis and was the motor of the rapid recovery.

The data set used in this analysis consists of 6839 plant-level observations for the years 1990–2002. The number of plants is 1180. From those, 211 plants (21%) appear all years of the sample. We use on average 53.7 individual observations per plant to construct the dispersion measures (with a minimum of 10 and a maximum of 1454 observations per plant). The paper industry represents 38% of the observations in the sample, the machinery manufacturing 47.8% and the electronic industry 14.2%. Descriptive statistics of the variables used in the analysis are presented in Table 2.

Table 2. Descriptive Statistics.

Variable	Mean	SD	Minimum	Maximum
Value added	29.983	25.095	0.367	535.163
Sales	146,497.2	155,321.8	46.706	3,386,051
SE	0.234	0.363	9.05e-08	9.174
SE^2	0.187	1.407	8.19e-15	84.163
CV	0.061	0.034	0.008	0.312
Gini	0.027	0.014	0.004	0.146
SD	0.068	0.046	0.007	0.499
RMD	0.019	0.011	0.002	0.119
Education	11.365	0.849	9.367	15.435
Age	39.187	3.802	25.640	51.543
Women	0.247	0.177	0.008	0.923
Seniority	109.086	67.664	0	450
Plant age	2.080	1.597	1	8
Plant capital	40.6567	68.5619	0	955.81
Size 1	0.2070	0.4052	0	1
Size 2	0.2696	0.4438	0	1
Size 3	0.5233	0.4994	0	1
Sector 1	0.3797	0.4853	0	1
Sector 2	0.4775	0.4995	0	1
Sector 3	0.1427	0.3498	0	1
ROA-Firm	8.7414	10.003	−21.079	38.048
TFP-Firm	6.3814	0.4675	2.03	8.088
VA-Firm	45,094.42	24,158.77	11,774.98	157,144.4
Change in sales	0.1048	0.4125	−1.995	2
Change in wage	0.1015	0.2876	−2	2
Change in employment	0.0414	0.2923	−1.705	2

As the time span is relatively large, 12 years, mean and standard deviations alone might not provide enough insight of the magnitude and relevance of each variable in different points in time. In what follows, we present a short description of the evolution of the key variables during the period 1990–2002. Evolution of within-plant wage dispersion is depicted in Fig. 1.

We find a moderate increase in wage dispersion during the years 1990–2000, although values converge to the levels of 1990 during the last years, especially 2002. This moderate increase is true for the whole sample of individuals, CV(1), as well as for within-plant wage dispersion, CV and SE. The variable CV(1) is obtained calculating the CV of all individuals who are included in the sample year by year. It is obtained from the individual database. CV and SE are the yearly average of the variables constructed to measure conditional and unconditional within-plant wage dispersion, and are obtained from the plant database. The shape of the dispersion distribution in this sample is relatively akin to that in Uusitalo and Vartiainen (2009). They find that wage differences have not increased during the years 1980–2002, but the differences across firms are increasing, and this is only partly accounted for by sorting between firms. The CV of wages of all individuals here, CV(1), ranges from 0.54 in year 1990 to 0.483 in year 2002. It increased constantly until year 1994 when it reached a level of 0.345, declining in the following years. Unconditional wage dispersion (measured as the CV of (log) wages within plant) experienced lesser changes: from 0.42 in year 1990 to 0.4 at the end of the period, reaching a

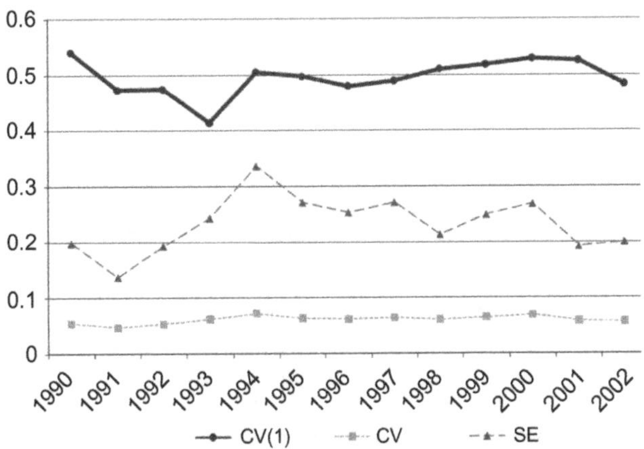

Fig. 1. Evolution of Wage Dispersion.

peak in year 1994, when the average CV of the three sectors was 0.46. This time of the economic cycle (around year 1994) faced a large reallocation of factors (labor and capital) across industries (from old-line manufacturing to the growing electronic industry sectors) and across firms within industries. We observe from Figs. 2 and 3 that electronic sector is the one with a major degree of wage dispersion throughout the years, while the paper industry has the most compressed wage structure within plants.

We observe that, although paper industry has the highest value added per worker, it has always experienced the lowest degree of within-plant

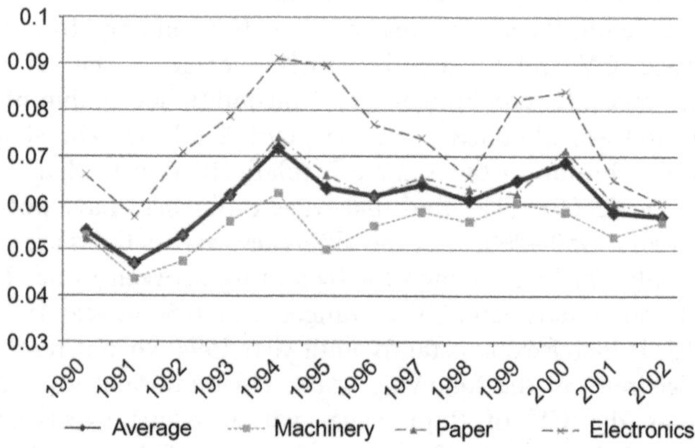

Fig. 2. Unconditional Wage Dispersion.

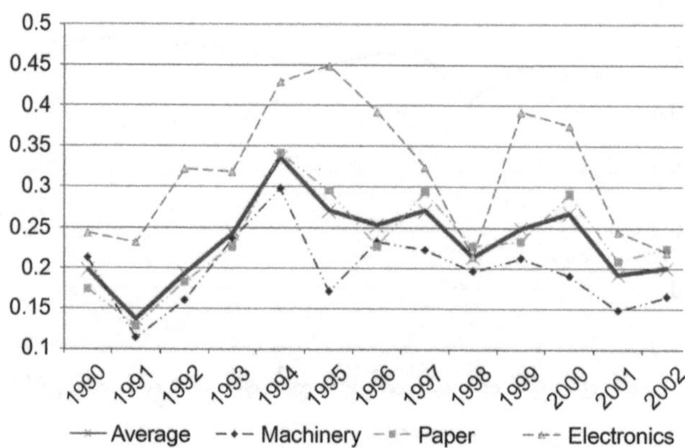

Fig. 3. Conditional Wage Dispersion.

wage dispersion. Patterns of productivity might have their origin in the economic turbulence of the period, while the pattern of wage dispersion could be determined by the strong trade unions in the paper industry, or the relatively homogeneous workforce. Uusitalo and Vartiainen (2009) stress that "relative wages have largely been determined by market forces," and centralized bargaining has a limited effect on the shape of wage distribution within plants in Finland. Different collective agreements set out minimum pay levels for each occupational category and job level, as well as general wage increases, which are usually specified in percentage terms. Still, the general increases often hardly exceed the sum of inflation and average productivity growth. Those general increases are not binding for the local parties, if they both agree to deviate from it. Nothing prevents a firm from increasing an individual's wage more than the general increase, and if the firm finds its jobs threatened, it can initiate negotiations on lower pay increases or even pay cuts. Some industries operate complicated collective agreements and allow adjusting for individual performance. Besides, bonuses and other payments are often used to adjust workers' remuneration to their actual productivity. Thus, even complying with general increases, firms that can sustain a decent productivity growth rate do have at least some freedom as to their internal wage structure.

Figs. 4 and 5 show the evolution of sales per person and value added per worker. These are the key dependent variables in this study as they are used as measures of labor productivity.

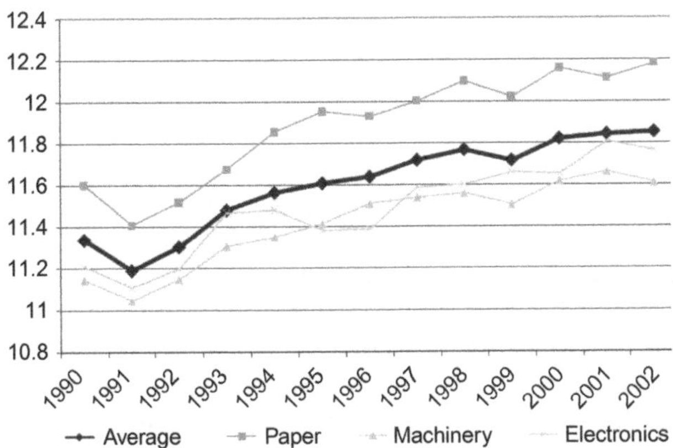

Fig. 4. Sales Per Person in the Euros.

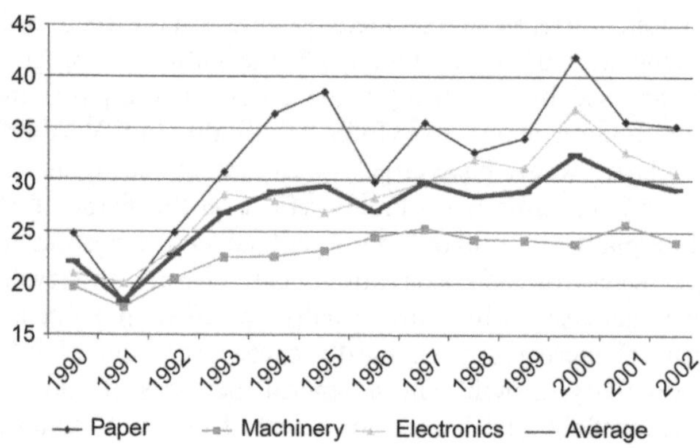

Fig. 5. Value Added, Hours Worked.

METHODOLOGY

Basic Specification

For a test of the tournament model by Lazear and Rosen (1981), we use a two-step procedure. In a first step, we compute within-plant conditional wage dispersion by calculating SE of wage regression for each plant and year separately, as in Winter-Ebmer and Zweimüller (1999). These SEs are used as explanatory variable in a plant-level performance regression.

The following regressions are run:

$$\text{In } W_{ijt} = \alpha_{0t} + \alpha_{1t} Y_{ijt} + \varepsilon_{ijt} \quad (1)$$

$$\text{In } P_{jt} = \beta_0 + \beta_1 \sigma_{jt} + \beta_2 \sigma_{jt}^2 + \beta_3 X_{jt} + \beta_4 Z_{jt} + v_j + \varepsilon_t + \mu_j \quad (2)$$

where the subscript i denotes individual, the subscript j denotes plant, and the subscript t denotes time period (year). W_{ijt} is the yearly wage (included performance-related pay and bonuses); Y_{ijt} is a matrix of individual characteristics like age, education, and gender; and ε_{ijt} is the error term. Eq. (1) is run for each plant and year separately. The SEs of these regressions σ_{jt} are used as a measure of within-plant conditional wage dispersion. These SEs and its squared are included as explanatory variable in the plant-level performance regression, Eq. (2). This measure of dispersion does not control for working hours: plants with a larger mix of part-time and full-time workers might experience larger dispersion, even when all workers receive similar hourly wage. We partly control for this limitation of the data, when we include in Eq. (1) control factors such as gender and education as part-time work is relatively more common among women and less educated workers.

In Eq. (2), plant performance P_{jt} is explained by the within-plant wage dispersion σ_{jt}, its squared σ_{jt}^2, aggregated characteristics of workers X_{jt}, and employer characteristics Z_{jt}. We use a two-way error component model, with random effects, where ν_j represents the random plant effect and ε_t is the time component. Eq. (1) is run for every year and firm separately, while Eq. (2) is run only once, with all firms and years pooled in the same data set.

Plant performance P_{jt} is measured as sales per person and value added per hours worked alternatively. We include both measures as they have been largely used in the literature, and explain the differences in results. The matrix X_{jt} contains average education attainment per plant, average worker age, proportion of women, and average seniority. The matrix Z_{jt} contains size, plant age and industry dummies, and plant capital. We control for plant-specific effects by estimating a panel data. We choose random effects specification to obtain precise estimates of the population parameters. In cases where the key explanatory variables do not vary much over time (like in our case, within-plant wage dispersion), fixed effects and first-differencing methods can lead to imprecise estimates.[1] Besides, as the time span is relatively large, we cannot claim that the individual effects might be time invariant. In the random effect specification, the plant effect v_j is assumed to be uncorrelated with the rest of the regressors X_{jt}, Z_{jt}, σ_{jt}, and σ_{jt}^2.

For a test of fair wage effort hypothesis, we estimate a performance equation, with unconditional wage dispersion as key explanatory variable. Unconditional wage dispersion refers to dispersion of wages within plant, regardless of individual characteristics. We use the CV of (log) wages as a measure of unconditional wage dispersion. The following equation is estimated:

$$\ln P_{jt} = \gamma_0 + \gamma_1 CV_{jt} + \gamma_2 X_{jt} + \gamma_4 Z_{jt} + v_j + \varepsilon_t + \mu_{jt} \quad (3)$$

where P_{jt} refers to plant-level productivity, CV_{jt} is the coefficient of variation of wages, X_{jt} is a matrix that contains aggregate worker characteristics, and Z_{jt} contains plant-level controls. The term v_j accounts for plant random effects, ε_t is the random time effects, and μ_{jt} is the error term.

Robustness Test

To test the robustness of our results, we include a battery of sensitivity analysis. First, we include unconditional indicators of intra-plant (log) wage dispersion in the analysis. Among those unconditional indicators are the Gini coefficient, the relative mean deviation, and the standard deviation in logarithm. We include them as explanatory variable in the performance Eq. (3), instead of the conditional wage dispersion variable.

To check whether the results are robust to the definition of performance, we estimate Eqs. (2) and (3), when performance is measured as (firm level) value added, (firm level) return of assets, and (firm level) total factor productivity.

To deal with the possible endogeneity of dispersion, lagged dispersion variables are used as proxy. Dispersion might be endogenous as plants adjust their level of wage dispersion to changes in productivity. We include dispersion in year $t-1$ as explanatory variable in the following regressions:

$$\text{In}\, P_{jt} = \beta_0 + \beta_1 \sigma_{jt-1} + \beta_2 \sigma^2_{jt-1} + \beta_3 X_{jt} + \beta_4 Z_{jt} + v_j + \varepsilon_t + \mu_{jt} \tag{4}$$

$$\text{In}\, P_{jt} = \gamma_0 + \gamma_1 CV_{jt-1} + \gamma_2 X_{jt} + \gamma_4 Z_{jt} + v_j + \varepsilon_t + \mu_{jt} \tag{5}$$

The static analysis presented above shows the relation between within-plant wage dispersion and labor productivity, but it is not definitive about causality. To circumvent this limitation of a static test, we propose a dynamic test, where we study whether wage dispersion is related to increases in sales, wages, or employment. To test whether plants with more dispersed wage structure grow faster (in terms of sales, wages, or employment growth), we estimate the following equations:

$$\Delta P_{jt} = \beta_0 + \beta_1 \sigma_{jt} + \beta_2 \sigma_{jt} + \beta_3 X_{jt} + \beta_4 Z_{jt} + v_j + \varepsilon_t + \mu_{jt} \tag{6}$$

$$\Delta P_{jt} = \gamma_0 + \gamma_1 CV_{jt} + \gamma_2 X_{jt} + \gamma_4 Z_{jt} + v_j + \varepsilon_t + \mu_{jt} \tag{7}$$

where ΔP_{jt} represents change in sales/wage/ employment from year t to $t+1$. In particular, the variable ΔP_{jt} is constructed as in Kawaguchi (2007) and Davis and Haltinwanger (1992):

$$\Delta P_{jt} = \frac{P_{jt+1} - P_{jt}}{(P_{jt+1} + P_{jt})/2} \tag{8}$$

This dependent variable takes a value between −2 and 2. This definition is useful when panels are unbalanced. It prevents the dependent variable to take the value of ∞ when the same plant is not observed the previous/next year, thus reducing the effect of extreme values.

RESULTS

Relation between Wage Dispersion and Labor Productivity

Table 3 presents estimates of the effect of conditional wage dispersion on plant performance. These estimates are obtained applying Generalized Least Squares (GLS) random effect estimation to Eq. (2). As measures of productivity, we alternate between sales per worker and value added per hours worked. As measure of dispersion, we use the standard deviation of log wages. We include in Table 3 the standard deviation of log wages lagged, to address simultaneity issues. We present random effects and fixed effect estimation, and a Hausman's test for random effects for every model specification. As we argue in the "Methodology" section, we use the coefficients obtained from random effects specification in the analysis, as random effects allow some unobserved characteristics to vary overtime.

Overall in the regressions we find a positive and concave quadratic relation between conditional wage dispersion and labor productivity. This relation is significant when sales per person is the dependent variable. The relation is also quadratic, although not significant, when value added plant is the dependent variable. This quadratic relation is what tournament models predict: while a certain degree of dispersion enhances productivity, too much of it can induce workers to engage in unproductive predatory practices.

Evaluating the elasticities at sample means, we calculate that a 10% in within-plant (conditional) wage dispersion leads to an increase in sales per person of 0.13%, and an increase in value added plant of 0.073%. This means that increasing conditional wage dispersion by 10% a year, an average plant would increase its sales per worker by 1904 euros/year. Sales per worker reach a maximum when the value of conditional wage dispersion is 3, while value added reaches a maximum when the value of conditional wage dispersion is 8.5. In our sample, 99% of the plants have conditional wage dispersion lower than 1.75. Thus, most plants are on the positive slope of the curve.

Table 3. Regression Results: Conditional Wage Dispersion.

Dependent Variable	Sales				Value Added			
	RE	FE	RE	FE	RE	FE	RE	FE
SE	0.060***	0.054**			0.034	0.022		
	(0.022)	(0.023)			(0.023)	(0.024)		
SE^2	−0.010*	−0.009			−0.002	−0.000		
	(0.006)	(0.006)			(0.006)	(0.006)		
Lagged SE			0.078***	0.071**			0.002	0.006
			(0.030)	(0.030)			(0.30)	(0.03)
Lagged SE^2			−0.021**	−0.020*			−0.001	−0.003
			(0.010)	(0.010)			(0.010)	(0.01)
Education	0.281***	0.286***	0.281***	0.284***	0.116***	0.067***	0.127***	0.073***
	(0.015)	(0.020)	(0.017)	(0.023)	(0.013)	(0.021)	(0.015)	(0.023)
Age	−0.001	0.008**	−0.006	0.008**	−0.008**	−0.005	−0.012***	−0.005
	(0.003)	(0.004)	(0.004)	(0.004)	(0.003)	(0.004)	(0.003)	(0.005)
Women	−0.203**	−0.60***	−0.17*	−0.70***	−0.23***	−0.64***	−0.24***	−0.66***
	(0.089)	(0.148)	(0.099)	(0.173)	(0.070)	(0.157)	(0.078)	(0.18)
Seniority	0.002***	0.002***	0.002***	0.002***	0.001***	0.001***	0.001***	0.001***
	(0.000)	(0.000)	(0.000)	(0.000)	(0.000)	(0.000)	(0.000)	(0.000)
Plant age	0.019*		0.027**		0.014**		0.018**	
	(0.010)		(0.011)		(0.007)		(0.008)	
Plant capital	0.002***	0.001***	0.002***	0.001***	0.002***	0.001**	0.002***	0.000**
	(0.000)	(0.000)	(0.000)	(0.000)	(0.000)	(0.000)	(0.000)	(0.000)
Overall R^2	0.2419	0.2130	0.2470	0.2058	0.2351	0.1269	0.2618	0.1358
Within R^2	0.1543	0.1570	0.1420	0.1467	0.0269	0.0324	0.0249	0.0316
Between R^2	0.2329	0.1903	0.2852	0.2126	0.2673	0.1200	0.3208	0.1450
No. of obs.	6724	6724	5463	5463	6724	6724	5463	5463
No. of plants	1019	1019	805	805	1019	1019	805	805
χ^2 test for RE	−192.63		94.52		130.01		114.52	

Note: Significant at 10% (*), 5% (**), and 1% (***) significance level. Standard error in parenthesis. Size and industry dummies are also included.

We also find a positive and significant relation between unconditional wage dispersion and plant productivity (see Table 4). This relation is positive and significant with measures of productivity, sales per person, and value added. Results not reported here find no evidence of a quadratic relation. Unconditional wage dispersion is key to study the influence of management's pay on work morale of the rest of the workforce, or the relations between different work groups, as discussed by Akerlof and Yellen (1990). In Akerlof and Yellen's (1990) framework, workers' taste for a fair wage implies that (a certain degree of) wage compression is an optimal firm wage strategy, as workers proportionally withdraw effort as their actual wage falls short of their fair wage. Contrary to what Akerlof and Yellen (1990) model predicts, our results show a positive relation between different measures of wage dispersion (among equal and unequal workers) and labor productivity (value added and sales per worker). However, this positive relation is not statistically significant when value added per worker is the dependent variable.

Sensitivity Analysis

Our key results are robust to the battery of sensitivity analysis performed. In few cases, we observe changes in significance, with no variation in the sign of the coefficients in any case. This is the case when we analyze different measures of dispersion, different measures of performance, different industries, and different average characteristics of plant workers. First, we observe in Table 5 that the positive and significant relation between sales per worker and dispersion holds for different definitions of dispersion. The coefficients range from 0.967 in the case of relative mean deviation to the coefficient of 0.3 in the case of standard deviation of (log) wages, with elasticities of 0.018 and 0.020.

These results do not change in sign when we include different measures of firm-level performance, like firm return on assets or firm value added (see Table 6). However, when firm total factor productivity is the dependent variable, the coefficient of our conditional wage dispersion measure becomes no significant.

In this paper, we analyze whether wage dispersion has an impact on productivity. But dispersion might be endogenous, and firms' increases in productivity might cause increases in dispersion. To address this problem, we include lagged values of dispersion in the analysis, as shown in Eqs. (4) and (5). Results are presented in alternate columns of Table 3 (in the case

Table 4. Regression Results: Unconditional Wage Dispersion.

Dependent Variable	Sales				Value Added			
	RE	FE	RE	FE	RE	FE	RE	FE
CV	0.429**	0.409**			0.538***	0.516***		
	(0.169)	(0.172)			(0.175)	(0.183)		
Lagged CV			0.424**	0.375*			0.025	−0.021
			(0.188)	(0.192)			(0.19)	(0.198)
Education	0.282***	0.286***	0.282***	0.285***	0.116***	0.066***	0.127***	0.073***
	(0.015)	(0.020)	(0.017)	(0.023)	(0.013)	(0.021)	(0.015)	(0.024)
Age	−0.000	0.009**	−0.006	0.007*	−0.006**	−0.003	−0.012***	−0.006
	(0.000)	(0.004)	(0.004)	(0.004)	(0.003)	(0.004)	(0.003)	(0.005)
Women	−0.203**	−0.59***	−0.166*	−0.70***	−0.23***	−0.64***	−0.24***	−0.66***
	(0.089)	(0.148)	(0.099)	(0.173)	(0.071)	(0.157)	(0.078)	(0.179)
Seniority	0.002***	0.002***	0.002***	0.002***	0.001***	0.001***	0.001***	0.001***
	(0.000)	(0.000)	(0.000)	(0.000)	(0.000)	(0.000)	(0.000)	(0.000)
Plant age	0.019**		0.027**		0.013*		0.018**	
	(0.011)		(0.011)		(0.007)		(0.008)	
Plant capital	0.002***	0.001***	0.002***	0.001***	0.002***	0.001**	0.002***	0.000*
	(0.000)	(0.000)	(0.000)	(0.000)	(0.000)	(0.000)	(0.000)	(0.000)
Overall R^2	0.2415	0.2129	0.2469	0.2057	0.2350	0.1278	0.2619	0.1358
Within R^2	0.1544	0.1570	0.1417	0.1463	0.0279	0.0334	0.0249	0.0315
Between R^2	0.2319	0.1899	0.2850	0.2127	0.2664	0.1200	0.3210	0.1452
No. of obs.	6724	6724	5463	5463	6724	6724	5463	5463
No. of plants	1019	1019	805	805	1019	1019	805	805
χ^2 test for RE	−177.92		67.06		114.96		95.57	

Note: Significant at 10% (*), 5% (**), and 1% (***) significance level. Standard error in parenthesis. Size and industry dummies are also included.

Table 5. Sensitivity Analysis: Different Measures of Performance.

Dependent Variable	Firm ROA		Firm Value Added		Firm TFP	
	RE	FE	RE	FE	RE	FE
SE	0.115**	0.129**	0.067***	0.073***	−0.001	−0.001
	(0.051)	(0.054)	(0.017)	(0.017)	(0.003)	(0.003)
SE^2	−0.026**	−0.030**	−0.02***	−0.02***	0.000	0.000
	(0.012)	(0.013)	(0.004)	(0.004)	(0.000)	(0.001)
Education	−0.036	−0.186**	0.127***	0.104***	−0.02***	−0.05***
	(0.027)	(0.048)	(0.011)	(0.015)	(0.002)	(0.003)
Age	−0.04***	−0.04***	−0.01***	−0.006**	−0.01***	−0.01***
	(0.006)	(0.009)	(0.002)	(0.003)	(0.000)	(0.001)
Women	−0.135	−0.144	−0.19***	−0.26***	−0.008	0.142***
	(0.136)	(0.372)	(0.055)	(0.000)	(0.008)	(0.023)
Seniority	0.001***	0.001***	0.001***	0.001***	−0.00***	−0.00***
	(0.000)	(0.000)	(0.000)	(0.000)	(0.000)	(0.000)
Plant age	0.037***		0.011*		−0.01***	
	(0.014)		(0.006)		(0.001)	
Plant capital	−0.000	−0.001*	0.00***	−0.00***	0.000***	−0.000
	(0.000)	(0.000)	(0.000)	(0.000)	(0.000)	(0.000)
Overall R^2	0.0503	0.0053	0.2597	0.1590	0.0395	0.0014
Within R^2	0.0098	0.0124	0.1061	0.1149	0.1869	0.2205
Between R^2	0.0791	0.0121	0.2665	0.1457	0.0112	0.0283
No. of obs.	5344	5344	6223	6223	6194	6194
No. of. plants	890	890	948	948	946	946
χ^2 test for RE	17.94		221.57		654.86	

Note: Significant at 10% (*), 5% (**), and 1% (***) significance level. Standard error in parenthesis. Size and industry dummies are also included.

of conditional wage dispersion) and Table 4 (in the case of unconditional wage dispersion). In the case of conditional wage dispersion, results do not differ in sign or significance form the initial analysis, when we include lagged values as explanatory variables. We only observe a change in significance (though not in sign), when unconditional wage dispersion is the main explanatory variable, and value added plant is dependent variable.

Table 7 presents the estimation of the dynamic analysis in Eqs. (6) and (7). In this case, we study whether wage dispersion is related to increases in sales, wages, or employment. The dynamic test reinforces the results obtained in the previous section. Plants with higher degree of wage dispersion (both conditional and unconditional) enjoy more growth, in terms of wage, sales, and employment. Coefficients are positive and significant. Again, in the case on conditional wage dispersion, we find evidence of a quadratic relation.

Table 6. Sensitivity Analysis: Different Measures of Dispersion.

Dependent Variable	Sales Per Person							
	RE	FE	RE	FE	RE	FE	RE	FE
CV	0.429**	0.409**						
	(0.169)	(0.172)						
Gini			0.743*	0.784*				
			(0.417)	(0.427)				
SD					0.300**	0.274**		
					(0.112)	(0.122)		
RMD							0.967*	1.018*
							(0.512)	(0.524)
Education	0.28***	0.29***	0.28***	0.29***	0.28***	0.29***	0.28***	0.29***
	(0.015)	(0.020)	(0.015)	(0.020)	(0.015)	(0.020)	(0.015)	(0.020)
Age	−0.000	0.009**	−0.001	0.008**	−0.000	0.008**	−0.000	0.008**
	(0.000)	(0.004)	(0.003)	(0.003)	(0.003)	(0.004)	(0.003)	(0.004)
Women	−0.203**	−0.59***	−0.203**	−0.6***	−0.20**	−0.59***	−0.202**	−0.59***
	(0.089)	(0.148)	(0.089)	(0.148)	(0.089)	(0.148)	(0.089)	(0.148)
Seniority	0.00***	0.00***	0.00***	0.00***	0.00***	0.00***	0.00***	0.00***
	(0.000)	(0.000)	(0.000)	(0.000)	(0.000)	(0.000)	(0.000)	(0.000)
Plant age	0.019**		0.019**		0.019*		0.019*	
	(0.011)		(0.011)		(0.011)		(0.011)	
Plant capital	0.00***	0.00***	0.00***	0.00***	0.00***	0.00***	0.00***	0.00***
	(0.000)	(0.000)	(0.000)	(0.000)	(0.000)	(0.000)	(0.000)	(0.000)
Overall R^2	0.2415	0.2129	0.2410	0.2126	0.2418	0.2131	0.2410	0.2126
Within R^2	0.1544	0.1570	0.1540	0.1566	0.1543	0.1569	0.1541	0.1567
Between R^2	0.2319	0.1899	0.2312	0.1895	0.2321	0.1902	0.2312	0.1895
No. of obs.	6724	6724	6724	6724	6724	6724	6724	6724
No. of plants	1019	1019	1019	1019	1019	1019	1019	1019
χ^2 test for RE	−177.92		−175.22		−178.34		−173.85	

Note: Significant at 10% (*), 5% (**), and 1% (***) significance level. Standard error in parenthesis. Size and industry dummies are also included.

Table 7. Sensitivity Analysis: Dynamic Analysis.

Dependent Variable	Change in Sales		Change in Wage		Change in Employment	
	RE	RE	RE	RE	RE	RE
SE	0.095***		0.054***		0.053***	
	(0.022)		(0.017)		(0.015)	
SE^2	−0.012**		−0.006		−0.005	
	(0.005)		(0.004)		(0.003)	
CV		0.800***		0.461***		0.605***
		(0.162)		(0.128)		(0.110)
Education	−0.017*	−0.017*	−0.03***	−0.03***	−0.03***	−0.03***
	(0.010)	(0.010)	(0.008)	(0.008)	(0.008)	(0.008)
Age	−0.17***	−0.02***	−0.02***	−0.02***	−0.02***	−0.02***
	(0.002)	(0.003)	(0.003)	(0.003)	(0.002)	(0.002)
Women	−0.28	−0.031	−0.035	−0.037	−0.063	−0.068
	(0.051)	(0.051)	(0.041)	(0.041)	(0.043)	(0.042)
Seniority	0.000**	0.000**	0.000	0.000	0.000***	0.000***
	(0.000)	(0.000)	(0.000)	(0.000)	(0.000)	(0.000)
Plant age	0.069***	0.069***	0.048***	0.048***	0.067***	0.067***
	(0.005)	(0.005)	(0.004)	(0.004)	(0.004)	(0.004)
Plant capital	0.000	0.000	−0.000	−0.000	−0.000**	−0.000*
	(0.000)	(0.000)	(0.000)	(0.000)	(0.000)	(0.000)
Overall R^2	0.0648	0.0650	0.0955	0.0953	0.1030	0.1046
Within R^2	0.0154	0.0166	0.0423	0.0430	0.0277	0.0301
Between R^2	0.2199	0.2141	0.2384	0.2357	0.2413	0.2391
No. of obs.	6724	6724	4795	4795	6724	6724
No. of plants	1019	1019	863	863	1019	1019

Note: Significant at 10% (*), 5% (**), and 1% (***) significance level. Standard error in parenthesis. Size and industry dummies are also included.

We have run an additional battery of sensitivity analysis to analyze whether our results are driven by industry considerations. First we run Eqs. (1) and (2) separately for the three subsectors of our sample. We also run Eqs. (1) and (2) separately for plants with average education of workers below (and above) the sample median, and for plants with average seniority below and above the sample median. With the first test, we address the issue of industry-specific differences (such as different industry level of collective bargaining, internationalization, technological restrictions, etc.). The second and third tests allow us to study whether conclusions differ depending on the specific characteristics of the workers employed (low skilled workers vs. high skilled workers), and the employer relations between different types of workers. Results for those tests are not reported here, but they are available to the reader upon request. Results do not differ considerably when we split the sample by the average education of workers, nor by the average worker seniority. When we split the sample by industry, we observe a consistent positive and significant relation between different measures of dispersion (conditional and unconditional) and different measures of performance (value added and sales) in the machinery manufacturing sector, while results in the rest of the sectors are in line with those presented on Tables 3 and 4 that refer to the aggregate sample. In all, a separate study of the different industries does not contradict our main results on the aggregate sample that suggest that the incentive effect of wage dispersion dominates fairness or sabotage considerations.

In short, in all sensitivity analysis performed, we observe a positive and significant or a not significant relation between wage dispersion and plant productivity, while no negative relation is found. This implies that theories supporting a certain degree of wage compression as optimal pay strategy do not receive enough support in the analysis.

CONCLUSIONS

This paper studies the relation between within-plant wage dispersion and labor productivity. Tournaments models argue for a degree of wage dispersion to motivate workers, while fair wage effort hypotheses stress the importance of within-firm wage compression to induce workers to exert effort. Previous empirical papers on this topic yield mixed results. In this essay, we try to add empirical evidence to this debate using Finnish data for the years 1990–2002.

Our main finding is a positive and significant relation between within-plant wage dispersion and productivity of labor. This positive relation holds for different measures of dispersion (both conditional and unconditional) and different definitions of productivity (value added per worker or sales per person). It also holds when we split the sample by industry, average education of the workforce, and average seniority. Our results are in line with a recent strand of the literature that finds a positive link between wage dispersion and firm performance, like Winter-Ebmer and Zweimüller (1999), Lallemand et al. (2004), and Grund and Westergaard-Nielsen (2008).

We also find evidence of a quadratic effect when sales per person is the dependent variable. This is the effect that tournament models predict: while a certain degree of dispersion enhances productivity, too much of it can induce workers to engage in unproductive predatory practices. Still, in our sample, conditional wage dispersion would lead to decreased sales when it reaches values above 3. In our sample, 99.8% of the observations are below this threshold. In general, our results suggest that the incentive effect of wage dispersion dominates fairness or sabotage considerations.

Our results suggest that the incentive effect of wage dispersion predicted by tournament models dominates fairness and sabotage considerations, even when this positive effect should be rather limited, taking into account the scarce significance found when plants value added per hours worked is the dependent variable.

On the other hand, fair wage models predict that lower levels of unconditional wage dispersion enhance motivation and improve labor productivity. Overall in the regression, we find a positive and significant or a non-significant relation between different measures of dispersion and labor productivity. We do not find evidence of a negative relation in any case. Thus, our findings do not support fair wage models of wage dispersion.

NOTE

1. Although random effects specification is preferred, both fixed effects and random effects are presented in the results tables. A Hausman's specification test, which tests the appropriateness of the random-effects estimator, is also presented.

ACKNOWLEDGMENTS

We would like to thank three anonymous referees and the editors (Solomon Polachek and Konstantinos Tatsiramos) for many useful comments and suggestions on an earlier version of this chapter. We are also grateful to Pekka Ilmakunnas and Statistics Finland for giving access to the data. Financial support from the Yrjo Jahsson Foundation is acknowledged.

REFERENCES

Akerlof, G., & Yellen, J. (1990). The fair wage effort hypothesis and unemployment. *The Quarterly Journal of Economics*, *105*(2), 255–283.

Asplund, R. (2004). *A macroeconomic perspective on education and inequality*. ETLA Discussion Paper 906.

Braakmann, N. (2008). *Intra-firm wage inequality and firm performance – First evidence from German linked employer-employee*. Data University of Lüneburg Working Paper Series in Economics 77, February 2008.

Burger, J. D., & Walkers, S. J. K. (2008). Testing fair wage theory. *Journal of Labor Research, 29*, 318–322.

Charnes, G., & Kuhn, P. (2005). *Pay inequality, pay secrecy and effort: Theory and evidence*. NBER Working Paper 11786, September 2005.

Cowherd, M. D., & Levine, D. I. (1992). Product quality and pay equity between lower-level employees and top management: An investigation of distributive justice theory. *Administrative Science Quarterly, 37*, 302–320.

Davis, S., & Haltinwanger, J. (1992). Gross job creation, gross job destruction, and employment reallocation. *Quarterly Journal of Economics, 107*(3), 819–863.

Frick, B., Prinz, J., & Winkelmann, K. (2003). Pay inequalities and team performance: Empirical evidence from the North American Major Leagues. *International Journal of Manpower, 24*, 472–488.

Grund, C., & Westergaard-Nielsen, N. (2008). The dispersion of employees' wage increases and firm performance. *Industrial and Labor Relations Review, 61*(4), 485–501.

Heyman, F. (2005). Pay inequality and firm performance: Evidence from matched employer-employee data. *Applied Economics, 37*, 1313–1327.

Hibbs, D. A., & Locking, H. (2000). Wage dispersion and productive efficiency: Evidence from Sweden. *Journal of Labor Economics, 18*(4), 755–781.

Hunnes, A. (2009). Internal wage dispersion and firm performance: White collar evidence. *International Journal of Manpower, 30*(8), 776–796.

Jirjahn, U., & Kraft, K. (2007). Intra-firm wage dispersion and firm performance – Is there a uniform relationship? *Kyklos, 60*(2), 231–253.

Kawaguchi, D. (2007). A market test for sex discrimination: Evidence from Japanese firm level panel data. *International Journal of Industrial Organization, 25*, 441–460.

Lallemand, T., Plasman, R., & Ryck, F. (2004). Intra-firm wage dispersion and firm performance: Evidence from employer-employee data. *Kyklos, 57*(4), 841–864.

Lazear. (1989). Pay inequality and industrial politics. *Journal of Political Economy, 95*, 561–580.

Lazear, E., & Rosen, S. (1981). Rank-order tournaments as optimum labor contracts. *Journal of Political Economy, 89*(5), 841–864.

Leonard, J. S. (1990). Executive pay and firm performance. *Industrial and Labor Relations Review, 43*, 13–29.

Levine, D. I. (1991). Cohesiveness, productivity and wage dispersion. *Journal of Economic Behaviour and Organization, 15*(2), 237–255.

Mahy, B., Rycx, F., & Volral, M. (2011a). Wage dispersion and firm productivity in different working environments. *British Journal of Industrial Relations, 49*(3), 460–485.

Mahy, B., Rycx, F., & Volral, M. (2011b). Does wage dispersion make all firms productive? *Scottish Journal of Political Economy, 58*(4), 455–489.

Martins (2008). Dispersion in wage premiums and firm performance. *Economic Letters, 101*, 63–65.

Milgrom, P., & Roberts, J. (1990). The efficiency of equity in organizational decision processes. *AEA Papers and Proceedings, 80*(2), 154–159.

Mondello, M., & Maxcy, J. (2009). The impact of salary dispersion and performance bonuses in NFL organizations. *Management Decision, 47*(1), 110–123.

Pfeffer, J., & Langton, N. (1993). The effect of wage dispersion on satisfaction, productivity, and worker collaboratively: Evidence from college and university faculty. *Administrative Science Quarterly*, *38*, 382–407.

Piekkola, H. (2002). *From creative destruction to human capital growth: Wage dispersion effects in Finland*. ETLA Discussion Paper 822.

Simmons, R., & Berri, D. J. (2011). Mixing the prince and the paupers: Pay and performance in the National Basketball Association. *Labour Economics*, *18*(3), 381–388.

Uusitalo, R., & Vartiainen, J. (2009). Finland: Firm factors in wages and wage changes. In E. P. Lazear & K. L. Shaw (Eds.), *The structure of wages: An international comparison* (pp. 149–178). Chicago, IL: The University of Chicago Press.

Winter-Ebmer, R., & Zweimüller, J. (1999). Intra-firm wage dispersion and firm performance. *Kyklos*, *52*, 555–572.

TENURE, WAGE PROFILES AND MONITORING

John G. Sessions and Nikolaos Theodoropoulos

ABSTRACT

Efficiency wage theory predicts that firms can induce worker effort by the carrot of high wages and/or the stick of monitoring worker performance. Another option available to firms is to tilt *the remuneration package over time such that the lure of high future earnings acts as a deterrent to current shirking. On the assumption that firms strive for the optimal trade-off between these various instruments, we develop a two-period model of efficiency wages in which increased monitoring attenuates the gradient of the wage-tenure profile. Our empirical analysis, using two cross sections of matched employer-employee British data, provides robust support for this prediction.*

Keywords: Monitoring; tenure; efficiency wages

JEL classifications: J33; J41; J54

New Analyses of Worker Well-Being
Research in Labor Economics, Volume 38, 105–162

ISSN: 0147-9121/doi:10.1108/S0147-9121(2013)0000038004

INTRODUCTION

> Personnel economics has grown over the past twenty years to become a major branch of labour economics. Although much has been learned, many important questions remain. For example, are worker wage profiles dependent on individual attributes or is the firm more important in determining wage growth. (Lazear, 2000)

A firm has a number of weapons in its arsenal that it can use to raise worker productivity. It can establish tournament competitions in which a rank-order prize structure awards the largest prize to the most productive worker, the second-largest prize to the second-most productive worker, and so on (Lazear & Rosen, 1981). It can implement contingent employment contracts in which wages are an increasing function of output, thereby inducing effort as workers strive to maximize realized earnings net of effort (Holmström, 1979). Or it can adopt a carrot and stick, efficiency-wage approach; paying a single wage that is independent of output but above the market clearing level, and dismissing any worker it detects as providing inadequate performance (Shapiro & Stiglitz, 1984).

Another line of attack is to *tilt* the remuneration package over time, paying workers less than the value of their marginal product when they are relatively short-tenured, and correspondingly more than the value of their marginal product when they are relatively long-tenured. Deferring compensation in this way bestows workers with ex post rents that they will be reluctant to jeopardize. If reducing effort increases the probability of involuntary termination, then upward sloping wage profiles raise the cost of shirking and encourage workers to raise effort (Adams & Heywood, 2011).

Firms therefore face optimal trade-offs between both the level and rate of change of remuneration and the quantity of resources they devote to monitoring. The former trade-off, between the level of remuneration and monitoring, has been examined extensively in the literature. Less attention, however, had been paid to the latter trade-off; the relationship between the slope of the wage-tenure profile and the level of monitoring.[1]

On the assumption that firms strive for the optimal trade-off between these various instruments, we hypothesize that increased monitoring leads to a decline in the slope of the wage-tenure profile. Since firms set wages and monitoring jointly as part of their profit-maximizing strategy, monitoring is an endogenous variable in the wage equation. To correct for endogeneity, we use an instrument that exploits variation in labor costs across firms. Our empirical analysis, using two cross sections of British matched employer–employee data, finds strong evidence in support of our theoretical prior. Following Barth (1997), we test for agency and human capital considerations by looking if the deferred compensation occurs in piece rate jobs and if firm specific human capital affects the trade-off between deferred compensation and monitoring. Our results suggest that deferred compensation does not occur in piece rate jobs and that the trade-off between deferred compensation and monitoring does not depend on the presence of firm-specific human capital. We also look at alternative interpretations of our results and find the effect to be mainly working through the disciplinary role of supervisors than a coordination role. Finally, fixed effects estimates suggest a causal effect.

We interpret our findings as further support of efficiency wage theory, and especially of the Lazear (1981) and Medoff and Abraham (1980) view that agency considerations are an important driver of the wage-tenure profile. Wages increase over time not only because workers become more productive, but because firms maximize their profits by optimally deferring pay.

The chapter is set out as follows: the second section discusses the wage-seniority nexus. The third section outlines the theoretical framework to our analysis while the fourth section discusses our data and methodology. The fifth section sets out the main results and the sixth section examines various mechanisms that may generate the results and looks at different interpretations. It also presents results from a fixed effects model and utilizes an alternative definition of supervision. Final comments are collected in the seventh section.

WAGES AND SENIORITY

Efficiency wage theory predicts that firms can elicit effort from their employees by paying supra-competitive, that is, efficiency wages and/or by devoting resources to monitoring. Jobs in which it is difficult to monitor worker performance will generally merit high pay, and vice versa. This trade-off between the *level* of remuneration and monitoring – a central tenet of Bulow and Summer's (1986) dual labor market hypothesis – has been examined extensively in the empirical literature. Supportive evidence is offered by Arai (1994a, 1994b), Bayo-Moriones et al. (2010), Cappelli and Chauvin (1991), Ewing and Payne (1999), Groshen and Krueger (1990), Konings and Walsh (1994), Krueger (1991), Kruse (1992), Machin and Manning (1992), Moretti and Perloff (2002), Raff and Summers

(1987), Rebitzer (1995), and Walsh (1999). Less sympathetic conclusions are drawn by Neal (1993), Fitzroy and Kraft (1986), and Brunello (1995).[2]

Another option available to the firm is to *tilt* the remuneration package over time such that pay increases with seniority. The correlation between seniority and pay is one of the most robust empirical findings in labor economics – for surveys of the theoretical and the empirical literature, see Hutchens (1989), Carmichael (1990), Polachek and Siebert (1993), and Lazear (2000). Received wisdom throughout most of the 1960s and 1970s as to the source of the relationship was that earnings were a reflection of human capital, workers becoming both more productive and better remunerated over time as the return to investments in training are realized (see Becker, 1962; Ben-Porath, 1967; Mincer, 1958). These investments may be specific or general; the former increasing a worker's productivity in the worker's current firm and the latter increasing a worker's productivity in any firm. Worker's paid fully (partially) for general (specific) training by accepting early career, that is, training pay less that the value of their marginal product to the firm. Latter career, that is, trained pay reflected the increase in worker productivity; fully in the case of general training and partially in the case of specific training. Since specific training is only of value within a worker's current firm, it is optimal for workers to neither pay the full cost nor reap the full benefit of such training – to do otherwise might tempt the firm into making redundancies in an attempt to replace trained with untrained workers. By setting trained pay below the value of a trained workers' marginal product, firms are deterred from laying-off trained workers and, accordingly, workers are persuaded to participate in specific training programs. In either case, an upward sloping wage profile emerges; wages increase with seniority because productivity increases with seniority.

The human capital explanation was challenged in a series of papers by Lazear (1979, 1981) and Medoff and Abraham (1980, 1981). Lazear argued that compulsory retirement and actuarially inequitable pension schemes that encouraged early retirement were anathema to human capital theory. Where is the logic in a human resource policy that pays, and thus evidently values, an employee today but which then either forces or induces him to quit tomorrow? Such policies were incompatible with the human capital view that longer-tenured workers were paid no more than their marginal product, especially when wages could be adjusted downwards if productivity declined with age.[3]

A number of wage setting models are able to explain the apparent failings of the human capital model. Freeman (1977) and Harris and

Holmström (1982) develop models in which risk averse workers prefer upward sloping wage profiles because they offer insurance against the possibility that the workers' future productivity is lower than anticipated. Another possibility is that workers prefer rising consumption profiles over their life cycle but find voluntary saving difficult. Upward sloping earnings profiles are therefore desirable because they represent a mechanism for forced-saving (Frank & Hutchens, 1993; Loewenstein & Sicherman, 1991; Neumark, 1995). And models of job search generally predict that more time in the labor market increases the chance of finding a better match and thus tends to be associated with higher earnings (Jacobson & LaLonde, 1993; Manning, 2000; Ruhm, 1991).[4]

Perhaps the most persuasive explanation is the agency approach developed by Lazear (1979, 1981). Lazear reconciled the various phenomena by focusing on contracts that discourage employee shirking and other malfeasance over an employee's life cycle, especially in situations where monitoring worker effort is problematic. The basic idea is that workers and firms enter into contracts, implicit or explicit, whereby workers are paid less than the value of their marginal product when they are in the early years of their job tenure, and correspondingly more than the value of their marginal product when they are in their later years. By deferring compensation in this way, workers are provided with ex post rents that they are reluctant to lose. If reducing effort increases the probability of involuntary termination, then upward sloping wage profiles raise the cost of shirking and encourage workers to raise effort.

Lazear's explanation cuts the link between productivity and pay; wages grow with seniority irrespective of how marginal product relates to seniority. And while it makes sense for the firm to pay wages in excess of the value of a worker's marginal product for a period of time, it would not make sense for the firm to do this indefinitely. There will come a point when the present discounted value of the worker's marginal product equals the present discounted value of his remuneration package. This would imply, from the firm's perspective, an optimal retirement date and hence the need for policies to force or encourage the worker's retirement.

The question as to whether it is human capital or agency considerations that drive the wage profile is not entirely academic. If human capital explanations are found wanting and agency considerations dominate, then issues arise concerning the credibility of long-term employment contracts. Firms will want to lose senior workers who are more expensive but perhaps not more productive. This could lead to time-consistency problems, with some firms finding it difficult to attract younger applicants because of their inability to guarantee long-term employment. If, on the other hand, the slope is primarily a reflection of human capital considerations, then such incentive-compatibility problems will not arise – older workers will be more productive *ceteris paribus*. In this case, the wage profile provides some indication of the return to investments in on-the-job training and education.[5]

Several studies have attempted to discriminate empirically between the two explanations. Hutchens (1987) focuses on the implicit trade-off between the use of deferred payment contracts and the difficulty of monitoring and finds that Lazear-type characteristics (i.e., wage profiles, mandatory retirement, pension schemes, long job tenures) tend not to be associated with jobs that are conducive to monitoring.

Lazear and Moore (1984) address the issue by considering the empirical evidence regarding the relative "flatness" of self-employed workers' wage profiles (Fuchs, 1981; Wolpin, 1977). Such a finding is puzzling since investments in physical capital would tend to depress observed wages for the early career self-employed, while subsequent returns to those investments would tend to raise observed wages. Both factors imply that, other things equal, the wage profiles of self-employed workers will be steeper than those of wage and salary workers.

Lazear and Moore (1984) rationalize the finding by highlighting the duality of principal and ownership intrinsic to self-employment. Observed wage profiles, they argue, are a reflection of the disharmony of interests prevalent in the employment relation that are, by definition, absent from self-employment. By raising the wage profile, employers are able to induce their employees to work harder, therefore raising the present value of the latter's lifetime earnings. The self-employed require no such internal incentive mechanism and thus may be used as a control group to test the theoretical prior that the profile is determined primarily by agency as opposed to human capital considerations.

Brown and Sessions (2006) generalize Lazear and Moore's approach by comparing the wage profiles of self-employed workers, wage and salary workers, and workers employed under performance related pay schemes. The latter, they argue, face an intermediate degree of agency consideration as compared to the two former, and if agency considerations are important then their profile should lay between those of self-employed workers and wage and salary workers. Both studies find convincing empirical support – Lazear and Moore from U.S. data, Brown and Sessions from British data – for the argument that agency considerations are extremely important in driving the wage-tenure profile.

THEORETICAL FRAMEWORK

We illustrate the theoretical underpinning to our analysis in the following stylized model. Assume that workers are homogenous risk neutral with a working life of two periods and separable periodic utility functions $u_t = m_t - e_t$, $t = 1, 2$, where m_t and e_t denote income and effort respectively in period t. Employed workers make a discrete, all or nothing choice regarding the provision of effort to their employer such that $e_t = (0, \overline{e})$, where $\overline{e} > 0$.[6] Firms have a reservation level of profit, $\hat{\pi} \geq 0$, and have access to a monitoring technology defined through the function $p(k)$, where k denotes the value of resources devoted to monitoring and $p(k) \in [0, 1]$ is the probability that a shirker, that is, a worker setting $e_t = 0$ will be detected. To avoid unnecessary complications, we assume that the criteria on which this judgment is based are verifiable by an independent arbitrator such that there is no dispute about the firm's assessment. Monitoring technology is described by $dp(k)/dk \equiv p'(k) > 0$, $d^2p(k)/dk^2 \equiv p''(k) < 0$, $p(0) = 0$ and $p(\tilde{k}) = 1$. It is thus technically possible for the firm to perfectly monitor worker performance. Since our focus of interest is not the optimal level of monitoring, however, we assume that production and monitoring technologies are such that it is always in the interests of the firm to monitor imperfectly. Detection of shirking implies instantaneous dismissal and unemployment utility $b \geq 0$.

We assume that workers produce revenue via a stochastic revenue function $y = f(e; \theta_i)$, where θ_i is a parameter representing a random shock to demand or productivity. We assume that θ_i takes one of two values; θ_H with probability s or θ_L with probability $(1 - s)$. θ_i impacts on revenue as follows:

$$f(\overline{e}, \theta_H) > f(\overline{e}, \theta_L) = f(0, \theta_H) > f(0, \theta_L) \tag{1}$$

Thus, the firm is unable to distinguish between "unlucky," that is, $\theta_i = \theta_L$ non-shirkers and "lucky," that is, $\theta_i = \theta_H$ shirkers and is therefore unable to dismiss workers without monitoring.

We envisage two types of employment contract: "spot-market" contracts of the form $(w, \overline{e})$ and "life-time" contracts of the form $(w_1, w_2, \overline{e}, \overline{e})$. The timing of events in a spot contract is as follows – see Fig. 1.

After the employment contract is signed, the worker makes a decision as to whether or not to shirk and the firm makes a decision as to whether or not to monitor. The state of nature is then revealed to both the worker and the firm and the amount of revenue is realized. Finally, if the worker is

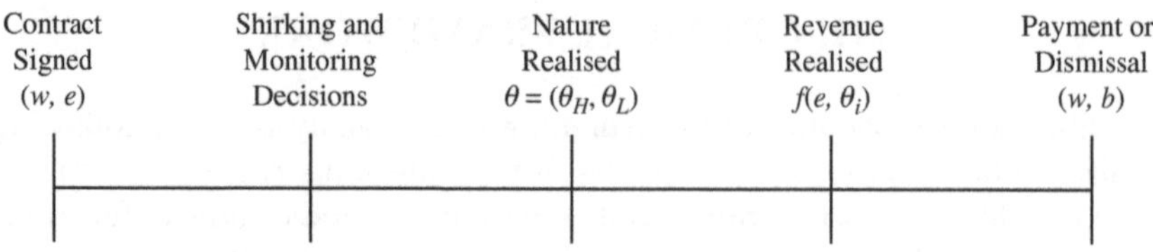

Fig. 1. Spot Contract Timings.

either not monitored or monitored and found not to have shirked, payment is made. If the worker is monitored and found to have shirked, he is dismissed and obtains unemployment utility b.

Firms offering spot contracts will endeavor to maximize their profits subject to the constraints that workers receive at least their reservation wage, $w^r = \bar{e} + b$, and that, once employed, they do not shirk. A spot contract will therefore necessitate workers being paid the lowest wage that satisfies the single period "non-shirking constraint." NSC:

$$w - \bar{e} \geq p(k)b + [1 - p(k)]w \tag{2}$$

Satisfaction of Eq. (2) implies an optimal viz. "efficiency" wage of $w^*(k) = b + e/p(k) > w^r$, such that workers receive some employment rents but are just indifferent between shirking and not shirking.

Consider now the specification of a two-period "lifetime" contract. We ignore discounting and assume, for simplicity, that monitoring is determined in period one for two periods. Firms offering such contracts will be faced, in the second period, with the same effort elicitation problem as those firms offering spot contracts such that $w_2^*(k) = w^*(k) = b + e/p(k)$ as before. In the first period, however, firms can set w_1 such that the worker's *lifetime* NSC is satisfied:

$$w_1 + w_2^* - 2\bar{e} \geq p(k)2b + [1 - p(k)](w_1 + w_2^* - \bar{e}) \tag{3}$$

Undetected shirkers enjoy utility of w_1 now and $w_2^* - \bar{e}$ tomorrow – that is, given w_2^*, workers will not shirk in period two.[7] Satisfaction of 3 implies an equilibrium first period wage of $w_1^* = b + \bar{e}$, with workers acquiring rents on account of the firm's inability to perfectly monitor. The firm, however, can reduce these rents by offering lifetime contracts that induce workers to queue up to access the second period wage that exceeds their reservation utility.

Since it is in the firm's interest to pay neither more nor less than the efficient wage levels $w^* = (w_1^*, w_2^*)$ as derived from the two non-shirking constraints (Eqs. (2) and (3)), we can substitute them directly into the firm's expected profit function:

$$E\{\pi(w, k; \theta_i)\} = E\{f(e_1; \theta_i)\} + E\{f(e_2; \theta_i)\} - [w_1 + w_2 + c(k)]$$

$$\Rightarrow$$

$$E\{\pi(w^*, k; \theta_i)\} = 2E\{f(\bar{e}; \theta_i)\} - \left\{ 2b + \left[\frac{1 + p(k)}{p(k)}\right]\bar{e} + c(k) \right\} \quad (4)$$

where $E\{f(e, \theta_i)\} = sf(e, \theta_H) + (1 - s)f(e, \theta_L)$ and $c(k)$, $\partial c(k)/\partial k \equiv c'(k) > 0$, is a function representing the cost of monitoring to the firm. Although it is in the firm's interest to pay workers their efficient wage, it can reduce these by increasing the resources it devotes to monitoring. The firm will therefore optimize profit with respect to k by equating the marginal benefit and marginal cost of increasing the quantity of resources devoted to monitoring:

$$\frac{\partial E\{\pi^*(w^*, k; \theta_i)\}}{\partial k} = \frac{p'(k^*)}{[p(k^*)]^2}\bar{e} - c'(k^*) = 0 \quad (5)$$

Workers employed under lifetime contracts thus face an upward sloping earnings profile:

$$\Delta w^*(k^*) = w_2^*(k^*) - w_1^* = \left[\frac{1 - p(k^*)}{p(k^*)}\right]\bar{e} > 0 \quad (6)$$

It is apparent from Eq. (6) that increased monitoring on the part of the firm assuages the slope of the experience-earnings profile:

$$\frac{\partial \Delta w(k^*)}{\partial k^*} = -\frac{p'(k^*)}{[p(k^*)]^2}\bar{e} < 0 \quad (7)$$

The above illustration is, clearly, highly simplified. Complications to the basic story could, for example, involve risk-averseness on the part of the worker. In such a situation, workers would prefer relatively flatter profiles, other things equal, especially if it is possible for the firm to make a type-2 error and inadvertently fire a non-shirker, if there is a chance that the firm will default on its promise of future high wages, or if the firm's survival in future periods is not guaranteed. Such risk would be especially pronounced in relatively smaller firms that, other things equal, will be more likely to go out of business and whose promise of future wage premia will be, consequently, less credible.

There is also the assumption that the choice over effort is dichotomous. In more general, continuous effort settings, the relationship between the level of pay and monitoring is less clear-cut. Fluctuations in the cost of monitoring will invoke both substitution and scale effects. An increase in the cost of monitoring will induce firms to place a greater reliance on wage incentives, but may also lead to a reduction in the desired level of effort itself, and this latter effect may conceivably outweigh the former (Allgullin & Ellingsen, 2002). Empirical analysis of this issue suggests that monitoring has a significant and negative impact on the wages of high-effort workers, but not on the wages of low-effort workers (Strobl & Walsh, 2007).[8]

DATA AND METHODOLOGY

Data

Our data are derived from the 1998 and 2004 *Workplace Employee Relations Survey* (WERS). These are the fourth and fifth installments of a government-funded series of cross-section surveys conducted at British workplaces. A workplace is defined as comprising the activities of a single employer at a single set of premises, for instance, a single branch of a bank, a car factory, or a school. The previous surveys were conducted in 1980, 1984, and 1990 without, however, offering the possibility to match employees with employers.

The sample of workplaces was randomly drawn from the Interdepartmental Business Register *IDBR*. This is maintained by the Office for National Statistics ONS and is considered to be the highest quality-sampling frame of workplaces defined as the activities of a single employer at a single set of premises available in Britain.

The survey comprises three main sections: The "Management Questionnaire" face-to-face interviews with senior managers with day-to-day responsibility for employee relations; the "Worker Representative Questionnaire"; and the "Employee Questionnaire". The survey population for the Management Questionnaire is all British workplaces barring those in agriculture, hunting and forestry, fishing, mining and quarrying, private households with employed persons, and extra-territorial organizations.

The response rate in the 1998 (2004) Management Questionnaire was 80% (64%). The respective figure for the Employee Questionnaire was 66% (61%). At those workplaces responding to the manager survey, a questionnaire was presented to 25 randomly selected employees in workplaces with more than 25 employees, or to all the employees in workplaces with fewer than 25 employees.[9]

For the purposes of our study, we combine data from the Management and Employee Questionnaires. Thus, our final 1998 (2004) sample comprises 21,301 (16,217) employees linked to a set of 1,451 (1,381) firms.[10]

Although there are limitations in the WERS data, they are extremely attractive in enabling the matching of employees within employers while also permitting controls for a detailed range of employer characteristics that might otherwise confound the relationship between wages, tenure, and monitoring. The uniqueness of the WERS data in clustering employees to a specific employer makes it the first British dataset that allows studying interactions between employees and employers. Further, the two cross sections allow us to examine the above relationship at different points in time. To our knowledge, there is no other study that has examined the relationship between the slope of the wage-tenure profile and the level of monitoring using matched employer–employee data.

Methodology

Our theoretical model implies an inverse relationship between the slope of the wage-tenure profile and the value of resources devoted to monitoring by the firms. To test this hypothesis empirically, we enter as explanatory variables into our econometric model interactions that capture the relationships between monitoring and tenure. To be specific, our equation of interest is:

$$w_{ij} = \alpha + \beta_0 m_j + (\beta_1 + \beta_2 m_j) t_{ij} + (\beta_3 + \beta_4 m_j)\left(\frac{t_{ij}^2}{100}\right) + \beta_5 \mathbf{X}_{ij} + \beta_6 \mathbf{Z}_j + u_{ij} \quad (8)$$

where $i = 1, \ldots, M$ and $j = 1, \ldots, N$ denote individual worker and firm-specific subscripts, respectively. The dependent variable w_{ij} denotes ln weekly wage earned by individual i at firm j, t_{ij} denotes the employment tenure of individual i at firm j, m_j denotes the level of monitoring within firm j, $\mathbf{X}_{ij}$ and $\mathbf{Z}_j$ denote vectors of individual and firm characteristics, respectively, and u_{ij}

denotes the error term. The relationship between monitoring and the gradient of the tenure profile is given by:

$$\frac{\partial w_{ij}}{\partial t_{ij}} = \beta_1 + \beta_2 m_j + 2(\beta_3 + \beta_4 m_j)\left(\frac{t_{ij}}{100}\right) \quad (9)$$

and

$$\frac{\partial^2 w_{ij}}{\partial t_{ij} \partial m_j} = \beta_2 + 2\beta_4\left(\frac{t_{ij}}{100}\right) \quad (10)$$

The testable hypothesis from our theoretical prior is that $\beta_2 + 2\beta_4 t_{ij} < 0$ such that wages rise more gradually with employee tenure as the level of monitoring within the firm increases.

We source the individual characteristics vector, $\mathbf{X}_{ij}$, from the Employee Questionnaire.

The control variables here are age[11] and age-squared/100, gender, ethnicity, married/cohabitation, having dependent children, long-term disability, educational and vocational qualifications. We also include dummy variables recording whether the employee has a fixed-term or temporary job, whether the employee is a trade union member, and five dummies capturing the amount of job training the employee has received over the previous year. Assumed that the nature of the job itself will impact upon the wage-tenure profile, we also include occupation fixed effects. Occupations will differ, for example, in terms of risk of injury or in the degree of autonomy they offer to employees, and it may be the case that those jobs which require more monitoring typically employ lower quality workers and pay less than other occupations, ceteris paribus. Table 1 provides definitions of the above variables and Table 2 the corresponding descriptive statistics. Descriptive statistics in Table 2 suggest that individual characteristics are similar across the two surveys.

Earnings were recorded as a categorical variable in *WERS*. The specific question in both surveys is:

> How much do you get paid for your job here, before tax and other deductions are taken out? If your pay changes before tax from week to week because of overtime, or because you work different hours each week, think of what you earn on average.

Respondents in the 1998 (2004) survey were asked to place their weekly pay level within 12 (14) bands, chosen to approximate decile bands and the top and bottom 5% of the earnings distribution as estimated from the *New Earnings Survey*. Table 3 provides the share of employees within each of the above pay bands.

Table 1. Variable List and Definitions – Employee Questionnaire.

Variable	Definition
Individual characteristics	
Age	Age in years mid-points[a]
Age-sq/100	Age squared divided by 100
Female	Female: 0–1 dummy
Minority	Ethnic minority: Black, Indian, Pakistani, Bangladeshi, Chinese: 0–1 dummy
Married/cohabiting	Living with spouse/partner: 0–1 dummy
Dependent children	Have dependent children: 0–1 dummy
Disability	Long standing health problem/disability that limit work, home or leisure time: 0–1 dummy
Academic qualifications	
Low CSE	GCSE Grades D–G: 0–1 dummy[b]
High CSE	GCSE Grades A–C: 0–1 dummy
A-Level	A level or equivalent: 0–1 dummy
Degree	Undergraduate Degree or equivalent: 0–1 dummy
Postgraduate	Postgraduate degree or equivalent: 0–1 dummy
Vocational	Recognized vocational qualifications, i.e., trade apprenticeship: 0–1 dummy[c]
Job characteristics	
ln wage	ln average gross weekly wage, mid-points between the upper and the lower band
ln lower wage limit	ln average gross weekly wage, aggregation of the lower bands
ln upper wage limit	ln average gross weekly wage, aggregation of the upper bands
Tenure	Years of work at this workplace mid-points of 5 bands
Instrumented tenure	Years of work of individual i in firm j minus average years of work in firm j
Tenure-sq/100	Tenure squared divided by 100
Instrumented tenure-sq/100	(Years of work of individual i in firm j square minus average years of work in firm j squared)/100
Fixed-term	Employed on a fixed term contract: 0–1 dummy
Temporary	Employed on a temporary contract: 0–1 dummy
Trade union member	Employee is a trade union member: 0–1 dummy
Occupational categories	
Manager	Manager and senior official: 0–1 dummy
Professional	Professional, i.e., lecturer, teachers, doctors: 0–1 dummy
Technical	Associate professional and technical: 0–1 dummy
Clerical	Clerical and secretarial typist, postal clerk, secretary: 0–1 dummy
Crafts	Craft and skilled service tool maker, electrician, fitter: 0–1 dummy
Services	Personal and protective service police officer, bar staff: 0–1 dummy

Table 1. (*Continued*)

Variable	Definition
Sales	Sales till operator, sales assistant: 0–1 dummy
Operatives	Operative and assembly line worker, packer, truck driver: 0–1 dummy
Training dummies	
Training days	Numbers of days training received in past 12 months:
Training days ($0 \leq TD < 1$)	Less than 1 day: 0–1 dummy
Training days ($1 \leq TD < 2$)	1 to less than 2 days: 0–1 dummy
Training days ($2 \leq TD < 5$)	2 to less than 5 days: 0–1 dummy
Training days ($5 \leq TD < 10$)	5 to less than 10 days: 0–1 dummy
Training days ($TD \geq 10$)	10 days or more: 0–1 dummy
Employee Monitoring	Supervision of other employees: 0–1 dummy[d]

[a]In 1998, there were seven age bands. In 2004, there were nine age bands.

[b]In 1998, the education question asked "What is the highest educational qualification you hold?" There were six education categories available: "GCSE grades D–G," "GCSE grades A–C," "A levels," "Degree," "Postgraduate degree," "None of these." In 2004, the education question asked "Which if any of the following academic qualifications have you obtained?" There were eight options: "GCSE grades D–G," "GCSE grades A–C," "1 GCE 'A' level grades A–E," "Two or more GCE 'A' levels grades A–E," "First degree," "Higher degree," "Other academic qualifications," "No academic qualifications."

[c]The vocational qualification question differs between 1998 and 2004. In 1998, employees were asked: "*Do you hold any recognized vocational qualifications, such as trade apprenticeship, NVQs, or a City and Guilds Certificate.*" Employees had to reply either "*Yes*" or "*No*". In 2004, employees were asked "*And which, if any, of the following vocational or professional qualifications have you obtained?*" Employees were provided with nine options: "Level 1 NVQ," "Level 2 NVQ," "Level 3 NVQ," "Level 4 NVQ," "Level 5 NVQ," "Completion of Trade Apprenticeship," "City and Guilds, RSA," "Other professional qualifications, e.g., qualified teacher, accountant, nurse," "No vocational or professional qualifications."

[d]This variable is available only in the 2004 survey.

Entries in Table 3 suggest an equal distribution of responses across the pay bands. Given that wages were recorded in bands, we construct an average measure of wages by taking the midpoints of each band and then aggregating.

Unfortunately, the WERS contains no information on the value of resources that firms expend on monitoring. It does, however, contain information on the number of employees who hold supervisory responsibilities. We therefore follow Leonard (1987), Gordon (1990, 1994), and Neal (1993) in proxying monitoring intensity via the proportion of supervisory employees within the firm.[12] Supervisors, which include foremen and line managers, are defined in the WERS as "… those people directly concerned

Table 2. Descriptive Statistics – Employee Questionnaire.

	1998		2004	
	Mean	Std. Dev.	Mean	Std. Dev.
Demographic				
Age	39.566	11.543	40.466	11.656
Age-sq/100	16.987	9.226	17.734	9.360
Minority	0.028	0.165	0.044	0.207
Female	0.507	0.499	0.530	0.499
Married/cohabiting	0.692	0.462	0.682	0.465
Dependent children	0.402	0.490	0.387	0.487
Disability	0.054	0.226	0.046	0.209
Education				
Low CSE	0.111	0.315	0.159	0.365
High CSE	0.261	0.439	0.261	0.439
A-Level	0.155	0.362	0.142	0.349
Degree	0.179	0.383	0.205	0.404
Postgraduate	0.061	0.238	0.067	0.249
Vocational	0.369	0.482	0.612	0.487
Occupation				
Managerial	0.105	0.306	0.111	0.315
Professional	0.158	0.365	0.123	0.328
Technical	0.096	0.295	0.160	0.367
Clerical	0.197	0.397	0.182	0.386
Crafts	0.079	0.270	0.070	0.256
Services	0.072	0.258	0.093	0.290
Sales	0.080	0.271	0.063	0.243
Operatives	0.089	0.285	0.077	0.266
Job				
Tenure	7.951	7.529	7.739	7.564
Instrumented tenure	3.395	7.529	5.989	7.564
Tenure-sq/100	1.199	1.675	1.171	1.679
Instrumented tenure-sq/100	0.682	1.012	0.930	1.420
Fixed-term	0.030	0.170	0.032	0.178
Temporary	0.035	0.185	0.044	0.205
Trade union member	0.388	0.487	0.362	0.480
Training				
Training days $0 \leq TD < 1$	0.085	0.279	0.091	0.287
Training days $1 \leq TD < 2$	0.143	0.350	0.150	0.357
Training days $2 \leq TD < 5$	0.214	0.410	0.220	0.414
Training days $5 \leq TD < 10$	0.093	0.290	0.099	0.299
Training days $TD \geq 10$	0.088	0.283	0.084	0.277

Table 2. *(Continued)*

	1998		2004	
	Mean	Std. Dev.	Mean	Std. Dev.
Wage				
ln weekly wage	5.399	0.822	5.687	0.766
ln lower wage limit	4.834	2.329	5.352	1.758
ln upper wage limit	5.541	0.711	5.789	0.703
Supervisor				
Supervisor/Foreman/Line manager	–	–	0.347	0.476
Number of observations	21,301		16,217	

Notes:
1. Samples include workers in the age group 18–60 years.
2. Means are weighted so that they are representative of the sampling population.
3. "–" implies that the variable is not present.

with the detailed supervision of work." The specific variable is derived from the following question asked in both the 1998 and 2004 management questionnaires:

> What proportion of non-managerial employees here have job duties that involve supervising other employees? (*BINVMANG*)

Managers were asked to indicate in which range their firm lay: 0% "None"; 1–19% "Just a few"; 20–39% "Some"; 40–59% "Around half"; 60–79% "Most"; 80–99% "Almost all"; and 100% "All."[13] The distribution of the index across the sample of firms in the raw 1998 (2004) data is provided in Table 4.

In terms of the firm characteristics vector, $\mathbf{Z}_j$, we drew from the Management Questionnaire which provides a large bank of information on workplace characteristics. We include in $\mathbf{Z}_j$ the size of the workplace as measured by the log number of employees in the firm, the log number of years the firm has been in operation, and the following share variables with respect to the total number of employees in the firm: eight occupational groups, women, ethnic minorities, part-time, trade union density, less than 20 and above 50 years old.

Given that the share of supervisors might systematically vary according to the industry, we control for industry fixed effects. We also include region fixed effects, and unemployment to vacancy rates by travel to work area to capture the tightness of the local labor market. Table 5 provides definitions of these workplace characteristics and Table 6 the corresponding

Table 3. The Pay Distribution Across Bands.

Pay Band	1998		2004	
	Mean	Observations	Mean	Observations
Less than £50	5.32	1,133	2.62	425
£51–£80	5.73	1,220	3.34	542
£81–£140	11.52	2,453	3.99	647
£111–£140	–	–	4.63	750
£141–£180	9.43	2,008	6.04	979
£181–£220	11.52	2,454	7.71	1,249
£221–£260	10.93	2,328	9.42	1,527
£261–£310	10.56	2,250	11.33	1,837
£311–£360	8.52	1,815	9.58	1,553
£361–£430	9.93	2,116	11.41	1,850
£431–£540	8.28	1,764	11.48	1,860
£541–£680	4.44	946	9.22	1,494
£681–£870	–	–	5.0	810
£681 or more	3.82	814	–	–
£871 or more	–	–	4.23	685
Percent observations	100.00	21,301	100.00	16,208

Notes: Respondents in the 1998 (2004) survey were asked to place their weekly pay level within 12 (14) bands, chosen to approximate decile bands and the top and bottom 5% of the *New Earnings Survey*. "–" implies the band was not available in the respective survey.

Table 4. Distribution of the Endogenous Monitoring Variable (BINVMANG).

Bands	1998		2004	
	Mean	Observations	Mean	Observations
None: 0%	10.30	225	13.22	301
Just a few: 1–19%	46.20	1,009	42.84	975
Some: 20–39%	27.52	601	30.01	683
Around half: 40–59%	7.60	166	8.66	197
Most: 60–79%	3.89	85	3.30	75
Almost all: 80–99%	2.15	47	1.23	28
All: 100%	2.34	51	0.75	17
Total number of observations (%)	100.00	2,184	100.00	2,276

Notes: Entries in the table are from the raw 1998 and 2004 WERS Management Questionnaire data after dropping missing information on monitoring (BINVMANG). There were 7 (19) missing observations in the 1998 (2004) survey, respectively.

Table 5. Variable List and Definitions – Management Questionnaire.

Variable	Definition
Firm characteristics	
BINVMANG	% of nonmanagerial employees have job duties that involve supervising other employees?
–	0% "None.": 0–1 dummy
–	1–19% "Just a few.": 0–1 dummy
–	20–39% "Some.": 0–1 dummy
–	40–59% "Around half.": 0–1 dummy
–	60–79% "Most.": 0–1 dummy
–	80–99% "Almost all.": 0–1 dummy
–	100% "All.": 0–1 dummy
ln size	ln of the total number of employees at the firm
ln age of firm	ln number of years the firm is operating
Industry classification	
Construction	Construction: 0–1 dummy
Education	Education: 0–1 dummy
Financial	Financial services: 0–1 dummy
Health	Health: 0–1 dummy
Hotels and restaurants	Hotels and restaurants: 0–1 dummy
Manufacturing	Manufacturing: 0–1 dummy
Other businesses	Other businesses: 0–1 dummy
Public administration	Public administration: 0–1 dummy
Transportation	Transportation: 0–1 dummy
Utilities	Electricity, water, gas: 0–1 dummy
Wholesale and retail	Wholesale and retail: 0–1 dummy
Training	
Firm specific training	Time new employees take to do their jobs as well as more experienced employees 0. None, 1. Just a few, 2. Some, 3. Around half, 4. Most, 5. Almost all, 6. All
Workforce	
Female	Share of females
Ethnic minority	Share of ethnic minorities
Less than 20	Share of less than 20 years old
More than 51	Share of more than 51 years old
Part-time	Share of part-time contracts
Trade union density	Share of employees belong to a trade union
Managers and seniors	Share of managers and senior officials
Professional	Share of professional staff
Technical	Share of technical staff
Clerical	Share of clerical staff
Craft	Share of craft staff
Protective and personnel	Share of protective and personnel service staff
Operative	Share of operative and assembly staff

Table 5. (*Continued*)

Variable	Definition
Sales	Share of sales staff
Region dummies	10 region dummies (Standard Statistical Region)
Other variables	
Unemployment-vacancy rate	Unemployment to vacancy rate by travel to work area (TWA)
Piece rates/measure of output	Individual performance/output measured/assessed by piece rates/other measures of output: 0–1 dummy[a]
Payment by result	If employees at the firm get paid by results: 0–1 dummy[b]
Disciplinary supervision role	Supervisors have the authority to dismiss employees for unsatisfactory performance: 0–1 dummy
Teamwork	Proportion if any of employees at this workplace work in formally designated teams 0. None, 1. Just a few, 2. Some, 3. Around half, 4. Most, 5. Almost all, 6. All

[a]Variable is only available in 1998.
[b]Variable is only available in 2004.

descriptive statistics. Descriptive statistics in Table 6 suggest that firm characteristics are similar across the two surveys.

As a baseline, we initially estimate Eq. (8) via ordinary least squares (OLS). Since firms set wages and monitoring jointly as part of their profit-maximizing strategy – recall the third section – monitoring is an endogenous variable in the wage equation and we therefore adopt an instrumental variable (IV) approach. This requires variables that influence monitoring but not wages, or the wage-tenure profile. Such variables are extremely difficult to identify, both theoretically and practically. Our preferred approach builds on the identification strategy of Goldin (1986) and Lemieux, Macleod, and Parent (2012) and corrects for endogeneity of monitoring in the wage equation by using variation in labor costs across firms. Our identification strategy therefore rests on the assumption that the instrumental variable only affects the wage-tenure profile through is effect on monitoring.

We proxy the cost of monitoring through the following question asked in the management questionnaire:

> About what proportion of this establishment's (sales revenue/operating costs) is accounted for by wages, salaries and other labour costs like pensions and national insurance? (*KPROSAL*)

Managers had to choose one of the following options: (1) 0–25%; (2) 25–49%; (3) 50–74%; (4) 75–100%. The variation of responses in the

Table 6. Descriptive Statistics: Firm Characteristics.

	1998		2004	
	Mean	Std. dev.	Mean	Std. dev.
Industry				
Manufacturing	0.154	0.361	0.157	0.364
Utilities	0.037	0.188	0.018	0.134
Construction	0.050	0.218	0.053	0.224
Wholesale and retail	0.139	0.346	0.096	0.294
Hotels and restaurants	0.042	0.202	0.029	0.168
Transportation	0.059	0.236	0.055	0.228
Financial	0.053	0.224	0.049	0.216
Other businesses	0.089	0.284	0.110	0.313
Public administration	0.089	0.285	0.076	0.266
Education	0.118	0.322	0.129	0.335
Health	0.121	0.326	0.163	0.369
Region				
East Anglia	0.037	0.191	0.084	0.277
East Midlands	0.086	0.281	0.071	0.256
London	0.124	0.329	0.100	0.300
North East	0.063	0.243	0.046	0.209
North West	0.091	0.287	0.143	0.350
Scotland	0.094	0.292	0.107	0.310
South East	0.192	0.393	0.119	0.324
South West	0.092	0.289	0.093	0.291
Wales	0.045	0.208	0.046	0.209
West Midlands	0.091	0.288	0.101	0.301
Share of workforce				
Females	0.495	0.289	0.511	0.292
Ethnic minorities	0.040	0.088	0.065	0.127
Young	0.055	0.102	0.055	0.098
Old	0.157	0.113	0.220	0.145
Part-time	0.241	0.264	0.249	0.255
Trade union density	0.361	0.344	0.307	0.317
Managers	0.091	0.100	0.099	0.106
Professional	0.141	0.217	0.132	0.201
Technical	0.084	0.154	0.125	0.198
Clerical	0.189	0.220	0.171	0.214
Craft	0.092	0.179	0.075	0.169
Protective and personnel	0.083	0.204	0.091	0.216
Operative	0.111	0.235	0.095	0.216
Sales	0.093	0.217	0.099	0.228
Firm characteristics				
ln size	4.710	1.207	4.627	1.543
ln Age of the Firm	2.618	2.305	2.829	2.873

Table 6. *(Continued)*

	1998		2004	
	Mean	Std. dev.	Mean	Std. dev.
Other variables				
Unemployment-vacancy rate	3.857	1.688	3.396	2.393
Piece rate/measure of output	0.087	0.282	–	–
Payment by result	–	–	0.277	0.447
Disciplinary supervision role	0.070	0.255	0.106	0.307
Teamwork	4.171	2.088	4.280	2.097
Firm specific training	2.022	1.850	1.689	1.592
Number of observations	21,301		16,217	

Note: Means are weighted; "–" implies that the variable is not present.

1998 (2004) sample were: (1) 23.24% (20.49%); (2) 23.74% (27.64%); (3) 26.21% (26.47%); (4) 26.81% (25.41%). These simple descriptive statistics show that there is a substantial variation on sales revenue/operating costs across firms. This is in line with Brown (1992) who argues against the assumption of a common fixed cost of monitoring across firms. Although the above question does not explicitly identify the cost of monitoring, we believe that it at least captures monitoring costs as monitoring costs are part of the firm's operating costs. Indeed, a simple correlation between *KPROSAL* (the instrument) and *BINVMANG* (the endogenous variable) provides a positive relationship for both surveys ($r = 0.25$ for 1998; $r = 0.30$ for 2004). We believe that this instrument is an exogenous shifter of monitoring as it purely captures labor costs. Further, this instrument is not a choice variable. An example of a choice variable would be that the firm sets targets on labor turnover. Setting targets on labor turnover could directly affect wages as well as work through many other potential channels to interact with wages besides just through its effect on the supervisor to staff ratio.

Tenure may also be viewed as an endogenous variable in a wage regression due to unobserved individual characteristics and to job match effects (Altonji & Shakotko, 1987; Topel, 1991). For instance, employees with a better match between their skills and those demanded in the job can stay longer with their employer, have higher productivity and earn more. Also, tenure can also be correlated with monitoring if firms with strong selectivity for long tenure employees have low or high monitoring efforts. For instance, firms can better retain the most able employees in a firm organization that easily reveals their ability. This also reduces the necessity of monitoring and thus biases our interaction effects. Thus, to correct for the above biases we instrument tenure by taking deviations of individual tenure from the average tenure of the firm the employee is observed (see also Altonji & Shakotko, 1987; Dustmann & Pereira, 2008; Topel, 1991; Zwick, 2012). We instrument t_{ij}, the mean tenure of individual i in firm j, by $\tilde{t}_{ij} = t_{ij} - \overline{t_j}$. We also define $\tilde{t}^2_{ij} = (t^2_{ij} - \overline{t^2_j})/100$. By construction, $\tilde{t}_{ij}$ and $\tilde{t}^2_{ij}$ are uncorrelated with unobserved individual characteristics and job match specific effects. When presenting our results, we label t_{ij} as "*Instrumented tenure*" and $\tilde{t}^2_{ij}$ as "*Instrumented tenure-Sq*/100."

RESULTS

Ordinary Least Squares

Our OLS estimates for 1998 and 2004 are reported in Table 7.

The regressions for both samples are generally well specified and the estimated coefficients are consistent with the standard human capital model of wages. Wages increase concavely with job tenure and are positively and significantly related to educational attainment and the amount of training undertaken in the previous 12 months. The returns to firm-specific tenure are lower than the returns to actual labor market experience as captured by age and age-squared/100.[14]

Marriage or cohabitation is associated with a positive wage premium, but having a dependent child has the opposite effect. We also note significant occupational differentials and evidence of racial and gender disadvantage. There are significant and positive returns to trade union membership while fixed-term and temporary employees receive lower wages than their permanent counterparts, other things equal. In terms of firm characteristics, pay is higher in larger firms but lower in firms the more skewed the age demographic, and in firms with a higher percentage of part-time employees.

In terms of our key regressor, it is evident that higher monitoring impacts negatively on the slope of the wage profile in both samples. In 1998, for example, a unit increase in monitoring reduces the slope of the wage profile by 0.20% for a worker with zero years of tenure, 0.18% for a worker with one year of tenure and 0.12% for a worker with five years of tenure. The respective figures for 2004 are 0.40%, 0.36%, and 0.21%.

Table 7. Ordinary Least Squares Estimates Dependent Variable – ln Weekly Wage.

	1998		2004	
	Coef.	St. error	Coef.	St. error
Monitoring	0.014**	0.006	0.012*	0.006
Monitoring×Tenure	−0.002	0.002	−0.004	0.003
Monitoring×Tenure-sq/100	0.008	0.008	0.019*	0.011
Tenure	0.033***	0.003	0.023***	0.004
Tenure-sq/100	−0.107***	0.107	−0.076***	0.021
Age	0.067***	0.002	0.057***	0.002
Age-sq/100	−0.079***	0.003	−0.065***	0.003
Low CSE	0.025*	0.013	0.088***	0.013
High CSE	0.088***	0.011	0.123***	0.013
A levels	0.149***	0.013	0.193***	0.015
Degree	0.349***	0.014	0.327***	0.015
Postgraduate	0.478***	0.020	0.410***	0.020
Vocational	0.059***	0.007	0.076***	0.008
Manager	0.905***	0.016	0.815***	0.017
Professional	0.715***	0.017	0.821***	0.019
Technical	0.450***	0.018	0.528***	0.017
Clerical	0.302***	0.015	0.359***	0.016
Craft	0.387***	0.017	0.363***	0.020
Services	0.145***	0.016	0.276***	0.019
Sales	0.131***	0.019	0.206***	0.022
Operative	0.161***	0.019	0.273***	0.019
Fixed term contract	−0.264***	0.021	−0.079***	0.021
Temporary	−0.310***	0.017	−0.302***	0.018
Female	−0.270***	0.009	−0.268***	0.009
Minority	−0.412***	0.024	−0.069***	0.019
Trade union member	0.224***	0.011	0.153***	0.009
Married/cohabiting	0.066***	0.008	0.030***	0.008
Dependent child	−0.088***	0.008	−0.085***	0.008
Disability	0.082***	0.015	−0.118***	0.017
Training less than 1 day	0.047***	0.014	−0.004	0.013
Training 1 to less than 2 days	0.094***	0.011	0.095***	0.011
Training 2 to less than 5 days	0.159***	0.010	0.155***	0.010
Training 5 to less than 10 days	0.198***	0.014	0.212***	0.014
Training 10 days or more	0.098***	0.014	0.125***	0.014
ln number of employees	0.038***	0.004	0.026***	0.002
Share of managers	−0.034	0.047	0.204***	0.044
Share of professional	−0.057*	0.032	0.001	0.031
Share of technical	−0.239***	0.034	0.024	0.029
Share of clerical	0.033	0.030	0.039	0.030
Share of craft	−0.108***	0.031	−0.109***	0.034
Share of services	−0.099***	0.028	−0.077**	0.031

***Table** 7.* (*Continued*)

	1998		2004	
	Coef.	St. error	Coef.	St. error
Share of operatives	−0.044	0.029	−0.049*	0.029
Share of sales	−0.108***	0.028	−0.098***	0.029
Share of women	−0.048**	0.023	−0.062**	0.026
Share of ethnic minorities	0.053	0.046	−0.035	0.036
Share of part-time	−0.926***	0.021	−0.842***	0.024
Share of union coverage	−0.003	0.017	−0.065***	0.015
Share of employees <20 years old	−0.139***	0.040	−0.038	0.044
Share of employees >50 years old	−0.256***	0.035	−0.064**	0.029
ln age firm	−0.006***	0.001	−0.0001	0.001
Unemployment-vacancy rate by TWA	−0.017***	0.002	−0.002	0.002
Constant	3.470***	0.058	3.908***	0.060
Observations	21,301		16,217	
R-squared	0.659		0.622	
Industry fixed effects	Yes		Yes	
Region fixed effects	Yes		Yes	
Clusters	1,451		1,381	

Note: Estimates are weighted and allow for clustering of employees within firms. Levels of significance: ***1%, **5%, *10%. The omitted category is a male white worker, with no education and no vocational qualification, holds a routine/unskilled occupation, has a permanent job contract, does not belong to a trade union, is not married or cohabiting, does not have dependent children, is in good health, did not have any training in the last 12 months, works in community services and lives in Yorkshire/Humberside.

Instrumental Variables – Two Stages Least Squares

Our instrumental variable estimates are set out in Table 8 for 1998 and Table 9 for 2004. The controls are exactly the same as in Table 7 except that in the first stage we use the instrument (KPROSAL) and its interactions with $\tilde{t}_{ij}$ and $\tilde{t}^2_{ij}$ in place of the endogenous monitoring variable (BINVMANG) and its interactions with tenure and tenure-squared/100. Since we interact our instrument (KPROSAL) with $\tilde{t}_{ij}$ and $\tilde{t}^2_{ij}$, the first stage involves three steps. The results are reported in four columns; columns 1–3 report the first-stage results and column 4 the second stage results.[15]

In column 1, the dependent variable is the endogenous variable (BINVMANG). There is a positive and statistically significant relationship between BINVMANG and KPROSAL suggesting that higher labor costs increase the likelihood that a firm monitors its employees. In column 2, the

Table 8. Instrumental Variables (2SLS) – 1998.

Dependent Variable	First Stage (Linear Probability Model)						Second-Stage	
	(1)		(2)		(3)		(4)	
	BINVMANG		BINVMANG×Tenure		BINVMANG×Tenure-sq/100		ln wage	
	Coef.	St. error	Coef.	St. error	Coef.	St. error	Coef.	St. error
KPROSAL	0.014*	0.008	–0.197*	0.113	–0.084***	0.025	–	–
KPROSAL×Instrumented Tenure	–0.001	0.002	0.084**	0.033	0.006	0.006	–	–
KPROSAL×Instrumented Tenure-sq/100	0.001	0.021	0.108	0.246	0.123***	0.046	–	–
BINVMANG	–	–	–	–	–	–	0.243	0.323
BINVMANG×Tenure	–	–	–	–	–	–	–0.082***	0.021
BINVMANG×Tenure-sq/100	–	–	–	–	–	–	0.349***	0.095
Instrumented Tenure	0.007	0.008	1.479***	0.090	0.136***	0.017	0.105***	0.022
Instrumented Tenure-sq/100	–0.025	0.058	–0.197	0.667	1.406***	0.126	–0.686***	0.161
Age	–0.005	0.005	–0.030	0.064	–0.002	0.012	0.066***	0.003
Age-sq/100	0.008	0.007	0.056	0.079	0.006	0.015	–0.077***	0.004
Low CSE	0.021	0.029	0.082	0.334	0.016	0.063	0.055***	0.014
High CSE	0.063**	0.025	1.009***	0.284	0.191***	0.053	0.097***	0.024
A levels	0.054*	0.030	0.813**	0.343	0.145**	0.065	0.157***	0.023
Degree	0.041	0.033	0.719*	0.378	0.141**	0.071	0.320***	0.020
Postgraduate	0.008	0.047	0.192	0.532	0.048	0.101	0.471***	0.021
Vocational	–0.058***	0.017	–0.518***	0.198	–0.080**	0.037	0.030	0.020
Manager	–0.070*	0.039	–1.357***	0.453	–0.264***	0.085	0.914***	0.030
Professional	–0.007	0.040	–0.783*	0.456	–0.167*	0.086	0.713***	0.018
Technical	0.033	0.040	–0.076	0.457	–0.038	0.086	0.460***	0.020
Clerical	–0.070**	0.035	–0.987**	0.400	–0.165**	0.076	0.272***	0.028
Craft	–0.175***	0.036	–1.508***	0.414	–0.237***	0.078	0.336***	0.060
Services	0.008	0.038	–0.794*	0.438	–0.146*	0.083	0.186***	0.017
Sales	–0.080*	0.041	–0.612	0.478	–0.090	0.090	0.136***	0.032
Operative	–0.014	0.035	–0.710*	0.405	–0.184**	0.076	0.222***	0.017
Fixed term contract	0.012	0.048	–0.528	0.549	–0.109	0.104	–0.212***	0.022
Temporary	0.033	0.041	–0.010	0.475	–0.038	0.090	–0.265***	0.021

Table 8. *(Continued)*

Dependent Variable	First Stage (Linear Probability Model)						Second-Stage	
	(1)		(2)		(3)		(4)	
	BINVMANG		BINVMANG×Tenure		BINVMANG×Tenure-sq/100		ln wage	
	Coef.	St. error	Coef.	St. error	Coef.	St. error	Coef.	St. error
Female	0.013	0.020	0.030	0.238	−0.022	0.045	−0.268***	0.010
Minority	−0.114**	0.051	−0.084	0.592	0.050	0.112	−0.122***	0.042
Trade union member	−0.027	0.022	0.043	0.252	0.042	0.047	0.166***	0.013
Married/cohabiting	0.014	0.021	0.050	0.225	0.011	0.042	0.071***	0.008
Dependent child	0.030	0.019	0.212	0.219	0.026	0.041	−0.077***	0.013
Disability	0.007	0.033	−0.381	0.376	−0.129*	0.071	−0.083***	0.015
Training less than 1 day	−0.018	0.029	0.055	0.334	0.014	0.063	0.027*	0.014
Training 1 to less than 2 days	0.023	0.025	0.768***	0.293	0.157***	0.055	0.103***	0.014
Training 2 to less than 5 days	0.077***	0.023	1.427***	0.365	0.253***	0.050	0.158***	0.029
Training 5 to less than 10 days	−0.031	0.031	0.089	.0354	0.044	0.067	0.192***	0.017
Training 10 days or more	0.047	0.031	1.301***	0.354	0.231***	0.067	0.152***	0.022
ln number of employees	0.113	0.006	0.674***	0.069	0.079***	0.013	0.037	0.037
Share of managers	0.358***	0.111	0.832	1.271	−0.048	0.241	0.162	0.127
Share of professional	0.404***	0.068	5.043***	0.785	0.860***	0.149	0.125	0.142
Share of technical	0.299***	0.071	4.050***	0.809	0.615***	0.153	−0.013	0.107
Share of clerical	0.441***	0.069	4.146***	0.794	0.625***	0.150	0.117	0.149
Share of craft	0.908***	0.065	8.781***	0.750	1.318***	0.142	0.079	0.305
Share of services	0.489***	0.061	4.230***	0.698	0.617***	0.132	0.081	0.165
Share of operatives	0.289***	0.055	3.156***	0.636	0.515***	0.120	0.023	0.098
Share of sales	0.634***	0.062	4.526***	0.706	0.602***	0.133	0.002	0.206
Share of women	−0.273***	0.055	−2.149***	0.633	−0.316***	0.120	−0.083	0.093
Share of ethnic minorities	−0.027	0.107	−0.744	1.220	−0.170	0.231	0.059	0.049
Share of part-time	−0.069	0.053	1.872***	0.614	0.370***	0.116	−0.945	0.032
Share of union coverage	0.006	0.035	−0.423	0.409	−0.135*	0.077	0.018	0.017
Share of employees <20 years old	0.514***	0.102	1.948*	1.164	0.227	0.220	−0.345**	0.169
Share of employees >50 years old	−0.590***	0.083	−6.817***	0.950	−1.160***	0.180	−0.280	0.203

ln firm age	−0.011***	0.004	−0.095**	0.045	−0.015*	0.008	−0.007	0.004
Unemployment-vacancy rate by TTWA	0.034***	0.006	0.167**	0.073	0.016	0.014	−0.019	0.012
Constant	0.521***	0.133	−1.330	1.525	−0.823***	0.289	3.607***	0.179
F-test for weak identification	$15.27_{3,\ 21301}$		$25.15_{3,\ 21301}$		$36.54_{3,\ 21301}$		–	
Observations	21,301		21,301		21,301		21,301	
R-squared centered	0.092		0.498		0.568		0.650	
R-squared uncentered	0.688		0.667		0.661		0.991	
Industry fixed effects	Yes		Yes		Yes		Yes	
Region fixed effects	Yes		Yes		Yes		Yes	
Clusters	1,451		1,451		1,451		1,451	

Notes: Estimates are weighted and allow for clustering of employees within firms. The endogenous variable (monitoring) is "BINVMANG." The instrument is "*KPROSAL*": "About what proportion of this firm's (sales revenue/operating costs) is accounted for by wages, salaries and other labour costs like pensions and national insurance?" "Tenure" is the endogenous variable, "Instrumented Tenure" is the instrument for "Tenure" and is constructed as deviations of employee tenure from the average tenure of the firm the employee works. Levels of significance: ***1%, **5%, *10%. "–" implies the variable is not present.

Table 9. Instrumental Variables (2SLS) – 2004.

Dependent Variable	First Stage (Linear Probability Model)						Second-Stage	
	(1)		(2)		(3)		(4)	
	BINVMANG		BINVMANG× Tenure		BINVMANG× Tenure-sq/100		ln wage	
	Coef.	Std. error	Coef.	St. error	Coef	St. error	Coef.	St. error
KPROSAL	0.049***	0.011	−0.297**	0.123	−0.070***	0.023	–	–
KPROSAL×Instrumented Tenure	0.000	0.004	0.111**	0.045	0.005	0.008	–	–
KPROSAL×Instrumented Tenure-sq/100	−0.010	0.022	−0.157	0.240	0.074	0.045	–	–
BINVMANG	–	–	–	–	–	–	0.212*	0.126
BINVMANG×Tenure	–	–	–	–	–	–	−0.059**	0.024
BINVMANG×Tenure-sq/100	–	–	–	–	–	–	0.302***	0.109
Instrumented Tenure	0.000	0.012	1.254***	0.124	0.036	0.023	0.090***	0.031
Instrumented Tenure-sq/100	0.032	0.062	0.613	0.658	1.418***	0.125	−0.515***	0.172
Age	−0.005	0.005	−0.001	0.058	0.002	0.011	0.055***	0.002
Age-sq/100	0.005	0.006	0.010	0.072	−0.000	0.013	−0.063***	0.003
Low CSE	−0.014	0.028	0.265	0.302	0.088	0.057	0.094***	0.014
High CSE	0.004	0.027	0.781***	0.292	0.185***	0.055	0.128***	0.014
A levels	−0.039	0.031	1.012***	0.335	0.256***	0.063	0.200***	0.017
Degree	−0.040	0.031	0.369	0.333	0.126**	0.063	0.329***	0.016
Postgraduate	0.013	0.041	0.216	0.439	0.073	0.083	0.410***	0.021
Vocational	−0.001	0.017	0.221	0.182	0.050	0.034	0.076***	0.008
Manager	0.058	0.036	0.242	0.393	−0.002	0.074	0.802***	0.019
Professional	0.003	0.039	−0.030	0.416	−0.034	0.079	0.814***	0.019
Technical	0.019	0.035	−0.539	0.376	−0.147**	0.071	0.523***	0.018
Clerical	0.054	0.033	0.064	0.361	−0.038	0.068	0.349***	0.018
Craft	0.027	0.040	0.184	0.433	0.005	0.082	0.352***	0.020
Services	−0.038	0.040	−0.774*	0.429	−0.156*	0.081	0.262***	0.021
Sales	0.037	0.043	−0.448	0.468	−0.130	0.089	0.220***	0.022

Operative	0.001	0.038	−0.222	0.410	−0.066	0.078	0.259***	0.019
Fixed term contract	0.025	0.044	−0.279	0.478	−0.060	0.091	−0.082***	0.022
Temporary	0.003	0.038	0.158	0.405	0.040	0.077	−0.309***	0.019
Female	0.009	0.019	−0.082	0.209	−0.015	0.039	−0.271***	0.009
Minority	0.036	0.039	0.004	0.423	0.004	0.080	−0.084***	0.020
Trade union member	−0.011	0.020	0.045	0.221	0.014	0.042	0.144***	0.010
Married/cohabiting	0.058***	0.018	0.466**	0.195	0.067*	0.037	0.024**	0.011
Dependent child	−0.036*	0.018	−0.362*	0.199	−0.053	0.037	−0.073***	0.010
Disability	−0.012	0.036	−0.090	0.386	−0.006	0.073	−0.124***	0.018
Training less than 1 day	−0.044	0.028	−0.766**	0.302	−0147**	0.057	0.009	0.016
Training 1 to less than 2 days	0.052**	0.024	−0.099	0.259	−0.059	0.049	0.099	0.013
Training 2 to less than 5 days	0.051**	0.022	0.560**	0.234	0.091**	0.044	0.145	0.013
Training 5 to less than 10 days	0.038	0.029	0.472	0.310	0.076	0.059	0.202***	0.015
Training 10 days or more	−0.019	0.031	0.343	0.333	0.064	0.063	0.134***	0.016
ln number of employees	0.070***	0.005	0.618***	0.061	0.100	0.011	0.019**	0.009
Share of managers	0.677***	0.098	5.621***	1.047	0.925***	0.199	0.085	0.097
Share of professional	0.323***	0.064	2.519***	0.686	0.443***	0.130	−0.068	0.051
Share of technical	0.379***	0.061	3.414***	0.660	0.607***	0.125	−0.059	0.059
Share of clerical	0.112*	0.061	0.837	0.652	0.176	0.124	0.032	0.032
Share of craft	0.298***	0.072	4.250***	0.777	0.788***	0.147	−0.131**	0.056
Share of services	0.497***	0.065	4.769***	0.703	0.838***	0.133	−0.132*	0.073
Share of operatives	0.030	0.060	0.796	0.646	0.145	0.123	−0.043	0.030
Share of sales	−0.247***	0.057	−0.737	0.617	−0.052	0.117	−0.071*	0.042
Share of women	−0.015	0.054	0.037	0.584	−0.011	0.111	−0.061**	0.027
Share of ethnic minorities	0.204***	0.076	3.113***	0.812	0.592***	0.154	−0.060	0.050
Share of part-time	−0.359***	0.051	−3.239***	0.543	−0.525***	0.103	−0.807***	0.053
Share of union coverage	−0.033	0.033	−0.837**	0.359	−0.166**	0.068	−0.063***	0.017
Share of employees <20 years old	0.556***	0.098	6.852***	1.053	1.207***	0.200	−0.159*	0.092
Share of employees >50 years old	0.110*	0.061	2.151***	0.658	0.419***	0.125	−0.092**	0.036
ln firm age	0.020***	0.002	0.150***	0.027	0.021***	0.005	−0.003	0.003
Unemployment-vacancy rate by TWA	−0.009*	0.005	0.001	0.055	0.004	0.010	−0.003	0.002
Constant	0.855***	0.126	−4.313***	1.345	−1.209***	0.256	3.906***	0.125

Table 9. *(Continued)*

Dependent Variable	First Stage (Linear Probability Model)						Second-Stage	
	(1)		(2)		(3)		(4)	
	BINVMANG		BINVMANG× Tenure		BINVMANG× Tenure-sq/100		ln wage	
	Coef.	Std. error	Coef.	St. error	Coef	St. error	Coef.	St. error
F-test for weak identification	$17.48_{3,\ 16217}$		$23.18_{3,\ 16217}$		$32.55_{3,\ 16217}$		–	
Observations	16,217		16,217		16,217		16,217	
R-squared centered	0.103		0.586		0.651		0.593	
R-squared uncentered	0.732		0.735		0.732		0.993	
Industry fixed effects	Yes		Yes		Yes		Yes	
Region fixed effects	Yes		Yes		Yes		Yes	
Clusters	1,381		1,381		1,381		1,381	

Notes: See previous Table; ***1%, **5%, *10%. "–" implies the variable is not present.

dependent variable is the interaction between BINVMANG and the endogenous tenure variable. There is a negative and significant relationship between KPROSAL and BINVMANG times tenure suggesting that monitoring decreases with increases in tenure and labor costs. The same pattern holds in column 3, where the dependent variable is BINVMANG times tenure-squared/100. As can be seen in columns 1–3 of Tables 8 and 9, the *F*-statistic for excluded instruments for each of the first three steps far exceeds the commonly used threshold of 10 suggesting that our instruments are not weak.

From column 4, it is evident that higher monitoring impacts negatively on the slope of the wage profile in both samples. In 1998, for example, a unit increase in monitoring reduces the slope of the wage profile by 8.2%, 7.5%, and 4.7% for a worker with zero, one and five years of tenure, respectively. The corresponding reductions in 2004 are 5.9%, 5.3%, and 2.9%.

The effect of monitoring on the shape of the wage-tenure profile is illustrated graphically in Fig. 2 for the 1998 sample and in Fig. 3 for the 2004 sample. Figures 2 and 3 plot simulated wage-tenure profiles over a range of monitoring (i.e., *BINVMANG* = 0, *BINVMANG* = 0.1, *BINVMANG* = 0.3 and *BINVMANG* = 0.6). For ease of graphical exposition, we set the constants in both graphs equal to zero.

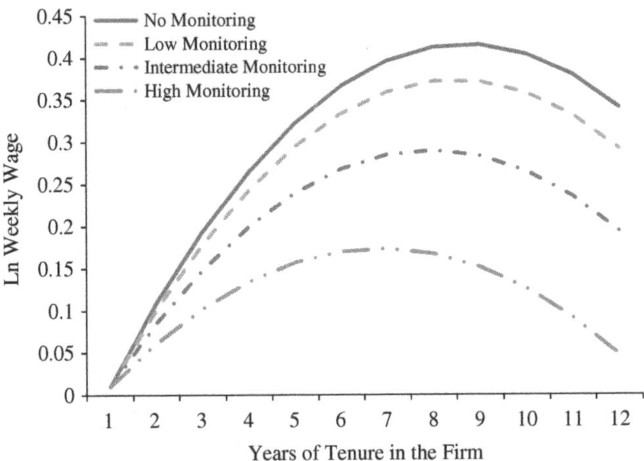

Fig. 2. Wages, Monitoring and Tenure – (1998). *Note*: Low, intermediate, and high monitoring are defined as when monitoring is equal to 0.1, 0.3, and 0.6, respectively. These values come from the distribution of the raw monitoring variable BINVMANG (see Table 4).

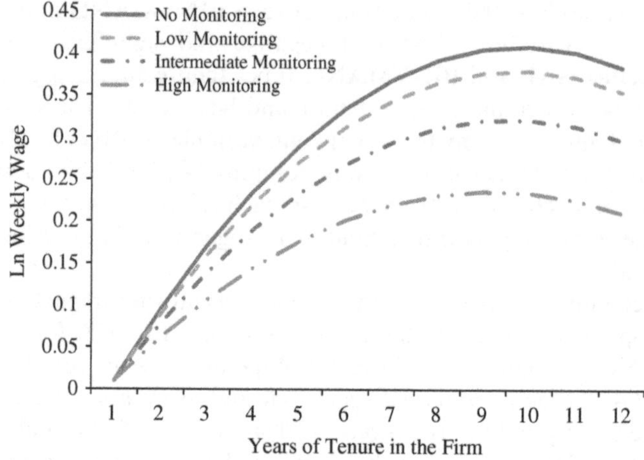

Fig. 3. Wages, Monitoring and Tenure – 2004. *Note*: Low, intermediate, and high monitoring are defined as when monitoring is equal to 0.1, 0.3, and 0.6, respectively. These values come from the distribution of the raw monitoring variable BINVMANG (see Table 4).

It is clear from both figures that there is a significant and consistent negative relationship between monitoring and the slope of the wage-tenure profile. In Fig. 2, wages peak at 7.65 years of tenure when $BINVMANG=0$, 7.43 years when $BINVMANG=0.1$, 6.91 years when $BINVMANG=0.3$, and 5.85 years when $BINVMANG=0.6$. In Fig. 3, wages peak at 8.74, 8.67, 8.52, and 8.18 years of tenure, respectively. We do not discuss the rest of the estimates obtained from the IV approach as they are in line with the OLS estimates discussed in the section "Ordinary Least Squares."

SENSITIVITY ANALYSES

To examine the robustness of our findings regarding the relationship between monitoring and the slope of the wage-tenure profile, Table 10 reports results from a battery of sensitivity tests.[16]

Piece Rates and Payment by Results

We pay specific attention to the effect of piece rates on the relationship between monitoring and the slope of the wage-tenure profile. Piece rates

Table 10. Robustness Checks Dependent Variable: Log Wage.

	(1)		(2)		(3)		(4)		(5)		(6)		(7)	
	1998		1998		2004		2004		1998		2004		2004	
	No Piece-Rates		Piece-Rates		No Payment-by-Result		Payment-by-Result		Firm-Specific Training		Firm-Specific Training		Employee-Recorded Monitoring	
	Coef.	St. error	Coef.	St. error	Coef.	St. error	Coef.	St. error	Coef.	St. error	Coef.	St. error	Coef.	St. error
BINVMANG	0.286	0.219	0.095	0.229	0.279**	0.137	−3.244	11.618	0.205**	0.097	0.141	0.387	3.957	2.491
BINVMANG×Tenure	−0.106***	0.034	−0.025	0.040	−0.075**	0.033	0.418	1.551	−0.075***	0.022	−0.051**	0.023	−1.632**	0.809
BINVMANG×Tenure-sq/100	0.431***	0.140	0.094***	0.157	0.385**	0.153	−1.960	6.837	0.314***	0.097	0.260**	0.122	7.384**	3.479
Instrumented Tenure	0.132***	0.037	0.054***	0.040	0.112**	0.044	−0.491	1.909	0.094***	0.022	0.094***	0.036	0.493**	0.239
Instrumented Tenure-sq/100	−0.822***	0.241	−0.342***	0.244	−0.646***	0.243	2.905	10.294	−0.598***	0.167	−0.447**	0.192	−2.617**	1.212
Firm training	–	–	–	–	–	–	–	–	0.008	0.006	0.016	0.011	–	–
BINVMANG×COTHJOB	–	–	–	–	–	–	–	–	0.0001	0.003	0.001	0.007	–	–
Instrumented Tenure×COTHJOB	–	–	–	–	–	–	–	–	0.002***	0.001	0.001	0.001	–	–
Instrumented Tenure-sq/100×COTHJOB	–	–	–	–	–	–	–	–	−0.014**	0.005	−0.004	0.008	–	–
Constant	3.658***	0.178	3.062***	0.234	3.853***	0.173	7.016	11.093	3.599***	0.087	3.818***	0.346	3.641***	0.409
Observations	19,434		1,867		11,722		4,495		21,301		16,217		15,797	
Industry FE	Yes		Yes		Yes		Yes		Yes		Yes		Yes	
Region FE	Yes		Yes		Yes		Yes		Yes		Yes		Yes	
Clusters	1,329		122		981		400		1,451		1,381		1,295	

Notes:

1. All specifications include the control variables as per Tables 8 and 9.
2. Estimates are weighted and allow for clustering of employees within firms.
3. COTHJOB refers to firm-specific training.
4. The estimation method across all columns is a 2SLS. For reasons of brevity we only report the second stages.
5. Levels of significance: ***1%, **5%.
6. "–" implies the variable is not present.

tend to occur in circumstances where monitoring costs are relatively low, minimal if any wages are deferred and little or no monitoring is undertaken. Indeed, in the extreme, the only monitoring undertaken is the counting of pieces. Firms may be inclined to reduce monitoring and to increase the use of deferred compensation when monitoring is difficult and/or expensive and when the counting of pieces becomes problematic. But this would imply that monitoring and deferred compensation go hand in hand – the circumstances in which monitoring costs are likely to be high are exactly those in which the incentives to defer compensation are likely to be highest.[17]

We expect monitoring problems to differ across piece rates and time rates jobs. In the 1998 data, we observe whether or not individual output is measured or assessed by piece rates, or any other measure of output. This information is not available in the 2004 data. However, in the 2004 data we observe whether or not the worker is paid by the amount of work he is doing or its value, rather than just the number of hours he works.

For the 1998 sample, we restrict our main specification to observations where individual output is not measurable by piece rates or by any other measure of output (column 1) and to jobs where output is measurable by piece rates or by any other measure of output (column 2). We do the same for the 2004 sample, restricting to observations where the worker is not paid by the amount done or its value (column 3), and to observations where the worker is paid by the amount done or its value (column 4).

The estimation strategy is a 2SLS, where we report only the second stage results for the main variables of interest. The results confirm the robustness of our key finding. According to a priori expectations, we find evidence that our main interaction term is negative and significant in jobs where output is not measurable, or no payment by result is made. In contrast, deferred compensation does not take place for jobs where output is measurable in pieces or where the employees are paid by the amount of work they do. This result is in line with Barth (1997) who finds that piece rates methods of pay have negligible return to seniority.

Firm Specific Human Capital

We also pay particular attention to firm specific human capital in our robustness checks since this may generate a trade-off between "apparent" deferred compensation – that is, the steepness of the tenure profile – and monitoring without any appeal to Lazear-type arguments (Barth, 1997). Firm specific capital, by its nature, creates a closer tie between firms and workers. As such, one might expect that a larger deviation from contractual effort is required to warrant the termination of employment, since in such a situation the firm will be losing all of the returns to its investments. Thus, the optimal detail and extent of monitoring may well differ as compared to workers lacking in firm specific human capital, for whom even a small deviation from anticipated effort renders them a liability.

We therefore include an additional regressor, COTHJOB, that proxies the extent of firm specific human capital in our specification as well as interactions between COTHJOB and the instrument KPROSAL, and between COTHJOB and $\tilde{t}_{ij}$ and $\tilde{t}^2_{ij}$.[18] The estimation strategy is 2SLS where we report only the second stage results for the main variables of interest. The estimates are set out in Table 10 (columns 5 and 6) and again emphasize the robustness of our central finding. The interaction estimates between instrumented monitoring and instrumented tenure and tenure-squared/100 remain significant after controlling for the various interactions firm specific human capital with other controls. The interaction effect between firm specific training and monitoring is negative and insignificant. Thus, the tradeoff between deferred compensation and monitoring does not depend on the presence of firm specific human capital. This result is in line with Barth (1997) who finds a small and negative interaction between firm specific skills and seniority.

Individual-Reported Monitoring

Because the monitoring variable is coming from the management questionnaire disregards managerial employees, we utilize information from the following question asked in the 2004, but not in the 1998, Employee Questionnaire:

> Do you supervise any other employees? A supervisor, foremen or line manager is responsible for overseeing the work of other employees on a day to day basis; yes/no?

Our aim here is to test whether our results are robust to an alternative, employee instead of employer reported measure of supervision that measures the total share of employees (managerial plus nonmanagerial) with supervisory responsibilities.[19] Given the dichotomous nature of the above question, we aggregated employees' responses by firm to get the total number of supervisors for each firm and divide them with the total number of employees in the firm. This ratio gives us the share of employees with supervisory responsibilities. We then instrument for monitoring and tenure as in the section "Methodology." The estimates from this exercise are reported in column 7 of Table 10 and follow the same pattern of results as reported in column 4 of Tables 8 and 9, confirming that wages rise more gradually with employee tenure as the level of monitoring increases.

The Role of Supervision – Helping or Disciplining?[20]

Given the difficulty of measuring the two main variables of interest – monitoring intensity and seniority wages – within WERS, we cannot rule out a priori that supervision might reflect non-monitoring considerations. Supervision could be interpreted as "helping" instead of "controlling" when the colleague who supervises does not really have a disciplinary function with respect to the employee who is supervised and when there is a manager whose duty is the control of effort of (both). In such a case, the role of a supervisor might be to coordinate production rather than to discipline underperforming employees.

To capture such an effect we incorporate triple interactions between monitoring, tenure and teamwork. The estimation method is again 2SLS and we present the second stage estimates of the variables of interest in Table 11. Columns 1 (1998) and 4 (2004) show that there is a negative and statistically significant effect of the triple interaction coefficient between monitoring, tenure and teamwork suggesting that supervisors may indeed also act as advisors in the production process.

To ascertain the disciplinary role of supervisors we add triple interactions between monitoring, tenure, and whether supervisors have the authority to make final decisions on dismissing workers for unsatisfactory performance. The results from this exercise are reported in columns 2 (1998) and 5 (2004) of Table 11. The triple interaction attains a negative and statistically significant coefficient that is considerably larger than the triple interaction coefficient emanating from the coordination effect.

To examine the relative importance of the coordination and disciplinary channels, we estimate the above interactions jointly (Table 11, columns 3 and 6) and find that statistical significance only remains for the disciplinary effect where the triple interaction coefficient between monitoring, tenure and supervisors dismissing employees for unsatisfactory performance is statistically significant at the 10% level. We interpret these results as suggestive, but not conclusive, that the disciplinary role of supervision dominates any coordination role and that the main mechanism through which our results operate is the controlling rather than advisory role of supervision.

Table 11. Productivity or Discipline Effect Dependent Variable: Log Wage.

	1998						2004					
	(1)		(2)		(3)		(4)		(5)		(6)	
	Coordination		Disciplinary		Both		Coordination		Disciplinary		Both	
	Coef.	St. error	Coef.	St. error	Coef.	St. error	Coef.	St. error	Coef.	St. error	Coef.	St. error
BINVMANG	0.717	0.454	0.370	0.260	0.274*	0.150	0.361	0.246	0.226*	0.119	0.156	0.124
BINVMANG×Tenure× Teamwork	−0.009*	0.005	–	–	0.044	0.029	−0.014**	0.007	–	–	0.001	0.026
BINVMANG×Tenure-sq/ 100×Teamwork	0.036	0.027	–	–	−0.238	0.149	0.060**	0.028	–	–	0.007	0.131
Instrumented Tenure× Teamwork	0.011**	0.004	–	–	−0.034	0.024	0.016	0.010	–	–	−0.004	0.030
Instrumented Tenure-sq/ 100×Teamwork	−0.075*	0.043	–	–	0.361	0.230	−0.077*	0.046	–	–	−0.0002	0.179
Teamwork	0.067**	0.029	–	–	−0.223	0.160	0.027***	0.009	–	–	0.0007	0.059
Instrumented Tenure	0.012	0.008	0.025***	0.008	0.002	0.010	0.029***	0.005	0.025*	0.014	0.026	0.017
Instrumented Tenure-sq/100	−0.028	0.062	−0.084*	0.049	0.038	0.085	−0.128***	0.030	−0.156**	0.078	−0.152	0.099
BINVMANG×Tenure× Disciplinary procedure	–	–	−0.063***	0.021	−0.344*	0.195	–	–	−0.061**	0.024	−0.056*	0.032
BINVMANG×Tenure-sq/100 ×Disciplinary Procedure	–	–	0.263***	0.095	1.777*	0.973	–	–	0.306***	0.112	0.178*	0.095
Instrumented Tenure× Disciplinary Procedure	–	–	0.060**	0.025	0.305*	0.175	–	–	0.068**	0.034	0.072	0.171

Table 11. *(Continued)*

	1998						2004					
	(1)		(2)		(3)		(4)		(5)		(6)	
	Coordination		Disciplinary		Both		Coordination		Disciplinary		Both	
	Coef.	St. error	Coef.	St. error	Coef.	St. error	Coef.	St. error	Coef.	St. error	Coef.	St. error
Instrumented Tenure-sq/ 100×Disciplinary procedure	–	–	−0.457***	0.173	−2.928*	1.581	–	–	−0.365**	0.186	−0.217	0.991
Disciplinary procedure	–	–	0.351***	0.121	1.887*	1.110	–	–	0.043	0.062	0.048	0.291
Observations	21,301		21,301		21,301		16,217		16,217		16,217	
Clusters	1,451		1,451		1,451		1,381		1,381		1,381	

Notes:
1. All specifications include the control variables as per Tables 8 and 9.
2. Estimates are weighted and allow for clustering of employees within firms.
3. Teamwork refers to the proportion of people in the workplace that work in formally designated teams.
4. Disciplinary procedure refers to supervisors that have the authority to dismiss employees for unsatisfactory performance.
5. The estimation method across all columns is a 2SLS. For reasons of brevity we only report the second stage results for the variables of interest.
6. Levels of significance: ***1%, **5%,*10%.
7. "–" implies the variable is not present.

Table 12. Fixed Effects Estimates Dependent Variable – ln Weekly Wage.

	1998		2004	
	Coef.	St. error	Coef.	St. error
KPROSAL×Instrumented Tenure	−0.003**	0.001	−0.004**	0.002
KPROSAL×Instrumented Tenure-sq/100	0.019**	0.009	0.025**	0.011
Instrumented Tenure	0.026***	0.003	0.025***	0.005
Instrumented Tenure-sq/100	−0.137***	0.025	−0.101***	0.031
Age	0.061***	0.002	0.053***	0.002
Age-sq/100	−0.069***	0.003	−0.061***	0.003
Low CSE	0.064***	0.012	0.076***	0.014
High CSE	0.098***	0.010	0.112***	0.013
A levels	0.167***	0.012	0.183***	0.015
Degree	0.320***	0.013	0.306***	0.015
Postgraduate	0.435***	0.018	0.397***	0.020
Vocational	0.021***	0.007	0.074***	0.008
Manager	0.913***	0.016	0.857***	0.018
Professional	0.727***	0.016	0.879***	0.019
Technical	0.456***	0.016	0.556***	0.018
Clerical	0.299***	0.014	0.391***	0.017
Craft	0.366***	0.017	0.431***	0.021
Services	0.179***	0.017	0.324***	0.020
Sales	0.131***	0.019	0.255***	0.024
Operative	0.235***	0.017	0.313***	0.020
Fixed term contract	−0.168***	0.019	−0.100**	0.021
Temporary	−0.248***	0.018	−0.303***	0.019
Female	−0.273***	0.008	−0.265***	0.009
Minority	−0.117***	0.021	−0.058***	0.019
Trade union member	0.173***	0.009	0.151***	0.010
Married/cohabiting	0.035***	0.008	0.027***	0.008
Dependent child	−0.066***	0.007	0.027***	0.008
Disability	−0.042***	0.014	−0.097***	0.017
Training less than 1 day	0.021*	0.012	0.001	0.014
Training 1 to less than 2 days	0.119***	0.010	0.095***	0.011
Training 2 to less than 5 days	0.150***	0.009	0.156***	0.011
Training 5 to less than 10 days	0.184***	0.012	0.207***	0.014
Training 10 days or more	0.125***	0.013	0.150***	0.015
Constant	3.627***	0.045	3.912***	0.051
Observations	21,301		16,217	
R-squared within	0.460		0429	
R-squared between	0.664		0.541	
R-squared overall	0.532		0.476	
Clusters	1,451		1,381	
Std. dev. of firm specific effect	0.404		0.404	

Table 12. *(Continued)*

	1998		2004	
	Coef.	St. error	Coef.	St. error
Std. dev. of idiosyncratic error term	0.452		0.447	
Intra-class correlation	0.444		0.449	
Corr(*u*, *Xb*)	0.266		0.164	

Notes:
1. Estimates allow for clustering of employees within firms.
2. The fixed effects specification estimates only individual characteristics as there is variation of individual characteristics within a firm. The firm specific variables are not identified as there is no variation of firm characteristics. Our main interactions (monitoring with tenure and tenure squared/100) survive in the fixed effects specification as there is variation in tenure within a firm.
3. Last row of the Table shows the correlation between unobserved firm specific effects and the other controls included in the specification.
4. Levels of significance: ***1%, **5%,*10%.

Fixed Effects Estimates

The results so far exploit variation in monitoring across firms. Since firms are observed only once we are not able to correct for possible fixed effects across firms. Thus, firm specific coefficients will not be identified as there is no variation in firms' characteristics. However, it is possible to use a fixed effects model as the interaction between monitoring and tenure will survive in the estimation because employees' characteristics (i.e., tenure) vary within a firm. In the fixed effects model the estimates (employee characteristics) are identified from within firm variation only and are measured as deviations from their sample mean. In other words, the fixed effects model identifies the effects off people with different tenure within firms. In this case, we remove the potential bias arising from heterogeneity within firms. The results from this exercise are reported in Table 12. The coefficients of the two main interaction terms remain statistically significant but their magnitudes are reduced compared to the IV estimates suggesting that there is in fact a causal relationship. The estimates suggest that firms that tend to pay more monitor the least the longer employees have been in the firm.[21] This result is in line with a view of agency problems within the firm may be a motivating factor behind deferred pay compensating schemes.

The alternative is to estimate a random effects model. The random effects approach goes beyond simply adjusting the standard errors for workplace clustering as it takes into account between firm heterogeneity. In

Table 13. Random Effects Estimates Dependent Variable – ln Weekly Wage.

	1998		2004	
	Coef.	St. error	Coef.	St. error
KPROSAL	0.004	0.007	0.008	0.008
KPROSAL×Instrumented Tenure	−0.004**	0.001	−0.004***	0.002
KPROSAL×Instrumented Tenure-sq/100	0.020**	0.008	0.024**	0.010
Instrumented Tenure	0.025***	0.003	0.024***	0.005
Instrumented Tenure-sq/100	−0.137***	0.024	−0.101***	0.030
Age	0.061***	0.002	0.054***	0.002
Age-sq/100	−0.069***	0.002	−0.062***	0.003
Low CSE	0.062***	0.012	0.081***	0.013
High CSE	0.101***	0.010	0.115***	0.013
A levels	0.168***	0.012	0.186***	0.015
Degree	0.325***	0.013	0.312***	0.015
Postgraduate	0.436***	0.017	0.401***	0.019
Vocational	0.020***	0.007	0.075***	0.008
Manager	0.912***	0.015	0.840***	0.017
Professional	0.722***	0.015	0.856***	0.019
Technical	0.458***	0.016	0.545***	0.017
Clerical	0.298***	0.014	0.380***	0.016
Craft	0.356***	0.016	0.404***	0.020
Services	0.188***	0.016	0.306***	0.019
Sales	0.166***	0.018	0.242***	0.023
Operative	0.224***	0.016	0.298***	0.019
Fixed term contract	−0.166***	0.019	−0.094***	0.021
Temporary	−0.249***	0.018	−0.303***	0.018
Female	−0.275***	0.008	−0.268***	0.009
Minority	−0.119***	0.020	−0.062***	0.019
Trade union member	0.171***	0.008	0.152***	0.099
Married/cohabiting	0.041***	0.007	0.028***	0.008
Dependent child	−0.068***	0.007	−0.082***	0.008
Disability	−0.048***	0.014	−0.106***	0.017
Training less than 1 day	0.020*	0.012	−0.001	0.013
Training 1 to less than 2 days	0.121***	0.010	0.094***	0.011
Training 2 to less than 5 days	0.125***	0.009	0.156***	0.010
Training 5 to less than 10 days	0.186***	0.012	0.208***	0.013
Training 10 days or more	0.128***	0.012	0.140***	0.014
ln number of employees	0.034***	0.005	0.028***	0.004
Share of managers	0.110*	0.067	0.172**	0.070
Share of professional	0.096**	0.044	0.0003	0.051
Share of technical	−0.049	0.047	0.007	0.047
Share of clerical	0.109**	0.044	0.041	0.049
Share of craft	−0.005	0.044	−0.103*	0.056
Share of services	0.097**	0.040	−0.085*	0.049

Table 13. (*Continued*)

	1998		2004	
	Coef.	St. error	Coef.	St. error
Share of operatives	0.013	0.039	−0.062	0.048
Share of sales	0.047	0.043	−0.098**	0.046
Share of women	−0.102***	0.038	−0.044	0.041
Share of ethnic minorities	−0.067	0.070	−0.022	0.056
Share of part-time	−0.904***	0.037	−0.852***	0.038
Share of union coverage	−0.018	0.022	−0.076***	0.026
Share of employees <20 years old	−0.218***	0.068	−0.057	0.071
Share of employees >50 years old	−0.270***	0.055	−0.080*	0.046
ln age firm	−0.002	0.002	0.0001	0.002
Unemployment-vacancy rate by TWA	−0.021***	0.004	−0.003	0.004
Constant	3.714***	0.072	3.956***	0.075
Observations	21,301		16,217	
Rho	0.127		0.145	
R-squared within	0.460		0.429	
R-squared between	0.664		0.805	
R-squared overall	0.532		0.622	
Industry dummies	Yes		Yes	
Region dummies	Yes		Yes	
Clusters	1,451		1,381	

Note: Estimates allow for clustering of employees within firms. Levels of significance: ***1%, **5%, *10%.

this case, the firm specific variables are identified as there is variation across firms. For instance, it could be the case that those firms which supervise more intensely have older employees on average and pay everyone less, producing a spurious correlation between monitoring, tenure and wages. However, the implicit assumption in the random effects model is that the firm specific effects are exogenous and completely orthogonal to the other control variables. If there is correlation between the means of the control variables and the firm specific effects, the random effects model will not produce efficient GLS-estimators and the fixed effects model is preferable (Mundlak, 1978). As shown in Table 12 (fixed effects tables, last row) there is significant correlation between the control variables and firm specific effects (Corr(u, Xb)). So, the fixed effects approach is preferable. For reasons of completeness, we report the random effects estimates in Table 13. It is unfortunate that the fixed and random effect estimates are not directly comparable as they are not estimated on the same control variables. However, it is comforting that the main result remains robust in the random effects specification.

FINAL COMMENTS

Efficiency wage theory predicts that firms can raise worker effort by paying supra-competitive, that is, efficiency wages and/or by devoting resources to monitoring. As argued by Lazear (1979, 1981), however, another option available to the firm is to strategically defer compensation, tilting the remuneration package over time such that the prospect of higher future earnings acts as a deterrent to current period shirking. Deferring compensation in this way drives a wedge between a worker's expected lifetime remuneration in the current job and that in any alternative job. As more pay is deferred, the cost of losing the current job increases and workers are induced to raise effort. This increase in equilibrium effort encourages workers to participate in deferred compensation schemes by allowing the overall employment package to be more generous than it might otherwise be. Lazear's position stands in stark contrast to the arguments that upward sloping earning profiles are used to attract workers with longer expected tenure (Salop & Salop, 1976), that workers may prefer such profiles as a forced saving mechanism (Neumark, 1995), or that it is the returns to investments in training that drive deferred compensation (Levine, 1993).

Our aim in this chapter has not been to distinguish empirically between the various competing explanations for upward sloping tenure-earnings profiles (see Flabbi & Ichino, 2001, for such an exercise). We have instead focused on the potential trade-off between the level of monitoring and the extent of deferred compensation, a trade-off that has been hitherto unexplored in the literature. Our theoretical analysis demonstrates this trade-off in a simple, two-period model of efficiency wages in which firms set wages and monitoring jointly as part of their profit-maximizing strategy. Our empirical analysis, which is based on two cross-section surveys of matched employer-employee British data, finds compelling evidence of an inverse relationship between the level of monitoring and the slope of the wage-tenure profile. The trade-off is robust to a number of refinements to our basic estimation strategy. In particular, it does not appear to depend on the presence or otherwise of either firm specific human capital or the payment of piece rates. Fixed effect estimates suggest a causal effect. Finally, although we find some evidence that supervision may also work through productivity increases by helping employees to increase their work effort through teamwork, the main channel comes through the disciplinary supervisor role.

Thus, our results may be interpreted as further evidence in favor of efficiency wage theory. They also support the (Cappelli & Chauvin, 1991; Lazear, 1979; Medoff & Abraham, 1980) view that both agency and human capital considerations are important conduits through which tenure impacts upon wages. Wages increase over time not only because workers become more productive, but because firms maximize their profits by optimally deferring pay. Whether or not, firms in other countries replicate this strategy is an issue for future research.

NOTES

1. Papers that have empirically examined this relationship, albeit not always directly, include Eaton and Rosen (1983), Hutchens (1987), Krueger (1991), Flabbi and Ichino (2001), Goerke (2001), Moretti and Perloff (2002), Bayo-Moriones, Galdon-Sanchez, and Güell (2010), Zwick (2011, 2012), Cataldi, Kampelmann, and Rycx (2011), and Freedman and Kosova (2012).

2. Recent theoretical work has questioned the notion that monitoring and pay are *generally* substitutable. Allgullin and Ellingsen (2002) argue that while lower monitoring costs induce a cut in the efficient wage, as firms substitute toward monitoring, this is only the case for a given level of effort. In such circumstances, firms will typically find it optimal to demand a higher level of effort from their workforce, and the impact of this on the level of pay is ambiguous.

3. Medoff and Abraham (1980, 1981) highlight a related conundrum in their analysis of data on pay and supervisor performance ratings. They found that although relative performance ratings within a particular job grade did not increase with experience in the job grade, relative pay did. Again, such a finding is incompatible with the human capital position that earnings increase with seniority because productivity increases with seniority.

4. Firms may also prefer steeper rather than flatter profiles on account of potential sorting effects. Delayed payment schemes will tend to attract employees who are relatively more committed to a long-term employment relationship which will, in turn, render training investments less risky for firms (Freedman & Kosova, 2012).

5. The profile may also affect quitting behavior. More experienced "generally" trained workers will have more flexibility in the labor market than "specifically" trained workers. But both types may have more options than senior workers whose rents primarily reflect agency considerations.

6. For a non-linear treatment of the effort level see Nantz and Sparks (1990).

7. Note the assumption that detected shirkers are fired and forced into *permanent* unemployment. This is an expository device. Allowing a more realistic scenario

whereby detected shirkers receive unemployment benefits in period one and then have a chance of obtaining a single period employment contract in period two would not change our qualitative results.

8. The relationship between monitoring and the experience-earnings profile under continuous effort is, to our knowledge, still to be investigated. A trade-off between the *level* of monitoring and the slope of the earnings profile has been found in more complex dichotomous effort models – see, for example, Bai (1997). Firms do not, however, restrict themselves to simple "detect and fire" technologies but often employ more sophisticated incentive schemes such as performance related pay, career tournaments, profit sharing and employee share-ownership.

9. Changes in the nature of interest in employment relations led to substantial redesign of the 2004 wave. A major modification was the incorporation of small workplaces, that is, those employing between 5 and 9 employees. There were also a number of changes to the format of the various survey questions (see Kersley et al., 2006).

10. We use the terms workplaces, establishments, and firms interchangeably.

11. As in Zwick (2011) we keep individuals in the age group 18–60 in order to avoid selectivity issues at the edges of the age distribution.

12. Such a proxy is not uncontentious. The share of supervisors might be high because monitoring is difficult (Allgullin & Ellingsen, 2002) while supervisors may spend only a fraction of their work-time monitoring (Rebitzer, 1995). Arai (1994a), Drago and Perlman (1989), Goldin (1986), Groshen and Krueger (1990), and Heywood, Jirjahn, and Wei (2008) support the use of supervision as a proxy for monitoring, although they acknowledge that supervision may occur for nonmonitoring purposes – for example, to coordinate production. Indeed, supervisors are likely to perform different functions at different firms, and firms may utilize alternative forms of technology to monitor employee performance, for example, computers.

13. There is clearly an issue as to managers reporting that either "all" or "none" of their nonmanagerial employees were involved in supervision. The former firms might be worker-owned cooperatives of some form while the latter could be employing other means of monitoring worker performance. In any case, there is significant cross firm variation in the responses provided to this question.

14. The literature on returns to tenure is still unsettled. For the United States, Abraham and Farber (1987) and Altonji and Shakotko (1987) find only modest returns to tenure. Topel (1991) using the same data but different methodology finds substantial returns to tenure. Altonji and Williams (1997) find that estimates lie in between those reported by Altonji and Shakotko (1987) and Topel (1991). Altonji and Williams (2005) find returns to tenure of about 10% in 10 years.

15. Given that wages and monitoring in WERS are coded in bands, we also experimented with the three-stage IV strategy developed by Kelejian (1971) and outlined in Wooldridge (2010, pp. 89–198) and Angrist and Pischke (2009, pp. 190–192) to ascertain the sensitivity of our results with respect to functional form. Since the consistency of the second stage estimates does not hinge on getting the functional form of the first-stage correct we prefer the standard 2SLS set-up over the three-stage approach. Our results remained robust to this experimentation. In the appendix, we outline how this alternative IV approach can be estimated, as well as the results from this approach (Tables A1–A3). For robustness, we also report results from two alternative interval regression models. Table A4 presents

the results from an interval regression obtained from the Kelejian three-step approach. Table A5 presents the results from a limited information maximum likelihood interval regression developed by Bettin and Lucchetti (2012).

16. In the WERS data there is no explicit information if an employee has a part-time contract. This is the reason why we do not include a part-time control in the baseline specification. To proxy for part-time employment at the individual level we use working hours per week and assume an individual to work part-time if he works less or equal to 30 hours per week. This part-time dummy attains a negative and highly statistically significant coefficient and reduces the main interaction coefficient (*BINVMANG*Tenure*) by 56 % in the 1998 sample and 33% in the 2004 sample. However, both the main interaction coefficients remain statistically significant in both samples.

17. According to MacLeod and Parent (1999) and Parent (2002), piece rates and easy monitoring tend to occur in jobs in which skills are easily learned, the motions are repetitive and in which the scope for learning new things and teamwork are minimal, and there is thus no incentive to defer.

18. The specific question (COTHJOB) asked in the management questionnaire is: "About how long does it normally take before new employees are able to do their job as well as more experienced employees already working here?" This training question is identical to that offered by the *Panel Study of Income Dynamics* (PSID) in the United States and is generally considered to be one of the most reliable measures of firm-specific training (see Barron, Berger, & Black, 1997).

19. The unconditional correlation between the raw monitoring variable coming from the management questionnaire and the constructed measure of supervision share coming from the employee questionnaire is 0.23.

20. We would like to thank an anonymous referee and the editor for suggesting this alternative interpretation of the results.

21. We remind the reader that we control for occupation fixed effects throughout.

ACKNOWLEDGEMENTS

We thank the sponsors of the Workplace Employment Relations Survey (WERS) – Department for Business Enterprise and Regulatory Reform, ACAS, ESRC, and PSI – and the UK Data Archive for access to the WERS data. Helpful comments were received from seminar participants at the Universities of Bath, Lancaster, and Sheffield and from participants at the Western Economic Association Annual Conference, the Royal Economic Society Annual Conference, the European Association of Labor Economists Annual Conference and the Work Pensions and Labor Economics Study Group. The normal disclaimer applies. We would like to thank the editors of this book, Solomon Polachek and Konstantinos Tatsiramos, and an anonymous referee for comments that substantially improved this chapter.

REFERENCES

Abraham, K. G., & Farber, H. S. (1987). Job duration, seniority, and earnings. *American Economic Review*, *77*, 278–297.

Adams, S. J., & Heywood, J. S. (2011). Does deferred compensation increase worker effort? *Manchester School*, *79*, 381–404.

Allgullin, M., & Ellingsen, T. (2002). Monitoring and pay. *Journal of Labor Economics*, *20*, 201–216.

Altonji, J. G., & Shakotko, R. A. (1987). Do wages rise with job seniority? *Review of Economic Studies*, *54*, 437–459.

Altonji, J. G., & Williams, N. (1997). The effects of labor market experience, job seniority, and job mobility on wage growth. In S. W. Polachek (Ed.), *Research in labor economics, 17* (pp. 233–276). London: JAI Press.

Altonji, J. G., & Williams, N. (2005). Do wages rise with seniority? A reassessment. *Industrial and Labor Relations Review*, *58*, 370–397.

Angrist, J. D., & Pischke, J.-S. (2009). *Mostly harmless econometrics: An empiricist's companion.* Princeton, NJ: Princeton Univertiy Press.

Arai, M. (1994a). An empirical analysis of wage dispersion and efficiency wages. *Scandinavian Journal of Economics*, *96*, 31–50.

Arai, M. (1994b). Compensating wage differentials versus efficiency wages: An empirical study of job autonomy and wages. *Industrial Relations*, *33*, 249–262.

Bai, C. (1997). Earnings profiles and monitoring under asymmetric information. *Economics Letters*, *57*, 219–225.

Barron, J. M., Berger, M. C., & Black, D. A. (1997). How well do we measure training? *Journal of Labor Economics*, *15*, 507–528.

Barth, E. (1997). Firm-specific seniority and wages. *Journal of Labor Economics*, *15*, 495–506.

Bayo-Moriones, A., Galdon-Sanchez, J. E., & Güell, M. (2010). Is seniority-based pay used as a motivational device? Evidence from plant level data. In S. W. Polachek & K. Tatsiramos (Eds.), *Research in labor economics, 30* (pp. 155–187). Bradford, UK: Emerald Group Publishing Limited.

Becker, G. S. (1962). Investments in human capital: A theoretical analysis. *Journal of Political Economy*, *70*, 9–49.

Ben-Porath, Y. (1967). The production of human capital and the life cycle of earnings. *Journal of Political Economy*, *75*, 352–365.

Bettin, G., & Lucchetti, R. (2012). Interval regression models with endogenous explanatory variables. *Empirical Economics*, *43*, 475–498.

Brown, C. (1992). Wage levels and methods of pay. *Rand Journal of Economics*, *23*, 366–375.

Brown, S., & Sessions, J. G. (2006). Some evidence on the relationship between performance related pay and the shape of the experience-earnings profile. *Southern Economic Journal*, *72*, 660–676.

Brunello, G. (1995). The relationship between supervision and pay: Evidence from the British new earnings survey. *Oxford Bulletin of Economics and Statistics*, *57*, 309–322.

Bulow, J. I., & Summers, L. H. (1986). A theory of dual labor markets with application to industrial policy, discrimination, and keynesian unemployment. *Journal of Labor Economics*, *4*, 376–414.

Cappelli, P., & Chauvin, K. (1991). An interplant test of the efficiency wage hypothesis. *Quarterly Journal of Economics*, *106*(3), 769–787.

Carmichael, L. (1990). Efficiency wage models of unemployment: One view. *Economic Inquiry, 282*, 269–295.

Cataldi, A., Kampelmann, S., & Rycx, F. (2011). Productivity-wage gaps among age groups: Does the ICT environment matter? *De Economist, 159*(2), 193–221.

Drago, R., & Perlman, R. (1989). Supervision and high wages as competing incentives: A basis for labor market segmentation theory. In R. Drago & R. Perlman (Eds.), *Microeconomic issues in labor economics*. London: Harvester Wheatsheaf.

Dustmann, C., & Pereira, S. (2008). Wage growth and job mobility in the United Kingdom and germany. *Industrial and Labor Relations Review, 61*, 374–393.

Eaton, J., & Rosen, H. (1983). Agency, delayed compensation and the structure of executive remuneration. *Journal of Finance, 385*, 1489–1505.

Ewing, B., & Payne, J. (1999). The trade-off between supervision and wages: Evidence of efficiency wages from the NLSY. *Southern Economic Journal, 66*, 424–432.

Fitzroy, F., & Kraft, K. (1986). Cooperation, productivity and profit sharing. *Quarterly Journal of Economics, 102*, 23–35.

Flabbi, L., & Ichino, A. (2001). Productivity, seniority and wages. *Labour Economics, 8*, 359–387.

Frank, R. H., & Hutchens, R. M. (1993). Wages, seniority and the demand for rising consumption profiles. *Journal of Economic Behaviour and Organisation, 21*, 251–276.

Freedman, M., & Kosova, R. (2012). Agency and compensation: Evidence from the hotel industry. *Journal of Law, Economics, and Organization, 31*, 214–236.

Freeman, S. (1977). Wage trends as performance displays productive potential: A model and application to academic early retirement. *Bell Journal of Economics, 8*, 419–443.

Fuchs, V. (1981). Self-employment and labor market participation of older males. *Journal of Human Resources, 18*, 339–357.

Goerke, L. (2001). On the relationship between wages and monitoring in shirking models. *Metroeconomica, 52*, 376–390.

Goldin, C. (1986). Monitoring costs and occupational segregation by sex: A historical analysis. *Journal of Labor Economics, 4*, 1–27.

Gordon, D. M. (1990). Who bosses whom? The intensity of supervision and the discipline of labor. *American Economic Review Papers and Proceedings, 80*, 28–32.

Gordon, D. M. (1994). Bosses of different stripes: A cross-national perspective on monitoring and supervision. *American Economic Review, 84*, 375–379.

Groshen, E., & Krueger, A. (1990). The structure of supervision and pay in hospitals. *Industrial and Labor Relations Review, 43*, 134S–146S.

Harris, M., & Holmström, B. (1982). A theory of wage dynamics. *Review of Economic Studies, 49*, 315–333.

Heywood, J. S., Jirjahn, U., & Wei, X. (2008). Teamwork, monitoring and absence. *Journal of Economic Behavior and Organization, 68*, 676–690.

Holmström, B. (1979). Moral hazard and observability. *Bell Journal of Economics, 9*, 74–91.

Hutchens, R. M. (1987). A test of lazear's theory of delayed payment contracts. *Journal of Labor Economics, 54*, 153–170.

Hutchens, R. M. (1989). Seniority, wages and productivity: A turbulent decade. *Journal of Economic Perspectives, 34*, 49–64.

Jacobson, L., & LaLonde, R. J. (1993). Earnings losses of displaced workers. *American Economic Review, 83*, 685–709.

Kelejian, H. H. (1971). Two stage least squares and econometric systems linear in parameters but nonlinear in endogenous variables. *Journal of the American Statistical Association, 96*, 373–374.

Kersley, B., Alpin, C., Forth, J., Bryson, A., Bewley, H., Dix, G., & Oxenbridge, S. (2006). *Inside the workplace: Findings from the 2004 workplace employment relations survey*. New York, NY: Taylor & Francis Group.

Konings, J., & Walsh, P. P. (1994). Evidence of efficiency wage payments in UK firm level panel data. *Economic Journal, 104*, 542–555.

Krueger, A. (1991). Ownership, agency and wages: An examination of franchising in the fast food industry. *Quarterly Journal of Economics, 106*, 75–102.

Kruse, D. (1992). Supervision, working conditions and the employer size effect. *Industrial Relations, 31*, 229–249.

Lazear, E. P. (1979). Why is there mandatory retirement? *Journal of Political Economy, 87*, 1261–1284.

Lazear, E. P. (1981). Agency, earnings profiles, productivity and hours restrictions. *American Economic Review, 71*, 606–620.

Lazear, E. P. (2000). The future of personnel economics. *Economic Journal, 110*, F611–F639.

Lazear, E. P., & Moore, R. L. (1984). Incentives, productivity, and labor contracts. *Quarterly Journal of Economics, 99*, 275–296.

Lazear, E. P., & Rosen, S. (1981). Rank order tournaments as optimal salary schemes. *Journal of Political Economy, 97*, 561–580.

Lemieux, T., Macleod, W. B., & Parent, D. (2012). Contract form, wage flexibility, and employment. *American Economics Review: Papers and Proceedings, 102*, 526–531.

Leonard, J. (1987). Carrots and sticks: Pay, supervision and turnover. *Journal of Labor Economics, 5*, S136–S152.

Levine, D. I. (1993). Worth waiting for? Delayed compensation, training and turnover in the United States and Japan. *Journal of Labor Economics, 11*, 724–752.

Loewenstein, G., & Sicherman, N. (1991). Do workers prefer increasing wage profiles? *Journal of Labor Economics, 9*, 67–84.

MacLeod, B., & Parent, D. (1999). Job characteristics and the form of compensation. In S. Polachek (Ed.), *Research in labor economics* (Vol. 18, pp. 177–242). Stamford, CT: JAI Press.

Manning, A. (2000). Movin' on up: Interpreting the earnings-experience profile. *Bulletin of Economic Research, 52*, 261–295.

Machin, S., & Manning, A. (1992). Testing dynamic models of worker effort. *Journal of Labor Economics, 10*, 288–305.

Medoff, J., & Abraham, K. (1980). Experience, performance and earnings. *Quarterly Journal of Economics, 95*, 703–736.

Medoff, J., & Abraham, K. (1981). Are those paid more really more productive? The case of experience. *Journal of Human Resources, 16*, 186–216.

Mincer, J. (1958). Investment in human capital and personal income distribution. *Journal of Political Economy, 66*, 281–302.

Moretti, E., & Perloff, J. (2002). Efficiency wages, deferred payments, and direct incentives in agriculture. *American Journal of Agricultural Economics, 842*, 1144–1155.

Mundlak, Y. (1978). On the pooling of time series ad cross section data. *Econometrica, 46*, 69–85.

Nantz, K., & Sparks, R. (1990). The labor-managed firm under imperfect monitoring: Employment and work effort responses. *Journal of Comparative Economics*, *14*, 33–50.

Neal, D. (1993). Supervision and wages across industries. *Review of Economics and Statistics*, *75*, 409–417.

Neumark, D. (1995). Are rising earnings profiles a forced-saving investment? *Economic Journal*, *105*, 95–106.

Parent, D. (2002). Matching, human capital and the covariance structure of earnings. *Labour Economics*, *9*, 375–404.

Polachek, S. W., & Siebert, W. S. (1993). *The economics of earnings*. Cambridge University Press.

Raff, D. M. G., & Summers, L. H. (1987). Did henry ford pay efficiency wages. *Journal of Labor Economics*, *5*, S57–S86.

Rebitzer, J. B. (1995). Is there a trade-off between supervision and wages? An empirical test of efficiency wage theory. *Journal of Economic Behaviour and Organization*, *28*, 107–129.

Ruhm, C. J. (1991). Are workers permanently scarred by job displacements. *American Economic Review*, *81*, 319–324.

Salop, J., & Salop, S. (1976). Self-selection and turnover in the labor market. *Quarterly Journal of Economics*, *90*, 619–627.

Shapiro, C., & Stiglitz, J. E. (1984). Equilibrium unemployment as a worker discipline device. *American Economic Review*, *74*, 433–444.

Strobl, E., & Walsh, F. (2007). Estimating the shirking model with variable effort. *Labour Economics*, *14*, 623–637.

Topel, R. (1991). Specific capital, mobility, and wages: Wages rise with job seniority. *Journal of Political Economy*, *99*, 145–176.

Walsh, F. (1999). A multi-sector model of efficiency wages. *Journal of Labor Economics*, *17*, 351–376.

Wolpin, K. (1977). Education and screening. *American Economic Review*, *67*, 949–958.

Wooldridge, J. M. (2010). *Econometric analysis of cross section and panel data*. Cambridge, MA: MIT Press.

Zwick, T. (2011). Seniority wages and establishment characteristics. *Labour Economics*, *18*, 853–861.

Zwick, T. (2012). Consequences of seniority wages on the employment structure. *Industrial and Labor Relations Review*, *65*, 108–125.

APPENDIX A

This appendix outlines the alternative IV strategy we refer to in footnote 15.

Let W be the outcome variable (ln weekly wages), M be (BINVMANG) the raw monitoring (endogenous variable), and Θ the exogenous variable (KPROSAL) that we are using to predict M. The procedure can be implemented manually in three steps:

Step 1: Estimate a nonlinear model (ordered probit) using Θ to predict M, get predicted value M^{**} (all the other controls variables $\boldsymbol{X}$ and $\mathbf{Z}$ as in Eq. (8) of the main, should be in the instrument list, see Wooldridge, 2010, p. 89). The results from this step are reported in Table A1.

Step 2: Regress M on M^{**}, get predicted value M^{***} (OLS regression). The results from this step are reported in Table A2.

Step 3: Regress W on M^{***} (OLS regression, including all the other controls). The results from this step are reported in Table A3. For completeness, we also estimate an interval regression (Table A4).

The difference of this approach with respect to the 2SLS set-up is that here we are using the nonlinear fitted value M as the instrument. Steps 2 and 3 still have a linear first stage. So this approach retains the properties of a standard IV estimator. The main advantage is that M^{**} usually predicts M more precisely than Θ does.

Further, the advantage of this approach over a two stage approach (i.e., nonlinear model using Θ to predict M^{**}, get predicted value M^{**}, and then regress W on M^{**}) is not a consistent estimator because the fitted values from the nonlinear first stage are not conditional means. They are probabilities. Angrist and Pischke, 2009 (pp. 190–192) refer to this approach as "Forbidden Regressions."

Table A1. Step 1. Ordered Probit Model Dependent Variable: Endogenous Monitoring (BINVMANG).

	1998		2004	
	Coef.	St. error	Coef.	St. error
KPROSAL	0.024***	0.008	0.049***	0.010
Tenure	0.003	0.005	0.008	0.006
Tenure-sq/100	−0.009	0.022	−0.035	0.027
Age	−0.007	0.005	−0.007	0.006
Age-sq/100	0.009	0.006	0.006	0.007
Low CSE	0.011	0.029	−0.031	0.031
High CSE	0.025	0.024	−0.021	0.030
A levels	0.011	0.028	−0.066*	0.034
Degree	0.029	0.030	−0.041	0.034
Postgraduate	0.021	0.053	0.014	0.045
Vocational	−0.054***	0.016	−0.018	0.018
Manager	0.008	0.035	0.057	0.040
Professional	0.033	0.036	−0.021	0.043
Technical	0.095***	0.036	−0.012	0.038
Clerical	0.044	0.032	0.045	0.037
Craft	−0.048	0.037	0.009	0.045
Services	0.059	0.037	−0.048	0.043
Sales	−0.062	0.042	0.021	0.051
Operative	−0.026	0.037	0.010	0.044
Fixed term	0.012	0.043	0.103**	0.048
Temporary	0.063	0.040	0.042	0.042
Female	−0.008	0.019	0.023	0.021
Minority	−0.082*	0.047	−0.008	0.044
Trade union member	−0.034*	0.019	−0.004	0.022
Married/cohabiting	0.014	0.018	0.039**	0.020
Dependent child	0.021	0.017	−0.011	0.020
Disability	0.020	0.032	0.004	0.040
Training less than 1 day	−0.048	0.028	−0.044	0.031
Training 1 to less than 2 days	0.018	0.023	0.071***	0.026
Training 2 to less than 5 days	0.042	0.021	0.056**	0.024
Training 5 to less than 10 days	−0.031	0.028	0.077**	0.031
Training 10 days or more	0.008	0.028	0.010	0.033
ln number of employees	0.124***	0.006	0.106***	0.006
Share of managers	0.128	0.090	0.409***	0.099
Share of professional	0.330***	0.062	0.526***	0.072
Share of technical	0.507***	0.065	0.520***	0.067
Share of clerical	0.372***	0.061	0.392***	0.069
Share of craft	0.737***	0.063	0.338***	0.078
Share of services	0.253***	0.056	0.714***	0.071
Share of operatives	0.306***	0.055	0.164**	0.068
Share of sales	0.589***	0.062	−0.013	0.068

Table A1. *(Continued)*

	1998		2004	
	Coef.	St. error	Coef.	St. error
Share of women	−0.106	0.053	−0.059	0.060
Share of ethnic minorities	0.080	0.099	0.078	0.083
Share of part-time	−0.009	0.052	−0.449***	0.056
Share of union coverage	−0.068	0.032	−0.020	0.036
Share of employees <20 years old	0.322***	0.097	0.684***	0.102
Share of employees >50 years old	−0.817***	0.075	0.051	0.066
ln age firm	0.001	0.003	0.029***	0.003
Unemployment-vacancy rate by TWA	0.019***	0.006	−0.006	0.005
Cutoff 1	−0.249		−0.453	
Cutoff 2	1.393		1.056	
Cutoff 3	2.270		2.120	
Cutoff 4	2.643		2.682	
Cutoff 5	2.952		3.121	
Cutoff 6	3.276		3.537	
Observations	21,301		16,217	
Log-Likelihood	−29134.02		−21201.68	
Industry FE	Yes		Yes	
Region FE	Yes		Yes	
Clusters	1,451		1,381	

Notes: The dependent variable is the raw monitoring variable BINVMANG. Estimates are weighted and allow for clustering of employees within firms. Levels of significance: ***1%, **5%,*10%.

Table A2. Step 2 – Ordinary Least Squares Dependent Variable: Endogenous Monitoring (BINVMANG).

	1998		2004	
	Coef.	St. error	Coef.	St. error
M**	0.951***	0.027	0.962***	0.021
Constant	0.512***	0.034	0.783***	0.021
Observations	21,301		16,217	
R-squared	0.052		0.089	
Clusters	1,451		1,381	

Notes: The dependent variable is the raw monitoring variable BINVMANG. Estimates are weighted and allow for clustering of employees within firms. Standard errors are bootstrapped using 500 replications. Levels of significance: ***1%.

Table A3. Step 3. OLS. Dependent Variable: ln Weekly Wage.

	1998		2004	
	Coef.	St. error	Coef.	St. error
KPROSAL×Instrumented Tenure	−0.012**	0.005	−0.017**	0.006
KPROSAL×Instrumented Tenure-sq/100	0.080**	0.035	0.112***	0.037
Instrumented Tenure	0.038***	0.008	0.040***	0.011
Instrumented Tenure-sq/100	−0.224***	0.061	−0.218***	0.060
M***	−0.039	0.178	0.105	0.113
Age	0.063***	0.003	0.055***	0.002
Age-sq/100	−0.071***	0.003	−0.063***	0.003
Low CSE	0.063***	0.013	0.104***	0.014
High CSE	0.110***	0.011	0.139***	0.013
A levels	0.173***	0.012	0.214***	0.016
Degree	0.340***	0.015	0.339***	0.015
Postgraduate	0.443***	0.019	0.420***	0.019
Vocational	0.016	0.012	0.079***	0.008
Manager	0.911***	0.016	0.794***	0.018
Professional	0.714***	0.019	0.809***	0.018
Technical	0.463***	0.023	0.516***	0.017
Clerical	0.295***	0.016	0.341***	0.016
Craft	0.335***	0.017	0.349***	0.019
Services	0.205***	0.023	0.257***	0.019
Sales	0.137***	0.024	0.213***	0.021
Operative	0.206***	0.016	0.253***	0.018
Fixed term	−0.162***	0.023	−0.087***	0.023
Temporary	−0.241***	0.025	−0.310***	0.018
Female	−0.279***	0.008	−0.271***	0.009
Minority	−0.125***	0.025	−0.076***	0.019
Trade union member	0.164***	0.011	0.142***	0.010
Married/cohabiting	0.050***	0.008	0.026***	0.009
Dependent child	−0.069***	0.007	−0.075***	0.009
Disability	−0.058***	0.014	−0.124***	0.017
Training less than 1 day	0.014	0.016	0.005	0.014
Training 1 to less than 2 days	0.122***	0.011	0.092***	0.013
Training 2 to less than 5 days	0.152***	0.011	0.145***	0.011
Training 5 to less than 10 days	0.184***	0.013	0.198***	0.015
Training 10 days or more	0.132***	0.012	0.128***	0.015
ln number of employees	0.036*	0.021	0.017*	0.010
Share of managers	0.105**	0.048	0.135**	0.059
Share of professional	0.083	0.064	−0.063	0.057
Share of technical	−0.052	0.092	−0.045	0.057
Share of clerical	0.099	0.072	0.024	0.044
Share of craft	0.006	0.129	−0.114	0.046
Share of services	0.097*	0.053	−0.120	0.074
Share of operatives	0.017	0.058	−0.056*	0.031

Table A3. (*Continued*)

	1998		2004	
	Coef.	St. error	Coef.	St. error
Share of sales	0.069	0.105	−0.093***	0.028
Share of women	−0.108***	0.030	−0.065**	0.027
Share of ethnic minorities	−0.064	0.044	−0.030	0.037
Share of part-time	−0.885***	0.026	−0.809***	0.049
Share of employees <20 years old	−0.320***	0.076	−0.150*	0.079
Share of employees >50 years old	−0.296**	0.143	−0.073**	0.030
ln age firm	−0.003***	0.001	−0.003	0.003
Unemployment-vacancy rate by TWA	−0.018***	0.004	−0.003	0.002
Constant	3.719***	0.118	3.907***	0.119
Observations	21,301		16,217	
R-squared	0.664		0.629	
Industry FE	Yes		Yes	
Region FE	Yes		Yes	
Clusters	1,451		1,381	

Notes: The dependent variable is the ln of weekly wages and the estimation method is an OLS. M*** is the predicted valued obtained from the second step OLS regression. Estimates are weighted and allow for clustering of employees within firms. Standard errors are bootstrapped using 500 replications. Levels of significance: ***1%, **5%,*10%.

Table A4. Step 3. Interval Regression. Dependent Variables: ln Lower and ln Upper Weekly Wages.

	1998		2004	
	Coef.	St. error	Coef.	St. error
KPROSAL×Instrumented Tenure	−0.011**	0.004	−0.010*	0.006
KPROSAL×Instrumented Tenure-sq/100	0.070**	0.028	0.076**	0.033
Instrumented Tenure	0.036***	0.006	0.029***	0.010
Instrumented Tenure-sq/100	−0.206***	0.048	−0.157***	0.053
M***	−0.006	0.151	0.098	0.101
Age	0.060***	0.002	0.051***	0.002
Age-sq/100	−0.070***	0.003	−0.059***	0.003
Low CSE	0.049***	0.010	0.092***	0.012
High CSE	0.096***	0.009	0.132***	0.012
A levels	0.143***	0.010	0.202***	0.014
Degree	0.288***	0.012	0.318***	0.013
Postgraduate	0.403***	0.016	0.382***	0.017
Vocational	0.022**	0.010	0.072***	0.007
Manager	0.815***	0.014	0.728***	0.016
Professional	0.654***	0.015	0.748***	0.017
Technical	0.431***	0.019	0.474***	0.015
Clerical	0.236***	0.012	0.293***	0.015
Craft	0.306***	0.014	0.319***	0.017
Services	0.192***	0.016	0.194***	0.017
Sales	0.123***	0.018	0.176***	0.019
Operative	0.184***	0.013	0.223***	0.016
Fixed term	−0.186***	0.017	−0.093***	0.021
Temporary	−0.233***	0.017	−0.279***	0.017
Female	−0.262***	0.007	−0.254***	0.008
Minority	−0.111***	0.022	−0.075***	0.017
Trade union member	0.158***	0.009	0.130***	0.009
Married/cohabiting	0.056***	0.007	0.024***	0.008
Dependent child	−0.074***	0.007	−0.075***	0.008
Disability	−0.078***	0.012	−0.113***	0.015
Training less than 1 day	0.020	0.012	0.001	0.012
Training 1 to less than 2 days	0.089***	0.009	0.081***	0.012
Training 2 to less than 5 days	0.129***	0.010	0.132***	0.010
Training 5 to less than 10 days	0.170***	0.011	0.179***	0.014
Training 10 days or more	0.114***	0.011	0.116***	0.013
ln number of employees	0.029	0.018	0.015	0.009
Share of managers	0.162***	0.045	0.146***	0.053
Share of professional	0.098*	0.055	−0.052	0.051
Share of technical	−0.048	0.077	−0.026	0.051
Share of clerical	0.098*	0.059	0.032	0.040
Share of craft	0.002	0.110	−0.103**	0.041
Share of services	0.039	0.043	−0.098	0.066

Table A4. *(Continued)*

	1998		2004	
	Coef.	St. error	Coef.	St. error
Share of operatives	−0.003	0.047	−0.050*	0.028
Share of sales	−0.010	0.085	−0.081***	0.025
Share of women	−0.110***	0.025	−0.063***	0.024
Share of ethnic minorities	0.057	0.039	−0.017	0.033
Share of part-time	−0.842***	0.019	−0.749***	0.044
Share of employees <20 years old	−0.262***	0.058	−0.164**	0.071
Share of employees >50 years old	−0.232*	0.122	−0.072***	0.027
ln age firm	−0.005***	0.001	−0.003	0.002
Unemployment-vacancy rate by TTWA	−0.016***	0.003	−0.003	0.002
Constant	3.783***	0.098	4.050***	0.107
Observations	23,301		16,217	
Log-likelihood	−44086.50		−35213.092	
Industry FE	Yes		Yes	
Region FE	Yes		Yes	
Clusters	1,451		1,381	

Notes: The estimation method is an interval regression model where the two dependent variables are the ln lower and ln upper weekly wage as reported in Table 2. M*** is the predicted valued obtained from the second step OLS regression. Estimates are weighted and allow for clustering of employees within firms. Standard errors are bootstrapped using 500 replications. Levels of significance: ***1%, **5%, *10%.

Table A5. Limited Information Maximum Likelihood (LIML) Interval Regression.

	1998		2004	
	Coef.	St. error	Coef.	St. error
BINVMANG	0.208*	0.112	0.211*	0.117
BINVMANG×Tenure	−0.049*	0.027	−0.041*	0.024
BINVMANG×Tenure-sq/100	0.206*	0.121	0.220**	0.110
Instrumented Tenure	0.066**	0.028	0.066**	0.032
Instrumented Tenure-sq/100	−0.417**	0.205	−0.389**	0.175
Sigma	0.408		0.412	
Wald test – Chi-square(3)	19.25		25.78	
Wald test *P* value	0.000557		0.000029	
Log-likelihood	−43882.3		−36352.7	
Observations	21,301		16,217	

Notes: Entries in the Table are estimated using the Bettin and Lucchetti (2012) IV interval regression (LIML) methodology with robust standard errors. We present only the second stage estimates. Thus, *BINVMANG* refers to instrumented monitoring, and *Tenure* refers to instrumented tenure. All control variables shown in Table 8 are included in these models. Levels of significance: **5%, *10%.

ARE DANGEROUS JOBS PAID BETTER? EUROPEAN EVIDENCE

Nikolaos Georgantzis and Efi Vasileiou

ABSTRACT

This article tests whether workers are indifferent between risky and safe jobs provided that, in labor market equilibrium, wages should serve as a utility equalizing device. Workers' preferences are elicited through a partial measure of overall job satisfaction: satisfaction with job-related risk. Given that selectivity turns out to be important, we use selectivity corrected models. Results show that wage differentials do not exclusively compensate workers for being in dangerous jobs. However, as job characteristics are substitutable in workers' utility, they could feel satisfied, even if they were not fully compensated financially for working in dangerous jobs.

Keywords: Satisfaction with job risk; compensating wage differentials; dangerous job

JEL classifications: C23; J31

New Analyses of Worker Well-Being
Research in Labor Economics, Volume 38, 163–192

ISSN: 0147-9121/doi:10.1108/S0147-9121(2013)0000038005

INTRODUCTION

When accepting a given job, a worker implicitly agrees with a whole set of costs and benefits associated to it. In fact, the benefits should, generally speaking, weakly offset the costs, making the worker prefer the job to unemployment and this specific job to other jobs available in the economy. This intuitive idea was formalized in the theory of compensating wage differentials[1] (CWDs), according to which, a worker's wage from a specific job should compensate his effort and other psychological costs and disutilities experienced as a consequence of the whole set of job characteristics.

In this framework, our paper focuses on a specific type of disutility experienced by workers, the likelihood of being physically or mentally injured while undertaking any of the tasks included in the job description (Wei, 1999). The main novelty of this paper is the distinction made between the effect of the wage differential for job riskiness on overall job satisfaction and the effectiveness of the differential to compensate for job riskiness alone.

Job riskiness is a central issue in labor market regulation in all modern countries. However, most of the studies on CWDs (Arabsheibani & Marin, 2000; Daniel & Sofer, 1998; Sandy & Elliott, 1996; Viscusi & Aldy, 2003; Wei, 1999) explore whether wages compensate workers for working in a dangerous jobs, but not whether this compensation is sufficient to offset the disutility suffered due to the risk, thus leaving unanswered questions like "Do wages behave as a utility-equalizing device in the sense of the theory of compensating differentials?" and "Would the premium offered by the market keep the worker in a dangerous work as satisfied as someone in a safer job?" For example, some studies have already found that wage differentials do not compensate for all working conditions (Baudelot & Gollac, 1993; Godechot & Gurgand, 2000). Godechot and Gurgand (2000) measure the effect of various job dis-amenities and efforts on a wage equation in order to test whether workers are sufficiently satisfied with their wage premium accounting for these dis-amenities or efforts. They find that while some bad working conditions may be sufficiently compensated for, it is also true that workers have distinct preferences and expectations for the compensation they should receive for each one of them.

Recent studies have explored the connection between various measures of job dis-amenities and job satisfaction. Clark and Postel-Vinay (2009) explore the effect of employment protection legislation and unemployment insurance benefits on satisfaction with security in Europe. They find that satisfaction with job security is negatively related to such legislation but positively affected by generous unemployment insurance benefits.

Furthermore, Böckerman et al. (2011) investigate how firm dynamics affect job satisfaction. They find that wage differentials do compensate for the negative effects of uncertainty in firms that have a high turnover of employees.

Lalive (2007) investigates the determination of individual wages and job satisfaction by using the National Longitudinal Survey of Youth in the United States. He shows that wage differentials do not compensate for work conditions. Stutzer and Frey (2008) using the German Socio-Economic Panel Study find that commuters report a lower level of subjective well-being, but, other things being equal, they do not get higher wages in response to this. Along this line, our study intends to address the above questions by using risk-related job satisfaction as a partial measure of overall job satisfaction. We assume that satisfaction with job-related risk will not vary with the wage rate if wages compensate exactly for working in risky jobs. Thus, concentrating only on workers' self-reported satisfaction, we test the applicability of the theory on compensating differentials to job riskiness.

Additionally, the examination of whether wage differentials act as a utility equalizing device on job risk makes it possible to correct for several potential biases related to the empirical estimations. In particular, we investigate the problem of sample selection. This may arise if the decision to work in a dangerous job is not random. For example, some workers may choose jobs with bad working conditions precisely because of the compensating differentials, while others may simply be less adverse to these kinds of jobs because of a different attitude toward risk.

This study is organized as follows: the second section begins by describing the framework of compensating differentials adapted to the issue of job risk. At the same time, the empirical biases usually found in the relevant literature are exposed. The third section presents the relationship between satisfaction and the theory of compensating differentials. The fourth section develops the test of compensating differentials for dangerous jobs. The fifth section gives background on the dataset and some preliminary evidence. The sixth section reports the results and the seventh section concludes.

THE THEORY OF COMPENSATING DIFFERENTIALS AND JOB RISK

The theory of compensating differentials tries to explain wage disparities in the labor market assuming that the employees have different preferences for different job attributes and that jobs are different too. The key implication of the theory is that, as long as all persons in the population agree on whether a particular job characteristic is "good" or "bad," those working under good conditions would be paid less (making workers "buy" the enjoyable environment) and those working under bad conditions would be paid more (Rosen, 1986). The theory is immediately applicable to the case of wage compensations for bearing the risk of injury or even death.[2] Most workers can be expected to value both higher wages and greater levels of safety, but some are presumed to be willing to accept some additional risk in exchange for a higher wage yielding the same overall level of utility. Thus, firms accounting for worker heterogeneity regarding the appropriate wage-safety trade-off may choose to invest in costly procedures, rather than economizing on safety and redistributing the savings among workers in the form of higher wages. This has important implications both for firm strategies and for public policy toward risky jobs.

Many empirical studies report a positive relationship between wages and unsafe working conditions. A survey of some earlier studies, together with an investigation into the variety of results, can be found in Marin and Psacharopoulos (1982). More recent surveys can be found in Meng and Smith (1990), Martinello and Meng (1992), Sandy and Elliott (1996), Daniel and Sofer (1998), Wei (1999), Arabsheibani and Marin (2000), and Viscusi and Aldy (2003). In general, the evidence is ambiguous. Some studies find that, while fatal risk has a positive and significant effect on wages, non-fatal risk tends to have negative and insignificant effects on wages (Arabsheibani & Marin, 2000). Some studies find that both variables have positive and significant effects (Garen, 1988). However, when some other factors are taken into account (such as union status or industry-level variables) the apparent ubiquity of the positive relationship between job risk and wages breaks down (Daniel & Sofer, 1998; Dorman & Hagstrom, 1998; Sandy & Elliott, 1996). Yet, the positive and statistically significant wage premium for fatal job risks provides the most robust empirical support for the theory of compensating differentials (Viscusi & Aldy, 2003). Some authors have recognized that the divergent results found in the literature on compensating differentials are due to the existence of several biases.

An omitted-variable bias due to the correlation between unobserved worker productivity (such as talent and innate ability) and job risk has been indicated by some authors (Brown, 1980; Duncan & Holmlund, 1983; Hwang, Reed, & Hubbard, 1992). For instance, more able workers are likely to earn higher wages, and these workers will probably "spend" some of their additional income on job amenities. Thus, more able workers will have higher wages and higher levels of the desired job amenities. Additionally, a major concern in the literature on compensating differentials is the issue of self-selection (Kostiuk, 1990; Lanfranchi et al., 2002; Lee, 1978; Purse, 2004). One reason is that, when fatality or injury risk is a normal good, employees with high earnings potential (e.g., better educated workers) will select themselves into safer jobs (Viscusi, 1978).

There are also several empirical studies that do not support the hypothesis of compensating wage differentials attributing the failure to market frictions and imperfect information (Arabsheibani & Marin, 2000; Bender & Mridha, 2011; Brown & Medoff, 1989; Daniel & Sofer, 1998; Dickens & Katz, 1987; Dorman & Hagstrom, 1998; Gronberg & Reed; 1994; Kruse, 1992; Krueger & Summer, 1988; Sandy & Elliott, 1996). More specifically, labor market segmentation and dualism theory predict a positive relationship between wages and good working conditions. The theory of labor market segmentation (see, e.g., Cahuc & Zajdela, 1991; Doeringer & Piore, 1971) initially distinguishes between two segments, one characterized by better, permanent, well-paid jobs with career prospects (the "primary segment") and the other having temporary, poorly paid jobs without any career prospects (the "secondary segment"). In a recent study Bender and Mridha (2011) show that the standard CWD theory does not necessarily hold because labor market forces may fail to induce firms to pay a CWD.

The literature also addresses problems with measuring risk compensation. The job risk has been measured in a number of ways and it relies, with few exceptions, upon risk measures which are available by industrial or occupational category (Arnould & Nichols, 1983; Brown, 1980; Dorman & Hagstrom, 1998; Garen, 1988; Thaler & Rosen, 1975). Few studies (Biddle & Zarkin, 1988; Böckerman & Ilmakunnas, 2006; Fairris, 1989; Gegax, Gerking, & Schulze, 1991; Hamermesh, 1978; Viscusi, 1978, 1979) have been based on workers' perception of their job risk. A possible explanation for the scarcity of subjective assessment studies on job riskiness is that most of the available datasets[3] do not include information on the worker's perceived job attributes.

In addition to the scarcity of the datasets which include the perceived individual risk, many researchers are reluctant to use subjective assessments of risk because part of the literature on psychology and economics has documented biases in individual assessments. The literature on risk perception found that individuals respond differently to risks depending on whether they are seen as violations of personal autonomy (Dorman, 1996; Starr, 1969). As a result, they feel a lower aversion to risks they take for themselves than to risks that they regard as being imposed on them by others. A second problem is that people tend to overestimate low probability events and to underestimate high probability ones (Kahneman & Tversky, 1979). This should also apply to job choice. For the overwhelming majority of jobs, the risk of a fatal accident is very low. From the evidence on how people make other types of decisions, it seems likely that most people ignore the probability of a fatal injury when choosing a job. Hence, if many people do not pay attention to such risks, employers have limited incentives to pay compensating differences. Thus, measured differences may not reflect workers' willingness to accept a compensation for taking those risks but, rather, employers' costs of providing the corresponding safety measures (Dickens, 1985). However, this suggests that many workers do not know how dangerous a job is when they take it, and learn over time. Thus, one can assume that individual perceptions when workers already have the job provide an accurate measure of job risk. Lastly, it is found that survey respondents overreact to newly identified risks. The original argument was advanced by Slovic in the 1970s (see Lichtenstein & Slovic, 1971). However, as stated by Viscusi and O'Connor (1984), these effects may not be as great in job safety contexts, probably because workers' familiarity with job risks make them less alarmed by information regarding a minor increase in risk.

This study assumes that self-reported information on job risk is a broad concept covering much more than the occupational accidents officially recognized by national insurance systems.[4] The way in which workers perceive their job dangerousness will be useful for an outsider evaluating job risk, and it probably affects economic outcomes. While it is unlikely to perceive the job risk as revealed in the labor market, a worker feeling that there is a high probability of being killed or suffering physical injury may be less motivated and may even leave the job voluntarily (Viscusi, 1979). Furthermore, depending on a job's dangerousness, a worker will be more or less likely to invest in firm-specific human capital that will increase his/her commitment to the employer. Therefore, this subjective indicator could be a substantial value for labor market analysis for firm strategies and economic policy toward risky jobs.

SATISFACTION AND COMPENSATING WAGE DIFFERENTIALS FOR JOB RISK

This section introduces some approaches used in the literature for testing the theory of compensating differentials that do not only rely on the hedonic wage methodology, but also on stated job satisfaction used as a subjective proxy of utility at work (Böckerman & Ilmakunnas, 2006; Böckerman et al., 2011; Clark, 2003; Godechot & Gurgand, 2000; Helliwell & Huang, 2010; Lalive, 2007; Stutzer & Frey, 2008).

To illustrate this framework, consider the linear specification:

$$U = \alpha + \beta X + \delta D + \gamma w \tag{1}$$

$$w = \phi + \mu D + \pi K \tag{2}$$

where U is job satisfaction, and X and K are vectors of exogenous variables. We denote by D the probability of injury on the job and define w as the worker's wage rate (or its natural logarithm), whereas α and ϕ are constants.

A CWD would imply that $\mu = -\delta/\gamma$.[5] Applying this in the wage Eq. (2) and then inserting the wage equation into the utility function (1) we get:

$$U = \alpha + \beta X + \pi\gamma K + \gamma\phi \tag{3}$$

In this setting, the existing literature proposes two ways of testing for CWDs when using job satisfaction as a proxy for utility.

Changing notations as: $\alpha' = \alpha + \gamma\phi$, $\beta' = \beta$, $\pi' = \gamma\pi$, one empirical strategy is to check whether $\delta' = 0$ holds in the job satisfaction equation

$$U = \alpha' + \beta' X + \pi' K + \delta' D \tag{4}$$

where wage is not included, assuming that satisfaction is independent of the working conditions. This empirical strategy is employed by Godechot and Gurgand (2000), Clark (2003), Böckerman and Ilmakunnas (2006), and Stutzer and Frey (2008).

Alternatively, CWDs can be tested by checking whether $\gamma' = 0$ in the job satisfaction equation

$$U = \alpha' + \beta X + \pi' K + \gamma' w \tag{5}$$

where dis-amenities are not included and which would imply that the wage differential offered by the market would be just enough to keep the worker on the same indifference curve. This test is applied by Lalive (2007).

Consistently with the above models, this study examines whether wages act as a utility equalizing device by assuming that satisfaction will not vary with the wage rate if wages compensate exactly for the bad working conditions. However, the main econometric issue is that the coefficient γ from the estimated model (Eq. (5)) should be unbiased. However, this may not be the case if some workers choose jobs with bad working conditions because of the compensating differentials while others prefer these jobs because they have different attitudes toward risk. Thus, the issue of self-selection is crucial to the analysis. This study attempts to provide unbiased estimates for γ. It thus relies on an endogenous switching regression model (Maddala, 1983).

A TEST OF COMPENSATING WAGE DIFFERENTIALS FOR RISKY JOBS USING ENDOGENOUS SWITCHING REGRESSION MODELS

Some workers may choose dangerous jobs because of the compensating differentials while others, with a lower aversion to danger, prefer riskier jobs and therefore make wage premiums unnecessary. Thus, the estimate of the necessary compensating differential will be biased downwards. Additionally, in the framework of the endogenous switching regression model, wages are allowed to be different across the two groups. Wages in dangerous jobs may be identified by different characteristics from those in safe jobs, so that the data should not be pooled. Suppose that employers give a wage premium to employees with individual characteristics such as education or experience in order to reduce the accidents in the jobs. Thus, two different regimes are distinguished, one for those working in a dangerous job and one for those working in a safe job.

The switching regression model estimates the following system describing log wages for dangerous (w_d) and for safe (w_s) jobs:

$$\text{Situation 1}: \quad w_d = \beta_d X + u_d \quad \text{for } C = 1 \tag{6a}$$

$$\text{Situation 2}: \quad w_s = \beta_s X + u_s \quad \text{for } C = 0 \tag{6b}$$

and one "selection" equation which determines which sector is chosen by the individuals, where C is the dangerous job choice:

$$\text{Dangerous Job Choice}: \quad C = \tau_3 Z + \upsilon_3 \quad \text{[reduced form]} \tag{7}$$

In the wage equations (6), w_d and w_s are the log hourly wages[6] of workers in dangerous and safe jobs, respectively, X is a vector of exogenous variables, while u_d, u_s are unobserved random errors. In Eq. (7), C is a binary variable for a dangerous job, taking the value 1 when the job is dangerous and 0 otherwise, Z is a vector of variables influencing the choice of a dangerous job and υ is an error term. Note that, in the reduced form (7), Z must contain all the X variables. Among the extra variables, there should be at least one which permits model identification. This variable is the instrument. This variable must affect wage only via its effect on the choice of a worker being in a dangerous job. In our model, the income of other household members is used as an instrument.[7]

Eq. (7) is estimated using a Probit model capturing sample selection. Inverse Mill ratios $\theta(Z\widehat{\delta})/\Phi(Z_i\widehat{\delta})$ are obtained, where $\theta(.)$ and $\Phi(.)$are, respectively, the probability density and cumulative functions of the standard normal distribution, which are then used to correct for selectivity bias and obtain unbiased estimates of the wages (6) by estimating

$$w_d = \beta_d X + \sigma_d \frac{\theta(Z\widehat{\delta})}{\Phi(Z_i\widehat{\delta})} \tag{8a}$$

$$w_s = \beta_s X - \sigma_s \frac{\theta(Z\widehat{\delta})}{1 - \Phi(Z_i\widehat{\delta})} \tag{8b}$$

assuming that the covariances σ_d, σ_s between the reduced-form Eq. (7) and the wage equations errors are nonzero. Estimates of σ_d, σ_s indicate the nature of self-selection into each sector. Positive selection into each sector implies a positive σ_d and a negative σ_s. In an economic context, positive selection means that workers select themselves into each one of the two sectors because of preferences or comparative advantages. Negative selection into a dangerous job implies that workers prefer to avoid dangerous jobs, but they seem to have chosen them because of the risk premium or because they could not find other jobs.

Note that, following Maddala (1983), one can rewrite Eqs. (8a) and (8b) as:

$$E(w) = \beta_s X + (\beta_d - \beta_s) X \Phi(Z_i\widehat{\delta}) + (\sigma_d - \sigma_s)\theta(Z_i\widehat{\delta}) \tag{9}$$

Assuming that both categories have identical coefficients ($\beta_d = \beta_s$ and $\gamma_d = \gamma_s$) for all X except for the constants, we rewrite Eq. (9), as follows, which is known as treatment effect model:

$$E(w) = \beta X + \alpha \Phi(Z_i\widehat{\delta}) + (\sigma_d - \sigma_s)\theta(Z_i\widehat{\delta}) \tag{10}$$

where α is equal to the difference in wages and captures the effect of a dangerous work on the wage.

Finally, Eq. (11) describes satisfaction with job-related risk, which is chosen instead of overall job satisfaction due to the exanimation of only one characteristic of the job: its dangerousness. Therefore, it is examined whether workers are sufficiently satisfied with their monetary compensation for this specific dis-amenity. As Adam Smith stated, jobs differ in many characteristics, all of which can give rise to compensating differentials. In this study, it is supposed that jobs differ in only one characteristic: the dangerousness of the job. The choice of this specific part of job satisfaction is very important in our framework as one could feel reasonably satisfied with the dangerousness of his/her job, but dissatisfied with many other aspects such as working times, security, and type of job. This is particularly true in the sense that a worker's wage might include compensation for job dangerousness but also for a variety of other dis-amenities. To ensure that this strategy correctly identifies the effect under study, employer characteristics that are controlled for in the model partly capture the role of the remaining job characteristics in wage determination.

$$S = \gamma X + \lambda(w_d - w_s) + \varepsilon \qquad \text{for } C = 1/0 \tag{11}$$

In Eq. (11), the satisfaction variable, S, is a latent one. The appropriate model is the ordered Probit model. In an ordered Probit model, the latent probability of reporting a job satisfaction level S^* is

$$S = \Phi^{-1}(S^*) = \gamma X + \lambda(w_d - w_s) + \varepsilon \qquad \varepsilon | X \sim Normal\ (0, 1)$$

where X is a vector of exogenous personal and work-related characteristics, γ is a vector of coefficients to be estimated, and ε indicates the error term. Assuming that $\mu_1 < \mu_2 < \ldots < \mu_j$ where $\mu_1, \ldots, \mu_j$ are the cutoff points for the latent variable:

$$S^* = \begin{cases} 0, & \text{if } S^* \leq \mu_1 \\ 1, & \text{if } \mu_1 \leq S^* \leq \mu_2 \\ \ldots & \\ j, & \text{if } S^* > \mu_j \end{cases}$$

the parameters γ and μ can be estimated by maximum likelihood.

The empirical strategy here is to check whether $\lambda = 0$,[8] which would imply that the wage differential offered by the market would be just enough to keep the worker on the same indifference curve. Thus, if wage differentials only reflect compensation for risky jobs, workers will not prefer jobs with high wages to jobs with low wages.[9] The alternative hypothesis of non-competitive determination of the wage structure $\lambda > 0$ or $\lambda < 0$ would indicate dualism of the labor market. If this alternative view of the labor market dominates the competitive view, one may find that wage increases/decreases will be reflected on higher/lower reported satisfaction levels (Clark, 2003).

JOB RISK, SATISFACTION, AND WAGES: FIRST EMPIRICAL EVIDENCE FROM A EUROPEAN SURVEY

Our analysis uses the EPICURUS dataset.[10] The survey includes general questions aimed at identifying the respondent's individual characteristics. Questions concerning age, gender, marital status, employment status, education, occupation, and socio-economic and labor market status characteristics are included. The respondent is also asked several questions related to income, and about aspects related to job satisfaction, as well as satisfaction with several features of work.

In this study, a sub-sample of 3,030 workers from France, Greece, the United Kingdom, and the Netherlands is used. The sample includes workers occupied in paid employment between 18 and 65 years of age. Self-employed, retired, and unemployed persons, as well as housewives and students are excluded in order to keep the sample homogeneous. Moreover, those whose highest qualification is third level education are excluded from the main questionnaire because the designers of this questionnaire decided to exclude individuals with an education level 5 or 6 (ISCED International Classification 1997) in order to keep the sample as homogeneous as possible. All workers were interviewed online with the exception of Greece where face-to-face interviews were conducted. The agency that ran the surveys for Greece, France, the United Kingdom, and the Netherlands suggested that it was not necessary or useful to apply weighing techniques on the data. All the employee groups were sufficiently represented. The fieldwork in the United Kingdom, which was done online, had a gross sampling based on age, gender, and education level. In the screening phase 654 persons were screened out, and 1002 respondents completed the interview. For Greece, in the screenings phase, 500 respondents were screened out because they did not belong to the target population, and 800 respondents received a complete interview. In the Netherlands in the screening phase 413 persons were screened out, and 1007 respondents completed the questionnaire.

We distinguish between workers who work in dangerous jobs and those who work in safe jobs based on the following question:

Question: "Would you say that your job is dangerous (risk of physical accidents, contact with dangerous products)?"

Response: "Frequently, sometimes, hardly ever."

If a worker replies that his/her job is dangerous: either frequently or sometimes, it indicates that he/she is working in a dangerous job. Alternatively, if a worker replies that his/her job is hardly ever dangerous, the worker is categorized as belonging to the safe job group.

The level of "satisfaction with job-related risk" is derived from the following question:

"How satisfied are you with your job's physical risk?"

The answers are ranked on a 1 (completely dissatisfied) to 10 (completely satisfied) scale.

Fig. 1 provides a first approach to the negative relation between risk at job and an individual's satisfaction with dangerousness at work. It is found on average that the workers who are most satisfied with job-related risk are in safe jobs and this difference is large (81.37%). Approximately only 18.63% of satisfied workers viewed their job as being dangerous. For those who are dissatisfied with their job risk, 61.58% of workers believe their job is dangerous. Thus, the fear of a job accident is confined to workers with

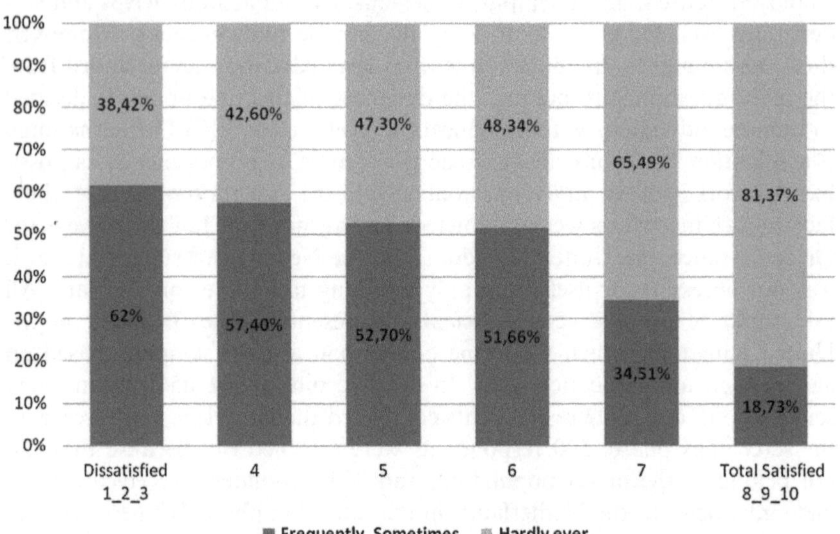

Fig. 1. Satisfaction with Job-Related Risk and Job Dangerousness.

low satisfaction in this domain. However, the raw correlation between job risk and satisfaction does not account for wages and the fact that we are comparing people with heterogeneous preferences facing different restrictions. Thus, the observed lower satisfaction of people who work in dangerous jobs might just reflect that these are people with different socio-demographic and socio-economic characteristics.

Table A1 presents sample statistics for workers occupied in dangerous and safe jobs, on the basis of their perception of job risk. Each of these variables affects wages and, at the same time, determines a worker's choice of a dangerous job. There is also substantial literature suggesting that women are more risk averse than men and those married with children are more risk averse than those without (DeLeire & Levy, 2004; Dohmen et al., 2005; Sloane & Grazier, 2006). Thus, workers with a strong aversion to risk will tend to make occupational choices which sort them into safer jobs. Hence, there are strong empirical results showing that workers sort into jobs on the basis of their preferences. Thus, it is difficult to separate compensating differentials from returns to skill where the employee is being rewarded for his ability to manage the risk inherent in a particular job. This skill might result from prior training or experience which enables some workers to be more productive in a dangerous job, but such characteristics may not be relevant to a safe job. For example, the fact that men are more likely to work in a dangerous job makes it possible that the "gender earnings gap" often found in empirical studies may be partly a compensation for job riskiness (Nielsen, 2005). Similarly, unionized workers are more likely to work in dangerous jobs than non-union workers. Previous empirical work has shown that unions raise the risk premium because they provide members with both more information about occupational risk and a mechanism for voicing their concerns about risk, something which is not available to non-union workers (Thaler & Rosen, 1975). So it is possible that some of the union wage differentials found in wage studies are actually a compensation for dangerous jobs. As stated before, one needs to account for possible biases arising from worker selection into risky or non-risky jobs when evaluating the compensating differentials hypothesis (Tables 1 and 2).

ECONOMETRIC RESULTS

Table 2 reports, the selectivity-corrected wage equations for workers in dangerous and safe jobs.[11] An important ingredient in the selectivity-corrected models is the instrument which permits model identification.

Table 1. Dangerous Choice, Probit Model, Marginal Effects.

Reduced Form		
Variables	Marginal effects	z-Value
Co_married	0.080	3.43***
Male	0.130	6.54***
Tenure	0.010	2.70***
Tenure^2/100	−0.039	3.32***
Sec education	−0.093	3.73***
Up_se education	−0.058	2.21***
Children	−0.008	0.40
Trade Unio Mb	0.121	4.75***
Managers	0.058	1.74*
Clerks	−0.159	5.92***
Craft_skilled	0.303	7.70***
Other occupat	0.133	4.41***
Private	−0.038	1.68*
Unempl Exp	0.053	1.51
Firm size < 99	0.092	3.35***
Firm size >100	0.017	0.70
Service sector	−0.038	1.23
Other sector	−0.068	1.96**
Greece	0.350	10.98***
France	0.239	8.03***
UK	0.116	3.91***
Household member's income	−0.041	1.92**
Log likelihood	−1624.76	
Pseudo R^2	0.18	
Observations	3,030	

Note: *, **, *** indicate significance at 10%, 5%, 1% levels, respectively.

In our model, this variable must affect wage only via its effect on the choice of a worker to be in a dangerous job. It has been argued that social background characteristics do not impact on the wage but on the job decision. To our knowledge only Daniel and Sofer (1998) have used two instruments for the choice of a risky job (the number of children and the log of the spouse's income). They found that both have significant effect on the choice of risky jobs. Accordingly, in this study, whether another household member has income[12] (*inco_household*) is used as an instrument for the choice of being in a risky job.[13]

Following Coles et al. (2007), one can suggest that job choice may be dependent on productivity-irrelevant characteristics. The identifying

Table 2. Selectivity-Corrected Wage Equations Models.

	Switching Regression Model				Treatment Effect Model	
	1		2		3	
	Dangerous choice		Safe choice		All workers	
	Coefficient	*t*-Stat	Coefficient	*t*-Stat	Coefficient	*t*-Stat
Co_married	0.080	2.07**	0.013	0.47	0.034	1.60
Male	0.212	3.19***	0.028	0.68	0.094	2.55**
Tenure	0.022	3.17***	0.015	3.07***	0.017	4.56***
Tenure^2/100	−0.053	2.18**	−0.014	0.87	−0.027	2.08***
Sec education	−0.017	0.35	0.165	4.00***	0.101	3.38***
Up_se education	0.077	1.72*	0.181	4.77***	0.143	5.40***
Trade Unio Mb	0.121	2.17**	−0.064	1.51	−0.002	0.08
Managers	0.201	3.59***	0.211	4.74***	0.203	6.30***
Clerks	0.017	0.18	0.215	4.59***	0.134	3.01***
Craft_skilled	0.184	1.58	−0.293	2.84***	−0.133	1.71*
Other occupat	0.162	2.34**	−0.015	0.31	0.044	1.07
Private	−0.172	4.54***	0.022	0.79	−0.041	2.02**
Unempl Exp	−0.076	1.42	−0.069	1.59	−0.074	2.49**
Firm size < 99	0.048	0.93	−0.037	0.97	−0.010	0.33
Firm size >100	0.002	0.06	0.053	1.81*	0.036	1.78*
Service sector	−0.102	2.31**	0.006	0.15	−0.029	1.09
Other sector	−0.089	1.53	0.025	0.49	−0.012	0.37
Greece	−0.749	5.57***	−1.242	13.27***	−1.073	13.36***
France	−0.025	0.25	−0.341	5.47***	−0.228	4.10***
UK	−0.409	6.49***	−0.492	12.02***	−0.458	14.12***
Worker being in dangerous job	–	–	–	–	−0.073	1.82*
Selection term	0.329	1.44	−0.540	2.93***	−0.458	3.22***
Constant	1.49	4.06***	1.689	19.28***	1.96	26.00***
Adjusted R^2	0.50		0.47		0.49	
Observations	1,096		1,934		3,030	

Note: *, **, *** indicate significance at 10%, 5%, 1% levels, respectively.

restriction chosen in our study, namely, the household member's income, conforms to the above intuition. In the market equilibrium envisaged here, there is a population of workers with different social background characteristics (Daniel & Sofer, 1998). In this case, workers who have a comparative advantage in taking safe jobs – that is, those who can be selective because of their extra household member's income – take employment in safe jobs and, in equilibrium, earn a lower average wage. Conversely, those who do not have the extra household member's income take more dangerous jobs and enjoy the corresponding wage premium. Additionally, in order to provide further evidence on the appropriateness of the chosen instrument the Staiger and Stock (1997) test for exogeneity is used. Staiger and Stock (1997) argue that, if the *F*-stat value associated with the chosen instruments in the first stage regression is above 10, then the quality of the instrument is acceptable. In this model the *F*-stat value is 11.1 indicating that the chosen instrument is adequate.

Reduced form Probit Equation

We start by presenting the results of the first step of the analysis, the reduced form choice Eq. (7) for the EU sample (Table 1). The estimation of the choice equation makes use of the Probit method to identify the factors that influence the decision of individuals to work in dangerous jobs. As expected, the household member's income, the variable that affects only the choice process, is highly significant. Those individuals whose family members provide the household with extra income are less likely to work in dangerous jobs, as compared to those who do not have an additional income from their family.

The results also confirm the picture which already emerges from the raw data (Table A1): the probability of choosing a dangerous job is higher if the worker is male, married, or having a partner. Educated workers are less likely to be in dangerous jobs. The probability of ending up in a dangerous job is an inverse U-shaped function of tenure with a maximum reached at around 13 years in the same job. This finding suggests that younger workers may be more willing to accept dangerous jobs since they are in the beginning of their careers and the possibility of finding a safer job is lower or it might simply be an age-related shift in preferences.

Union membership affects positively the choice process. However, this result should be interpreted with caution. Many authors emphasize that there is a possible endogenous relationship between union status and the choice of a dangerous job (Biddle & Zarkin, 1988). It could be the case that workers in dangerous jobs are more likely to be unionized in order to facilitate communication with the hierarchy or co-workers.

Country-specific effects show that workers in Greece are more willing to accept dangerous jobs, followed by French and to a lower extent by British workers. This may signal the importance of having a "job" even if it is dangerous in countries such as Greece or France with relatively high unemployment rates.

The above results confirm the idea that people do not choose jobs at random. It seems that this is particularly important when comparing what influences the choice of occupation among different groups of workers, as specific groups may have particular preferences. Thus, previous estimates of wage premium for dangerous jobs are misleading since they may confound equalizing wage effects with inter-personal differences. As stated before, one needs to account for any biases arising from worker selection into risky or non-risky jobs when evaluating the compensating differentials hypothesis.

Is Selectivity Important?

The results for the reduced form Probit can be used to control for sample selection when estimating wage equations for workers observed in dangerous and safe jobs. Table 2, columns 1 and 2 present the estimates for these wage Eqs. (8a) and (8b). It is found that there is no effect of self-selection of workers into dangerous jobs and a positive selection of workers into safe jobs. There is evidence of positive selection into safe jobs since the significant negative coefficient on the inverse Mills ratio (*selection term*) implies that those less likely to work in dangerous jobs are those workers with high unobserved components of safe job wages. A more straightforward interpretation is that those choosing safe jobs have a comparative advantage or a preference for this kind of jobs. Thus, if workers in safe jobs moved to dangerous jobs they might be less satisfied as they put more weight on security than on wages, in which case the wage premium would not be enough to equalize their utility.

Table 2, column 3 presents the estimates of the treatment effect model (Eq. (10)). One of the principal findings from the switching regression results of Table 2 (columns 1 and 2) still holds for the single-equation estimates, with a significant correlation between the errors in the wage and choice equations. Workers with positive unmeasured components of safe jobs earnings are less likely to work in dangerous jobs. While the single-equation results are consistent with the two-sector model, their validity is rejected by the F-test.[14]

Which Is the Effect of Job Risk in Wage Determination?

Table 2 (columns 1 and 2) reveals that the variables do not have the same influence in both wage equations. The two most important results are the positive effect of union status for workers in dangerous jobs and the non-significant effect for workers in safe jobs. In the literature, it is usually stated that the presence of unions endows workers with some market power, a situation which is not considered in the pure theory of compensating differentials. An explanation usually put forward suggests that union workers may be better informed than non-union workers to have access to reliable information on risk and may be able to employ it more effectively when bargaining (Thaler & Rosen, 1975). Thus, some studies find that unionized workers obtain substantially higher compensations for fatal risk (Gegax et al., 1991). In addition, sociologists argue that workers are only compensated for bad working conditions when the bad quality of the job is publicly recognized (Baudelot & Gollac, 1993). Unions are therefore the only means for everyone to recognize whether a working condition is good or bad.

The remaining findings are consistent with the implications of the theoretical literature on wages, according to which males have higher wages than women in dangerous jobs. Returns to schooling are significant in both equations. Being married is significant in the wage equations for workers in dangerous jobs.

The two wage equations for workers in dangerous and safe jobs can be used to compute the wage differential for each person in the sample. The wage rate for workers in safe jobs is 9 percent higher than for workers in dangerous jobs. Suppose that we erroneously pool the data and do not correct for selectivity. The wage differential would then be biased downward by 6.2 percent.[15] If instead we correct for selectivity but still erroneously pool the data (the Treatment Effect model, Table 2, column 3), the wage differential is also underestimated by 7.3 percent.

Are Wages a Utility Equalizing Device in the Sense of the Theory of Compensating Differentials?

The four countries examined in this study are very different in terms of labor demand and supply and institutional factors such as labor market centralization and union membership rates. For instance, an issue that often raises debate on the validity of the theory of compensating differentials is its assumption of a perfectly competitive labor market. If the labor market is not perfectly competitive, the CWDs may be weak or even absent. The countries studied here have different labor market conditions. On one hand, in the United Kingdom the labor market is characterized by higher flexibility and employers must propose a higher risk premium, in order to attract workers, whereas in France and Greece the labor market is more centralized and wage determination is coordinated by institutional mechanisms in which the individualization of wages is not completely developed (Brizard, 2004) (Tables 3 and 4).

Additionally, some studies find that CWDs are inversely correlated with unemployment. Thus, in countries where unemployment is relatively low and, consequently, job opportunities wider (like in our case, the United Kingdom), workers earn a higher risk premium. Purse (2004) points out that workers confronted with a higher level of unemployment, especially those with a low level of education and few marketable skills, may be much less likely to quit their job, irrespective of whether or not it is hazardous. If

Table 3. Satisfaction with Risk Equation (Ordered Probit).

Variables	1		2	
	Coefficient	*t*-Values	Coefficient	*t*-Values
Male	−0.011	0.27	–	–
Tenure	−0.008	1.22	–	–
Tenure^2/100	0.031	1.52	–	–
Sec education	0.055	1.09	0.025	0.67
Up_se education	0.189	3.57***	0.147	2.85***
Unemployment experience	−0.224	3.11***	−0.190	2.81***
Trade Union Mb	−0.191	3.97***	–	–
Service sector	−0.168	2.76***	−0.203	−2.16**
Other sector	−0.092	1.23	−0.126	0.70
Managers	0.204	3.00***	0.175	2.88***
Clerks	0.235	3.85***	0.196	3.08***
Craft_skilled	−0.136	1.70*	−0.027	0.22
Other occupat	0.078	1.29	0.092	1.62
Interaction terms				
Wage differentials × UK	−0.704	6.26***	−0.689	6.21***
Wage differentials × France	−0.125	0.77	−0.071	0.79
Wage differentials × Greece	−0.548	5.36***	−0.252	1.75*
Wage differentials × male	–	–	−0.470	4.13***
Wage differentials × tenure	–	–	−0.017	1.18
Wage differentials × Tenure^2	–	–	0.006	1.33
Wage differentials × Trd.Un.	–	–	−0.100	1.12
Adjusted R^2	0.08		0.09	
Observations	3,030			

Note: *, **, *** indicate significance at 10%, 5%, 1% levels, respectively.

Table 4. Overall Job Satisfaction (Ordered Probit).

Variables	Coefficient	t-Values
Male	−0.128	2.93***
Tenure	−0.005	0.85
Tenure^2/100	0.033	1.68*
Sec education	−0.012	0.25
Up_se education	−0.067	1.28
Unemployment experience	−0.109	1.59
Trade Union Mb	−0.126	2.72***
Service sector	−0.001	0.01
Other sector	−0.030	0.41
Managers	0.190	2.83***
Clerks	0.215	3.57***
Craft_skilled	−0.027	0.33
Other occupat	0.172	2.79***
Interaction terms		
Wage differentials*Greece	0.121	1.09
Wage differentials*France	0.615	3.88***
Wage differentials*UK	0.349	3.03***
Observations	3,027	

Note: *, **, *** indicate significance at 10%, 5%, 1% levels, respectively.

this is the case in countries such as Greece and France, where the unemployment rate is higher compared to the United Kingdom, the risk premium would be smaller or even absent. We address this issue by the use of appropriate interaction terms rather than estimating a different model for each country which would require a higher number of observations per country.

As mentioned above and according to the theory of compensating differentials, the wage differential that enters into satisfaction equations should be zero. Therefore, it would be expected that the coefficient of the wage differential estimated from these equations should not be significant. The econometric evidence from the risk-specific partial satisfaction regression (Table 3) shows that the wage differential yields lower satisfaction for Greek and British workers. This could probably mean that if dangerous jobs are also the low-paid ones, workers could be dissatisfied even if risk were compensated for, because even well-paid individuals would be paid less if they were in a dangerous job. In other words, risk is not fully compensated in the labor marker, thus reducing satisfaction. This result suggests that the market might possibly not clear, implying that workers who choose a dangerous job do so because they have no other alternative. In this line Purse (2004), who criticized the perfect mobility assumption, pointed out that "if workers do not have the freedom to change jobs when faced with unacceptable risks arising from their work, the presumed imperative placed on employers by the market to compensate them is correspondingly reduced. In the real world, workers are completely free to change jobs whenever they feel inclined to do so" (p. 598). In the estimates reported in Table 3, it is also interesting to note that, in the second specification, the interaction term between wage differentials and trade union is not significant, whereas in the first specification, unionized workers are less satisfied with their job riskiness. This suggests that unionized workers' wages capture the corresponding workers' dissatisfaction (Table 5).

As a robustness test, we rerun the whole estimation using the measure of overall job satisfaction instead of satisfaction with job risk (see Table 4). It

Table 5. Wage Equation, OLS Estimation.

Variables	Coefficient	*t*-Stat
Dangerous job	−0.062	3.22***
Married	0.054	3.14***
Male	0.131	7.80***
Tenure	0.020	6.34***
$\text{Tenure}^2/100$	−0.038	3.71***
Sec education	0.061	2.81***
Up_se education	0.113	5.00***
Trade Union Mb	0.039	2.08*
Managers	0.229	8.66***
Clerks	0.128	5.35***
Craft_skilled	0.039	0.40
Other occupat	0.090	3.63***
Private	−0.048	2.72**
Unemployment Experience	−0.062	2.19**
Firm size < 99	0.015	0.75
Firm size > 100	0.044	2.14**
Service sector	−0.053	1.94*
Other sector	−0.047	1.57
Greece	−0.955	43.40***
France	−0.172	8.50***
UK	−0.430	16.26***
Constant	1.912	35.53***
Observations	3,030	
Adjusted R^2	0.49	

is found that higher wage differentials do yield extra satisfaction for French and British workers. This may be explained by the fact that wage is not the only argument in a worker's utility function. People could feel satisfied with their jobs even if they were not sufficiently compensated for working in a dangerous one. An explanation could be provided by using the multidimensional model of overall job satisfaction (Skalli et al., 2008). According to this model, overall utility of a job is the result of an aggregation of all sub-utilities related to a different mix of job characteristics (such as working conditions, security, type of work, and wages).

An individual could remain equally satisfied with his/her job if certain characteristics of the job changed, like for example, when working conditions deteriorate but this is accompanied by a permanent job contract in a way that the overall job satisfaction remains the same. Thus, two different mixes of characteristics for the same job may be viewed by the worker as equally attractive, provided that a low content in one desirable property is compensated by an increase in another.

In this way, a worker may be willing to accept voluntarily a risky job if he/she is compensated with more of another desirable attribute in a way that his/her satisfaction remains the same; for example, a risky job which provides more security in terms of unemployment expectations, more convenient working time schedules, and not particularly higher wages as wages present only one dimension of a job among others.

CONCLUSIONS

This study tests the central implication of the theory of compensating differentials that workers are indifferent between risky and safe jobs in labor market equilibrium as long as wages serve as a utility equalizing device. Using satisfaction with job-related risk as a partial measure of overall job satisfaction, we examine whether wage differentials act as a utility equalizing device counterbalancing job risk. We have used a selectivity corrected model in order to overcome biases present in previous related studies. It turns out that it is important to adjust for selectivity.

The econometric evidence shows that the wage premium for being in a dangerous job is not sufficient to equalize workers' risk-related partial utility across job types. This could probably mean that dangerous jobs are also low-pay ones. Nevertheless, the wage differential yields higher overall job satisfaction and this probably says that workers are, in general, happy with their wages, although not sufficiently compensated for their job's riskiness. An explanation for this is that different job characteristics are substitutable, making a worker with low potential earnings in a safe job willing to accept a riskier job if he/she is sufficiently compensated with more of another desirable attribute. Thus, policies focusing on job characteristics reflected on overall job satisfaction would be as important as policies focusing on the level of pay. This, however, requires the design of a regulatory framework that promotes the transition of workers from one state (low pay/low quality) to another (high pay/high quality) by improving the dynamics that lead to jobs of superior quality and by encouraging occupational and regional mobility. And probably this is even more crucial in countries with a high level of employment protection, where as stated by Gielen and Tatsiramos (2012) it induces the employed worker to stay in a low satisfaction job until a better job is found.

Policymakers should aim at designing specific measures which, apart from the objective risk of a job, take into account the subjective perception of workers regarding their jobs' riskiness. Firms could also benefit from findings like those presented here to improve their workers' satisfaction using less costly strategies.

Future research could check the robustness of our results in a broader set of countries. It would also be necessary to extend the analysis to part-time jobs which seem to constitute an especially interesting field for job risk management by regulators and firms.

NOTES

1. First proposed by Adam Smith (1991) in the *Wealth of Nations*, followed by Mincer (1958), Becker (1964), and Rosen (1986).

2. An important strand of empirical studies have investigated the relationship between a wage premium and undesirable working conditions other than risky jobs (for a review, see Rosen, 1986). Bad working conditions usually refer to dangerous and stressful conditions at the workplace (Duncan & Holmlund, 1983; French & Dunlap, 1998), inconvenient location and commuting time (Stutzer & Frey, 2008), shift work and flexible working hours (Gariety & Shaffer, 2001; Kostiuk, 1990; Lanfranchi et al., 2002), and perception of job instability measured by product market volatility (Moretti, 2000; Magnani, 2002).

3. To the knowledge of the authors, the University of Michigan's Survey of Working Conditions (SWC), the Quality Employment Survey (QES), and the EPICURUS dataset are the only datasets including a subjective risk variable obtained from workers' perception of their jobs' dangerous and unhealthy conditions. However, the other two studies are cross-sectional data obtained from American respondents. Thus, the dataset analyzed here is the only one with a panel structure including a question on perceived job risk by European workers.

4. As argued by Viscusi (1993), the ideal risk measure would reflect subjective assessment of the risk of a job by both the workers and the firm, but in practice we have a less perfect measure. The only exception known which used linked firm-worker data is the paper by Dale-Olsen (2006) and Lalive et al. (2006).

5. Note that $\mu > 0$ or $\mu < 0$ are sufficient conditions to reject the theory.

6. These are wage averages obtained by dividing the total regular monthly income from the main employment by the total amount of hours worked usually, excluding overtime.

7. The appropriateness of the chosen instrument is discussed in detail in the sixth section.

8. One may argue that this empirical model focuses only on injury risk. But in reality the wage is (potentially) affected by many different compensating differentials. If these are correlated with injury risk, it would bias the results that are being generated here. However, one should consider (i) which attributes should be included and which ones should not, (ii) the potentially relevant attributes are not necessarily observable, and (iii), even if they were, the resulting model would be a very complex one.

9. The differential $w_d - w_s$ is the predicted value difference of wages for dangerous and safe jobs for each worker.

10. This survey was elaborated in 2004 by the EPICURUS team in the framework of a European project under the Fifth Framework Programme "Improving Human Potential" (contract number: HPSE-CT-2002-00143). The variables included in our model are defined in Table A2.

11. For comparison, Table 5 contains OLS estimates of wages including "job risk" as a dummy variable.

12. The household income includes labor and capital income of other household members.

13. The variable "number of children" is not significant in the Probit equation.

14. The F-test for the equality of coefficients in the two groups is $F(20, 3030) = 5.42$ with $Pr > F$ 0.000 and is therefore significantly different from zero.

15. The wage OLS estimation is reported in Table 5.

ACKNOWLEDGMENTS

We acknowledge financial support by the EU (EPICURUS project), the Spanish Ministry of Science and Innovation (ECO2011-23634), and Junta de Andalucía (P07-SEJ-03155). Comments by Dr. Ali Skalli and two anonymous referees are gratefully acknowledged.

REFERENCES

Arabsheibani, G., & Marin, A. (2000). Stability of estimates for the compensation of the danger. *Journal of Risk and Uncertainty*, *20*, 247–269.

Arnould, R., & Nichols, L. (1983). Wage-risk premiums and workers' compensation: A refinement of estimates of compensating wage differentials. *Journal of Political Economy*, *91*, 332–340.

Baudelot, C., & Gollac, M. (1993). Salaires et conditions de travail. *Economie et Statistique*, *265*, 65–84.

Becker, G. (1964). *Human capital*. Chicago, IL: The University of Chicago Press.

Bender, K., & Mridha, H. (2011). The effect of local area unemployment on compensating wage differentials for injury risk. *Southern Economic Journal*, *78*, 287–307.

Biddle, J. E., & Zarkin, G. (1988). Worker preferences and market compensation for job risk. *Review of Economics and Statistics*, *70*, 660–667.

Böckerman, P., & Ilmakunnas, P. (2006). Do job disamenities raise wages or ruin job satisfaction? *International Journal of Manpower*, *27*, 290–302.

Böckerman, P., Ilmalunnas, P., & Johansson, E. (2011). Job security and employee well-being: Evidence form matched survey and register data. *Labour Economics*, *18*, 547–554.

Brizard, A. (2004). *1999–2002: Des hausses de salaires de moins en moins individualisees*. Premières Informations, Premières Synthèses, DARES, n° 22.1.

Brown, C. (1980). Equalizing differences in the labour market. *Quarterly Journal of Economics*, *94*, 113–34.

Brown, C., & Medoff, J. (1989). The employer size-wage effect. *Journal of Political Economy*, *97*, 1027–1059.

Cahuc, P., & Zajdela, H. (1991). Comment expliquer le dualisme du marché du travail à partir de comportements rationnels? *Revue Economique*, *3*, 469–491.

Clark, A. (2003). *Looking for labour market rents with subjective data*. Mimeo. Paris: DELTA.

Clark, A., & Postel-Vinay, F. (2009). Job security and job protection. *Oxfort Economics Papers*, *61*, 207–239.

Coles, M., Lanfranchi, J., Skalli, A., & Treble, J. (2007). Pay, technology, and the cost of worker absence. *Economic Inquiry*, *45*, 268–285.

Dale-Olsen, H. (2006). Estimating worker' marginal willingness to pay for safety using linked employer-employee data. *Economica*, *73*, 99–127.

Daniel, C., & Sofer, C. (1998). Bargaining, compensating wage differentials, and the dualism of the labor market: Theory and evidence for France. *Journal of Labor Economics*, *16*, 546–575.

DeLeire, T., & Levy, H. (2004). Worker sorting and the risk of death on the job. *Journal of Labor Economics*, *22*, 925–953.

Dickens, W. (1985). Occupational safety and health regulation and irrational behavior: A preliminary analysis. In J. D. Worrall & D. Appel (Eds.), *Workers' compensation benefits: Adequacy, equity and efficiency* (pp. 19–40). New York, NY: ILR Press.

Dickens, W., & Katz, L. (1987). Where have all the good jobs gone?: Deindustrialization and theories of dual labour markets. In K. Lang & J. Leonard (Eds.), *Unemployment and the structure of labour markets*. New York, NY: Basil Blackwell.

Doeringer, P., & Piore, M. (1971). *Internal labor markets and manpower analysis*. New York, NY: D.C. Heath and Company.

Dohmen, T., Falk, A., Huffman, D., Sunde U., Schupp, J., & Wagner, G., (2005). *Individual risk attitudes: New evidence from a large, representative, experimentally-validated survey*. IZA Discussion Paper No. 1730.

Dorman, P. (1996). *Markets and mortality: Economics, dangerous work and the value of human life*. Cambridge: Cambridge University Press.

Dorman, P., & Hagstrom, P. (1998). Wage compensation for dangerous work revisited. *Industrial and Labour Relations Review*, *52*, 116–35.

Duncan, G., & Holmlund, B. (1983). Was Adam Smith right after all? Another test of the theory of compensating wage differentials. *Journal of Labour Economics*, *1*, 367–379.

Fairris, D. (1989). Compensating wage differentials in the union and nonunion sectors. *Industrial Relations*, *28*, 356–372.

French, T., & Dunlap, J. (1998). Compensating wage differentials for job stress. *Applied Economics*, *30*, 1067–1075.

Garen, J. (1988). Compensating wage differentials and the endogeneity of job riskiness. *The Review of Economics and Statistics*, *70*, 9–16.

Gariety, B., & Shaffer, S. (2001). Wage differentials associated with flexitime. *Monthly Labor Review*, *124*, 68–75.

Gegax, D., Gerking, S., & Schulze, W. (1991). Perceived risk and the marginal value of safety. *Review of Economics and Statistics*, *73*, 589–596.

Gielen, A., & Tatsiramos, K. (2012). *Quit behavior and the role of job protection*. Labour Economics, *19*(4), 624–632.

Godechot, O., & Gurgand, M. (2000). Quand les salariés jugent leur salaire. *Economie et Statistique*, *331*, 3–24.

Gronberg, T., & Reed, W. (1994). Estimating workers' marginal willingness to pay for job attributes using duration data. *Journal of Human Resources*, *24*, 911–931.

Hamermesh, D. S. (1978). Economic aspects of job satisfaction. In O. Ashenfelter & W. Oates (Eds.), *Essays in labour market analysis* (pp.53–72). New York, NY: Wiley.

Helliwell, J. F., & Huang, H. (2010). How's the job? Well-being and social capital in the workplace. *Industrial and Labor Relations Review*, *63*, 205–227.

Hwang, H., Reed, R., & Hubbard, C. (1992). Compensating wage differentials and unobserved productivity. *Journal of Political Economy*, *100*, 835–58.

Kahneman, D., & Tversky, A. (1979). Prospect theory: An analysis of decisions under risk. *Econometrica*, *47*, 263–291.

Kostiuk, P. F. (1990). Compensating differentials for shift work. *Journal of Political Economy*, *98*, 1055–75.

Krueger, A., & Summer, L. (1988). Efficiency wages and the inter-industry wage structure. *Econometrica*, *56*, 259–293.

Kruse, D. (1992). Supervision, working conditions and the employer size-wage effect. *Industrial Relations*, *31*, 229–49.

Lalive, R. (2007). Do wages compensate for workplace amenities? *Applied Economics Quarterly*, *53*, 273–298.

Lalive, R., Ruf, O., & Zweimuller, J., (2006). *Wages and risks at the workplace: Evidence from linked firm-worker data*. mimeo, University of Zurich.

Lanfranchi, J., Ohlsson, H., & Skalli, A. (2002). Compensating wage differentials and shift work preferences. *Economics Letters*, *74*, 393–398.

Lee, L. (1978). Unionism and wage rates: A simultaneous equations model with qualitative and limited dependent variables. *International Economic Review*, *19*, 415–433.

Lichtenstein, S., & Slovic, P. (1971). Reversals of preference between bids and choices in gambling situations. *Journal of Experimental Psychology*, *89*, 46–55.

Maddala, G. (1983). *Limited dependent and qualitative variables in econometrics*. Cambridge: Cambridge University Press.

Magnani, E. (2002). Product market volatility and the adjustment of earnings to risk. *Industrial Relations*, *41*, 304–328.

Marin, A., & Psacharopoulos, G. (1982). The reward of risk in the labor market: Evidence from the United Kingdom and reconciliation with other studies. *Journal of Political Economy, 90*, 827–853.

Martinello, F., & Meng, R. (1992). Work-place Risks and the value of hazard avoidance. *Canadian Journal of Economics, 25*, 333–345.

Meng, R., & Smith, D. (1990). The valuation of risk death in public sector decision-making. *Canadian Public Policy, 16*, 137–144.

Mincer, J. (1958). Investment in human capital and the personal income distribution. *Journal of Political Economy, 66*, 281–302.

Moretti, E. (2000). Do wages compensate for risk of unemployment? Parametric and semiparametric evidence from seasonal jobs. *Journal of Risk and Uncertainty, 20*, 45–66.

Nielsen, A. (2005). *Gender wage gap is feminist fiction?* Retrieved from http://www.iwf.org/articles/article_detail.asp?ArticleID = 749

Purse, K. (2004). Work-related fatality risks and neoclassical compensating wage differentials. *Cambridge Journal of Economics, 28*, 597–617.

Rosen, S. (1986). The theory of equalizing differences. In O. Ashenfelter & P. R. G. Layard (Eds.), *Handbook of labor economics* (Vol. 1, pp. 641–692). Amsterdam: North-Holland.

Sandy, R., & Elliott, R. (1996). Unions and risk: Their impact on the compensation for fatal risk. *Economica, 63*, 291–309.

Skalli, A., Theodossiou, I., & Vasileiou, E. (2008). Jobs as lancaster goods: Facets of job satisfaction and overall job satisfaction. *Journal of Socio-Economics, 37*, 1906–1920.

Sloane, P., & Grazier, S. (2006). *Accident risk, gender, family status and occupational choice in the UK*. IZA Discussion Paper No. 2302.

Smith, A. (1991[1776]). *Recherches sur la nature et les causes de la richesse des Nations*. Paris: Flammarion-GF.

Staiger, D., & Stock, J. H. (1997). Instrumental variables regression with weak instruments. *Econometrica, 65*, 363–376.

Starr, C. (1969). Social benefits vs technological risk. *Science, 19*, 1232–1238.

Stutzer, A., & Frey, B. (2008). Stress that doesn't pay: The commuting paradox. *Scandinavian Journal of Economics, 110*, 339–366.

Thaler, R., & Rosen, S. (1975). The value of saving a life: Evidence from the labour market. In N. Terleckyj (Ed.), *Household production and consumption* (pp. 265–300). New York, NY: Columbia University Press.

Viscusi, W. K. (1978). Wealth effects and earnings premiums for job hazards. *The Review of Economics and Statistics, 60*, 408–419.

Viscusi, W. K. (1979). *Employment hazards: An investigation of market performance*. Cambridge: Harvard University Press.

Viscusi, W. K. (1993). The value of risks to life and health. *Journal of Economic Literature, 31*, 1912–1946.

Viscusi, W. K., & Aldy, J. E. (2003). The value of a statistical life: A critical review of market estimates throughout the world. *Journal of Risk and Uncertainty, 27*, 5–76.

Viscusi, W. K., & O'Connor, C. (1984). Adaptive responses to chemical labeling: Are workers Bayesian decision makers? *American Economic Review, 74*, 942–956.

Wei, X. (1999). Estimating British workers' demand for safety. *Applied Economics, 31*, 1265–1271.

APPENDIX

Table A1. Sample Descriptive Statistics.

Variables	Safe Jobs	Dangerous Jobs
	Mean (SD)	
Satisfaction with the job-related risk (1 to 10)	7.3(2.6)	5.07(2.8)
Overall Job Satisfaction (1 to 10)	6.8(2.01)	6.5(2.1)
Net hourly wage (euros)	7.8(4.8)	6.7(5.1)
Household member's income	0.65	0.59
Male (dummy)	0.40	0.67
Married (dummy)	0.67	0.71
Tenure (years in firm)	8.1(8.8)	8.7(8.5)
Primary education (dummy)	0.19	0.31
Sec education (dummy)	0.41	0.41
Up_se education (dummy)	0.39	0.28
Member of Union (dummy)	0.17	0.29
Managers (dummy)	0.15	0.18
Clerks (dummy)	0.38	0.12
Craft_skilled (dummy)	0.06	0.24
Sales (dummy)	0.18	0.15
Other occupat (dummy)	0.23	0.31
Unemployment experience (dummy)	0.09	0.10
Industrial sector (dummy)	0.10	0.22
Service sector (dummy)	0.75	0.64
Other sector (dummy)	0.15	0.14
Private (dummy)	0.69	0.67
France (dummy)	0.25	0.28
The Netherlands (dummy)	0.29	0.17
Greece (dummy)	0.14	0.33
The UK (dummy)	0.32	0.22
Observations	1,934	1,096

Table A2. Variable List.

Variables	Definition
Satisfaction with Physical risk (1 to 10)	Standardized score of an individual's satisfaction with risk, which is measured on an 11 point scale of 0 = not at all satisfied to 10 = very satisfied
Overall Job Satisfaction	Standardized score of an individual's overall job satisfaction, which is measured on an 11 point scale of 0 = not at all satisfied to 10 = very satisfied
Dangerous jobs	Dummy variable equal to 1 if the individual replies that his/her job is dangerous frequently or sometimes and 0 otherwise
Net hourly wage	Log of CPI-deflated hourly wage in euros
Age (years)	Age of the respondent in years (18–65)
Male	Dummy variable equal to 1 if the respondent is a man
Married	Dummy variable equal to 1 if the respondent is married or cohabits
Tenure (years in firm)	Number of years of the respondent with current employer
Low education	Dummy variable – Less than second stage of secondary level education
Sec education	Dummy variable – Second stage of secondary level education
Up_se education	Dummy variable – Post-secondary level education
Member of Union	Dummy variable equal to 1 if the respondent is in a trade union
Managers	Dummy variable – Managers and Professionals and associate professional
Clerks	Dummy variable – Clerks and service occupations
Craft_skilled	Dummy variable – Craft, related trades workers, plant, machine operators, and assemblers
Sales	Dummy variable – Service and Sales workers
Other occupat	Dummy variable – Armed forces – other occupations
Unemployment experience	Dummy variable equal to 1 if the respondent has weeks of unemployment during the last year and 0 otherwise
Working in private sector	Dummy variable equal to 1 if the respondent works in the private sector
Industrial sector	Dummy with value 1 for workers in the agricultural sector, manufacturing and electricity, mining, and gas and water supply sector
Service sector	Dummy with value 1 for workers in the service sector; wholesale, hotels, transport, financial intermediation, real estate, education, health, and social work
Other sector	Dummy with value 1 for workers in the sector of other activities
Firmsize_24	Dummy variable equal to 1 if the respondent works in a firm with number of employees:1–24 people
Firm size_99	Dummy variable equal to 1 if the respondent works in a firm with number of employees: 25–99 people

Table A2. *(Continued)*

Variables	Definition
Firm size more than 100	Dummy variable equal to 1 if the respondent works in a firm with number of employees: more than 100 people
Countries	Dummy variables for the following countries: France, Great Britain, Greece, and the Netherlands
Household member's income	Dummy variable with value 1 if the respondent has a member in the family who provides the household with extra income and 0 otherwise

INVOLUNTARY UNEMPLOYMENT AND EFFICIENCY-WAGE COMPETITION

Marco Guerrazzi

ABSTRACT

This chapter introduces a model of efficiency-wage competition along the lines put forward by Hahn (1987). Specifically, I analyze a two-firm economy in which employers screen their workforce by means of increasing wage offers competing one another for high-quality employees. The main results are the following. First, using a specification of effort such that the problem of firms is well-behaved, optimal wage offers are strategic complements. Second, the symmetric Nash equilibrium can be locally stable under the assumption that firms adjust their wage offers in the direction of increasing profits by conjecturing that any wage offer above (below) equilibrium will lead competitors to underbid (overbid) such an offer. Finally, the exploration of possible labor market equilibria reveals that effort is counter-cyclical.

Keywords: Efficiency-wages; wage competition; Nash equilibria; effort

JEL classifications: C72; E12; E24; J41

New Analyses of Worker Well-Being
Research in Labor Economics, Volume 38, 193–210

ISSN: 0147-9121/doi:10.1108/S0147-9121(2013)0000038006

INTRODUCTION

Discussing the actual possibility of involuntary unemployment equilibria, Hahn (1987) sketches a model economy in which a finite set of firms is engaged in a wage competition process within an efficiency-wage setting. In that paper, resuming some arguments of Cournot's (1838) output-quantity game, Hahn (1987) describes a situation in which under a persistent excess of labor supply, firms do not cut wages not only because this would lower their profitability, but also because wage cuts would enhance the productivity of their competitors. Building on this strategic framework, Hahn (1987) argues that involuntary unemployment is well defined, compatible with rationality, and not inconsistent with an equilibrium of the model economy.

The main goal of Hahn's (1987) model is to show that firms might find unprofitable to voluntary agree on a generalized wage reduction in order to reduce equilibrium unemployment.[1] However, important aspects of the efficiency-wage competition process in which firms are assumed to be engaged are left unexplored. For instance, although reaction functions are explicitly derived, nothing is said about the strategic relation among the optimal wage offers put forward by competing firms. Moreover, the achievement of a Nash equilibrium in the efficiency-wage competition process is taken for granted without specifying which kind of out-of-equilibrium adjustment might lead to the mutual consistency among firms' wage offers. In addition, on a genuine macroeconomic perspective, there is no discussion about the cyclical behavior of effort.

After its publication, Hahn's (1987) model has been revisited (inter alia) by van de Klundert (1988) and, more recently, by Jellal and Wolff (2002). In the context of segmented labor markets, both contributions derive Stackelberg versions of Hahn's (1987) framework by assuming that firms in the primary sector act as leaders by setting efficiency-wages while employers in the secondary sector act as followers by paying competitive wages fixed at the reservation level. However, to the best of my knowledge, the gaps of the seminal Cournot version reviewed above had never been filled.[2] As a consequence, in the present contribution I aim at accomplishing this task. Specifically, I build a two-firm efficiency-wage model in which each competitor tries to overbid the wage offer of the other employer aiming at maximizing its profits. Consistently with Akerlof (1984) and Hahn (1987), I assume that for each firm the efficiency of the employed labor force is positively correlated to its own wage offer but negatively correlated to the offer put forward by the other firm.

Within this framework, I discuss the shape of the strategic relation among optimal wage offers and their link with the corresponding iso-profit curves. Thereafter, considering the most recurrent adjustment mechanisms exploited in similar game-theoretic contexts (e.g., Kopel, 1996; Varian, 1992), I consider the way in which the wage strategy prevailing in the symmetric Nash equilibrium can actually be achieved. Furthermore, taking into account possible labor market equilibria, I discuss effort cyclicality.

The main results of this theoretical exploration are the following. First, using a specification of effort such that the problem of the representative firm is well-behaved in the sense that it does not deliver corner solutions, optimal wage offers are strategic complements, i.e., whenever the competitor increases (decreases) its wage offer, the optimal response for each firm is to raise (decrease) its wage offer as well. Second, the symmetric Nash equilibrium exists but is unstable under the traditional cobweb adjustment. In other words, when the game is played by means of alternate wage offers there is no way to achieve the Nash equilibrium. Instead, I show that such an allocation can be locally stable under the assumption that each firm continuously adjusts its optimal wage offer in the direction of increasing profits by conjecturing that any wage offer above (below) equilibrium will lead the competitor to underbid (overbid) such an offer. Moreover, the analysis of possible labor market equilibria reveals that effort is counter-cyclical, i.e., consistently with efficiency-wage models in which unemployment acts as a worker discipline device (e.g., Guerrazzi, 2008; Uhlig & Xu, 1996), equilibria with higher (lower) unemployment are characterized by higher (lower) effort levels.

This chapter is arranged as follows. The second section describes the model. The third section derives the symmetric Nash equilibrium. The fourth section investigates its local dynamics. The fifth section discusses possible labor market outcomes and the cyclicality of effort. Finally, the sixth section concludes.

THE MODEL

The model economy is populated by two identical firms indexed by $i = 1, 2$ and a mass L^S of identical workers that inelastically supply their labor services. As in Solow (1979), each firm seeks to maximize its profit (π_i) by taking into account that it can simultaneously set employment (L_i) and the real wage (w_i). Furthermore, as in Akerlof (1984) and Hahn (1987), the efficiency of employed labor force (e_i) is assumed to positively depend on the wage offer carried out by the firm that actually provides the job but negatively correlated to the wage offer put forward by the other firm. Therefore, the problem of each firm is given by

$$\max_{L_i,w_i} \pi_i = F_i(e_i(w_i, w_j)L) - w_i L_i \qquad i,j = 1,2 \tag{1}$$

where $F_i(\cdot)$ is the production function of firm i while $\partial e_i(\cdot)/\partial w_i > 0$ and $\partial e_i(\cdot)/\partial w_j < 0$.

The first-order conditions (FOCs) for the problem in Eq. (1) are the following:

$$L_i : F_i'(e_i(w_i, w_j)L_i)e_i(w_i, w_j) = w_i \qquad i,j = 1,2 \tag{2}$$

$$w_i : F_i'\ (e_i(w_i, w_j)L_i)\frac{\partial e_i(w_i, w_j)}{\partial w_i} = 1 \qquad i,j = 1,2 \tag{3}$$

Exploiting the FOCs in Eqs. (2) and (3), the Solow (1979) condition can be conveyed as

$$\frac{(\partial e_i(w_i, w_j)/\partial w_i)w_i}{e_i\left(w_i, w_j\right)} = 1 \qquad i,j = 1,2 \tag{4}$$

The expression in Eq. (4) states that in order to maximize profits, each firm has to set a real wage such that the effort-wage elasticity is equal to 1 no matter the shape of the production function.[3] From a mathematical perspective, the Solow (1979) condition is both necessary and sufficient if and only if – in addition to Eq. (4) – even second-order conditions are met and this happens when the effort function is concave; indeed, under effort convexity profit maximization would lead competing firms to settle in a corner solution by pushing employment toward the full employment allocation by questioning the possibility of involuntary unemployment. In this case, provided that the individual wage offers imply a positive level of effort, firms – just like in a competitive environment – will always prefer lower wages.[4] Taking into account those arguments, in the remainder of the chapter I will exploit a concave effort function by considering employment adjustments that occur along the (decreasing) labor demand schedules of each firm.

From a game-theoretical point of view, the intriguing feature of the framework outlined in Eqs. (1)–(4) is that the Solow (197) condition does depend not only on the wage offer of the individual firm but also on the wage offer put forward by its competitor. As a consequence, similarly to the situation described by Cournot (1838) in the context of output-quantity competition, the two firms are in a situation of strategic interaction regarding wages. Specifically, the optimal wage offer of firm 1 depends on the offer put forward by firm 2 and vice versa.

In order to derive explicit results, it is obviously necessary to define production and effort functions. First, along the lines put forward by Akerlof (1982) and, more recently, by Alexopoulos (2004), for each firm, the production function is assumed to be the following:

$$F_i(e_i(w_i, w_j)L_i) = (e_i(w_i, w_j)L_i)^{\alpha} \qquad 0<\alpha<1 \qquad i,j=1,2 \tag{5}$$

where α measures the curvature of the (convex) production possibility set.

Furthermore, for each firm, the effort function is assumed to be given by

$$e_i(w_i, w_j) = (\kappa + w_i - w_j)^{\beta} \qquad \kappa>0 \qquad 0<\beta<1, \qquad i,j=1,2 \tag{6}$$

where κ conveys productivity shocks while β is the curvature of the effort function.[5]

The expression in Eq. (6) suggests that the efficiency of the employed labor force is an exponential concave function that encloses an erratic positive term affecting the production possibilities of firms. Moreover, such a function increases (decreases) as the wage differential between the two firms becomes wider (tighter). Anecdotal evidence and empirical tests of efficiency-wage theories are consistent with this formulation (e.g., Huang, Hallam, Orazem, & Paterno, 1998; Krueger & Summers, 1988; Raff & Summers, 1987). In addition, on a theoretical ground, the effort function in Eq. (6) can be interpreted as the upshot of a utility maximization process in which workers have fairness concerns about relative wages as well as quadratic costs associated to effort provision.[6] A pictorial representation of Eq. (6) is given in Fig. 1.

It is worth noting that under concavity the existence of an interior solution that fulfils the Solow (1979) condition implies that the vertical intercept of Eq. (6) has to be negative. As a consequence, for each firm, the wage offer of its competitor cannot be lower than κ.

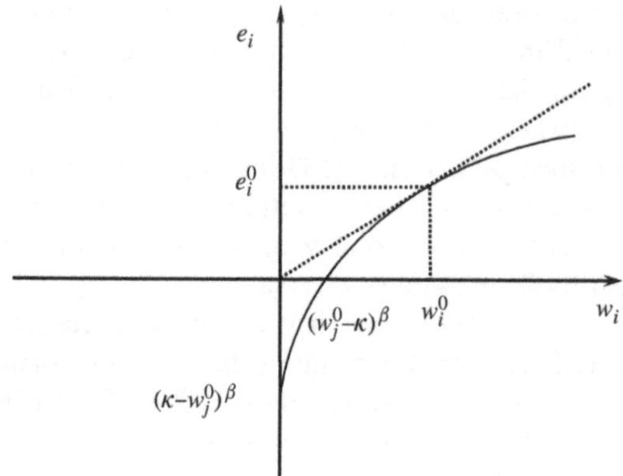

Fig. 1. Effort Function.

NASH EQUILIBRIUM

Combining Eqs. (4) and (6) it becomes possible to derive the reaction functions (f_i) of the two firms; indeed, straightforward algebra leads to following linear expression:

$$w_i = \frac{1}{1-\beta}w_j - \frac{\kappa}{1-\beta} \qquad i,j=1,2 \tag{7}$$

The positive slope of the function in Eq. (7) shows that the optimal wage offers of the two firms are strategic complements, i.e., whenever the competitor increases (decreases) its wage offer, the optimal response for each firm is to rise (decrease) its wage offer as well. Technically speaking, the rationale for such a behavior is straightforward. Everything else being equal, assuming the concavity of Eq. (6), an increase (decrease) of the wage offer carried out by the competitor reduces (increases) workers' effort provision by leading the U-shaped wage-effort ratio to shift right (left). As a consequence, in order to restore efficiency, each firm has to increase (decrease) its offer as well.

The Nash equilibrium is found where the two reaction functions intersect each other. Therefore, the symmetric optimal wage strategy is given by

$$w_i^* = \frac{\kappa}{\beta} \qquad i,j=1,2 \tag{8}$$

Plugging the result in Eq. (8) into Eq. (6) shows that in equilibrium workers are paid more than their individual efficiency. From a formal point of view, this result comes from the fact that when the effort function is concave, κ^{β} is lower than κ/β for all the positive values of κ. An illustration of the Nash equilibrium is given in Fig. 2.

The diagram in Fig. 2 shows the reaction functions of the two firms together with equilibrium iso-profit curves, i.e., the iso-profit curves associated with the wage strategy in Eq. (8). In general, for each firm, those curves are non-linear functions such as

$$w_j = \kappa + w_i - \left(\left(\frac{\overline{\pi}_i}{\Phi} \right)^{(1-\alpha/\alpha)} w_i \right)^{1/\beta} \qquad i,j = 1,2 \tag{9}$$

where $\Phi \equiv (1-\alpha)\alpha^{\alpha/1-\alpha}$ while $\overline{\pi}_i$ is a constant level of profit.

The set of non-linear functions conveyed by Eq. (9) is represented by reverse-U-shaped curves with a vertical intercept equal to κ which reach their maximum in the point when they intersect the relevant reaction function. In other words, consistently with the textbook definition of a Nash equilibrium (e.g., Varian, 1992), when firm 2 decides to pay κ/β it is in the best interest of firm 1 to pay κ/β as well and vice versa, so that none of the two players will have incentives to deviate from such a wage strategy. Moreover, for each firm, higher (lower) iso-profit curves are associated with lower (higher) levels of profit. Furthermore, it is worth noting that in Fig. 2 the equilibrium iso-profit curves of the two firms intersect each

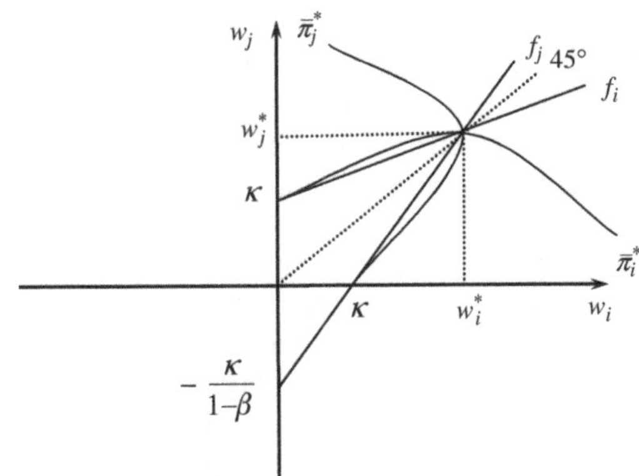

Fig. 2. Nash Equilibrium.

other. As in Cournot's (1838) output-quantity competition, this geometrical feature conveys the non-cooperative feature of the Nash wage equilibrium derived in this strategic context.

LOCAL DYNAMICS

Before discussing possible labor market outcomes, it is necessary to say something about the way in which the wage strategy in Eq. (8) can actually be reached; indeed, if starting from a different allocation there was no way to achieve it, then such a symmetric wage distribution, together with its labor market implications, would lose a great deal of its practical significance.

Assuming adjustments to lagged wage signals, i.e., adjustments grounded on alternate wage offers, the Nash equilibrium is stable if and only if firm 1's reaction function is steeper than firm 2's reaction function (e.g., Kopel, 1996). Taking the result in Eq. (7) into account, this happens whenever

$$\frac{1}{(1-\beta)^2} < 1 \tag{10}$$

The inequality in Eq. (10) could be hypothetically verified by assuming a strong degree of convexity of the effort function in Eq. (6). This stability requirement, taking into account the slope of Eq. (7), would also lead to overturn the result on complementarity derived in the previous section by conveying the substitutability of optimal wage offers. However, as stated in the second section, under effort convexity the Solow condition in Eq. (4) is totally inconsistent with firms' maximum profit problem so Eq. (8) would fail to identify the optimal response for each competitor's wage offer; indeed, exploiting a convex effort function, the reaction function in Eq. (8) would actually detect the *worse* wage reply, i.e., the wage offer that leads to minimum profits.

Considering those arguments, it becomes possible to state that as far as effort concavity is concerned – together with its well-behaved solutions – the inequality in Eq. (10) cannot be verified so that under the traditional cobweb adjustment the symmetric Nash equilibrium is unstable. Specifically, unless the starting wage strategy coincides with the one in Eq. (8), optimal wage offers explode or implode depending on whether their initial values are above or below κ/β.

The badly behaved dynamic patterns conveyed by effort concavity raise the issue of finding another possible mechanism able to describe how the Nash equilibrium might be actually reached. In this regard, a different type of micro-founded (or behavioral) adjustment can be derived by assuming that each firm adjusts its wage offer in the direction of increasing profits (e.g., Varian, 1992). In this case, adjustments are simultaneous and the out-of-equilibrium dynamics of real wages is described by

$$\dot{w}_i = \gamma\left(\frac{\partial \pi_i(w_i, \hat{w}_j(w_i))}{\partial w_i}\right) \qquad \gamma > 0 \qquad i,j = 1,2 \tag{11}$$

where $\hat{w}_j(w_i)$ is the conjecture of firm i about the wage behavior of firm j while γ is a constant that conveys the speed of out-of-equilibrium adjustments.

Considering the properties of mutual consistency of a Nash equilibrium stressed above, I assume that each firm conjectures the wage behavior of its competitor by means of the following conjectural or "learning" rule:

$$\hat{w}_j(w_i) = \frac{\kappa}{\beta} + \lambda_i\left(w_i - \frac{\kappa}{\beta}\right) \qquad i,j = 1,2 \tag{12}$$

where λ_i is a constant that conveys the so-called conjectural variation, i.e., the "expected" variation of the wage offer put forward by firm j when firm i marginally changes its own proposal.

For each firm, Eq. (12) can be interpreted as a Stackelberg leadership rule that approximates competitor's reaction function; indeed, the nearer λ_i to the shape of the optimal response function, the closer Eq. (12) to Eq. (7). Formally speaking:

$$\lim_{\lambda_i \to (1/1-\beta)} \hat{w}_j(w_i) = -\frac{\kappa}{1-\beta} + \frac{1}{1-\beta} w_i \qquad i,j = 1,2 \tag{13}$$

In addition to the asymptotic result in Eq. (13), the main implications of Eq. (12) can be summarized as follows. First, consistent with the static case developed by Hahn (1987) and warmly supported by a number of game theorists who question the rationality of adjustments occurring outside Nash equilibria (e.g., Bacharach, 1976), the suggested learning rule implies that when firm i decides to bid the equilibrium wage offer it conjectures that its competitor will do the same by warding off any out-of-equilibrium dynamics and confirming κ/β as the stable wage strategy.[7] However, the range of possibility covered by Eq. (12) is wider; indeed, depending on the sign and the magnitude of λ_i, Eq. (12) also defines the conjectures of firm i about the proposal of firm j outside the Nash equilibrium. Specifically, if λ_i is equal to zero, then each firm neglects the strategic interaction between its own behavior and the behavior of its competitor. In other words, in this case, each firm thinks that for any given wage offer the competitor will leave its proposal unaltered by playing the equilibrium wage strategy. Furthermore, when λ_i is positive (negative), then firm i conjectures that any wage offer above equilibrium will lead firm j to overbid (underbid) such an offer.

Taking into consideration Eq. (12), the Jacobian matrix (J) of the dynamic system in Eq. (11) evaluated in Eq. (8) is given by

$$J \equiv \begin{bmatrix} \Omega(\beta - 1 + \lambda_1) & \Omega \\ \Omega(\beta - 1 + \lambda_2) & \Omega \end{bmatrix} \tag{14}$$

where $\Omega \equiv \gamma\alpha^{(1/1-\alpha)}\beta^2(\beta\kappa^{\beta-1})^{(\alpha/1-\alpha)-1}\kappa^{\beta-3} > 0$.

A sufficient requirement for the local stability of the dynamic system in Eq. (11) is the negativity (positivity) of the trace (determinant) of J. Straightforward calculations suggest that the trace (Tr(J)) and the determinant (Det(J)) are equal to

$$\mathrm{Tr}(J) = \Omega(\beta + \lambda_1) \tag{15}$$

$$\mathrm{Det}(J) = \Omega(\lambda_1 - \lambda_2) \tag{16}$$

The results in Eqs. (15) and (16) show that local stability requires λ_1 (λ_2) to be negative and higher than β (λ_1) in modulus.[8] Obviously, this means that the symmetric Nash equilibrium can be locally stable when each firm adjusts its wage offers in the direction of increasing profits by conjecturing that any wage offer above (below) equilibrium will lead its competitor to underbid (overbid) such an offer.[9]

From an economic point of view, those dynamic findings imply that convergence toward the symmetric wage strategy in Eq. (8) requires that each firm myopically perceives a certain degree of substitution among the optimal wage offers put forward by its competitor. In this strategic framework, such a misperception could be achieved by assuming that κ is subject to idiosyncratic shocks that – for each firm – systematically fades the correct perception of actual competitor's reaction function.[10] Along this way, avoiding the issue of (unrealistic) corner solutions together with inconsistent reactions functions, the model economy recovers the stability requirement of the game of alternate wage offers.

LABOR MARKET OUTCOMES

Plugging Eq. (8) into Eq. (6) and then substituting in Eq. (2) allows to derive the equilibrium aggregate demand for labor. Specifically, in the symmetric Nash equilibrium the quantity of labor services demanded by the two competing firms amount to

$$L^D = n\beta^{1/1-\alpha}(\kappa)^{-\left(1-\alpha\beta/1-\alpha\right)} \tag{17}$$

where $n = 2$.

The result in Eq. (17) allows to characterize labor market tightness in a precise manner. In details:

- if $L^D < L^S$, then the model economy experiences an involuntary unemployment rate equal to $(L^S - L^D)/L^S$ as in the seminal Hahn's (1987) contribution;
- if $L^D = L^S$, then there prevails full employment which would coincides with the Nash wage equilibrium; and
- if $L^D > L^S$, then firms are rationed in the labor market so that actual employment is equal to L^S and each firm would have $1/n(L^D - L^S)$ vacant positions. However, as suggested by Weiss (1991, p. 21), such an allocation cannot be a proper equilibrium; indeed, the shortage of labor would lead firms to increase their wage offers until L^D and L^S become equal.[11] In such a situation, the dynamic adjustments described in the previous section would fail to hold because firms would have to compete not only for the quality of workers but also for their (scant) services. As a consequence, in addition to Eq. (11), the analysis of this scarcity scenario would require the definition of the out-of-equilibrium dynamics for the employment level in the two firms.[12]

Since the chapter focuses on the properties of the wage strategy in Eq. (8), I will discuss the cyclicality of effort under the first two points. Within those scenarios, taking into account movements in κ, the result in Eq. (17) can be exploited to discuss how equilibrium employment reacts to effort movements. Specifically, plain differencing suggests that effort is counter-cyclical, i.e., equilibria with higher (lower) unemployment are characterized by higher (lower) effort levels. Such an effort pattern is perfectly consistent with the idea underlying efficiency-wage models in which involuntary unemployment acts as a worker discipline device. In this class of models popularized by Shapiro and Stiglitz (1984), involuntary unemployment is the threat that prevents workers from shirking. As a consequence, an increase (decrease) in unemployment should lead workers with jobs to work harder (slowly), making them more (less) efficient (e.g., Guerrazzi, 2008; Uhlig & Xu, 1996).

Although in the efficiency-wage competition model developed in the second section the payment of an efficiency-wage is not related to the shirking motivation, effort is counter-cyclical as well. However, there is an important difference between this model and the efficiency-wage models with shirking workers; indeed, in those models the counter-cyclicality of effort emerges as the result of a Marxian (or Ricardian) endogeneity of labor supply (e.g., Bowles, 1985; Drago, 1989–1990). By contrast, in the model economy developed in the second section such a counter-cyclicality is the upshot of a wage competition process engaged by firms in the attempt to hire workers of higher quality in a technology scenario characterized by decreasing returns with respect to labor.

CONCLUDING REMARKS

This chapter provides a model of efficiency-wage competition along the lines put forward by Hahn (1987). Specifically, I build a two-firm efficiency-wage model in which workers' effort attainable by the representative firm is an increasing function of its own wage offer but declining in the offer put forward by its competitor. As a consequence, employers screen their workforce by means of increasing wage offers competing one another for high-quality employees.

The main results achieved in this theoretical analysis can be summarized as follows. First, using a specification of effort such that the maximum profit problem of the representative firm is well-behaved in the sense that it does not deliver corner solutions, optimal wage offers are strategic complements, i.e., whenever the competitor increases (decreases) its wage offer, the optimal response for each firm is to rise (decrease) its wage offer as well. Second, the symmetric Nash equilibrium can be locally stable under the assumption that each firm adjusts its optimal wage offer in the direction of increasing profits by conjecturing that any wage offer above (below) equilibrium will lead the competitor to underbid (overbid) such an offer. Finally, the exploration of possible labor market equilibria reveals that effort is counter-cyclical, i.e., equilibria with higher (lower) unemployment are characterized by higher (lower) effort levels.

NOTES

1. By contrast, macroeconomic interventions such as expansionary monetary policies could be more effective in this direction.

2. A more general Stackelberg version of Hahn's (1987) model in which wages are endogenously determined is derived in Appendix A.

3. An equivalent reading of the Solow (1979) condition provides that firms set the wage–employment pair in order to minimize the cost of labor in terms of efficiency, i.e., in order to minimize the wage-effort ratio (e.g., Lindbeck & Snower, 1987).

4. Formally speaking, when the effort function is convex, the Solow (1979) selects an allocation in which profits are at their minimum level; indeed, under effort convexity, the Hessian matrix of the maximum problem in Eq. (1) evaluated in the wage pair conveyed by Eq. (4) is positive definite. In the context of the optimal-growth model, the same issue is addressed by Guerrazzi (2012).

5. Akerlof (1984) and Hahn (1987) consider a similar effort function that also positively depends on unemployment. In a subsequent part of the paper, I will show that this disciplining effect of unemployment endogenously emerges from the simplest formulation in Eq. (6).

6. See Appendix B.

7. The dynamic system in Eq. (11) has the nice feature to verify Nash stationarity, i.e., its steady-state coincides with the Nash equilibrium of the game at hand (e.g., Sandholm, 2005).

8. Under reasonable calibrations, e.g., $\alpha = 2/3$, $\beta = 1/2$, $\kappa = \gamma = 1$, $\lambda_1 = -0.7$, and $\lambda_2 = -0.8$, J displays two complex-conjugate eigenvalues with negative real part. In this case, convergence toward the Nash equilibrium occurs though convergent oscillations.

9. It is worth noting that without any conjectural variations, i.e., $\lambda_i = 0$, the dynamic system would display a saddle-note bifurcation without any guide for dynamics. Moreover, when each firm conjectures that any wage offer above (below) equilibrium will lead each competitor to overbid (underbid) such an offer, i.e., $\lambda_i > 0$, the Nash equilibrium is locally unstable.

10. In the context of exchange rate dynamics, Gourinchas and Torell (2001) argue that idiosyncratic shocks might lead to systematic biases in individual forecasts.

11. It is worth noting that in this case the value of the marginal productivity of labor is higher than the level satisfying the Solow (1979) condition. Specifically, when firms are rationed in the labor market the effort-wage elasticity is lower than one. The same possibility is contemplated in dynamic efficiency-wage models developed, inter alia, by Faria (2000) and Guerrazzi (2008).

12. More technically, when the Nash equilibrium depicts a situation in which the two firms are rationed in the labor market it becomes necessary to study a 4×4 dynamic system in w_1, w_2, L_1, and L_2 whose resting point is the full employment allocation without any room for involuntary unemployment.

13. Identical firms can play those different roles if, for instance, the labor market is segmented and there are relevant mobility costs that workers have to bear in order to switch from one segment to another.

14. When the wage offer of firm 1 is lower than the one of firm 2, firm 1's profits are very low. Under those circumstances, the iso-profit curves of firm 1 become convex.

15. From a psychological point of view, the fair wage theory developed by Adams (1963) is an economic implementation of the theory of cognitive dissonance put forward by Festinger (1957).

REFERENCES

Adams, J. S. (1963). Wage inequities, productivity and work quality. *Industrial Relations: A Journal of Economy and Society*, *3*(1), 9–16.

Akerlof, G. A. (1982). Labor contracts as partial gift exchange. *Quarterly Journal of Economics*, *79*(4), 543–569.

Akerlof, G. A. (1984). Gift exchange and efficiency-wage theory: Four views. *American Economic Review*, 74(2), 79–83.

Alexopoulos, M. (2004). Unemployment and the business cycle. *Journal of Monetary Economics*, *51*(2), 277–298.

Bacharach, M. (1976). *Economics and the theory of games*. London: Macmillan.

Bowles, S. (1985). The production process in a competitive economy: Walrasian, Neo-Hobbesian, and Marxian models. *American Economic Review*, *75*(1), 16–36.

Cournot, A. (1838). *Recherces sur les Principes Mathematiques de la Theorie de la Richesse*. Paris: L. Hachette.

Drago, R. (1989–1990). A simple Keynesian model of efficiency wages. *Journal of Post Keynesian Economics*, *12*(2), 171–182.

Faria, J. R. (2000). Supervision and effort in an intertemporal efficiency wage model: The role of the solow condition. *Economics Letters*, *67*(1), 93–98.

Faria, J. R. (2005). Profitability, investment, and efficiency wages. *Journal of Applied Mathematics and Decision Sciences*, *2005*(4), 201–211.

Festinger, L. (1957). *A theory of cognitive dissonance*. Stanford, CA: Stanford University Press.

Gourinchas, P. O., & Torell, A.(2001). *Exchange rate dynamics, learning and misperception*. NBER Working Paper, No. 9391.

Guerrazzi, M. (2008). A dynamic efficiency-wage model with continuous effort and externalities. *Economic Issues*, *13*(2), 37–58.

Guerrazzi, M. (2012). The animal spirits hypothesis and the Benhabib-farmer condition for indeterminacy. *Economic Modelling*, *29*(4), 1489–1497.

Hahn, F. H. (1987). On involuntary unemployment. *Economic Journal*, Supplement: Conference Papers, pp. 1–16.

Huang, T.-L., Hallam, A., Orazem, P. F., & Paterno, E. M. (1998). Empirical tests of efficiency wage models. *Economica*, *65*(257), 125–143.

Jellal, M., & Wolff, F.-C. (2002). Dual labor market and strategic efficiency wage. *International Economic Journal*, *17*(3), 99–112.

Kahneman, D., Knetsch, J. L., & Thaler, R. H. (1986a). Fairness as a constraint on profit seeking: Entitlements in the market. *American Economic Review*, *76*(4), 728–741.

Kahneman, D., Knetsch, J. L., & Thaler, R. H. (1986b). Fairness and the assumption of economics. *Journal of Business*, *59*(4), S285–S300.

Kopel, M. (1996). Simple and complex adjustment dynamics in cournot duopoly models. *Chaos, Solitons & Fractals*, *7*(12), 2031–2048.

Krueger, A. B., & Summers, L. H. (1988). Efficiency wages and the inter-industry wage structure. *Econometrica*, *56*(2), 259–293.

Lindbeck, A., & Snower, D. J. (1987). Efficiency-wages versus insiders and outsiders. *European Economic Review*, *31*(1–2), 407–416.

Raff, D. M. G., & Summers, L. H. (1987). Did Henry Ford pay efficiency wages. *Journal of Labor Economics*, *5*(4), S57–S86.

Sandholm, W. H. (2005). Excess payoff dynamics and other well-behaved evolutionary dynamics. *Journal of Economic Theory*, *124*(2), 149–170.

Shapiro, C., & Stiglitz, J. (1984). Equilibrium unemployment as a worker discipline device. *American Economic Review*, *74*(3), 433–444.

Solow, R. M. (1979). Another possible source for wage stickiness. *Journal of Macroeconomics*, *1*(1), 79–82.

Uhlig H., & Xu, Y. (1996). *Effort and the cycle: Cyclical implications of efficiency wages.* Tilburg University Discussion Paper No. 49.

van de Klundert T. (1988). *Wage-differential and employment in a two-sector model with a dual labour market.* Research Memorandum, Department of Economics, Tilburg University.

Varian, H. R. (1992). *Microeconomic analysis* (3rd ed.). New York, NY: W.W. Norton.

Weiss, A. (1991). *Models of unemployment, layoffs, and wage dispersion.* Oxford: Clarendon Press.

APPENDIX A: STACKELBERG EQUILIBRIA

In this section I derive the Stackelberg equilibrium of the model economy described in the second section. This exercise is relegated in this appendix because the effort function in Eq. (6) delivers meaningful equilibria of this kind if and only if its curvature is quite strong, i.e., whenever β is close to zero.

Without loss of generality, I assume that firm 1 is the leader while firm 2 is the follower.[13] In this case, firm 1 will try to maximize its profits by taking into account that firm 2 will adhere to its own reaction function. Therefore, firm 1's problem becomes

$$\max_{L_1, w_1} \ \pi_1 = F_1(e_1(w_1, w_2)L_1) - w_1 L_1 \tag{A.1}$$

s.to

$$w_2 = -\frac{1}{1-\beta}\kappa + \frac{1}{1-\beta}w_1 \tag{A.2}$$

Taking into account Eq. (6), the solution of the problem in Eqs. (A.1) and (A.2) provides the following wage distribution:

$$w_1^S = \frac{\kappa}{\beta}\left(1 + \frac{1}{1-\beta}\right) \tag{A.3}$$

$$w_2^S = \frac{\kappa}{\beta}\left(1 + \frac{1}{(1-\beta)^2}\right) \tag{A.4}$$

The results in Eqs. (A.3) and (A.4) show that in the Stackelberg equilibrium firm 2 pays more than firm 1. As a consequence, firm 2 will be more efficient and will achieve higher profits; indeed, consistently with textbook results derived in the context of output competition (e.g., Varian, 1992), under complementarity among optimal wage offers, leadership is never preferred. Furthermore, non-uniform wage and profit distributions reveal that Stackelberg equilibria can provide a theoretical underpinning for segmented (or dual) labor markets (e.g., Jellal & Wolff, 2002; van de Klundert, 1988). An illustration is given in Fig. A.1.

The diagram in Fig. A.1 recalls that the Stackelberg equilibrium is found where the highest iso-profit curve of firm 1 is tangent with reaction function of firm 2.[14] Moreover, it is worth noting that w_1^S does not satisfy the Solow (1979) condition; indeed, in the Stackelberg equilibrium the leader

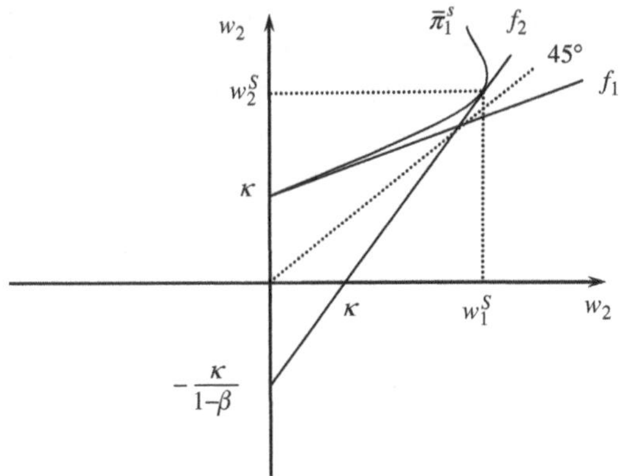

Fig. A.1. Stackelberg Equilibrium.

effort-wage elasticity is higher than 1. This possibility is contemplated by Faria (2005) who develops an inter-temporal model with investment and efficiency-wages.

APPENDIX B: EFFORT MICRO-FOUNDATION

In this section I sketch a possible micro-foundation for the effort function in Eq. (6). Straightforward integration suggests that the problem of the representative worker called in to provide effort for firm i should be given by

$$\max_{e_i} \quad U=(\kappa+w_i-w_j)^\beta e_i-\frac{1}{2}e_i^2+\varphi \qquad i,j=1,2 \tag{B.1}$$

where φ is a constant that without loss of generality can be normalized to zero.

On worker's side, the expression in Eq. (B.1) can be interpreted as follows. First, κ conveys the intrinsic motivation of the worker, i.e., the measure of the marginal utility of providing effort which does not depend on wages. This parameter can well follow a stochastic process by mirroring the behavior of erratic productivity shocks. Moreover, along the arguments put forward by Adams (1963) and, more recently, by Kahneman, Knetsch, and Thaler (1986a, 1986b), the wage differential (w_i-w_j) can be thought as the (simplest) functional form catchwing worker's perception of being treated fairly by job offering firms.[15] As a consequence, when a firm decides to pay less than the other such a behavior will be perceived as unfair so that the representative worker will adjust effort provision downward until a mutual fair treatment is psychologically restored. Obviously, a positive wage premium will lead the worker to do the opposite.

PLAYING HARD TO GET: THEORY AND EVIDENCE ON LAYOFFS, RECALLS, AND UNEMPLOYMENT

Núria Rodríguez-Planas

ABSTRACT

This paper is the first to present empirical evidence consistent with models of signaling through unemployment and to uncover a new stylized fact using the 1988–2006 Displaced Worker Supplement (DWS) of the Current Population Survey (CPS), namely that, among white-collar workers, post-displacement earnings fall less rapidly with unemployment spells for layoffs than for plant closings. Because high-productivity workers are more likely to be recalled than low-productivity ones, they may choose to signal their productivity though unemployment, in which case the duration of unemployment may be positively related to post-displacement wages. Identification is done using workers whose plant closed as they cannot be recalled, and no incentives to signal arise.

Keywords: Asymmetric information; laid-off workers; recalls; unemployment; wages

JEL Classifications: J60; J30

New Analyses of Worker Well-Being
Research in Labor Economics, Volume 38, 211–258

ISSN: 0147-9121/doi:10.1108/S0147-9121(2013)0000038007

INTRODUCTION

Since the seminal work by Akerlof (1970), many economists have analyzed how informational asymmetries affect the behavior of economic agents. This is especially true in regard to the labor market, where the effect of imperfect information about workers' productivity on labor market outcomes has long been recognized.[1] In spite of this extensive theoretical interest, empirical evidence on the extent of the problem in the labor market has, until recently, been relatively sparse.[2] In these papers, worker quality is imperfectly observed, and so potential employers must contend with the possibility of hiring a "lemon." When faced with an adverse shock, employers prefer dismissing low productivity workers. As a result, in equilibrium, employed workers are more productive than the unemployed, or certain types of displaced workers are more productive than other types. If employers believe that the least productive workers are concentrated in the pool of unemployed workers, or certain types of unemployed workers, they may use the employment history of the worker as a sorting criterion.

Although these papers provide empirical evidence that potential employers are aware of the existence of adverse selection in the labor market, they do not analyze whether workers, who are likely to have private information on their productivity, take costly actions to signal to prospective employers' favorable information. Rodríguez-Planas (2009) develops a theoretical model that suggests that at least some aspect*s* of the search decisions of workers on temporary layoff may have a signaling component.[3] The main idea behind Rodríguez-Planas' paper is that high-productivity laid-off workers are more likely to be recalled by their former employer than low-productivity laid-off workers. Thus, they may choose to remain unemployed rather than to accept a low-wage job. If so, unemployment can serve as a signal of productivity.[4]

The contribution of the current paper is to develop an empirical implication of this model, namely that post-displacement earnings do not fall as rapidly with unemployment-spell length for laid-off workers compared to workers displaced by plant closing as they cannot be recalled.[5] Using 1988–2006 Displaced Workers Supplements to the Current Population Survey (CPS), this paper offers quantitative empirical evidence consistent with signaling through unemployment among white-collar workers. Most importantly, it uncovers a new empirical fact about white-collar laid-off workers in the United States.

The identification strategy that we follow is to use workers displaced through plant closings to control for all factors affecting earnings and the duration of unemployment not associated with having a positive probability of recall. The assumption is that workers displaced through plant closings cannot be recalled, which, in the Rodríguez-Planas' model implies that they will not have any incentives to signal through unemployment. Therefore, the empirical hypothesis is that post-displacement earnings fall *less* rapidly with unemployment spells for layoffs than for plant closings. While this identification strategy is similar to that of Gibbons and Katz (1991), it is important to note that this paper does *not* rely on Gibbons and Katz's lemon effect of layoffs per se; because even *within* each of the layoff and plant closing samples, there is heterogeneity in worker's ability unobservable to potential employers. This implies that the relevant comparative statics are the difference in the *slope* of post-displacement wage against unemployment duration between layoffs and plant closings (not the difference in level). Thus, the results from this paper cannot be interpreted as evidence either for or against the presence of the type of asymmetric information studied in Gibbons and Katz (1991).[6]

The empirical findings are consistent with the signaling model of unemployment for white-collar workers. We find that white-collar workers' post-displacement earnings do not fall as rapidly with unemployment-spell length for laid-off workers compared to workers displaced by plant closings. No such differential effect between layoffs and plant closings is found among blue-collar workers. As explained below, the lack of effects for the blue-collar sub-sample is also consistent with the model, because the information content of a recall is small when employers lack the ability to act on this information.[7] Additional evidence that supports the model is provided. In support of the signaling explanation, we demonstrate that the estimates from the white-collar sub-sample are surprisingly robust to inclusion of region, industry, occupation dummies, and pre-displacement earnings. This suggests that the patterns encountered are not simply due to differences in the sector of the economy in which workers were employed. Finally, the paper explores whether the empirical findings are also compatible with explanations other than signaling.

The next two sections discuss the literature review and present background information on the relevance of recalls in the labor market. The fourth section four presents a simple version of the model demonstrating that the intuition holds in equilibrium and develops the empirical implication of the model. The fifth section five describes the data, and reports the results. The sixth section six concludes.

LITERATURE REVIEW

While there is a vast literature on signaling through education, empirical evidence on signaling through a costly action other than education is, to the best of my knowledge, scarce. Weiss (1995) provides a thorough review of early studies on signaling through education. More recently, several authors have developed models of symmetric employer learning where they assume that employers statistically discriminate among prospective workers on the basis of a signal (usually education) which is related to the (unobserved) ability of a worker. Using the NLSY, Farber and Gibbons (1996), and Altonji and Pierret (1997, 2001) test the symmetric employer learning model and find evidence supportive of learning being symmetric across employers. Bauer and Haisken-DeNew (2001) and Galindo-Rueda (2002) obtain similar findings for white-collar workers in Germany and workers in the United Kimgdom, respectively. Lange (2007) provides an estimate for the speed of employer learning, and Arcidiacono, Bayer, and Hizmo (2010) provide evidence that education (specifically, attending college) plays a much more direct role in revealing (as opposed to signaling) ability in the college labor market.

Several authors have made an attempt to distinguish between symmetric and asymmetric employer learning by introducing endogenous mobility in their models.[8] The first author do to this, Schönberg (2007) finds evidence supportive of asymmetric employer learning for college graduates, but not for high school graduates. Similarly, Zhang (2007) also finds evidence supportive of adverse selection in the labor market by examining the impact of education on wages for individuals with different job turnover patterns using a three-period model. Using a model where firms compete for workers through bidding wars, Pinkston (2009) finds evidence of both public learning and asymmetric information in the labor market. In contrast with the paper at hand, all of these papers exploit the empirical methodology first developed by Altonji and Pierret, that is, they use education as the identifying variable.[9] In addition, they focus their analysis on testing adverse selection in the labor market as opposed to workers' signaling (through an action other than education.)

Finally, an additional related strand of the literature is the one first developed by Waldman (1984) and based on the idea that promotions serve as a signal of worker ability. Although this line of research has received considerable theoretical attention (Bernhardt, 1995; Chang & Wang, 1996; Golan, 2005; Milgrom & Oster, 1987; Ricart i Costa, 1988; Owan, 2004; Waldman, 1990; Zabojnik & Bernhardt, 2001), it is only recently that the idea has been tested empirically. To the best of my knowledge, DeVaro and Waldman (2012) were the first ones to empirically test the promotion-as-signal hypothesis and to find support for their theory. They derive two predictions consistent with their model. First, workers with high levels of education are promoted faster. Second, the wage increase associated with a promotion decreases with education. Using proprietary data from a single, large American firm in the financial services industry, they find empirical support for both predictions. Similarly, Belzil and Bognanno (2005) find evidence consistent with the promotion-as-signal hypothesis using an eight-year panel of promotion histories of 30,000 American executives. And DeVaro, Ghosh, and Zoghi (2007) study discrimination in promotion decisions using a promotion discrimination model based on job assignment signaling. Using personnel data from a large U.S. firm and data from the National Compensation Survey, the authors find strong empirical support for their model's predictions concerning promotion probabilities, whereas empirical support is mixed for the model's predictions concerning the wage growth attached to promotions. While in these models it is the employer who signals (through promotions) the worker ability, in the current paper it is the worker who decides whether she wants to take a costly action to signal favorable information to prospective employers.

SOME STYLIZED FACTS ON LAYOFFS AND RECALLS

Many laid-off workers in the United States are rehired by their former employers. Early work by Lilien (1980) documented that over 70% of workers laid off in U.S. manufacturing in the 1970s were subsequently rehired by their former employers. Katz (1986) finds that this process is also widespread outside manufacturing. More recently, the Mass Layoff Statistics program reports that over half of employers reporting a layoff in 2008 indicated that they anticipated some type of recall (U.S. Bureau of Labor Statistics, 2009). It also reports that among all establishments expecting to recall workers, most employers (88%) expected to recall at least half of the separated employees. Finally, even in the midst of the current recession, the evidence indicates that about one fifth of laid-off workers who landed new positions within the last year were rehired by the same employer that had let them go (CNNmoney.com, 2009).

Studies by Robertson (1989), Corak (1996), and De Raaf, Motte, and Vincent (2003) present comparable figures for Canada. Although temporary layoffs are thought to be quantitatively more important in North America than in Europe – mainly due to the tighter recruitment and dismissal regulations existing in the old continent – empirical evidence has also found that this phenomenon exist in many European countries. For instance, Jensen and Svarer (2003) report that about half of all unemployment spells in Denmark were due to temporary layoffs. Similarly, Jansson (2002) calculates that about 45% of all transitions from unemployment in Sweden ended with the worker returning to the previous employer. In other European countries the recall rate has been estimated to be close to one-third: 37% in Spain, 32% in Austria, and 26% in Germany (Alba-Ramírez, Arranz-Muñoz, & Muñoz-Bullón, 2007; Fischer & Pichelmann, 1991; and Mavroramas & Orme, 2004, respectively).

In the United States, most recalls take place within the first three months and few occur after six months. For instance, Katz and Meyer (1990) find that the recall hazard becomes quite low after about 25 weeks of unemployment. Similarly, Katz (1986) finds that almost no recalls occur after 26 weeks. More recently, the Mass Layoff Statistics 2009 program reports that 60% (85%) of those employers expecting to recall workers expect to do so within three (six) months.

At the same time, most layoffs in the United States find jobs within 3 months. For instance, in the sample used in this paper, 70% of laid-off workers displaced from white-collar jobs find a job within 3 months (the average unemployment spell of laid-off workers displaced from white-collar jobs is 12.31 weeks – with a standard error of 16.92 –, and the median is at 6 weeks of unemployment.) Using a very different sample of displaced workers, Anderson (1992) also finds that about 70% of workers expecting a recall have exited unemployment within the first 12 weeks of their unemployment spell.

MODEL OF SIGNALING THROUGH UNEMPLOYMENT AND EMPIRICAL PREDICTIONS

The main idea behind Rodríguez-Planas' paper is that workers know their levels of productivity with their original employers, which are correlated with their probabilities of recall and with their productivity with a *new* employer.[10] At displacement, laid-off workers with favorable information may choose to remain unemployed rather than to accept a low-wage job, in which case, unemployment can serve as a signal of productivity. The contribution of the current paper is to develop an empirical implication of this model, namely that post-displacement earnings do not fall as rapidly with unemployment-spell length for laid-off workers compared to their counterparts being displaced by plant closing, and to test it. For the paper to be self-contained, this section first presents the theoretical model. We then explain the empirical implication of this model and discuss the empirical implementation.

The Model

There are two periods. In the first period, there are two types of laid-off workers: those who were of high productivity with the original employer (G-type workers) and those who were of low productivity with the original employer (B-type worker). The productivity of a G-type worker with the original employer is H and that of a B-type worker is L, with $0 < L < H$. I assume that there is a continuum of workers of each type, t, where $t = B$ or G. The cumulative distribution of all workers is normalized to "1." The proportion of G-type workers (respectively, B-type workers) is α (respectively, $1 - \alpha$), where $0 < \alpha < 1$.

Both the worker and the original employer know the worker's type, t, with that particular employer. However, laid-off workers are assumed to look identical to other potential employers. G-type workers are more likely to be of high productivity with a new employer than B-type workers. Specifically, a type-t worker will be of high productivity with a new employer (that is, with productivity equal to H) with probability p_t, $t = B$ or G and $0 < p_B < p_G < 1$. Viewed alternatively, some workers are better than others, but even good workers perform badly on some jobs and bad workers perform well on others. After the worker remains with an employer for one period, his productivity with that particular employer is revealed to both the worker and the employer, but not to other employers.

At the beginning of period one, prospective employers simultaneously offer laid-off workers a first-period wage. Workers observe that wage and choose either to work for a new employer – accepting the highest wage offered (randomizing in case of a tie) – or to become unemployed. If the worker becomes unemployed, his current income is U, where $U \geq 0$. One can think of U as unemployment insurance (UI). I assume that U is financed by a constant payroll tax, ζ, on all workers. I also assume that $U < L - \zeta$, to prevent workers always preferring unemployment over a job. To reduce the notational burden, I will set the reservation value to $U_0 \equiv U + \zeta$.

At the beginning of period two, the original employer recalls those former workers who are still unemployed with probability r_t, $t=B$, or G. I assume that $r_B<r_G\leq 1$. This assumption guarantees that the employer is more likely to recall high-productivity workers than low-productivity workers. For simplicity, I set $r_B=0$, (that is, the previous employer does not recall those workers who are of low productivity at his firm). Because I assumed that $r_B=0$, let $r_G=r$. Prospective employers observe that some unemployed workers are not recalled and they simultaneously offer them a wage. Unemployed workers accept the highest wage offered (randomizing in case of a tie). Workers work over the course of period two and retire at its end.

For notational simplicity, I assume that there is no discounting between periods. Workers maximize expected lifetime income. A large finite number of employers exist, and they maximize the present value of profits. Therefore, each period employers offer a wage equal to workers' (expected) productivity. Workers and firms are risk-neutral, and they know the population parameters: α, r, p_t, H, and L. I also assume that once a worker accepts a job offer, he is precluded from receiving a future offer from a new employer; and that after accepting an offer, workers cannot quit to return to a former employer. The latter assumption is consistent with the empirical evidence, which indicates that most workers who expect to be recalled remain unemployed instead of taking some interim job (Anderson, 1992; Katz, 1986; and Katz & Meyer, 1990, among others). Moreover, it is plausible that workers who believe that they are on temporary layoffs will consider – at least during the first few weeks – their laid-off time as time off from work to spend fixing up the house or catching up on personal things to do. Finally, this is not an unusual assumption in the theoretical literature on layoffs (Akerlof, Rose, & Yellen, 1990; Feldstein, 1976; Pissarides, 1982).[11]

A perfect Bayesian equilibrium in this model is a strategy combination of workers and firms and a belief structure of firms such that a worker cannot increase his total expected life-time earnings by changing his first-period choice of being unemployed or taking a first-period job given the wage schedules being offered, and a firm cannot increase its expected profit by offering a different contingency wage schedule given workers' strategies and its beliefs. All proofs are in the appendix.

Let w_G and w_B be the expected productivity of a G-type worker and a B-type worker, respectively, at a new job, where w_G and w_B are defined as:

$$w_G=p_GH+(1-p_G)L$$

and

$$w_B = p_B H + (1 - p_B) L$$

The first theorem characterizes all equilibria in which some or all workers choose unemployment in the first period.

Theorem 1. A necessary condition for a perfect Bayesian equilibrium in which some workers choose to remain unemployed is:

$$(1 - p_B) \geq \frac{L - U_0}{H - L} \tag{1}$$

Note that H and L are, respectively, the maximum and minimum wages that firms would offer to workers who are unemployed one period. $L - U_0$ is also the minimum loss incurred by a worker who refuses a first-period job. Thus, when Eq. (1) does not hold, the minimum cost of signaling by choosing unemployment exceeds the maximum potential expected gain.

To establish sufficiency, lemmas 1–3 characterize three classes of unemployment equilibrium; one, and only one, of these exists when (1) holds. These perfect Bayesian equilibria are: (a) All G-type workers are unemployed in the first period. B-type workers may be all employed (the fully-separating equilibrium for which conditions are given in lemma 1); (b) Some employed and some unemployed (the semi-separating equilibrium for which conditions are given in lemma 2); or (c) All unemployed (the pooling equilibrium for which conditions are given in lemma 3). The parameters values uniquely determine which of these equilibria applies. For brevity, I examine below only the conditions under which Lemma 1 holds. The characterization of Lemmas 2 and 3 can be found in Rodríguez-Planas' (2009) *Oxford Economic Paper*.

Lemma 1. For parameter values such that:

$$r(1 - p_G) - p_B \geq \frac{L - U_0}{H - L} \tag{2a}$$

and

$$p_G - 2p_B < \frac{L - U_0}{H - L} \tag{2b}$$

the unique perfect Bayesian equilibrium is one in which all G-type workers reject the first-period offer and all B-type workers accept it.

When conditions (2a) and (2b) hold, the minimum cost of signaling by choosing unemployment is smaller than the maximum potential gain of G-type workers, but greater than the maximum potential gain of B-type workers. Because of informational asymmetries and the existence of recalls among laid-off workers, accepting a job right away is sufficiently damaging to the future employment prospects of a laid-off worker that he may choose unemployment even if there is no disutility from work. Since G-type workers have higher productivity with their former employers and are more likely to be recalled than B-type workers, they have greater incentives to signal their productivity through unemployment. When conditions (2a) and (2b) hold, all G-type workers choose to reject the first-period market offer, whereas all B-type workers accept it.

In this model, the equilibrium with no voluntary unemployment is also possible. However, under certain conditions, this equilibrium fails to satisfy the Cho-Kreps intuitive criterion. The intuitive criterion in this model is as follows: Starting from an equilibrium with no voluntary unemployment, a worker choosing to wait unemployed is implicitly making the following statement: "I must have a positive probability of being recalled because those workers with no probability of being recalled would not choose unemployment, even if employers believed that only the high-productivity laid-off workers choose unemployment."[12]

Fig. 1 illustrates the region where each of the equilibrium prevails.[13] L1 illustrates the equilibrium in Lemma 1, where only G-type workers choose unemployment; L2 illustrates the equilibrium in Lemma 2, where all G-type and some B-type workers choose unemployment, and L3 illustrates the equilibrium in Lemma 3, where all workers choose unemployment. The figure also shows the region where no unemployment arises. Notice that no unemployment arises in regions with high values of p_G. There are two reasons for this. In the region where the values of p_G are high relative to those of p_B (upper LHS of Fig. 1), as the probability of a G-type worker of being a high-productivity worker with a new employer increases so does his cost of signaling relative to his potential expected gain, reducing the G-type worker's incentives to signal through unemployment.

In contrast, in the region where the values of p_G approach those of p_B (upper RHS of Fig. 1), the information content of the signal decreases since the comparative advantage of G-type workers in the spot market relative to B-types is reduced, making it less worthwhile to signal through unemployment. Fig. 1 also shows that as the probability of a B-type worker of being a high-productivity worker with a new employer, p_B, decreases

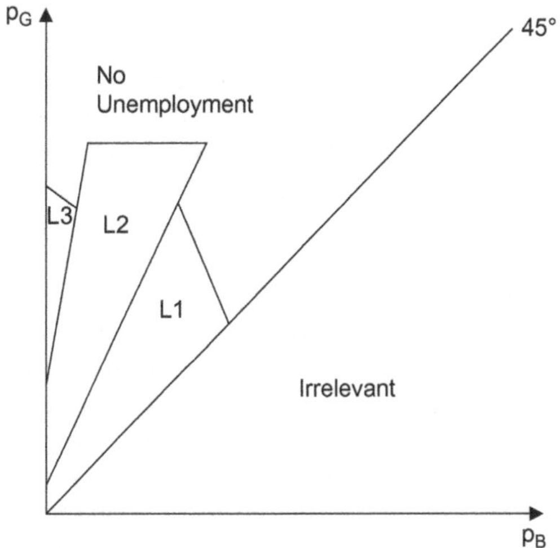

Fig. 1. Region Where Each of the Equilibrium Prevails.

relative to p_G, B-type worker's incentive to behave strategically and to choose unemployment instead of a low-wage job increases.

In the separating equilibria – the fully (lemma1) and the semi-separating (lemma 2) equilibria – the post-displacement earnings of permanently laid-off workers who accept jobs at the end of period one are lower than those of observationally equivalent permanently laid-off workers who are unemployed during the first period.[14] The next section presents the empirical implementation of this prediction and finds evidence consistent with the theoretical model using the Displaced Workers Supplement to CPS.

Empirical Implementation

In the signaling model described above, high-productivity laid-off workers are more likely to be recalled by their former employer than low-productivity laid-off workers. Thus, they may choose to remain unemployed rather than to accept a low-wage job. If so, unemployment can serve as a signal of productivity. In this case, unemployment duration may be positively related to post-displacement earnings even among laid-off workers who are not recalled. However, in the real world, the relation between earnings of displaced workers and unemployment duration is determined by many other factors, such as unobserved heterogeneity, loss of human capital, stigma, or discouraged workers' effect.[15] Most of these factors imply a negative relation between post-displacement earnings and length of unemployment. For simplicity, the theoretical model does not consider all of the above-mentioned factors that lead to the well-documented negative relationship between post-displacement earnings and unemployment duration. Adapting the model to incorporate the negative effect of unemployment on earnings would not change the model's main prediction, namely that asymmetric information and the high ex ante rate of recall lead to a positive relationship between post-displacement earnings and duration of unemployment for laid-off workers, holding everything else constant.

To isolate the effects of asymmetric information in the U.S. labor market, I must control for all other factors affecting earnings and the duration of unemployment not associated with having a positive probability of recall. To do so, I use workers displaced through plant closings. I assume that workers displaced when the plant closes cannot be recalled, an assumption that, in this model, implies that they have no incentive to signal their productivity through unemployment. In the model presented above, workers displaced through plant closings would always accept the first-period job in equilibrium. Thus, the model does not imply a positive relationship between unemployment duration and post-displacement earnings for workers displaced because of plant closings.[16]

Therefore the empirical hypothesis is that post-displacement earnings fall *less* rapidly with unemployment spells for layoffs than for plant closings. To formally test this hypothesis, the following regression is estimated, separately for white-collar and blue-collar workers:

$$Y_i = \alpha_0 + \sum_{j=1}^{4} \alpha_j D_i^j + \beta_0 C_i + \sum_{j=1}^{4} \beta_j Z_i^j + X'_i \delta + \xi_i \tag{3}$$

where D_i^j are four dummies for worker i initial length of joblessness, for $i = 1, \ldots N$; $D_i^1 = 1$ if the worker's initial length of joblessness is 1–4 weeks long, and 0 elsewhere; $D_i^2 = 1$ if the worker's initial length of joblessness is 5 to 12 weeks long, and 0 elsewhere; $D_i^3 = 1$ if the worker's initial length of joblessness is 13–24 weeks long, and 0 elsewhere; and $D_i^4 = 1$ if the worker's initial length of joblessness is more than 24 weeks long, and 0 elsewhere; C_i is a dummy for cause of displacement for worker i for $i = 1, \ldots N$ ($C_i = 1$ if the worker is laid off, and 0 if the worker is displaced through plant closings); $Z^j{}_i$ is the interaction between the layoff dummy and D_i^j dummies; and

X_i is a vector of observable pre-displacement characteristics that includes the log real pre-displacement weekly earnings, a spline function in previous tenure (with breaks at 1, 2, 3, and 6 years), three dummies for completed education (one for "high school graduate"; one for "some college"; and one for "college graduate or above"), an "advance notice" dummy, year-of-displacement dummies; previous-industry and previous-occupation dummies; experience and its square; a gender dummy; marriage dummy; a non-white dummy; and three region dummies. All regressions use the Huber/White estimator of variance. The LHS variable is the logarithm of the post-displacement weekly earnings.

Using the notations from Eq. (3), the prediction would translate to: $\beta_1 > 0$, $\beta_2 > 0$, $\beta_3 > 0$, $\beta_4 > 0$.

While it is true that a straight read from the theoretical model would imply a stronger test, namely, $\beta_4 > \beta_3 > \beta_2 > \beta_1 > 0$, this is no longer the case if workers' recall expectations were to fall after a certain length of the unemployment spell as they do in real world. Indeed, the theoretical model presented in this paper illustrates that when workers know their levels of productivity with their original employers, which are correlated with their probabilities of recall and with their productivity with a *new* employer, those who expect to be recalled may wait unemployed instead of accepting a low wage job with a new employer. By doing so they signal to prospective employers that they are higher productivity workers. Because most recalls in the United States occur between 1 and 3 months, and practically none occur after 6 to 9 months as explained in the third section, as the probability of recall converges toward zero, the expected benefits from waiting unemployed fall, decreasing the incentives to signal. Thus, a weaker, yet more realistic implication of the model is that post-displacement wages do *not* fall as rapidly with unemployment-spell length for laid-off workers compared to workers displaced to plant closings.

Because many fewer white-collar jobs than blue-collar jobs are covered by collective-bargaining agreements involving explicit layoff rules and recall-by-seniority rules, the degree of discretion over whom to lay off and recall is likely to be higher in white- than blue-collar jobs, and thus, the information content of a layoff and a recall is considerably higher in white- than blue-collar jobs (Gibbons & Katz, 1991; Hu & Taber, 2011). Therefore, the model would predict a stronger positive relationship between post-displacement earnings and duration of unemployment among workers laid-off from white-collar jobs than among those laid off from blue-collar jobs. As in Gibbons and Katz (1991) and Hu and Taber (2011), the analysis is done separately for blue- and white-collar workers.

Finally, we also test whether our data support the well-documented negative relationship between post-displacement earnings and unemployment duration among workers displaced through plant closings: $\alpha_1 < 0$, $\alpha_2 < 0$, $\alpha_3 < 0$, $\alpha_4 < 0$.

The results presented below are robust to modifying the length of the joblessness dummies, and to using an alternative specification including length of joblessness and its square (instead the dummies).

THE DATA AND RESULTS

The Data

The data used is from the Displaced Workers Supplements (DWS) to the CPS between 1988 and 1992 and between 1996 and 2006 (all years included) and restricts the analysis to individuals who *permanently* lost a job within three years prior to the survey date.[17] The reason for excluding the supplements from 1984, 1986, and 1994 is that they do not include one of the key variables for the analysis: the variable "initial length of unemployment spell."[18] Prior to 1994, the DWS asked respondents if, in the prior five years, they had lost or left a job owing to a plant closing, slack work, a position or shift abolished, or other reasons. However, because many researchers highlighted the problem of recall bias when using the DWS, starting in 1994, the Bureau of Labor Statistics decided to ask about employment status in the past three years instead of the past five years.[19] For consistency purposes, I only used workers who had reported losing a job in the last three years in the 1988, 1990 and 1992 DWS, but the results presented below are robust to including workers who reported losing a job in the last five years.[20]

The DWS only asks follow-up questions about at most one lost job. If an individual lost multiple jobs, she was only asked about the job that had been held the longest. The post-displacement wage is for the current job held at the survey date, which is not necessarily the first job since displacement. To guaranty that the key variable "Initial unemployment spell" is from the spell *immediately* preceding the current job, I have excluded multiple job losers included in the sample. The sample is further restricted to workers between the ages of 20 and 61 who were permanently displaced from a private-sector, full-time job because of a plant closing, slack work, or abolishment of a position or shift. I used permanently displaced workers in an attempt to identify a sample of workers who did *not* return to their previous jobs (and similar wages).[21] I focus on workers displaced from full-time jobs in an attempt to identify a sample of workers with strong attachments to the labor force. Like in Gibbons and Katz (1991), I classified as laid-off workers those displaced because of slack work or a position or shift that was eliminated. The sample is restricted to those individuals who were re-employed in wage-and-salary employment at the survey date and who had re-employment earnings of at least $40 a week. Earnings are deflated by the gross domestic product (GDP) deflator (base year = 2000). The white-collar sample consists of workers whose pre-displacement occupations were in the managerial and professional specialties or in the technical, sales, and administrative support specialties, while the blue-collar sample consists of workers who, in their pre-displacement job, were craft and kindred workers, operatives, laborers, transport operatives, or service workers. Workers in agriculture and construction industries are excluded.[22]

The main focus of the present analysis is to analyze how the post-displacement earnings vary by cause of displacement and with the length of the unemployment spell. Descriptive statistics of the sample are reported in Table 1. The data are divided in twenty groups, classifying by blue-collar/white-collar, length of unemployment spell, and layoff/plant closing. The length of unemployment spell is divided in five groups: (1) no unemployment; (2) 1–4 weeks unemployed; (3) 5–12 weeks unemployed; (4) 13–24 weeks unemployed; (5) more than 24 weeks unemployed. Sample means and standard deviations for all of the variables are displayed in the cells. The key variables are displayed in the first three rows: (1) the logarithm of the previous weekly earnings; (2) the logarithm of the real weekly current earnings; and (3) the change in the logarithm of real weekly earnings. Focusing first on white-collar workers, while the post-displacement earnings of workers displaced through plant closings fall with their unemployment spell, no such pattern is observed among layoffs within the first 6 months of the unemployment spell. For blue-collar workers, the post-displacement earnings fall with the unemployment spell for both layoffs and plant closings, but they fall *less* rapidly for layoffs than for plant closings – this (raw) differential pattern between layoffs and plant closings is statistically significant as can be seen in the first column of Table A1 for white-collar workers and Table A4 for blue-collar workers.

Unfortunately, the DWS does not allow to distinguish between workers who quit from those who were laid off by the firm. This is a concern because workers who become unemployed because they have quit often engage in job search prior to quitting, which is likely to lead to a shorter

Table 1. Descriptive Statistics for Displaced Workers Reemployed at Survey Date, DWS 1988–2006.

Weeks Unemployed	0 Weeks		1–4 Weeks		5–12 Weeks		13–24 Weeks		25 + Weeks	
	Plant closing	Layoff	Plant closing	Layoff	Plant closing	Layoff	Plant closing	Layoff	Plant closing	Layoff
A: White-collar workers at displacement										
Log of previous weekly earnings	6.538	6.452*	6.411	6.456	6.508	6.517	6.484	6.552	6.420	6.600***
	(.595)	(.675)	(.649)	(.645)	(.601)	(.634)	(.620)	(.629)	(.633)	(.664)
Log of current weekly earnings	6.476	6.336**	6.292	6.320	6.282	6.371	6.244	6.304	5.970	6.125
	(.790)	(.943)	(.921)	(.895)	(.890)	(.834)	(.965)	(.954)	(.911)	(1.156)
Change in log real weekly earnings	−.062	−.116	−.119	−.134	−.226	−.146	−.240	−.248	−.455	−.471***
	(.588)	(.785)	(.769)	(.797)	(.798)	(.719)	(.893)	(.848)	(.788)	(1.032)
Previous tenure (years)	7.529	6.612*	4.476	3.863*	6.463	4.332**	5.520	5.476	7.565	6.120**
	(7.390)	(7.140)	(5.775)	(4.636)	(7.474)	(5.637)	(6.637)	(6.011)	(7.520)	(7.007)
Unemployment spell (weeks)	0	0	2.240	2.400**	8.832	8.676	18.714	18.923	48.378	45.103
	(0)	(0)	(1.180)	(1.188)	(2.392)	(2.415)	(3.533)	(3.640)	(23.921)	(24.600)
Advance notice (%)	.619	.337***	.518	.302***	.485	.304	.484	.354***	.632	.273***
	(.486)	(.473)	(.500)	(.459)	(.501)	(.460)	(.501)	(.479)	(.483)	(.446)
Male (%)	.519	.446**	.462	.469	.467	.477**	.460	.434	.353	.516***
	(.500)	(.498)	(.499)	(.500)	(.500)	(.500)	(.500)	(.497)	(.479)	(.501)
Age	40.703	40.264	37.728	38.449	40.069	39.772	40.031	42.099**	41.813	42.529**
	(9.685)	(10.162)	(9.711)	(9.861)	(10.028)	(9.767)	(9.963)	(9.607)	(9.814)	(9.290)
Currently married (%)	.692	.617**	.596	.528**	.609	.610	.540	.605	.679	.637
	(.462)	(.487)	(.491)	(.500)	(.489)	(.488)	(.500)	(.490)	(.468)	(.482)
Black (%)	.043	.063	.058	.099**	.080	.053	.056	.073	.114	.093
	(.204)	(.243)	(.234)	(.300)	(.272)	(.224)	(.230)	(.261)	(.319)	(.292)
High school dropout (%)	.011	.010	.025	.025	.033	.013**	.012	.022	.047	.028
	(.104)	(.098)	(.155)	(.157)	(.179)	(.112)	(.111)	(.147)	(.211)	(.164)
High school graduate (%)	.241	.218	.261	.228	.245	.186**	.217	.179***	.295	.204
	(.428)	(.413)	(.440)	(.420)	(.431)	(.389)	(.414)	(.384)	(.457)	(.404)
Some college (%)	.319	.349	.342	.331	.328	.313	.354	.336	.389	.329
	(.467)	(.477)	(.475)	(.471)	(.471)	(.464)	(.480)	(.473)	(.489)	(.471)
College graduate or above (%)	.430	.424	.373	.417	.394	.488**	.416	.464	.269	.439***
	(.496)	(.495)	(.484)	(.493)	(.490)	(.500)	(.494)	(.500)	(.445)	(.497)
Number of observations	370	413	448	593	274	549	161	274	193	289

B: Blue-collar workers at displacement										
Log of previous weekly earnings	6.302	6.163***	5.967	5.996	6.050	6.076	6.071	6.219**	6.063	6.120
	(.514)	(.563)	(.550)	(.540)	(.542)	(.524)	(.557)	(.558)	(.521)	(.508)
Log of current weekly earnings	6.222	6.087*	5.936	5.935	5.896	5.986*	5.866	5.873	5.741	5.765
	(.712)	(.961)	(.604)	(.664)	(.615)	(.555)	(.653)	(1.079)	(.622)	(.777)
Change in log real weekly earnings	−.080	−.076	−.031	−.061	−153	−.090	−.205	−.345	−.322	−.354
	(.625)	(.918)	(.491)	(.588)	(.546)	(.428)	(.520)	(1.092)	(.576)	(.722)
Previous tenure (years)	8.119	5.051***	4.699	3.293***	5.214	3.568***	6.552	4.300***	7.517	5.473***
	(8.777)	(6.863)	(6.119)	(4.896)	(6.578)	(4.943)	(7.4653)	(5.419)	(7.782)	(6.617)
Unemployment spell (weeks)	0	0	2.301	2.358	8.878	8.322***	19.130	19.023	48.541	48.540
	(0)	(0)	(1.140)	(1.212)	(2.388)	(2.380)	(3.753)	(3.886)	(25.263)	(23.841)
Advance notice (%)	.505	.235***	.475	.235***	.441	.240***	.435	.282***	.559	.338***
	(.501)	(.425)	(.500)	(.424)	(.498)	(.428)	(.498)	(.451)	(.498)	(.474)
Male	.783	.772	.626	.687*	.664	.610	.536	.706***	.571	.636
	(.413)	(.421)	(.485)	(.464)	(.473)	(.488)	(.500)	(.456)	(.496)	(.482)
Age	39.986	37.837	37.187	35.389***	39.013	37.913	39.572	39.563	41.847	40.091
	(10.384)	(10.787)	(10.875)	(9.741)	(9.901)	(11.208)	(10.802)	(10.545)	(10.362)	(10.280)
Currently married (%)	.712	.630*	.618	.559*	.605	.569	.601	.592	.635	.586
	(.454)	(.484)	(.486)	(.497)	(.490)	(.496)	(.491)	(.493)	(.483)	(494)
Black (%)	.061	.073	.096	.114	.097	.099	.109	.092	.106	.111
	(.240)	(.260)	(.295)	(3187)	(296)	(.299)	(312)	(.290)	(.309)	(.315)
High school dropout (%)	.085	.087	.210	.168	.160	.112	.196	.184	.182	.207
	(.279)	(.282)	(.408)	(.374)	(.367)	(.316)	(.398)	(.389)	(.387)	(.460)
High school graduate (%)	.491	.408*	.462	.456	.450	.447	.406	.368	.488	.384**
	(.501)	(.492)	(.499)	(.498)	(.498)	(.498)	(.493)	(.484)	(.501)	(.488)
Some college (%)	.307	.377	.260	.282	.286	.294	.297	.276	.265	.298
	(.462)	(.486)	(.439)	(.450)	(.453)	(.456)	(.459)	(.448)	(.442)	(.454)
College graduate or above (%)	.118	.128	.068	.094	.105	.147	.101	.172*	.065	.111
	(.323)	(.335)	(.251)	(.292)	(.307)	(.355)	(.303)	(.379)	(.247)	(.315)
Number of observations	212	289	385	553	238	313	138	174	170	198

Note: The numbers in parenthesis are standard deviations. All weekly wages are deflated by the GDP deflator (base year = 2000).
*Difference in the means between layoff and plant closing are significantly different at the 90% confidence level.
**Difference in the means between layoff and plant closing are significantly different at the 95% confidence level.
***Difference in the means between layoff and plant closing are significantly different at the 99% confidence level.

unemployment spell before getting their next job (such a worker is also less likely to decline job offers that come up during the unemployment spell in hope of a recall from the company from which he quit). To the extent that we may have quitters in our data, this adds noise into our analysis. We have tried to address this concern in the following two ways. First, in the section "Alternative Explanations", we re-estimate the model distinguishing by whether workers received advanced notice (and thus were able to begin search prior to being displaced). We find that the effect holds for those who did *not* receive advance notice. Second, we re-estimated the model using *only* workers with a positive unemployment spell (who are more likely to be non-quitters). In this case, we find a similar pattern as the one presented in the main text (results available from the author upon request).

The Results

White-Collar Workers

The first and second columns of Table 2 display the α_j coefficients for white-collar workers displaced through plant closings, and the β_j coefficients for white-collar laid-off workers, respectively, for $j=1$ to 4. Table 2 also reports the p-value for the joint Z test of the one-sided alternative hypothesis: $\beta_1 > 0, \beta_2 > 0, \beta_3 > 0, \beta_4 > 0$.[23] Columns 1 and 2 of Table 2 show that, for white-collar workers, post-displacement earnings fall *less* with the unemployment spell for layoffs than for plant closings. All of the four β_j coefficients, for $j=1$ to 4, are sizeable and positive. Moreover, although only β_2 is statistically significant, the p-value for the Z test of the joint hypothesis: $\beta_1 > 0, \beta_2 > 0, \beta_3 > 0, \beta_4 > 0$ is significant at the 5% level, indicating that there is a differential effect by cause of displacement in the relationship between post-displacement earnings and unemployment duration for white-collar workers. Notice that these effects might understate the true signaling effect of unemployment for the following three reasons. First, some laid-off workers included in the sample could end up returning to their original employer and thus they should have higher re-employment wages and shorter initial spells of joblessness than workers who do not return to the original employers.[24] Second, some of the layoffs in the sample are likely to be determined by strict seniority systems. Third, as we may have quitters in our sample, this adds noise to our estimation.

The stronger effect is found between 1 and 3 months, which is when most recalls occur in the United States.[25] As the probability of recall converges toward zero, the expected benefits from waiting unemployed fall,

Table 2. Post-Displacement Earnings Equation (Workers Reemployed at Survey Date DWS 1988–2006).

	White-Collar Workers at Displacement		Blue-Collar Workers at Displacement	
	Plant closing	Layoff	Plant closing	Layoff
	(1)		(2)	
No unemployment		−.050		−.013
(β_0 for layoffs)		(.049)		(.062)
1–4 weeks	−.082*	+.050	−.045	−.022
(α_1 for plant closings and β_1 for layoffs)	(.048)	(.066)	(.050)	(.069)
5–12 weeks	−.158***	+.131*	−.151***	+.113
(α_2 for plant closings and β_2 for layoffs)	(0.58)	(.074)	(0.54)	(.073)
13–24 weeks	−.192**	+.065	−.181***	−.104
(α_3 for plant closings and β_3 for layoffs)	(.073)	(.095)	(.061)	(.106)
More than 24 weeks	−.407***	+.052	−.327***	+.005
(α_4 for plant closings and β_4 for layoffs)	(.064)	(.096)	(.060)	(.086)
$\alpha_1 < 0, \alpha_2 < 0, \alpha_3 < 0, \alpha_4 < 0$	Z = 4.82		Z = 2.64	
	Prob > Z = 0.000		Prob > Z = 0.008	
$\beta_1 > 0, \beta_2 > 0, \beta_3 > 0, \beta_4 > 0$	Z = 2.00		Z = 0.00	
	Prob > Z = 0.045		Prob > Z = 1.000	
Sample size	3,564		2,670	

Note: The numbers in parentheses are robust standard errors. All weekly wages are deflated by the GDP deflator (base year = 2000). Additional covariates include: the log real pre-displacement weekly earnings, a spline function in previous tenure (with breaks at 1, 2, 3, and 6 years), three dummies for completed education (one for "high school graduate"; one for "some college"; and one for "college graduate or above"), an "advance notice" dummy, year-of-displacement dummies; previous-industry and previous-occupation dummies; experience and its square; a gender dummy; marriage dummy; a non-white dummy; and three region dummies. Column (1) matches column (10) in Table A1; and column (2) matches column (10 in Table A4).

*Estimate significantly different from zero at the 90% confidence level.

**Estimate significantly different from zero at the 95% confidence level.

***Estimate significantly different from zero at the 99% confidence level.

decreasing the incentives to signal. Thus, any signaling that may occur among laid-off workers in the U.S. labor market should be observed mainly within the time that prospective employers are most likely to infer that workers are waiting for recall.

Table A1 highlights the robustness of these results to inclusion of control variables for white-collar workers. While parameters change some when introducing demographic variables – moving from columns (1) to (2) in Table A1 – , and when introducing schooling – moving from columns (2) to (3), all of the relevant coefficients change very little thereafter. It is particularly striking that controls for occupation, industry, region, and pre-displacement earnings – columns (8) through (10) of Table A1 – seem to make little difference in the final result, which suggest that the patterns encountered are not simply due to differences in the sector of the economy in which workers were employed.

As explained earlier, the results presented below are robust to modifying the length of the joblessness dummies and to using an alternative specification including length of joblessness and its square (instead of the dummies). Finally, the results are also robust to performing the analysis separately by gender.

One interesting question is whether the most able workers at a plant about to shut down (which is frequently anticipated by employees as news of closure often leaks months ahead of time) begin looking for other jobs early on, which may lead to a shorter unemployment spell. For this to explain our findings, one would need to see that the pre-displacement wages of workers displaced through plant closings are higher the shorter their unemployment spell. We do not have a panel of wages prior to displacement, so we cannot look at this directly. However, our best evidence is to look at wage differences prior to displacement. Column 3 of Table A2 displays the coefficients of interest after estimating our main specification with pre-displacement log wage as the LHS variable. None of the coefficients of interest are statistically significant. Moreover, when we test whether there is a monotonic pattern among workers displaced due to plant closings, we reject the hypothesis:

$$\alpha_1 > \alpha_2 > \alpha_3 > \alpha_4$$

corroborating that there is no pattern of pre-displacement wages decreasing with unemployment spell among these workers.[26] It is interesting to note that although the coefficients on the interaction dummies are not statistically significant, we cannot reject that the hypothesis:

$$\beta_1 < \beta_2 < \beta_3 < \beta_4$$

at the 5% level, suggesting that white-collar laid-off workers who wait longer unemployed are those who had higher pre-displacement productivity ones – as hypothesized by the theoretical model.

Finally, we propose an alternative specification, which estimates a similar equation as the one in the main text but replaces the left-hand side

(LHS) variable, the post-displacement log wage, by the change in the log wages (i.e., the log of the post-displacement wage minus the log of the pre-displacement wage) after displacement and no longer includes the pre-displacement wage in the right-hand side (RHS) of the equation. This specification has the advantage, relative to a specification in levels, that person-specific fixed-effects are differenced out in the LHS. It is practically equivalent to using a difference-in-difference methodology where the wage change of laid-off workers is compared to the wage change of workers displaced due to plant closing – this is the specification used by Gibbons and Katz (1991) and Hu and Taber (2011), among others. The assumption is that the relationship between wage change and unemployment spell between laid-off workers and those displaced due to plant closings only differs due to the signaling component of recalls among laid-off workers. This specification is presented in column 1 of Table A2 for white-collar workers, and its results are similar to those presented in the main text.

Blue-Collar Workers
For blue-collar workers, I do not find evidence that post-displacement earnings of laid-off workers fall *less* with unemployment spell than for workers displaced through plant closings, as one would expect from the model if most recalls in blue-collar jobs are driven by seniority rules, and therefore lack of information content. Notice that only two of the four β_j coefficients, for $j=1$ to 4, are positive (although not statistically significant), as shown in column 4 of Table 2, and that the p-value for the Z test of the hypothesis: $\beta_1>0$, $\beta_2>0$, $\beta_3>0$, $\beta_4>0$ is not statistically significant, indicating that there is no evidence of a differential effect by cause of displacement in the relationship between post-displacement earnings and unemployment duration for blue-collar workers.[27] It is common in this literature not to find effects for blue-collar workers as many of the layoffs and recalls among this group are based on seniority-based rules (see Gibbons & Katz, 1991; Hu & Taber, 2011) (Tables 3 and 4).

In contrast with the robustness of the results to inclusion of control variables for white-collar workers, the estimates for blue-collar workers are quite sensitive to the introduction of region and year dummies, and pre-displacement wages, as shown in Table A4. According to the first four columns of Table A4, all of four β_j coefficients, for $j=1$ to 4, are positive, and although they are not as large as those observed in the white-collar subsample, the null hypothesis: $\beta_1>0$, $\beta_2>0$, $\beta_3>0$, $\beta_4>0$ is rejected at the 5% level, indicating a differential pattern between layoffs and plant closings (similar to the one observed for white-collar workers). However, moving

Table 3. Post-Displacement Earnings Equation, Workers Reemployed at Survey Date DWS 1988–2006 (White-Collar Workers at Displacement).

Unemployment Spell	No Advance Notice		Received Advance Notice		UI Receipt		No UI Receipt		Exhaust UI		Did Not Exhaust UI		Recession Years		Expansion Years	
$N=3{,}564$	PC		Layoff		PC	Layoff	PC	Layoff	PC	Layoff	PC	Layoff	PC	Layoff	PC	Layoff
	(1)		(2)		(3)		(4)		(5)		(6)		(7)		(8)	
No unemployment		−.065		−.025		−.327		−.374		−.354		−.040		−.056		−.054
(β_0 for layoffs)		(.079)		(.054)		(.273)		(.049)		(.312)		(.050)		(.072)		(.061)
1–4 weeks	−.048	+.045	−.110*	+.080	+.001	+.510*	−.049	+.025	−.544	+.715*	−.041	+.019	−.060	.065	−.097	+.048
(α_1 for plant closings and β_1 for layoffs)	(.070)	(.092)	(.065)	(.087)	(.218)	(.300)	(.050)	(.068)	(.290)	(.408)	(.047)	(.066)	(.058)	(.091)	(.062)	(.083)
5–12 weeks	−.113	+.098	−.215**	+.167	+.170	+.498*	−.169	+.073	−.248	+.607	−.132**	+.100	−.107	−.025	−.178**	+.189***
(α_2 for plant closings and β_2 for layoffs)	(.073)	(.095)	(.093)	(.111)	(.202)	(.280)	(.098)	(.115)	(.370)	(.448)	(.056)	(.073)	(.004)	(0.125)	(.072)	(0.088)
13–24 weeks	−.264*	+.216*	−.114*	−.176	+.231	+.319	−.446*	+.218	+.156	+.069	−.221***	+.122	−.140	−.000	−.202**	+.084
(α_3 for plant closings and β_3 for layoffs)	(.129)	(.149)	(.068)	(.136)	(.198)	(.279)	(.230)	(.271)	(.220)	(.341)	(.083)	(.108)	(.091)	(.136)	(.092)	(.117)
More than 24 weeks	−.487***	+.191	−.385***	−.102	+.026	+.347	−.659***	+.136	−.164	+.345	−.431***	+.0522	−.294***	+.075	−.450***	+.044
(α_4 for plant closings and β_4 for layoffs)	(.137)	(.168)	(.067)	(.106)	(.199)	(.282)	(.198)	(.248)	(.194)	(.321)	(.110)	(.147)	(.103)	(.136)	(.078)	(.122)
$\alpha_1<0$, $\alpha_2<0$, $\alpha_3<0$, $\alpha_4<0$	$Z=2.22$ Prob > $\lvert Z\rvert=0.026$ Prob > $Z=0.017$		$Z=3.35$ Prob > $\lvert Z\rvert=0.001$ Prob > $Z=0.000$		$Z=0.00$		$Z=2.45$ Prob > $Z=1.000$		$Z=0.00$		$Z=2.48$ Prob > $Z=0.014$		$Z=2.38$ Prob > $\lvert Z\rvert=1.000$		$Z=8.29$ Prob > $\lvert Z\rvert=0.013$	
$\beta_1>0$, $\beta_2>0$, $\beta_3>0$, $\beta_4>0$	$Z=2.00$ Prob > $\lvert Z\rvert=0.045$ Prob > $Z=1.000$		$Z=0.00$ Prob > $\lvert Z\rvert=1.000$ Prob > $Z=0.043$		$Z=2.69$		$Z=2.18$ Prob > $Z=0.007$		$Z=2.01$		$Z=2.04$ Prob > $Z=0.029$		$Z=0.00$ Prob > $\lvert Z\rvert=0.044$		$Z=2.02$ Prob > $\lvert Z\rvert=0.042$	
Sample size	2,109		1,455		1,454		2,100		441		3,087		911		2,653	

Note: See Table 2. Sample sizes do not add to 3,564 because for several observations information on UI receipt or UI exhaustion was missing.

Table 4. Post-Displacement Earnings Equation Workers Reemployed at Survey Date DWS 1988–2006 (White-Collar Workers at Displacement).

Unemployment spell	1 year of tenure or less		Tenure greater than 1 year		No change in occupation		Occupation change		No change in industry		Industry Change	
$N=3{,}564$	PC	Layoff	PC	Layoff	PC	Layoff	PC	Layoff	PC	Layoff	PC	Layoff
	(1)		(2)		(1)		(2)		(3)		(4)	
No unemployment		−.018		−.050		−.044		−.089		.013		−.160*
(β_0 for layoffs)		(.138)		(.052)		(.039)		(.145)		(.050)		(.095)
1–4 weeks	−.161	+.121	−.075	−.002	−.044	+.029	−.105	+.090	−.043	−.019	−.160**	+.212*
(α_1 for plant closings and β_1 for layoffs)	(.126)	(.158)	(.050)	(.078)	(.038)	(.058)	(.136)	(.172)	(.061)	(.081)	(.079)	(.121)
5–12 weeks	+.094	−.043	−.215***	+.174**	−.148***	+.099	−.142	+.225	−.137*	+.079	−.176**	+.243*
(α_2 for plant closings and β_2 for layoffs)	(.120)	(.155)	(.069)	(.088)	(.057)	(.073)	(.137)	(.175)	(.081)	(.093)	(.085)	(.125)
13–24 weeks	−.017	+.087	−.222***	+.042	−.244***	+.144	−.104	−.065	−.023	−.138	−.309**	+.273*
(α_3 for plant closings and β_3 for layoffs)	(.179)	(.197)	(.081)	(.111)	(.094)	(.115)	(.137)	(.187)	(.073)	(.111)	(.123)	(.155)
More than 24 weeks	−.440*	+.206	−.394***	+.010	−.452***	+.099	−.302**	+.004	−.353***	−.079	−.439***	+.205
(α_4 for plant closings and β_4 for layoffs)	(.249)	(.295)	(.060)	(.105)	(.078)	(.114)	(.140)	(.201)	(.105)	(.163)	(.083)	(.131)
$\alpha_1<0, \alpha_2<0, \alpha_3<0, \alpha_4<0$	$Z=0.00$ Prob $>Z=1.000$		$Z=4.18$ Prob $>Z=0.000$		$Z=2.87$ Prob $>Z=0.004$		$Z=2.07$ Prob $>Z=0.038$		$Z=2.00$ Prob $>\|Z\|=0.046$		$Z=3.75$ Prob $>\|Z\|=0.000$	
$\beta_1>0, \beta_2>0, \beta_3>0, \beta_4>0$	$Z=0.00$ Prob $>Z=1.000$		$Z=2.05$ Prob $>Z=0.040$		$Z=1.99$ Prob $>Z=0.046$		$Z=0.00$ Prob $>Z=1.000$		$Z=0.00$ Prob $>\|Z\|=1.000$		$Z=2.64$ Prob $>\|Z\|=0.008$	
Sample size	945		2,619		2,358		1,206		1,864		1,700	

Note: See Table 2 in the main paper. Tenure refers to pre-displacement tenure. In column (2) the null hypothesis tested was H_0: $\beta_2>0, \beta_3>0, \beta_4>0$ (instead of H_0: $\beta_1>0, \beta_2>0, \beta_3>0, \beta_4>0$).

from columns (4) to (5) in Table A4 cuts the coefficient of β_1 by half and also reduces the size of the other coefficients of interest (reversing the sign of β_3) leading to an insignificant p-value for the Z test of the hypothesis: $\beta_1 > 0$, $\beta_2 > 0$, $\beta_3 > 0$, $\beta_4 > 0$. The size of all of four β_j coefficients changes further (becoming negative for three of the β_j) when pre-displacement wage is added as a control. This suggest that workers' heterogeneity explains most of the differential pattern between layoffs and plant closings displaced from blue-collar jobs – notice that no such effect was found for white-collar workers.

As we did for workers displaced from white-collar jobs, we explore whether there is any monotonic pattern between unemployment spell and pre-displacement wages for workers displaced through plant closings. Column 3 of Table A5 shows that there is no pattern of pre-displacement wages decreasing with unemployment spell. If anything we observe that all blue-collar workers displaced through plant closings have lower pre-displacement earnings than laid-off workers, but no monotonic pattern seems to emerge. Finally, we also estimate the alternative specification with the wage change as the LHS variable (shown in column 1 of Table A5). The results are similar to those found in our main specification, namely, there is no evidence of a differential effect by cause of displacement in the relationship between post-displacement earnings and unemployment duration.

Alternative Explanations

An important question is: Are there alternative explanations other than signaling for the findings among white-collar workers? For instance, one may be concerned if the main results of the paper are driven by differences in the composition of the pool of laid-off workers and that of workers displaced through plant closings. We shall explore this from several perspectives, such as, in terms of advance notice receipt, UI receipt, and whether the worker lost her job during an expansion or recession period.

Much evidence suggests that advance notice yields a productive pre-displacement search (Addison & Blackburn, 1994; Podgursky & Swaim, 1987). If so, one may be concerned that a pre-displacement search among displaced workers may be affecting the above results.[28] Moreover, notified workers may differ from their non-notified counterparts in some unmeasured way (Ruhm, 1992). In such a case, one would want to distinguish between those workers who were notified in advance and those who were not. While the prediction should hold for workers who do not receive advance notice, it is unclear whether such result ought to hold for workers who received advance notice. Assuming that (1) productive pre-displacement search occurs among workers who receive advance notice, (2) prospective employers observe the pre-displacement search time, and (3) the longer the pre-displacement notice the more productive the worker's search, the model would predict that a differential pattern by cause of displacement. Unfortunately, Addison and Blackburn's results (1994) provide no evidence of monotonically increasing benefits from longer pre-displacement written notice. Moreover, they do not find evidence of any incremental value to receiving extended written notice rather than informal notice. Thus, the signaling model would not necessarily predict a positive relationship between post-displacement earnings and the length of unemployment among laid-off workers. Column 1 of Table 3 display the estimates for workers who did not receive advance notice. These results are consistent with the signaling model of unemployment. As shown in column 2 of Table 3, this pattern is not observed among workers who received advance notice of displacement. As mentioned earlier, this unobserved pattern may result from complex reasons. Despite its interest, the topic lies beyond the scope of the present paper.[29]

Because the search behavior of UI recipients may differ from that of non-recipients, or because UI recipients may differ from their non-recipients counterparts in some unmeasured way, we distinguish between those workers who received UI benefits and those who did not in columns (3) and (4) of Table 3. For similar reasons, the analysis is also done by distinguishing between those who exhausted UI and those who did not in columns (5) and (6) of Table 3. For all subgroups, the *p*-value for the Z test of the null hypothesis: $\beta_1 > 0$, $\beta_2 > 0$, $\beta_3 > 0$, $\beta_4 > 0$ is significant at the 5% level, providing evidence consistent with the signaling model of unemployment.

One may also wonder whether our finding is driven by whether workers lost their job during an expansion or recession period. A priori, we would expect the information content of layoffs and recalls to be stronger during expansions than recessions as many more workers lose their jobs when there is an economic slowdown. To explore this, I have re-estimated the main specification dividing the sample in two based on whether the worker lost her job during a global recession or not. Following the IMF, a global recession would take a slowdown in global growth to 3% or less. By this measure, three periods from 1985 to 2006 qualify: 1990 to 1993, 1998, and 2001 to 2002. Results for white-collar workers are displayed in columns 7 and 8 of Table 3. As expected, our stylized fact is driven by the expansion periods.

Another concern is that this result may be explained by alternative signaling stories. For example, one could assume that, contrary to the model in this paper, longer unemployment after any kind of displacement signals lower ability. This is consistent with post-displacement wages falling with the duration of the initial unemployment spell. If a layoff is also a signal of productivity (as in Gibbons & Katz, 1991), then the market knows more about workers who were laid off than they know about workers displaced by a plant closing, and consequently, future signals of productivity (unemployment) will then have less of an effect on wages of workers who were laid off. However, such alternative signaling model relies on the assumption that layoffs are lemons. While this result has been questioned by many (see Krashinsky, 2002, and Song, 2007, among others), it is easy to check whether it holds with the current data set. When estimating Gibbons and Katz's (1991) specification using the data from the current paper, I find that white-collar workers displaced through layoffs did *not* have lower post-displacement wages than workers displaced through plant closings – the coefficient on the layoff dummy is –.008 (standard error = .028), ruling out that the results of this paper are another test of the "layoffs and Lemons" story. Alternatively, we have also tested Gibbons and Katz's "layoffs as lemons" hypothesis within the framework of equation (3) in the main test. To do so, we must test the following null hypothesis:

$$dY/dL = \beta_0 + \beta_1 D_1 + \beta_2 D_2 + \beta_3 D_3 + \beta_4 D_4 < 0$$

When we do so, we reject this hypothesis for white-collar workers ($Z = 0.00$ and $\text{Prob} > Z = 1.000$).[30]

Firm- Specific, Industry-Specific, and Occupation-Specific Human Capital

Firm- specific, industry- specific, and occupation-specific human capital is an important issue to address when studying post-displacement earnings of workers. Below, we analyze the relevance of each of this three different types of human capital in explaining why post-displacement wages don't fall so much even in the case of workers who lost a white-collar job and are not recalled. We find that the new stylized fact in this paper is driven by workers with seniority in their former job, workers who stay in the same occupation that was held prior to displacement, and workers who switch industries.

To explore the relevance of firm-specific human capital we follow Carmichael (1983) and use years working in the same firm before being displaced as a good approximation of firm-specific human capital. We then estimate our baseline specification separately for workers with 1 year of tenure or less, on the one hand, and those with more than 1 year of tenure, on the one hand. Columns 1 and 2 in Table 4 display the results. The estimates reveal that the differential effect by cause of displacement in the relationship between post-displacement earnings and unemployment duration holds *only* among white-collar workers who have more than 1 year of tenure with the former employer, revealing that firm-specific human capital is at least part of the explanation why post-displacement wages don't fall so much even in the case of white-collar workers who are not recalled. Moreover, this also suggest that some time may have to elapse before the current employer can accurately evaluate workers' productivity (perhaps because the employer cannot learn the workers' productivity until the workers learns the job), implying that layoffs (and subsequently recalls) after brief employment spells signal little information to prospective employers.

Neal (1995) and Parent (1999) emphasized in their studies that "workers apparently receive compensation for some skills that are neither completely general nor firm-specific but rather specific to their industry or line of work." Recently, the relevance of industry-specific human capital in the United States has been questioned by Neal (1999), Parent (2000), Gibbons, Katz, Lemieux, & Parent (2005), and Kambourov and Manovskii (2009), among others. More specifically, these authors have found that when occupational experience is also taken into account, it is occupational experience rather than industry experience that is of primary importance in explaining wages. Others have also found evidence consistent with a substantial fraction of workers' human capital being occupation specific in the United States (McCall, 1990; Shaw, 1984, 1987). Evidence of human capital being occupation specific has also been found in other countries, such as Sweden (Kwon & Meyersson Milgrom, 2004), the United Kingdom (Zangelidis, 2008), or Canada (Kambourov, Manovskii, & Plesca, 2005). Ultimately, whether the findings in the current paper are driven by occupation-specific or industry-specific human capital is an empirical question that we can address here.[31] Columns 3–6 in Table 4 aim at this by presenting estimates of the variables of interest obtained by estimating the baseline specification using only workers for whom: (i) no occupation change has occurred after displacement; (ii) occupation change has occurred after displacement, (iii) no industry change has occurred after displacement; and (iv) industry change has occurred after displacement. These estimates indicate that post-displacement earnings fall *less* with the unemployment spell for white-collar laid-off workers who find a job in the same occupation than for those displaced through plant closings who also find a job in the same occupation (shown in column 3), and for white-collar laid-off workers who change industry than for those displaced through plant closings who also change industry (shown in column 6). All of the four β_j coefficients, for $j=1$ to 4, in columns 3 and 6 are positive, and (although not statistically significant at the individual level) the *p*-value for the joint Z test of the hypothesis: $\beta_1>0$, $\beta_2>0$, $\beta_3>0$, $\beta_4>0$ is significant at the 5% level, indicating that there is a differential effect by cause of displacement in the relationship between post-displacement earnings and unemployment duration for white-collar workers who stay in the same occupation (column 3) or who change industries (column 6). These findings are suggestive of the relevance of occupation-specific versus industry-specific human capital among white-collar workers, and consistent with the most recent literature on the topic.[32]

While no such effect is found when restricting the sample to those cases in which occupation change has occurred (column 4 of Table 4), this is not necessarily evidence against the signaling model as the occupation-specific human capital is lost with the switch of occupation, and therefore the signaling content of the layoff is not as relevant for the new employer. Finally, it is also important to highlight that the significant effect among industry switchers is *not* driven by differential industry changes between layoffs and plant closings occurring at different points of the unemployment spell. A simple comparison of the percentage of industry change in our data that take place among workers displaced through plant closings with the percentage in which the same type of change occurs among laid-off workers at different points of the unemployment spell does not suggest that industry changes are more common for layoffs than plant closings at any point of the unemployment spell. Table A7 shows the probability of staying in the same industry for white-collar displaced workers by cause of displacement and length of the unemployment spell and no statistically significant differences are found across the two groups.

CONCLUSION

This paper is particularly timely given the recent waves of layoffs in the economy, especially because it uncovers a new empirical fact in the United States, namely that, among white-collar workers, post-displacement earnings do not fall as rapidly with unemployment-spell length for laid-off workers compared to workers displaced by plant closings.[33],[34] These findings are consistent with an asymmetric information model of layoffs that explicitly considers the possibility of recall, and therefore suggest that at least some aspects of the search decisions of white-collar workers on temporary layoff in the United States may have a signaling component. Finally, the paper explores alternative explanations for these results. It finds that the results are robust across several subgroups of white-collar workers – regardless of their UI receipt status, or their work experience – and that they are driven by those who experience no occupation change, suggesting that signaling is more relevant when the amount of human capital transmitted is higher.

While the empirical results are consistent with a signaling through unemployment model, we acknowledge that the nature of asymmetric information makes it difficult to conduct direct empirical tests.[35] In addition, we recognize that frequently the data available are not rich enough to precisely distinguish between all potential explanations. Superior data, when they exists, usually restrict the analysis to very specialized settings, such a single firm – as in DeVaro and Waldman (2012) – or to a narrowly defined group of workers – as in Acemoglu and Pischke (1998).[36] Nonetheless, this paper provides additional evidence suggestive that explanations of asymmetric information are important. In "Layoffs and Lemons," Gibbons and Katz showed that prospective employers understood adverse selection in the labor market. The results in this paper indicate that workers may also be aware of the existence of adverse selection and of its consequences on their behavior. This finding implies a need for differential unemployment policies by cause of displacement and type of job (blue-collar versus white-collar).

NOTES

1. Spence (1973), Waldman (1984), Greenwald (1986), McCormick (1990), Ma and Weiss (1993), Riordan and Staiger (1993), Gottfries and McCormick (1995), Montgomery (1999), Strand (2000), and Eriksson (2002), among others.

2. Gibbons and Katz (1991), Canziani and Petrolongo (2001), Kugler and Saint-Paul (2004), Schönberg (2007), Hu and Taber (2011), Kahn (2013), and Zhang (2007).

3. In this (as well as in the current chapter), temporary laid-off workers are laid-off workers who *initially* expected to be recalled to their former job despite not having a definite recall date. However, it is important to notice that these ex ante

temporary layoffs may end up *not* being recalled to their former employer, and ex post becoming permanent layoffs and having to find a new job with a *new* employer.

4. Ma and Weiss (1993), and Gottfries and McCormick (1995), have also developed models in which least-able workers choose low-skilled jobs and more-able ones choose unemployment. While Rodríguez-Planas' paper analyses the effect of recalls on workers' unemployment when employers have better information about their workers than outside firms do, Ma and Weiss, and Gottfries and McCormick focus on the interaction between signaling and testing.

5. Recalled laid-off workers return to their old employer (and most likely to their old job) and therefore their earnings losses are small relative to permanently displaced workers (Katz & Meyer, 1990). The prediction of the model is for permanently displaced workers, and the empirical analysis is also done for permanently displaced workers.

6. See Krashinsky (2002), and Song (2007), for evidence against Gibbons and Katz's lemons effect.

7. We follow Gibbons and Katz (1991), and Hu and Taber (2011), and focus our analysis on white-collar workers. That said, we present main results for blue-collar workers. The reason these authors focused on white-collar workers is that the occupation was a rough proxy for whether a job is covered by collective bargaining agreements which typically have seniority-based rules and are considerably more common among blue-collar jobs. As a referee pointed out for this comparison to be relevant in this chapter, it must be that collective bargaining agreements also stipulate seniority-based rules for recalls. The empirical evidence is indeed consistent with firms that have inverse seniority layoff rules also have seniority recall rules which lead to extensive use of temporary layoffs and recalls over the business cycle (Freeman, 1980; http://saleshq.monster.com/training/articles/1055-legal-tips-for-managers-layoffs, and http://www.referenceforbusiness.com/encyclopedia/Kor-Man/Layoffs.html, among others).

8. They endogenize mobility by adding non-pecuniary job characteristics to the workers' utility function following Neal (1998) and Acemoglu and Pischke (1998).

9. One exception to the use of the methodology developed by Altonji and Pierret is Kahn (2013). This author also develops a model of asymmetric learning that nests the symmetric learning case and allows the degree of asymmetry to vary. The novelty of her model is that it derives a new dependent variable for identifying employer learning: the variance in pay changes. Kahn (2013) finds evidence supportive of asymmetric information.

10. An underlying assumption is that employers have discretion over whom to layoff and recall. In practice, employers may rehire according to a seniority rule.

11. This assumption could be endogenized into the model. For instance, we could assume that the employer bears a cost of hiring someone that may be recalled. The market would then offer an even lower wage to laid-off workers, and those laid-off workers who think that they will be recalled would have a higher incentive to wait unemployed. Alternatively, we could assume that workers bear a cost of generating a job offer or a once-for-all cost of changing jobs.

12. See Rodríguez-Planas (2009), for proofs on the existence of the equilibrium with no voluntary unemployment, uniqueness of the equilibrium, and equilibrium refinements.

13. Fig. 1 has been computed for parameter values $\alpha = 0{,}4$; $r = 0{,}5$; $H = 5$; $L = 1$; $U = 0{,}6$; and $\zeta = 0{,}2$. For other parameter values, some region may cease to exist but the sorting is always the same.

14. It is unclear whether this prediction would hold when all workers choose unemployment (lemma 3) because accepting a first-period job is an out-of-equilibrium strategy. However, an equilibrium in which all laid-off workers choose unemployment is quite unlikely in the United States. For example, in the DWS sample of laid-off workers used in the next section, more than 10 percent of laid-off workers find jobs without an intervening unemployment spell.

15. Unfortunately, as the data we use do not contain information on wage offers that the worker turns down during his unemployment spell, we cannot identify whether the main factor contributing to duration of the unemployment spell is the workers declining offers or the worker not searching for work.

16. To generate some unemployment among workers displaced through plant closings, some frictional unemployment is needed. Adding frictional unemployment for both laid-off workers and workers displaced through plant closings into this model does not alter the results of this chapter.

17. Although the model is about how having recall expectations affects displaced workers' behavior, the predictions of the model are for workers who are permanently displaced. So a priori, the DWS is a good data set. That said, one may be concerned if no laid-off worker expected to be recalled in our dataset. After 1994, the DWS asked workers whether they expected to be recalled to their former employer. We can thus explore whether workers in our sample expected to be recalled. While *no* workers displaced through plant closing expect to be recall, we do observe that some laid-off workers expected a recall. Between 3.5 and 8 percent of blue-collar workers in our sample (depending on the survey year) reported that they expected to be recalled. Among white-collar workers, the percentage is lower, as expected, as it ranges between 1.4 and 2.3 percent. The fact that these numbers are lower than those mentioned in Section 3 of the paper is consistent with many laid-off workers returning to the former employer.

18. The variable "initial unemployment spell" was added starting in 1988, however, due to an error this variable was *not* collected for all displaced workers who were re-employed at the survey date in the 1994 supplement.

19. Recall bias arises because respondents forget less salient events from the distant past and fail to report them. Carrington (1990), Topel (1990), Evans and Leighton (1995), Oyer (2004), and Song (2007), are some of the researchers who have found evidence of recall bias when using the DWS.

20. In order to explore whether recall bias was affecting the results, the analysis was also done using workers who had reported losing a job in the last *two* years. The results in this chapter are also robust to such sensitivity analysis. Estimates are available from the author upon request.

21. Katz and Meyer (1990), find that the post-displacement hourly earnings of workers with unemployment spells ending in recall are similar to their pre-displacement hourly earnings.

22. I did not include agricultural workers because they tend to have a large number of jobs with a pronounced seasonal pattern. Workers displaced from construction jobs were eliminated from the sample because formulating an appropriate definition of permanent displacement from a construction job is difficult.

23. To test this one-sided alternative, I have used bootstrapping with 1,000 iterations. When one obtains a p-value less than 0.050 it implies that we cannot reject our joint hypothesis: $\beta_1 > 0, \beta_2 > 0, \beta_3 > 0, \beta_4 > 0$.

24. The DWS is known to overstate what would be considered job displacement because some laid-off workers end up returning to their original employer after the survey date. This occurs despite the fact that workers entering my sample are re-employed at survey date and have answered "yes" to the question: "In the past 3 years, have you left or lost a job because of a plant closing, an employer going out of business, or a layoff from which you were *not* recalled, or other similar reasons?"

25. See evidence presented earlier in the third section.

26. We also tested the following hypothesis and could not reject it: $\alpha_1 > \alpha_2 > \alpha_3 > \alpha_4 > 0$.

27. Following an anonymous referee suggestion, we have tested whether there is a differential pattern between workers losing a blue-collar and white-collar job. To do so, we pooled all workers and estimated the main specification adding a dummy indicating whether the worker lost a white-collar or blue-collar job plus interactions between this variable and the main variables (the layoff dummy, the unemployment spell dummies, and the interactions between the unemployment spell dummies and the layoff dummy). The analysis is shown in Appendix Table A3. The tests of the hypothesis at the bottom of the table corroborate the differential pattern between blue-collar and white-collar workers.

28. Notice that workers displaced by plant closings also receive advance notice (shown in the descriptive statistics Tables 1). It is likely that in this case employees knew about the plant closing ahead of time and thus began searching for a new job early on.

29. A concern raised by an anonymous referee is that our empirical finding may be due to the fact that the most able workers at a plant about to shut down knew months ahead of time about the closing and, thus, they have been looking for other jobs early on. This would explain their relatively shorter unemployment spell and higher post-displacement wages soon after displacement. That said, it is important to notice that this does not seem to be supported by the data as the positive pattern between unemployment spell and reemployment wage for layoffs versus plant closings is *not* observe among those who received advanced notice.

30. We thank an anonymous referee for this suggestion.

31. We thank an anonymous referee for suggesting this line of analysis.

32. This analysis has also been conducted with the sample of workers who were displaced from a blue-collar job. We find that the difference in post-displacement earnings between white-collar and blue-collar workers is generated by firm-specific and occupation-specific human capital. It is interesting to note that the post-displacement earnings of workers who change industries do not fall as rapidly with unemployment-spell length for laid-off workers compared to workers displaced by plant closing regardless of whether they lost a blue-collar or white-collar job.

33. Every day one can read several articles on layoffs in the press. For instance, on December 22, 2008, CNNMoney.com reported that: "As the recession has worsened, companies have ratcheted up layoffs. (...) Reports show that nearly 1 in 4 companies plan layoffs, and 1 million job cuts are forecasted."

34. As explained in the third section, recalls continue to be important in the current recession. According to the Mass Layoff Statistics program over half of

employers reporting a layoff in 2008 indicated that they anticipated some type of recall (US Bureau of Labor Statistics, 2009). It also reports that among all establishments expecting to recall workers, most employers (88%) expected to recall at least half of the separated employees. Finally, even in the midst of the current recession, the evidence indicates that about one fifth of laid-off workers who landed new positions within the last year were rehired by the same employer that had let them go (CNNmoney.com, 2009).

35. This has also been acknowledged by Gibbons and Katz (1991), Hu and Taber (2011), Schönberg (2007), Kahn (2013), Pinkston (2009), and Zhang (2007), among others.

36. Acemoglu and Pischke (1998), analyze the German Apprenticeship labor market.

ACKNOWLEDGMENTS

I especially thank Kevin Lang for his much-appreciated support and guidance. I also thank the extremely valuable suggestions and comments from three anonymous referees and the Editor, Solomon Polachek. Finally, George Akerlof, Eli Berman, William Dickens, Lawrence Katz, and Andrew Weiss have provided comments of earlier versions of this chapter. I acknowledge financial support from the Spanish ministry of Education and Science (grant MICINN2009-11857), the Generalitat de Catalunya (grant SGR2009-57), and Barcelona Graduate School of Economics.

REFERENCES

Acemoglu, D., & Pischke, J. (1998). Why do firms train? Theory and evidence. *Quarterly Journal of Economics*, *113*, 78–118.

Addison, J., & Blackburn, M. (1994). The worker adjustment and retraining notification act. *Journal of Economic Perspectives*, *8*(1), 181–190.

Akerlof, G. (1970). The market for lemons: Qualitative uncertainty and the market mechanism. *Quarterly Journal of Economics*, *84*, 488–500.

Akerlof G., Rose, A., & Yellen, J. (1990, May). *Waiting for work*. NBER Working Paper No. 3385. Cambridge, MA: NBER.

Alba-Ramírez, A., Arranz-Muñoz, J. M., & Muñoz-Bullón, F. (2007). Exits from unemployment: recall or new job. *Labour Economics*, *14*, 788–810.

Altonji, J., & Pierret, C. (1997). Employer learning and the signaling value of education. In I. Ohashi & T. Tachibanaki (Eds.), *Industrial relations, incentives and employment* (pp. 159–195). London: Macmillan.

Altonji, J., & Pierret, C. (2001). Employer learning and statistical discrimination. *Quarterly Journal of Economics*, *116*, 313–350.

Anderson, P. (1992). Time-varying effects of recall expectations, a reemployment bonus, and job counseling on unemployment durations. *Journal of Labor Economics*, *10*(1), 99–115.

Arcidiacono, P., Bayer, P., & Hizmo, A. (2010). Beyond signaling and human capital: Education and the revelation of ability. *American Economic Journal: Applied Economics*, *2*(4), 76–104.

Bauer, T., & Haisken-DeNew, J. (2001). Employer Learning and the Returns to Schooling. *Labour Economics*, *8*, 161–180.

Belzil, C., & Bognanno, M. (2005). *The promotion dynamics of American executives*. Mimeo. Temple University, Philadelphia, PA.

Bernhardt, D. (1995). Strategic promotion and compensation. *Review of Economic Studies*, *62*, 315–339.

Canziani, P., & Petrolongo, B. (2001). Firing costs and stigma: A theoretical analysis and evidence from microdata. *European Economic Review*, 45, 1877–1906.

Carmichael, L. (1983). Firm-specific human capital and promotion ladders. *Bell Journal of Economics*, *14*(1), 251–258.

Carrington, W. J. (1990). *Specific human capital and worker displacement*. Ph.D Dissertation. Chicago, IL: University of Chicago.

Chang, C., & Wang, Y. (1996). Human capital investment under asymmetric information: The pigovian conjecture revisited. *Journal of Labor Economics*, *14*, 505–519.

Corak, M. (1996). Unemployment insurance, temporary layoffs and recall expectations. *Canadian Journal of Economics*, *29*, 1–7.

DeVaro, J., & Waldman, M. (2012). The signaling role of promotions: Further theory and empirical evidence. *Journal of Labor Economics*, *30*(1), 91–147.

DeVaro, J., S. Ghosh, & C. Zoghi. (2007, 4th August). *Job characteristics and labor market discrimination in promotions: New theory and empirical evidence*. Working Paper. Cornell University, Ithaca, NY.

Dickler, J. (2009, 28 July). Laid-off workers get their jobs back. CNNmoney.com.

Farber, H. S., & Gibbons, R. (1996). Learning and wage dynamics. *Quarterly Journal of Economics*, *111*, 1007–1047.

Feldstein, M. (1976). Temporary layoffs in the theory of unemployment. *Journal of Political Economy*, *84*, 937–957.

Eriksson, S. (2002). *Imperfect information, wage formation, and the employability of the unemployed.* Working Paper 17, Institute for Labour Market Policy Evaluation, Uppsala, Sweden.

Evans, D. S., & Leighton, L. S. (1995). Retrospective bias in the displaced worker surveys. *Journal of Human Resources*, *30*(2), 386–396.

Fischer, G., & Pichelmann, K. (1991). Temporary layoff unemployment in Austria: Empirical evidence from administrative data. *Applied Economics*, *23*, 1447–52.

Freeman, R. (1980). The effect of unionism on workers attachment to firms. *Journal of Labor Research*, *1*(1), 29–61.

Galindo-Rueda, F. (2002). *Employer learning and schooling-related statistical discrimination in Britain*. Discussion Paper. IZA, Bonn, Germany.

Galindo-Rueda, F. (2002, November). *Endogenous wage and capital dispersion, on-the-job search and the matching technology*. IZA Discussion Paper No. 625.

Gibbons, R., & Katz, L. (1991). Layoffs and lemons. *Journal of Labor Economics* (October), 351–380.

Gibbons, R., Katz, L. F., Lemieux, T., & Parent, D. (2005). Comparative advantage, learning, and sectoral wage determination. *Journal of Labor Economics*, *23*(1), 681–724.

Golan, L. (2005). Counteroffers and efficiency in labor markets with asymmetric information. *Journal of Labor Economics*, *23*, 373–393.

Gottfries, N., & McCormick, B. (1995). Discrimination and open unemployment in a segmented labour market. *European Economic Review*, 39, 1–15.

Greenwald, B. (1986). Adverse selection in the labor market. *Review of Economic Studies*, *53*(3), 325–347.

Hu, L., & Taber, C. (2011). Displacement, asymmetric information, and heterogeneous human capital. *Journal of Labour Economics*, *29*(1), 113–152.

Jansson, F. (2002). Rehires and unemployment duration in the Swedish labour market: New evidence of temporary layoffs. *Labour*, *16*, 311–45.

Jensen, P., & Svarer, M. (2003). Short- and long-term unemployment: How do temporary layoffs affect this distinction? *Empirical Economics*, *28*, 23–44.

Kahn L. B., (2013). Asymmetric information between employers. *American Economic Journal: Applied Economics*, *5*(4), 165–205.

Kambourov, G., I. Manovskii, &, M. Plesca. (2005). *Returns to government sponsored training.* Mimeo. University of Pennsylvania, Philadelphia, PA.

Kambourov, G., & Manovskii, I. (2009). Occupational specificity of human capital. *International Economic Review*, *50*, 63–112.

Katz, L. (1986). *Layoffs, recall and the duration of unemployment.* NBER Working Paper No. 1825. Cambridge, MA: NBER.

Katz, L., & Meyer, B. (1990). Unemployment insurance, recall expectations, and unemployment outcomes. *Quarterly Journal of Economics* (November), 973–1002.

Krashinsky, H. (2002). Evidence on adverse selection and establishment size in the labor market. *Industrial and Labor Relations Review*, *56*(1), 84–96.

Kugler, A., & Saint-Paul, G. (2004). How do firing costs affect worker flows in a world with adverse selection? *Journal of Labor Economics*, *22*, 553–584.

Kwon, I., & Meyersson Milgrom, E. M. (2004). *Boundaries of internal labor markets: The relative importance of firms and occupations.* Mimeo. Stanford University Graduate School of Business, Stanford, CA.

Lange, F. (2007). The speed of employer learning. *Journal of Labor Economics*, *25*, 1–35.

Lilien, D. (1980). The cyclical importance of temporary layoffs. *Review of Economics and Statistics*, *57*, 24–31.

Ma, A., & Weiss, A. (1993). A signaling theory of unemployment. *European Economic Review*, 37, 135–157.

Mavromaras, K. G., & Orme, C. D. (2004). Temporary layoffs and split population models. *Journal of Applied Econometrics*, *19*, 49–67.

Milgrom, P., & Oster, S. (1987). Job discrimination, market forces, and the invisibility hypothesis. *Quarterly Journal of Economics*, *102*, 453–476.

McCall, B. P. (1990). Occupational matching: A test of sorts. *Journal of Political Economy*, *98*(1), 45–69.

McCormick, B. (1990). A theory of signaling during job search, employment efficiency and "stigmatized" jobs. *Review of Economic Studies*, *57*, 299–313.

Montgomery, J. (1999). Adverse selection and employment cycles. *Journal of Labor Economics*, *17*, 281–297.

Neal, D. (1995). Industry-specific human capital: Evidence from displaced workers. *Journal of Labor Economics, 13*(4), 653–677.

Neal, D. (1998). The link between ability and specialization: An explanation for observed correlations between wages and mobility rates. *Journal of Human Resources, 33*, 173–200.

Neal, D. (1999). The complexity of job mobility among young men. *Journal of Labor Economics, 17*(2), 237–261.

Oyer, P. (2004). Recall bias among displaced workers. *Economics Letters, 82*(3), 397–402.

Owan, H. (2004). Promotion, turnover, earnings, and firm-sponsored training. *Journal of Labor Economics, 22*, 955–978.

Parent, D. (1999). Wages and mobility: The impact of employer-provided training. *Journal of Labor Economics, 17*(2), 298–317.

Parent, D. (2000). Industry-specific capital and the wage profile: Evidence from the national longitudinal survey of youth and the panel study of income dynamics. *Journal of Labor Economics, 18*(2), 306–323.

Pinkston, J. (2009). A model of asymmetric employer learning with testable implications. *Review of Economic Studies, 76*(1), 367–394.

Pissarides, C. (1982). Job search and the duration of layoff unemployment. *Quarterly Journal of Economics, 97*(4), 595–612.

Podgursky, M., & Swaim, P. (1987). Job displacement and earnings loss: Evidence for the displaced worker survey. *Industrial and Labor Relations Review, 41*, 17–29.

De Raaf, S., Motte, A., & Vincent, C. (2003). *The dynamics of reliance on EI benefits: Evidence from the SLID. The earnings supplement project*. Working Paper Series 03-0. Social Research and Demonstration Corporation (SDRC), Ottawa, Canada.

Ricart i Costa, J. (1988). Managerial task assignment and promotion. *Econometrica, 56*, 449–466.

Riordan, M., & Staiger, R. (1993). Sectoral shocks and structural unemployment. *International Economic Review, 34*, 611–629.

Robertson, M. (1989). Temporary layoffs and unemployment in Canada. *Industrial Relations, 28*, 82–90.

Rodríguez-Planas, N. (2009). A signaling model of temporary layoffs. *Oxford Economic Papers, 61*(3), 566-585.

Ruhm, C. (1992). Advance notice and post-displacement joblessness. *Journal of Labor Economics, 10*(1), 1–32.

Shaw, K. (1984). A formulation of the earnings function using the concept of occupational investment. *Journal of Human Resources, 14*, 319–40.

Shaw, K. (1987). Occupational change, employer change, and the transferability of skills. *Southern Economic Journal, 53*, 702–19.

Schönberg, U. (2007). Testing for asymmetric employer learning. *Journal of Labor Economics, 25*, 651–691.

Song, Y. (2007). Recall bias in the displaced workers survey: Are layoffs really lemons? *Labour Economics, 14*, 335–345.

Spence, M. (1973). Job market signalling. *Quarterly Journal of Economics, 87*, 355–74.

Strand, J. (2000). Wage bargaining and turnover costs with heterogeneous labor asymmetric information. *Labour Economics, 7*, 95–116.

Topel, R. (1990). Specific capital and unemployment: Measuring the costs and consequences of job loss. *Carnegie-Rochester Conference Series in Public Policy, 33*(Autumn), 181–214.

United States Bureau of Labor Statistics. (2009). *Extended mass layoff in 2008*. Report. Washington, DC: United States Department of Labor.

Waldman, M. (1984). Job assignment, signaling, and efficiency. *Rand Journal of Economics*, *15*, 255–267.

Waldman, M. (1990). Up-or-out contracts: A signaling perspective. *Journal of Labor Economics*, *8*, 230–250.

Weiss, A. (1995). Human capital vs signaling explanation of wages. *Journal of Economic Perspectives*, *9*(4), 133–154.

Zabojnik, J., & Bernhardt, D. (2001). Corporate tournaments, human capital acquisition, and the firm size-wage relation. *Review of Economic Studies*, *68*, 693–716.

Zangelidis, A. (2008). Occupational and industry specificity of human capital in the British labour market. *Scottish Journal of Political Economy*, *55*(4), 420–443.

Zhang Y. (2007, November 1). Employer learning under asymmetric information: The role of job mobility.

APPENDIX

Table A1. Post-Displacement Earnings Equation Workers Reemployed at Survey Date DWS 1988–2006 (White-Collar Workers at Displacement).

Unemployment Spell	(1)		(2)		(3)		(4)	
$N = 3{,}564$	PC	Layoff	PC	Layoff	PC	Layoff	PC	Layoff
No unemployment		−.140**		−.099*		−.110*		−.103
(β_0 for layoffs)		(.062)		(.060)		(.058)		(.057)
1–4 weeks	−.184***	+.170**	−.148**	+.131	−.125**	+.122	−.103*	+.104
(α_1 for plant closings and β_1 for layoffs)	(.060)	(.084)	(.057)	(.081)	(.055)	(.078)	(.054)	(.077)
5–12 weeks	−.194***	+.230**	−.158**	+.180**	−.140**	+.139	−.134**	+.133
(α_2 for plant closings and β_2 for layoffs)	(.068)	(.089)	(.066)	(.087)	(.064)	(.085)	(.063)	(.084)
13–24 weeks	−.232***	+.200*	−.190**	+.165	−.196**	+.157	−.194**	+.133
(α_3 for plant closings and β_3 for layoffs)	(.086)	(.113)	(.085)	(.112)	(.081)	(.108)	(.081)	(.108)
More than 24 weeks	−.508***	+.298***	−.427***	+.195*	−.360***	+.134	−.369***	+.110
(α_4 for plant closings and β_4 for layoffs)	(.077)	(.113)	(.074)	(.109)	(.071)	(.106)	(.070)	(.105)
$\alpha_1 < 0, \alpha_2 < 0, \alpha_3 < 0, \alpha_4 < 0$	$Z = 12.27$ Prob > |Z|=.0000		$Z = 10.03$ Prob > |Z|=.0000		$Z = 5.85$ Prob > |Z|=.0000		$Z = 5.09$ Prob > |Z|=.0000	
$\beta_1 > 0, \beta_2 > 0, \beta_3 > 0, \beta_4 > 0$	$Z = 4.57$ Prob > |Z| = .0000		$Z = 3.18$ Prob > |Z|=.0001		$Z = 2.44$ Prob > |Z|=.015		$Z = 2.24$ Prob > |Z|=.025	
Constant	6.476*** (.041)		Yes		Yes		Yes	
Married, race, gender			Yes		Yes		Yes	
Education					Yes		Yes	
Exp., exp^2							Yes	
R-squared	.0151		.0738		.1341		.1485	

Unemployment spell	(5)		(6)		(7)		(8)	
$N = 3{,}564$	PC	Layoff	PC	Layoff	PC	Layoff	PC	Layoff
No unemployment		−.071		−.065		−.045		−.060
(β_0 for layoffs)		(.057)		(.057)		(.056)		(.057)
1–4 weeks	−.100*	+.082	−.082	+.079	−.078	+.075	−.064	+.062
(α_1 for plant closings and β_1 for layoffs)	(.055)	(.077)	(.055)	(.076)	(.055)	(.076)	(.055)	(.075)
5–12 weeks	−.147**	+.137	−.136**	+.143*	−.127**	+.135	−.130**	+.138*
(α_2 for plant closings and β_2 for layoffs)	(.063)	(.083)	(.063)	(.082)	(.064)	(.082)	(.063)	(.082)
13–24 weeks	−.209***	+.107	−.199**	+.103	−.190**	+.092	−.186**	+.086
								(.103)
(α_3 for plant closings and β_3 for layoffs)	(.081)	(.106)	(.080)	(.106)	(.080)	(.105)	(.077)	
More than 24 weeks	−.398***	+.082	−.401***	+.097	−.401***	+.102	−.401***	+.102
(α_4 for plant closings and β_4 for layoffs)	(.071)	(.105)	(.071)	(.105)	(.070)	(.105)	(.070)	(.104)
$\alpha_1 < 0$, $\alpha_2 < 0$, $\alpha_3 < 0$, $\alpha_4 < 0$	$Z = 4.20$		$Z = 3.61$		$Z = 3.11$		$Z = 2.77$	
	Prob > |Z|=.0000		Prob > |Z|=.0000		Prob > |Z|=.002		Prob > |Z|=.006	
$\beta_1 > 0$, $\beta_2 > 0$, $\beta_3 > 0$, $\beta_4 > 0$	$Z = 2.04$		$Z = 2.10$		$Z = 2.06$		$Z = 2.00$	
	Prob > |Z|=.041		Prob > |Z|=.036		Prob > |Z|=.039		Prob > |Z|=.045	
Constant	Yes		Yes		Yes		Yes	
Married, race, gender, education, exp., and $\exp^2$	Yes		Yes		Yes		Yes	
Year dummies, years since displacement, region	Yes		Yes		Yes		Yes	
Pre-displacement tenure spline			Yes		Yes		Yes	
Advance notice					Yes		Yes	
Industry							Yes	
Occupation								
Pre-displacement wage								
R-squared	.1726		.1761		.1774		.1909	

Table A1. *(Continued)*

Unemployment Spell	(9)		(10)	
$N = 3{,}564$	PC	Layoff	PC	Layoff
No unemployment		−.056		−.050
(β_0 for layoffs)		(.057)		(.049)
1–4 weeks	−.062	+.058	−.082*	+.050
(α_1 for plant closings and β_1 for layoffs)	(.055)	(.075)	(.048)	(.066)
5–12 weeks	−.133**	+.140*	−.158***	+.131*
(α_2 for plant closings and β_2 for layoffs)	(.064)	(.082)	(0.58)	(.074)
13–24 weeks	−.189**	+.087	−.192**	+.065
(α_3 for plant closings and β_3 for layoffs)	(.078)	(.103)	(.073)	(.095)
More than 24 weeks	−.405***	+.099	−.407***	+.052
(α_4 for plant closings and β_4 for layoffs)	(.070)	(.104)	(.064)	(.096)
$\alpha_1 < 0$, $\alpha_2 < 0$, $\alpha_3 < 0$, $\alpha_4 < 0$	$Z = 2.75$ Prob > $\lvert Z \rvert$=.006		$Z = 4.82$ Prob > $Z = 0.000$	
$\beta_1 > 0$, $\beta_2 > 0$, $\beta_3 > 0$, $\beta_4 > 0$	$Z = 2.01$ Prob > $\lvert Z \rvert$=.044		$Z = 2.00$ Prob > $Z = 0.045$	
Constant	Yes		Yes	
Married, race, gender, education, exp., and exp^2	Yes		Yes	
Year dummies, years since displacement, region	Yes		Yes	
Pre-displacement tenure spline	Yes		Yes	
Advance notice	Yes		Yes	
Industry	Yes		Yes	
Occupation	Yes		Yes	
Pre-displacement wage			Yes	
R-squared	.1922		.3193	

Note: See Table 2. Column (10) matches column (1) in Table 2.

Table A2. Wage Change Equation, Workers Reemployed at Survey Date, DWS 1988–2006 (White-Collar Workers at Displacement).

	Wage change		Post-displacement wage		Pre-displacement wage	
	Plant closing	Layoff	Plant closing	Layoff	Plant closing	Layoff
	(1)		(2)		(3)	
No unemployment (β_0 for layoffs)		−.048 (.049)		−.050 (.049)		−.008 (.034)
1–4 weeks (α_1 for plant closings and β_1 for layoffs)	−.091* (.049)	+.046 (.067)	−.082* (.048)	+.050 (.066)	.029 (.034)	.012 (.046)
5–12 weeks (α_2 for plant closings and β_2 for layoffs)	−.170*** (0.59)	+.126* (.074)	−.158*** (0.58)	+.131* (.074)	.037 (0.037)	.013 (.049)
13–24 weeks (α_3 for plant closings and β_3 for layoffs)	−.193** (.076)	+.055 (.098)	−.192** (.073)	+.065 (.095)	.005 (.048)	.032 (.061)
More than 24 weeks (α_4 for plant closings and β_4 for layoffs)	−.407*** (.066)	+.030 (.098)	−.407*** (.064)	+.052 (.096)	.003 (.041)	+.070 (.056)
$\alpha_1 < 0, \alpha_2 < 0, \alpha_3 < 0, \alpha_4 < 0$	$Z = 4.79$ Prob $> Z = 0.000$		$Z = 4.82$ Prob $> Z = 0.000$		n.a.	
$\alpha_1 > \alpha_2 > \alpha_3 > \alpha_4$	n.a.		n.a.		$Z = 0.00$ Prob $> Z = 1.000$	
$\beta_1 > 0, \beta_2 > 0, \beta_3 > 0, \beta_4 > 0$	$Z = 2.16$ Prob $> Z = 0.031$		$Z = 2.00$ Prob $> Z = 0.045$		$Z = 2.04$ Prob $> Z = 0.041$	
$\beta_1 < \beta_2 < \beta_3 < \beta_4$	n.a.		n.a.		$Z = 2.00$ Prob $> Z = 0.046$	
Sample size	3,564		3,564		3,564	

Note: n.a., not applicable. The numbers in parentheses are robust standard errors. All weekly wages are deflated by the GDP deflator (base year = 2000). Additional covariates include: a spline function in previous tenure (with breaks at 1, 2, 3, and 6 years), three dummies for completed education (one for "high school graduate"; one for "some college"; and one for "college graduate or above"), an "advance notice" dummy, year-of-displacement dummies; previous-industry and previous-occupation dummies; experience and its square; a gender dummy; marriage dummy; a non-white dummy; and three region dummies. In addition, column (2) has pre-displacement wage as a RHS variable.

*Estimate significantly different from zero at the 90% confidence level.

**Estimate significantly different from zero at the 95% confidence level.

***Estimate significantly different from zero at the 99% confidence level.

Table A3. Post-Displacement Earnings Equation, Workers Reemployed at Survey Date, DWS 1988–2006.

	Plant closing	Layoff
Blue-collar No unemployment (β_0 for layoffs)		−.004
		(.060)
White-collar No unemployment (β_0 +WCβ_0 for layoffs)		−.055
		(.049)
Blue-collar		
1–4 weeks	−.033	−.025
(α_1 for plant closings and β_1 for layoffs)	(.045)	(.068)
5–12 weeks	−.139***	+.099
(α_2 for plant closings and β_2 for layoffs)	(0.53)	(.073)
13–24 weeks	−.169**	−.119
(α_3 for plant closings and β_3 for layoffs)	(.059)	(.107)
More than 24 weeks	−.325***	−.009
(α_4 for plant closings and β_4 for layoffs)	(.059)	(.086)
White-collar		
1–4 weeks	−.089*	+.053
(α_1 + WCα_1 for plant closings and β_1 + WCβ_1 for layoffs)	(.048)	(.067)
5–12 weeks	−.158**	+.130*
(α_2 + WCα_2 for plant closings and β_2 + WCβ_2 for layoffs)	(0.57)	(.074)
13–24 weeks	−.194***	+.072
(α_3 + WCα_3 for plant closings and β_3 + WCβ_3 for layoffs)	(.073)	(.096)
More than 24 weeks	−.417***	+.062
(α_4 +WCα_4 for plant closings and β_4 + WCβ_4 for layoffs)	(.063)	(.095)
$\alpha_1 < 0$, $\alpha_2 < 0$, $\alpha_3 < 0$, $\alpha_4 < 0$	$Z = 3.82$ Prob > $Z = 0.000$	
α_1 + WC$\alpha_1 < 0$, α_2 +WC$\alpha_2 < 0$, α_3 + WC$\alpha_3 < 0$, α_4 +WC$\alpha_4 < 0$	$Z = 4.14$ Prob > $Z = 0.000$	
$\beta_1 > 0$, $\beta_2 > 0$, $\beta_3 > 0$, $\beta_4 > 0$	$Z = 0.00$ Prob > $Z = 1.000$	
β_1 + WCβ_1 >0, β_2 + WC$\beta_2 > 0$, β_3 + WC$\beta_3 > 0$, β_4 + WC$\beta_4 > 0$	$Z = 3.35$ Prob > $Z = 0.000$	
Sample size	6,234	

Note: The numbers in parentheses are robust standard errors. See notes in Table 2 in the paper. WCα_1 , WCα_2 , WCα_3 , WCα_4 are the coefficients of the interaction between the white-collar dummy and the different unemployment spell dummies. And WCβ_1, WCβ_2, WCβ_3, WCβ_4 are the coefficients of the interaction between the white-collar dummy and the interactions between the layoff dummy and the different unemployment spell dummies.

Table A4. Post-Displacement Earnings Equation Workers Reemployed at Survey Date DWS 1988–2006 (Blue-Collar Workers at Displacement).

Unemployment spell	(1)		(2)		(3)		(4)	
$N = 2{,}670$	PC	Layoff	PC	Layoff	PC	Layoff	PC	Layoff
No unemployment		−.136*		−.101		−.119		−.105
(β_0 for layoffs)		(.075)		(.077)		(.076)		(.075)
1–4 weeks	−.286***	+.135	−.219***	+.108	−.163***	+.094	−.144***	+.073
(α_1 for plant closings and β_1 for layoffs)	(.058)	(.086)	(.055)	(.084)	(.055)	(.082)	(.055)	(.081)
5–12 weeks	−.326***	+.226*	−.276***	+.228*	−.243***	+.209**	−.245***	+.214**
(α_2 for plant closings and β_2 for layoffs)	(.063)	(.090)	(.060)	(.088)	(.059)	(.082)	(.059)	(.085)
13–24 weeks	−.357***	+.144	−.258***	+.068	−.224***	+.054	−.219***	+.031
(α_3 for plant closings and β_3 for layoffs)	(.074)	(.124)	(.071)	(.122)	(.068)	(.118)	(.067)	(.117)
More than 24 weeks	−.481***	+.160	−.408***	+.130	−.358***	+.128	−.360***	+.106
(α_4 for plant closings and β_4 for layoffs)	(.068)	(.104)	(.067)	(.103)	(.066)	(.101)	(.065)	(.099)
$\alpha_1 < 0$, $\alpha_2 < 0$, $\alpha_3 < 0$, $\alpha_4 < 0$	$Z = 32.73$ Prob > $\lvert Z \rvert$=.0000		$Z = 31.62$ Prob > $\lvert Z$ =.0000		$Z = 11.22$ Prob > $\lvert Z \rvert$=.0000		$Z = 10.05$ Prob > $\lvert Z \rvert$=.0000	
$\beta_1 > 0$, $\beta_2 > 0$, $\beta_3 > 0$, $\beta_4 > 0$	$Z = 4.57$ Prob > $\lvert Z \rvert$=.0000		$Z = 2.09$ Prob > $\lvert Z \rvert$=.036		$Z = 2.05$ Prob > $\lvert Z \rvert$=.040		$Z = 2.00$ Prob > $\lvert Z \rvert$=.045	
Constant	6.222*** (.049)		Yes		Yes		Yes	
Married, race, gender			Yes		Yes		Yes	
Education					Yes		Yes	
Exp., $\exp^2$							Yes	
R-squared	.0270		.0816		.1377		.1513	

Table A4. *(Continued)*

Unemployment spell	(5)		(6)		(7)		(8)	
$N = 3,564$	PC	Layoff	PC	Layoff	PC	Layoff	PC	Layoff
No unemployment		−.046		−.041		−.041		−.043
(β_0 for layoffs)		(.066)		(.066)		(.066)		(.065)
1–4 weeks	−.142***	+.032	−.135***	+.033	−.135***	+.033	−.132***	+.032
(α_1 for plant closings and β_1 for layoffs)	(.055)	(.074)	(.056)	(.075)	(.056)	(.075)	(.056)	(.075)
5–12 weeks	−.241***	+.199**	−.235***	+.200**	−.235***	+.200**	−.230***	+.183**
(α_2 for plant closings and β_2 for layoffs)	(.059)	(.080)	(.060)	(.081)	(.060)	(.081)	(.059)	(.080)
13–24 weeks	−.233***	−.023	−.233***	+.003	−.233***	−.003	−.229***	−.014
(α_3 for plant closings and β_3 for layoffs)	(.068)	(.111)	(.068)	(.111)	(.068)	(.111)	(.067)	(.111)
More than 24 weeks	−.405***	+.072	−.406***	+.073	−.406***	+.073	−.409***	+.075
(α_4 for plant closings and β_4 for layoffs)	(.065)	(.092)	(.065)	(.092)	(.065)	(.092)	(.064)	(.092)
$\alpha_1 < 0$, $\alpha_2 < 0$, $\alpha_3 < 0$, $\alpha_4 < 0$	$Z = 9.18$		$Z = 8.22$		$Z = 8.22$		$Z = 8.8$	
	Prob > |Z|=.0000		Prob > |Z|=.0000		Prob > |Z|=.0000		Prob > |Z|=.0000	
$\beta_1 > 0$, $\beta_2 > 0$, $\beta_3 > 0$, $\beta_4 > 0$	$Z = 0.00$		$Z = 2.08$		$Z = 2.08$		$Z = 0.00$	
	Prob > |Z|=1.000		Prob > |Z|=.037		Prob > |Z|=.037		Prob > |Z|=1.000	
Constant	Yes		Yes		Yes		Yes	
Married, race, gender, education, exp., and exp^2	Yes		Yes		Yes		Yes	
Year dummies, years since displacement, region	Yes		Yes		Yes		Yes	
Pre-displacement tenure spline			Yes		Yes		Yes	
Advance notice					Yes		Yes	
Industry							Yes	
Occupation								
Pre-displacement wage								
R-squared	.2123		.2145		.2145		.2294	

Unemployment spell	(9)		(10)	
$N = 3{,}564$	PC	Layoff	PC	Layoff
No unemployment		−.038		−.013
(β_0 for layoffs)		(.065)		(.062)
1–4 weeks	−.128**	+.023	−.045	−.022
(α_1 for plant closings and β_1 for layoffs)	(.055)	(.074)	(.050)	(.069)
5–12 weeks	−.227***	+.175**	−.151***	+.113
(α_2 for plant closings and β_2 for layoffs)	(.059)	(.079)	(0.54)	(.073)
13–24 weeks	−.231***	−.018	−.181***	−.104
(α_3 for plant closings and β_3 for layoffs)	(.067)	(.111)	(.061)	(.106)
More than 24 weeks	−.409***	+.067	−.327***	+.005
(α_4 for plant closings and β_4 for layoffs)	(.065)	(.092)	(.060)	(.086)
$\alpha_1 < 0$, $\alpha_2 < 0$, $\alpha_3 < 0$, $\alpha_4 < 0$	$Z = 8.82$		$Z = 2.64$	
	Prob > |Z|=.000		Prob > Z = 0.008	
$\beta_1 > 0$, $\beta_2 > 0$, $\beta_3 > 0$, $\beta_4 > 0$	$Z = .000$		$Z = .000$	
	Prob > |Z|=1.000		Prob > |Z|=1.000	
Constant	Yes		Yes	
Married, race, gender, education, exp., and exp^2	Yes		Yes	
Year dummies, years since displacement, region	Yes		Yes	
Pre-displacement tenure spline	Yes		Yes	
Advance notice	Yes		Yes	
Industry	Yes		Yes	
Occupation	Yes		Yes	
Pre-displacement wage			Yes	
R-squared	.2337		.3193	

Note: See Table 2. Column (10) matches column (2) in Table 2.

Table A5. Wage Change Equation, Workers Reemployed at Survey Date, DWS 1988–2006 (Blue-Collar Workers at Displacement).

	Wage change		Post-displacement wage		Pre-displacement wage	
	Plant closing	Layoff	Plant closing	Layoff	Plant closing	Layoff
	(1)		(2)		(3)	
No unemployment (β_0 for layoffs)		−.006 (.066)		−.013 (.062)		−.044 (.042)
1–4 weeks (α_1 for plant closings and β_1 for layoffs)	.020 (.052)	−.058 (.073)	−.045 (.050)	−.022 (.069)	−.148*** (.038)	+.081 (.051)
5–12 weeks (α_2 for plant closings and β_2 for layoffs)	−.091 (0.57)	+.065 (.077)	−.151*** (0.54)	+.113 (.073)	−.136*** (0.041)	+.110** (.055)
13–24 weeks (α_3 for plant closings and β_3 for layoffs)	−.141** (.063)	−.173 (.111)	−.181*** (.061)	−.104 (.106)	−.090*** (.048)	+.155** (.111)
More than 24 weeks (α_4 for plant closings and β_4 for layoffs)	−.263*** (.063)	−.063 (.090)	−.327*** (.060)	+.005 (.086)	−.146*** (.044)	+.129** (.060)
$\alpha_1 < 0, \alpha_2 < 0, \alpha_3 < 0, \alpha_4 < 0$	$Z = 0.00$ Prob > $Z = 1.000$		$Z = 2.64$ Prob > $Z = 0.008$		$Z = 8.06$ Prob > $Z = 0.000$	
$\alpha_1 > \alpha_2 > \alpha_3 > \alpha_4$	n.a.		n.a.		$Z = 0.00$ Prob > $Z = 1.000$	
$\beta_1 > 0, \beta_2 > 0, \beta_3 > 0, \beta_4 > 0$	$Z = 0.00$ Prob > $Z = 1.000$		$Z = .000$ Prob > $\|Z\| = 1.000$		$Z = 4.73$ Prob > $Z = 0.000$	
$\beta_1 < \beta_2 < \beta_3 < \beta_4$	n.a.		n.a.		$Z = 0.00$ Prob > $Z = 1.000$	
Sample size	2,670		2,670		2,670	

Note: n.a., not applicable. The numbers in parentheses are robust standard errors. All weekly wages are deflated by the GDP deflator (base year = 2000). Additional covariates include: a spline function in previous tenure (with breaks at 1, 2, 3, and 6 years), three dummies for completed education (one for "high school graduate"; one for "some college"; and one for "college graduate or above"), an "advance notice" dummy, year-of-displacement dummies; previous-industry and previous-occupation dummies; experience and its square; a gender dummy; marriage dummy; a non-white dummy; and three region dummies. In addition, column (2) has pre-displacement wage as a RHS variable.

*Estimate significantly different from zero at the 90% confidence level.

**Estimate significantly different from zero at the 95% confidence level.

***Estimate significantly different from zero at the 99% confidence level.

Table A6. Probability of staying in the same occupation for Displaced Workers, Workers Reemployed at Survey date, DWS 1988–2006 (White-Collar Workers at Displacement).

Weeks unemployed	0 weeks		1–4 weeks		5–12 weeks		13–24 weeks		25+ weeks	
	Plant closing	Layoff	Plant closing	Layoff	Plant closing	Layoff	Plant closing	Layoff	Plant closing	Layoff
Probability of staying in the same occupation	.746	.676**	.667	.675	.602	.663*	.665	.653	.585	.609
	(.436)	(.469)	(.472)	(.469)	(.490)	(.473)	(.474)	(.477)	(.495)	(.485)
Number of observations	370	413	448	593	274	549	161	274	193	289

Note: The numbers in parenthesis are standard deviations. All weekly wages are deflated by the GDP deflator (base year = 2000).
* Difference in the means between layoff and plant closing are significantly different at the 90% confidence level.
** Difference in the means between layoff and plant closing are significantly different at the 95% confidence level.

Table A7. Probability of staying in the same industry for Displaced Workers. Workers Reemployed at Survey date, DWS 1988–2006 (White-Collar Workers at Displacement).

Weeks unemployed	0 weeks		1–4 weeks		5–12 weeks		13–24 weeks		25+ weeks	
	Plant closing	Layoff	Plant closing	Layoff	Plant closing	Layoff	Plant closing	Layoff	Plant closing	Layoff
Probability of staying in the same industry	.600	.598	.542	.536	.489	.515	.472	.504	.404	.433
	(.491)	(.491)	(.499)	(.499)	(.500)	(.500)	(.501)	(.501)	(.492)	(.496)
Number of observations	370	413	448	593	274	549	161	274	193	289

Note: The numbers in parenthesis are standard deviations. All weekly wages are deflated by the GDP deflator (base year = 2000).

ECONOMIC AND HEALTH IMPLICATIONS OF LONG-TERM UNEMPLOYMENT: EARNINGS, DISABILITY BENEFITS, AND MORTALITY

Kenneth A. Couch, Gayle L. Reznik,
Christopher R. Tamborini and Howard M. Iams

ABSTRACT

Data from the 1984 Survey of Income and Program Participation *are linked to longitudinal records from the Social Security Administration to examine the relationship between the long-term unemployment that prime-aged (ages 25–55) male workers experienced around the time of the 1980–1982 twin recessions with earnings, receipt of either Disability Insurance or Supplemental Security Income (DI-SSI) benefits, and mortality. Separate estimations are made for those who voluntarily and involuntarily left employment and the combined sample of these two groups. We find that 20 years later, long-term joblessness was associated*

New Analyses of Worker Well-Being
Research in Labor Economics, Volume 38, 259–305

ISSN: 0147-9121/doi:10.1108/S0147-9121(2013)0000038008

with significantly lower earnings and higher likelihoods of the receipt of DI-SSI benefits as well as mortality.

Keywords: Earnings; mortality; social security disability insurance; supplemental security income; unemployment; recession; health

JEL classifications: H55; I31; J31; J63; J65

INTRODUCTION

The economic literature regarding the impact of job loss on prime-aged (ages 25–55) workers has often focused on those who left employment involuntarily due to business closure and found work again within a year (Couch & Placzek, 2010; Jacobson, LaLonde, & Sullivan, 1993). However, the experience of the recession which began following the peak of the business cycle in December of 2007 and officially ended with the trough that occurred in June of 2009 reminds us that many prime-aged workers experience periods of unemployment that extend beyond a year. Moreover, there are reasons for becoming unemployed other than job displacement.

In this chapter, we examine the earnings and health experiences of a group of workers in the 1984 *Survey of Income and Program Participation* (SIPP) who at the time of the survey had not been employed for more than two weeks in the past one to three years. The earliest time that they could have become jobless (at ages 25–55) was in 1981, squarely within the window of the twin recessions that in combination extended from January 1980 to November 1982. The third year in which the individuals examined in this study might have left their jobs, 1983, would be in the wake of the downturn.

The early 1980s recession was considered the most severe in post-World War II history in the United States prior to the Great Recession. Peak unemployment, based on the *Current Population Survey* (CPS), occurred at 10.8 percent in December of 1982. At the time, it was the highest level observed since the data began being collected in 1948. The only other peak, over 9.0 percent in the historical series, occurred during the Great Recession at 10.0 percent in October of 2009.

The early 1980s recession was followed by a period of sluggish employment growth (Jacobson et al., 1993). The unemployment rate remained over 8.0 percent for more than two years during the twin recessions of the early 1980s. In contrast, in the Great Recession, the unemployment rate was over 8.0 percent for just over three years. The sustained higher unemployment rates observed in the Great Recession were driven by mean and median weeks of unemployment that exceeded those observed in the downturn of the early 1980s by almost 4 months (Farber, 2013, Figure 2).

Nonetheless, in the post-World War II experience of the United States, these two periods are most similar in terms of the labor market difficulties experienced by workers. In this study, by examining workers who left employment around the time of the recession of the early 1980s, we hope to gain some insight into the magnitude of effects the Great Recession may have on outcomes of the long-term jobless.

In the analysis that follows, we use individual fixed-effects and propensity score matching methods to examine those who were unemployed at the time of the survey, comparing them to other individuals who were employed and highly attached to the labor market. We make use of annual longitudinal earnings data obtained through a link to the Social Security Administration's (SSA) Summary Earnings Record (SER) to examine workers' covered earnings for 20 years beyond when they report leaving their jobs. Similarly, we make use of a linkage between the 1984 SIPP panel and the Master Beneficiary Record (MBR), the Supplemental Security Record (SSR), and the Numident File of the SSA to examine the impact of joblessness on the receipt of either Social Security Disability Insurance or Supplemental Security Income (DI-SSI) benefits and mortality over an observational period that extends 20 years beyond job loss.

Only a few other studies have been able to observe the effects of job loss, voluntary or involuntary, on worker outcomes for such a long follow-up period. Von Wachter, Song, and Manchester (2009) study the impact of the early 1980s recession on long-term earnings losses of prime-aged job separators using a one percent extract of the SSA's Master Earnings File (MEF) combined with other administrative sources. Sullivan and Von Wachter (2009a, 2009b) similarly provide evidence regarding the impact of job separations and mass layoffs on the mortality of prime-aged workers who lost jobs in the early 1980s recession in the state of Pennsylvania. These prior studies focus on workers who were unemployed for relatively short periods of time, less than a year. Neither examines the receipt of DI-SSI benefits. We extend these prior analyses by focusing on workers who report being without a job for as long as three years, using a different but nationally-representative data set, and examining the outcomes of earnings, receipt of DI-SSI benefits, and mortality for workers who were prime-aged at the time they separated from employment.

Throughout the analysis, we focus on three groups: (1) all individuals unemployed in the 1984 SIPP who report having lost their job in the interval from 1981–1983; (2) all individuals in the first group who report the reason for their job loss was due to layoff or being fired; and (3) all individuals in the first group who report leaving employment voluntarily. The estimates for group (1) expand the traditional discussion of job loss from those who leave employment due to slack demand and find work again relatively quickly to others who experience long-term joblessness during a recession. The second and third groups divide the first into involuntary and voluntary separators.

The analysis also addresses a potential criticism, which is that the event of job loss, particularly for voluntary leavers, may be related to underlying health problems (Stewart, 2001). A prior analysis (Rupp & Davies, 2004) of self-reported work limitations in the 1984 SIPP and subsequent DI or SSI benefit receipt finds that there is a significant predictive association between these variables. That is to say, pre-existing health problems may both predicate the job loss and drive related outcomes (earnings, DI-SSI receipt, and mortality). To explore this issue, we provide additional estimates where we screen the samples to exclude individuals who report pre-existing work-limiting health conditions prior to and through the year of job loss. As robustness checks, we also provide propensity score matching estimates of the main results to more directly control for differences that may occur between those in the sample who have left jobs and those who remained employed (Browning, Dano, & Heinesen, 2006; Dustmann & Windmeijer, 2000). Additional sensitivity analyses allow for individuals to have earnings and health functions differentiated by factors such as income level, education, and pre-existing health conditions. Prior analyses (Dustmann & Windmeijer, 2000) have established that the response of health behaviors of individuals to unexpected changes in wage trajectories would depend on their prior level and trajectory.

We find that long-term joblessness has a consistent negative association with future earnings and a positive relationship with the subsequent probability of receiving DI-SSI benefits and mortality in the samples that contain all job leavers. The observed declines in earnings are largest for those who leave employment involuntarily, and the increase in the likelihood of receiving DI-SSI benefits is largest for those who leave employment voluntarily; however, long-run effects on mortality are similar for those who leave their jobs voluntarily and involuntarily.

For all job leavers, the estimated reduction in future earnings and the likelihood of receipt of DI-SSI are moderated once those with pre-existing health conditions are removed from the samples. The likelihood of dying within the first 20 years beyond job loss for the average job loser does not change meaningfully when those with pre-existing health conditions are excluded from the estimations. Across sub-groups, removing those with pre-existing health conditions results in equal (and large) proportional earnings losses across voluntary and involuntary job leavers. In the analysis of the increased probability of receiving DI-SSI benefits, the likelihood among voluntary leavers falls well below that for the involuntarily unemployed once those with pre-existing conditions are removed from the estimation samples. The results for earnings and DI-SSI receipt demonstrate that estimates based on samples of involuntary job losers are less likely to be influenced by self-selection based on pre-existing health problems that limit work activity than those of unemployed workers in general. The results described here do not exhibit a great deal of sensitivity to the robustness checks conducted in the paper.

Our estimates indicating sizeable long-term earnings losses for workers who experienced joblessness during the 1980–1982 recession are larger, as one might expect, than those reported by Von Wachter et al. (2009) for job leavers who were more quickly re-employed, but are largely consistent with other studies which have also examined workers who had more intermittent employment patterns (Couch & Placzek, 2010; Jacobson et al., 1993). Further, our estimates showing that long-term joblessness (both involuntary and voluntary) also has a significant impact on mortality are similar in magnitude to those reported by Sullivan and Von Wachter (2009a, 2009b) for workers who separated from employment in Pennsylvania during the early 1980s recession but returned to work within a year. Together, our results based on the SIPP-SSA data confirm patterns of the long-term impact of involuntary unemployment on earnings and mortality reported by other researchers, while extending them to the receipt of Disability or Supplemental Security Income benefits as well. Additionally, by demonstrating the role of pre-existing health conditions in driving earnings and health outcomes among samples of the involuntarily and voluntarily unemployed, we provide useful information for researchers who do not have this information available in their estimation samples.

The paper proceeds with a discussion of the prior literature. This is followed by a description of the methods used in the analysis and the available data. The empirical results are followed by our conclusions.

PRIOR LITERATURE

The majority of prior studies on the experiences of prime-age workers who lose their jobs have examined the impact on earnings of involuntary job losses related to slack demand. Job separations can be voluntary, and analytically, a concern has been that earnings losses and other outcomes in that situation may be related to unobserved personal characteristics, such as health (Stewart, 2001), rather than specifically having lost a job. By focusing attention on those who involuntarily lose jobs due to layoffs that occur in periods of slack demand, analysts have sought to focus on the impact of that event on workers when the change in employment status is arguably less related to individual choice.

A great deal has been learned from studying the experiences of workers displaced from employment due to slack demand. Regardless of the data source, during ordinary business cycle conditions, prime-aged workers (25–55) who lose their jobs would expect to have a 10–15 percent long-term loss of their earnings (see the discussion in Couch & Placzek, 2010). During recessionary periods, there is evidence that over short time horizons (3–6 years) earnings losses are larger, ranging from 20 to 25 percent (Couch, Jolly, & Placzek, 2011; Couch & Placzek, 2010; Jacobson et al., 1993). The only existing study that examines long-term earnings losses from the 1980s recession, the same event we examine here, finds that earnings losses for displaced workers who are reemployed within a year stabilize at around 20 percent (Von Wachter et al., 2009) in the long-term. Together, these studies suggest that between 10 and 20 percent of wages are determined by skills that are valuable only to one's current employer, that is, due to specific skills.[1]

Because of economists' focus on understanding the underlying determinants of payments for skills in the labor market, most studies require that workers be re-employed to enter their samples. However, many studies also provide estimates of earnings losses if workers who are not re-employed quickly are included in the estimation samples. Those estimates are more comparable to the ones provided in this study and they (Couch & Placzek, 2010; Jacobson et al., 1993) suggest that the range of estimates of proportional earnings losses shifts upwards by 10–15 percentage points (implying 20–40 percent long-term earnings losses) if continuously unemployed (or intermittently employed) workers beyond the point of job displacement are included in the estimations.

Neither administrative nor national survey based data sources containing the necessary labor market information to determine why workers change employment tend to contain health information on prime-aged workers. As a result, health-related impacts for prime-aged workers who experience job loss have not been widely studied. Only two groups of authors, to our knowledge, have examined health-related outcomes for prime-aged workers who experience job loss in the United States. The work of Sullivan and Von Wachter (2009a, 2009b) examines mortality among a group of Pennsylvania workers displaced in the early 1980s recession in Pennsylvania. In that research, cumulative impacts on mortality of 10–15 percent are reported. As previously discussed, one potential complaint about those estimates is that the displacements might have been correlated with poor prior health and that the impacts on mortality are in part driven by this factor. The other work which has examined a health-related outcome of prime-aged workers in the United States who experience job loss is the work of Gruber and Madrian (1997) which analyzed the relationship between job loss and subsequent health insurance coverage using the same 1984 SIPP data employed in this study.[2]

While the body of prior research is thin regarding the health impacts of employment separation among prime-aged job losers, there is a sizeable literature on the topic for older workers. Primarily, this is due to the availability of the *Health and Retirement Study* (HRS) which collects data on individuals ages 51 and older that facilitate studies of the inter-relationship between later life work activities and health. Using those data, researchers have documented not only the decline in earnings associated with late life job loss (Chan & Stevens, 2000; Couch, 1992), but also its association with a broad range of health behaviors. For example, Gallo et al. (2006) explore the impact of involuntary job loss on mental health while Siegel, Bradley, Gallo, and Kasl (2003) document the impact of involuntary job loss for married men on the mental health of their wives. Gallo et al. (2004) explore the relationship between involuntary job loss and the risk of heart attack or stroke. Deb, Gallo, Ayyagari, Fletcher, and Sindelar (2011) additionally explore the relationship between involuntary job loss, BMI, and consumption of alcohol. Gallo, Brand, Teng, Leo-Summers, and Byers (2009) examine whether self-reports of work limitations among older workers who experience job displacement are associated with later functional disability, reporting that this is generally not a concern among males. The studies cited here are not meant to be exhaustive but do give an indication of the much richer range of health-related topics that have been explored in relation to late life job loss.

While the preponderance of studies based on the HRS have reported declines in health associated with job displacement, that view is not universal. Salm (2006) uses HRS data from 1994 to 2002 to examine a range of health outcomes employing a differences-in-differences estimation approach focusing on a group of workers who lost their jobs due to firm closure. The study (p. 1076) examines "self-reported changes in health, limitations in activities of daily living (ADL), subjective longevity expectations, depression, and physician diagnosed mental health conditions." The author concludes (p. 1076) that, "There is no negative effect of job loss on health." The primary explanation provided for this difference in results relative to others who have used the HRS data to examine similar outcomes is that examining workers who leave work due to exogenous events potentially removes biases that may be present when workers already in poor health leave work either at their own discretion or when laid off by their employer due to reasons such as low productivity.

This study contributes to the much smaller literature on the long-term health impacts of job loss among prime-aged workers. We examine the experiences of prime-aged males who have sustained periods of joblessness in contrast to prior research that has primarily focused on those who are quickly re-employed. Our reason for focusing on this sub-group of workers is to examine individuals whose experiences in the early 1980s recession were similar to those who have had the most adverse employment experiences in the United States during the Great Recession. We examine a group of workers who report being unemployed for one to three years and provide separate analyses for those who voluntarily and involuntarily separated from employment. The analysis of workers who were involuntarily unemployed is similar to many other analyses except that we focus on workers who have had worse unemployment experiences. Our additional examination of voluntary job leavers extends the frame of analysis to the broader social concern of what happens to the long-term unemployed during a severe recession. We estimate earnings losses and the relationship of job loss to mortality in a manner similar to the prior literature but also provide an extension of the existing literature on health impacts by analyzing the association between unemployment and the subsequent receipt of disability benefits (DI-SSI).

Because the prior literature has established that individuals with pre-existing health conditions are likely to be found unemployed (Stewart, 2001) and further that those very conditions can be related to the outcomes we study (Rupp & Davies, 2004), we explore whether pre-existing health limitations play an important role in determining outcomes for the long-term unemployed. Our approach is to first provide gross estimates of the association between job leaving and outcomes (earnings, DI-SSI receipt, and mortality) but then to remove from the sample those who reported pre-existing health limitations. This allows us to look at the impact of job loss on a group that reports being healthy prior to the event. We find that the exclusion of individuals who had pre-existing health limitations moderates but does not eliminate the observed relationship between job loss and the outcomes studied. In subsequent analyses, we also provide additional robustness checks using propensity score matching estimators and models that allow for greater variation in individual profiles in earnings and health. The qualitative results of the study are robust to these variations in approach.

METHODS

We make use of a panel individual fixed-effects model in the main analysis. This approach is common in the literature used to examine the impacts of job loss (Couch & Placzek, 2010; Jacobson et al., 1993; Von Wachter et al., 2009). Although most papers focus on workers who report leaving their jobs due to slack demand, workers may still differ from each other and time invariant heterogeneity can be captured with a fixed-effects model. Since we also examine workers who voluntarily separate from employment, it is especially important to control for some of the systematic differences that are likely to exist across individuals in that sample. We will discuss the fixed-effects methodology before describing the additional procedures used in robustness checks.

The fixed-effects methodology compares the experiences of workers who have sustained periods of unemployment to a comparison group of workers who did not report the loss of a job during the same period of time and exhibit a similar extent of labor market attachment. Define Y_{it} to be the outcome of interest for individual i at time t. X_{it} contains regressors related to the outcome of interest for individual i at time t. Let k index time relative to job loss with negative values representing years prior to the event, zero the year of the loss, and positive values afterwards. Then, a standard panel individual fixed-effects estimator can be written as:

$$Y_{it} = \beta X_{it} + \sum_{k=-2}^{k=20} D_{it}^{k}\gamma_k + \varphi_i + \varepsilon_{it} \tag{1}$$

β is a set of parameters relating regressors to the outcome of interest. D_{it}^{k} is a categorical variable that for each person (i) year (t) observation marks its timing relative to job loss. The parameters, γ_k, gauge the difference in the outcome variable for the group that experiences job loss relative to the comparison group for each period k. In cases where the dependent variable takes the values of zero or one, this estimation method is a linear probability model with individual fixed-effects. Fixed-effects models have been employed as linear probability models in looking at other categorical health related-outcomes related to unemployment such as the loss of health insurance (Gruber & Madrian, 1997).[3] Standard errors are corrected for clustering of observations at the individual level.

Building off of the fixed-effects approach, the analysis of the relationship between earnings and health found in Dustmann and Windmeijer (2000) indicates that those paths and interactions between them may vary greatly based on factors such as age, education, prior health conditions, and the initial level of earnings. To explore whether differences in the levels or trends in paths that vary due to these factors would influence our primary findings, we provide additional estimates of results based on Eq. (1) that include interactions between age, age-squared, and year of observation with the level of education. Interactions are also included between age and age-squared and whether the individual was above or below median income in 1980. We provide estimates here for the sample which omits workers with pre-existing health conditions to demonstrate that this does not substantially impact those estimates. We also estimated the fixed-effects models with the relevant interactions with all observations while interacting age and age-squared with pre-existing health conditions and found similar results. For purpose of brevity, those additional results are not included in the paper.

A second set of robustness checks are performed based on propensity score matching estimators. The concern addressed by these estimators is that those individuals who are observed without a job in our sample may be selected differently than those individuals in the comparison group in important dimensions not controlled for by the fixed-effects estimator (Browning et al., 2006). Matching each jobless person to a similar comparison person, thus, might result in different findings.

We employ the well-known programs written by Becker and Ichino (2002) to perform the scoring using logistic regression while focusing on the outcome being examined in the last year of the analysis, 20 years after job leaving.[4] We provide estimates based on two of the matching procedures, nearest neighbor estimation using random draws to break ties where multiple matches are available and kernel weighting. As the notation that underlies these estimators is well known and available in Becker and Ichino (2002), we do not reproduce it here.

DATA

Source

Data are drawn from wave 3 of the 1984 SIPP.[5] The SIPP is a nationally representative data set that surveys individuals every four months but elicits monthly dated information from respondents at each interview. The SIPP data used in this study are linked to several administrative files of the SSA: the SER, the MBR, the SSR, and the Numident File.

The linkage to the SER allows us to observe Social Security-covered earnings of the sample participants before and after the SIPP itself. The years of earnings used in the analysis extend from 1979 through 2003. These years of information allow us to observe earnings for individuals for at least two years prior to the point of job loss. We follow workers for 20 years beyond the time they report their job loss. The linkage to the MBR provides information on whether the individual has ever received Social Security DI. The SSR provides information on take-up of SSI, which is a means-tested program that provides cash assistance to disabled non-elderly adults. The Numident file validates dates of death. Weights that maintain the national representation of the data while correcting for attrition due to the inability to link individuals across the SIPP and these sources of additional information are used throughout the analysis.[6] Kim and Tamborini (2012), McNabb, Timmons, Song, and Puckett (2009), and Tamborini and Iams (2011, appendix) provide more detailed information on SSA's administrative records and data matching.

Samples

Within the Education and Work History topical module of the 1984 SIPP, respondents are asked if they are currently employed. If they are unemployed, they are asked when they last worked for more than two consecutive weeks and what the reason was for their job loss. We select respondents in the survey who reported the year of job loss from 1981 to 1983. Thus, we examine workers who report within the SIPP that they have been unemployed for one to three years. Responses for the reason for job loss include the possibility of being laid off or discharged. We use this response as being indicative of involuntary job loss. Similarly, unemployed workers may report they lost their last job for a number of reasons that would typically not be considered involuntary: (1) Found a better job,

(2) Did not like working conditions, (3) Dissatisfied with earnings, (4) Family or personal reasons, (5) Did not like location, or (6) Other. We code persons who left employment for these reasons as being voluntary job leavers. We omit workers who leave employment due to retirement from the analysis. In the study, we provide estimates for voluntary and involuntary job leavers as well as the combined group of the long-term unemployed.

Similar to the studies of workers impacted by the twin recessions of the early 1980s provided in Jacobson et al. (1993) and Von Wachter et al. (2009), we focus the analysis on prime-aged workers by restricting the sample to persons who would be at least age 25 but no older than 55 in 1980, the year prior to the first year (1981) in which the job losses we examine could have occurred. We also restrict our sample to men to focus on a group with greater attachment to the labor market. As we move forward in the observational period, we also restrict age in each calendar year in some of our estimations. These cutoffs vary by the outcome examined and are identified in a subsequent section.

From these individuals, we construct the analysis sample by first allowing those who report being currently unemployed to remain in the sample as long as they have five positive years of earnings in the period from 1980 through 1988, but we require the two annual observations in the years preceding the reported loss of employment to be positive.[7] This allows individuals who have years of non-earnings associated with their reported unemployment to remain in the sample. Then, a comparison group is similarly constructed from individuals who are employed at the time of the survey who are required to have positive years of earnings in the years 1980 through 1984. For both the job leavers and the comparison group, individuals are allowed to remain in the sample as long as they meet the selection criteria up to the point when they die. Those who receive DI-SSI benefits are allowed to remain in the sample as long as they meet other selection criteria.[8]

In examining the receipt of DI-SSI (non-elderly) benefits, we merge those two outcomes into one combined variable of disability. For that analysis, we use the same sample selection strategy as for the earnings analysis. Individuals are required to have at least five positive years of earnings in the period from 1980 through 1988 along with positive earnings in the two years prior to separation from employment. They are retained in the sample as long as they meet this criterion up to the point of DI-SSI benefit receipt. The coding of the outcome variable reflects having ever received DI or SSI benefits. So, individuals who die within the observational period of the study who have not yet received DI-SSI benefits have their data beyond that point set to missing. Those who receive DI-SSI before dying remain coded as having received benefits. The same individuals used in the earnings analysis are also used to examine mortality.

A potential criticism of studying health-related outcomes among those who leave employment, particularly those who voluntarily separate, is that the employment change itself may be associated with an underlying health problem (Browning et al., 2006; Stewart, 2001). This health problem, in turn, is responsible for the differences in outcomes relative to those who do not report experiencing long-term unemployment.

To explore this issue, we provide an initial set of estimates for the samples of the long-term unemployed and the voluntary and involuntary separators already described. Then, we screen the samples using a set of retrospective questions regarding pre-existing health conditions contained in SIPP's Health and Disability topical module, which was collected at the same time as the Education and Work History module. The SIPP asks respondents, does some "health or condition limit the type or amount of work … [you] can do?" It also asks respondents the year when this condition began. The SIPP also asks, "Does …'s health or condition prevent … from working at a job or business?" Again, the survey asks what year this problem arose. We make use of these two sets of questions and remove anyone from the estimation samples who reports that either of these conditions began prior to or during the year of their reported job loss. This strategy allows us to explore the influence of pre-existing health problems on earnings, receipt of DI-SSI, and mortality.

Measures: Dependent Variables

For the earnings analysis, the dependent variable is individuals' annual Social Security covered earnings. For the years of data used in the analysis, more than 90 percent of all workers in the United States were covered by the Social Security system so this source of earnings information is fairly comprehensive. One disadvantage is that these data are capped at the threshold of earnings that are taxable under the Social Security system;[9] however, studies that have used other administrative records have also imposed caps on their earnings to reduce the influence of outliers (Couch & Placzek, 2010; Jacobson et al., 1993). Similarly, survey-based data sources commonly contain censoring thresholds on earnings.[10] The earnings are stated in real 2008 dollars.

For the analysis of receipt of DI-SSI benefits, we make use of information available in the matched Master Beneficiary Record and Supplemental Security Record to date respondents' first entitlement to Social Security DI-SSI benefits for the disabled non-elderly.[11] The dependent variable in this case is coded as a zero prior to the first date of receipt and with the value of one afterward. Using this coding scheme, the parameters γ_k capture the difference in the cumulative distribution of receipt of DI-SSI benefits between those who experience a sustained period of unemployment and those who do not.

For the analysis of mortality, dates of death from the Numident File are used. Prior to the year of death, the dependent variable is coded as zero. Afterwards it is coded as one. Using this coding scheme, the parameters γ_k capture the difference in the cumulative distribution of mortality between those who experience a sustained period of unemployment and those who do not.

Measures: Independent Variables

The main independent variables measure the impact of joblessness on the three outcomes specified above: (a) earnings, (b) receipt of DI-SSI benefits, or (c) mortality, depending on the analysis. Specifically, a series of dichotomous variables measure the timing of the job loss for each person-year. For example, the year before the job loss $(t-1)$ is measured by the dummy variable D_{-1} and the year after $(t+1)$ is captured by the variable D_1. A series of these dummy variables (from $t-2$ to $t+20$) captures the persistent effects of the job loss. In addition to this set of dummy variables measuring the timing of the job loss, we also include age, age-squared, and calendar year dummies representing the year in which we observe either earnings, receipt of DI-SSI benefits, or mortality.

We restrict age in each calendar year to be less than 60 for the estimation of earnings and less than 65 for the receipt of DI-SSI benefits. There is no age restriction on the sample for the estimation of mortality. Within each sample, when a person-year observation exceeds these age thresholds, we set the observation to missing.

Summary Statistics of Sample

Panel A of Table 1 presents basic descriptive information on the primary sample in 1980, the last year prior to the job loss window. There are 140

Table 1. Descriptive Statistics in 1980.

Variables	Continuously Employed		Job Leavers					
	Mean	SE	All		Involuntary		Voluntary	
			Mean	SE	Mean	SE	Mean	SE
Panel A: Full analysis sample								
Earnings	$44,193	235	$29,781	1,252	$31,863	1,604	$26,704	1,971
Age	37.5	0.11	36.4	0.59	36.1	0.78	36.8	0.92
N (persons)	6,389		234		140		94	
Panel B: Respondents with pre-existing health limitations excluded								
Earnings	$44,424	241	$31,132	1495	$32,891	1,727	$26,910	2,870
Age	37.3	0.11	35.8	0.70	35.9	0.87	35.4	1.18
N (persons)	6,055		168		116		52	

Notes: Data use SIPP person weights adjusted for non-matches. All estimates are in 2008 dollars. The jobless sample includes individuals who were unemployed in 1984, last reported working for two consecutive weeks in 1981–1983, had five years of positive earnings in 1980–1988, and had positive earnings two consecutive years prior to their job loss. Continuously employed includes respondents who were employed in 1984 and who had positive earnings in 1980–1984.

involuntary, 94 voluntary, and 234 total job separators who enter the sample. There are 6,389 people in the comparison group of the continuously employed. As can be seen, the average age of job leavers (36.4) in 1980 is similar to the continuously employed (37.5). Among the job leavers, there does not appear to be much difference in the average age of voluntary (36.8) and involuntary leavers (36.1). While the average ages across these groups are similar, their levels of earnings in 1980 are quite different. Job leavers have lower earnings on average, $29,781, relative to the continuously employed, $44,193. Voluntary leavers also have lower average earnings ($26,704) than the involuntary job losers ($31,863). These differences point to the importance of controlling for differences across individuals in the levels of earnings prior to leaving employment as we do using the fixed-effect estimator employed in the analysis.

Panel B of Table 1 contains similar descriptive information on the samples screened to remove those with pre-existing health conditions. Across the samples shown in Panels A and B, the levels of average earnings reported across groups do not vary by more than $1,250. Average ages across the two panels also do not vary by more than one year. Thus, screening for pre-existing health conditions does not fundamentally alter the average characteristics of the estimation samples. The greatest impact is on sample size where the group of all job leavers is reduced by 28 percent, falling from 234 to 168 observations. The reductions are concentrated among the voluntary leavers with 42 respondents, or 45 percent, of the sample removed. Among involuntary leavers, 24 respondents, or 17 percent, of the sample are removed when we screen for pre-existing health conditions.

Based on the literature, one would expect to observe that those in the sample who had been unemployed for longer periods would be more likely to have reported a health condition prior to leaving employment. Table 2 shows the percent of individuals in our sample with pre-existing health conditions. There, 5.2 percent of those in the comparison group reported a pre-existing health condition whereas 29 percent of those in the jobless sample did. Those who lost their job in 1981 and remained unemployed in 1984 had a very high rate of pre-existing health conditions, 45.3 percent, while those who separated from employment in 1983 and remained unemployed in 1984 had a lower rate of pre-existing health conditions, 21 percent.

Across the categories of involuntary and voluntary job leavers, the percentages of each sample reporting a health limitation prior to employment separation were 15.9 and 48.2 percent, respectively. Thus, there are substantial numbers of individuals in the sample who report pre-existing conditions particularly among those who voluntarily leave employment. The fixed-effects estimates that do not remove from the sample those who report pre-existing conditions no doubt conflate the impact of job loss as well as prior health limitations on later outcomes. Removing those with

Table 2. Percent with Pre-Existing Health Conditions, by Jobless Category and Year of Job Loss.

	Continuously Employed	Job Leavers		
	%	All	Involuntary	Voluntary
		%	%	%
Continuously Employed	5.2			
Lost Job in:				
1981		45.3	31.0	73.6
1982		40.5	27.3	55.9
1983		21.0	8.6	40.4
1981, 1982, or 1983		29.0	15.9	48.2

Notes: Data use SIPP person weights adjusted for non-matches.

pre-existing conditions from the sample provides a direct method of controlling for the impact of prior health problems on outcomes related to job loss. Additionally, we explore other approaches to controlling for the impact of pre-existing conditions in our robustness checks, such as controlling for additional covariates that might influence the evolution of health and wages, as well as by directly matching those who lost jobs to comparable individuals in the comparison group.

MAIN RESULTS

Earnings Estimates for Full Sample

Fig. 1 contains estimates of the parameters (γ_k) from equation (1) that measure the relationship between unemployment and earnings in each subsequent year relative to the time of the initial employment separation for the primary samples contained in Panel A of Table 1. As can be seen in the

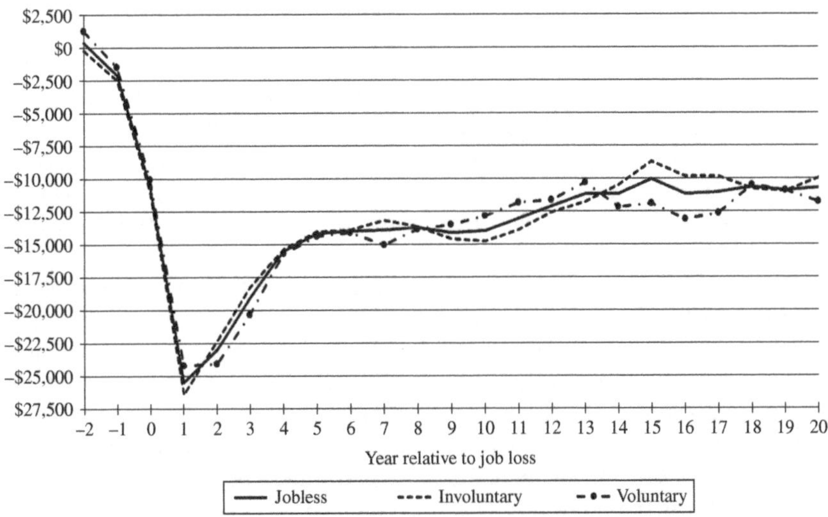

Fig. 1. Fixed-Effects Estimates of Annual Social Security Earnings for Jobless Men Prior to Age 60. *Notes*: Models control for age, age squared, and calendar year in each person-year. Standard errors are clustered at the individual level. Data use SIPP person weights adjusted for non-matches.

figure, immediately after the job loss there is a sharp drop in earnings that never fully recovers despite the fact that individuals in the sample are followed for 20 years. The year after the loss of employment, the estimated earnings losses for the involuntary, voluntary, and combined groups of job leavers are $26,421, $24,226, and $25,499, respectively. The 20th year beyond the reported loss of employment, the sustained earnings losses remain at $10,014, $11,803, and $10,710 for the three groups. Relative to their earnings in 1980, these estimates represent sustained losses of 31, 45, and 36 percent. The largest long-term percentage losses of earnings are observed among the group of individuals who voluntarily leave their prior jobs. In addition, this group had lower earnings prior to the job loss.

All of the estimates of earnings losses discussed here that occur after the point of employment separation are statistically significant at the .05 level.[12] The estimated impact of the job loss on earnings is not significantly different from zero in the two years prior to job loss. This is indicative that the method used for controlling for heterogeneity in the analysis is performing well in equalizing cross-group differences prior to the job loss.

Receipt of DI-SSI Benefits for Full Sample

Fig. 2 contains estimates based on the primary analysis sample for the difference in the cumulative distribution function of the fraction of individuals who had ever received DI-SSI benefits across the groups of those who are unemployed at the time of the 1984 SIPP survey and the comparison group. As can be seen in the figure, in the year after leaving employment, the rate of DI-SSI receipt increases more rapidly for voluntary job leavers, as would be expected, than for those who leave involuntarily.

By the fourth year after job loss, when the probability of having received DI-SSI benefits for voluntary leavers is 20 percentage points higher than for the comparison group and the involuntary leavers have an increased likelihood of 10 percentage points, all of the parameter estimates are statistically significant at the .01 level and remain so throughout the follow-up period. Twenty years after leaving employment, the increased probability of having received DI-SSI benefits is 22 percentage points for the involuntary and 28 for the voluntary leavers. The average increase for all job leavers is 25 percentage points. As was the case with earnings, there was no significant impact of job leaving on DI-SSI receipt in the two years prior to separating from employment. Also, there is no statistically significant effect within the year of job leaving itself.

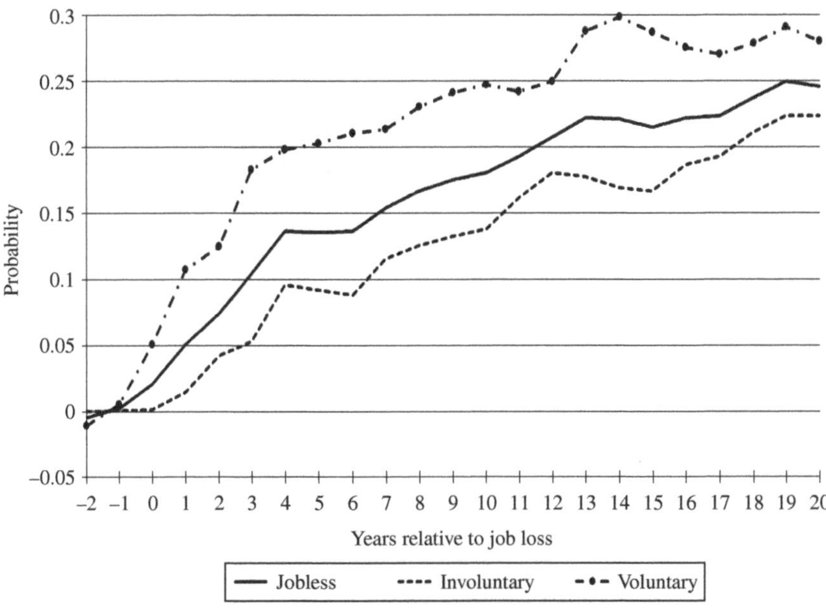

Fig. 2. Fixed-effects Estimates of Disability Receipt (DI or SSI) for Jobless Men Prior to Age 65. *Notes*: Models control for age, age squared, and calendar year in each person-year. Standard errors are clustered at the individual level. Data use SIPP person weights adjusted for non-matches.

To investigate the basic pattern of long-term findings presented in the paper, we also ran a series of linear probability models for the samples examining whether the categorical outcomes (DI-SSI receipt and mortality) were significantly related to job loss. Those estimates for DI-SSI receipt for the full sample are contained in Appendix B, Table B1, Panel A. There it can be seen that the estimates using a single record of data for each individual give virtually identical parameter estimates as those used to plot Fig. 2.

Mortality for Full Sample

Fig. 3 contains estimates of the relationship of long-term joblessness to mortality using the primary estimation sample shown in Panel A of Table 1. In the figure, there are clear increases in the likelihood a person has died among the voluntary and involuntarily unemployed (and for the

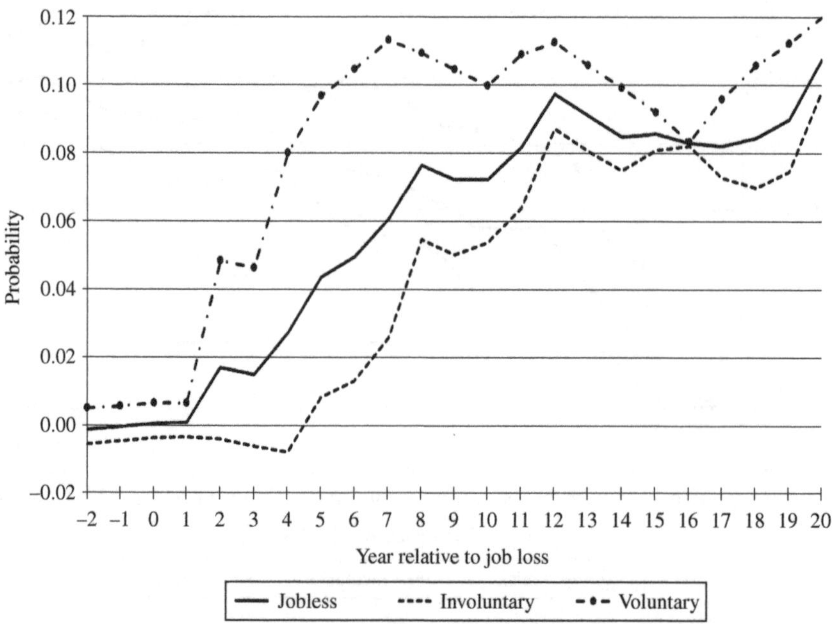

Fig. 3. Fixed-Effects Estimates of Mortality for Jobless Men. *Notes*: Models control for age, age squared, and calendar year in each person-year. Standard errors are clustered at the individual level. Data use SIPP person weights adjusted for non-matches.

combined group) but the initial impact appears larger among voluntary separators. However, the plotted estimates are not significant for all three groups (voluntary, involuntary, and all leavers) until the eighth year after job loss. From the tenth year forward, the estimated increase in the likelihood of having died across the three groups narrows. At twenty years after becoming unemployed, the probability of having died increases by 10 percentage points for the involuntary and 12 for the voluntary leavers, relative to the comparison group. The sample average for all job leavers is an increased risk of mortality of 11 percentage points 20 years after becoming unemployed. Thus, there do not appear to be appreciable differences across the voluntary and involuntarily unemployed in our sample in terms of their increased long-term risk of mortality. Again, as in the case of earnings and DI-SSI receipt, the estimated relationship between job leaving on mortality was not statistically significant for the two years prior to separating from employment.

Estimates for linear probability models that explore the increase in mortality related to job loss are reported in Appendix B, Table B2, Panel A. The estimates are similar to those in Fig. 3 for the 20th year following job loss. The range of estimates is from a 7 percentage point increase in mortality for the involuntarily displaced to 9 for the voluntary leavers. The average increased likelihood of dying for all job leavers is estimated to be 8 percentage points.

Earnings Estimates for the Sample Screened for Pre-Existing Health Problems

Fig. 4 contains estimates of the association between long-term unemployment and subsequent earnings using the estimation sample shown in Panel B of Table 1, which removes individuals with pre-existing health conditions. As can be observed in the figure, there are sharp reductions in

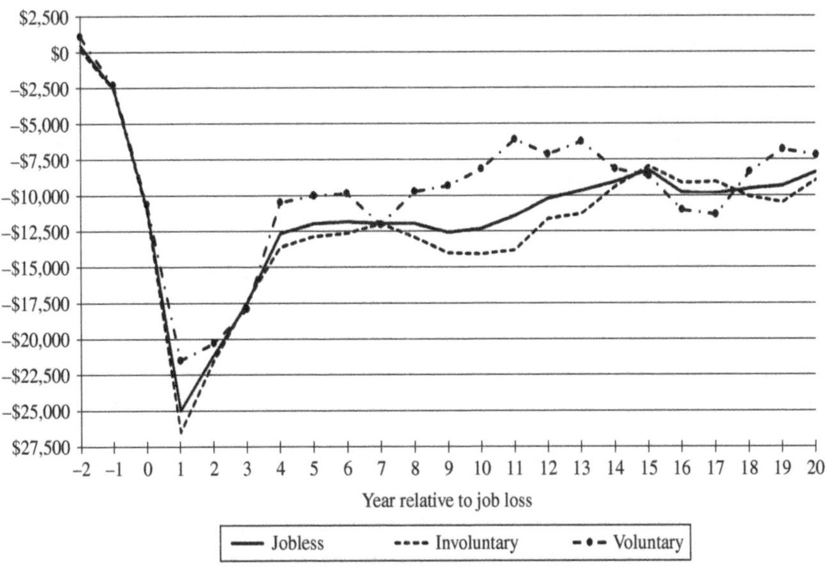

Fig. 4. Fixed-Effects Estimates of Annual Social Security Earnings for Jobless Men Prior to Age 60, Respondents with Pre-Existing Health Limitations Removed. *Notes*: Models control for age, age squared, and calendar year in each person-year. Standard errors are clustered at the individual level. Data use SIPP person weights adjusted for non-matches.

earnings in the year following job loss across all job leavers and voluntary and involuntary separators.

All of the points plotted in the figure for the involuntary and combined group of all leavers are statistically significant at the .05 level.[13] All but three of the points plotted are significant at the .10 level among the smaller group of voluntary leavers. Twenty years after the beginning of a spell of long-term unemployment, the average job loser experiences an \$8,410 reduction in annual earnings with the typical involuntary and voluntary separators having losses of \$8,952 and \$7,196, respectively. These represent losses of 27 percent for each group relative to their 1980 earnings.

To recall, estimates of earnings losses for a sample unscreened for pre-existing health conditions were presented in the section "Earnings Estimates for Full Sample." In that analysis, the percentage loss of earnings for all job leavers after 20 years was 36 percent and for involuntary and voluntary separators, it was 31 percent and 45 percent, respectively. There is little change in the estimated earnings losses for the involuntary job leavers and for the full sample. Among voluntary leavers, the estimates of earnings losses fall from 45 to 27 percent once those with pre-existing conditions are removed from the sample. These results suggest that health does not play a dominant role in driving the earnings reductions observed following job loss when pre-existing health conditions cannot be measured, but is an important consideration among samples of individuals voluntarily choosing to leave employment.

Receipt of DI-SSI Benefits for Sample Screened for Pre-Existing Health Problems

Fig. 5 contains estimates of the association between long-term unemployment and the subsequent receipt of DI-SSI benefits using the sample screened for pre-existing health problems contained in Panel B of Table 1. What can be seen in the figure is that after the job loss, the probability of receipt of DI-SSI among all workers who separate from employment begins to rise and then climbs steadily for the next 20 years. The same pattern is observed among those who leave employment involuntarily. For those who voluntarily separated from employment, the increase in the probability of DI-SSI receipt appears to plateau at around 12 percentage points beyond the 12th year after they leave their job. All of the parameters shown in the figure beyond the 7th year following job loss are statistically significant at the .05 level, except for two estimates among voluntary leavers that are

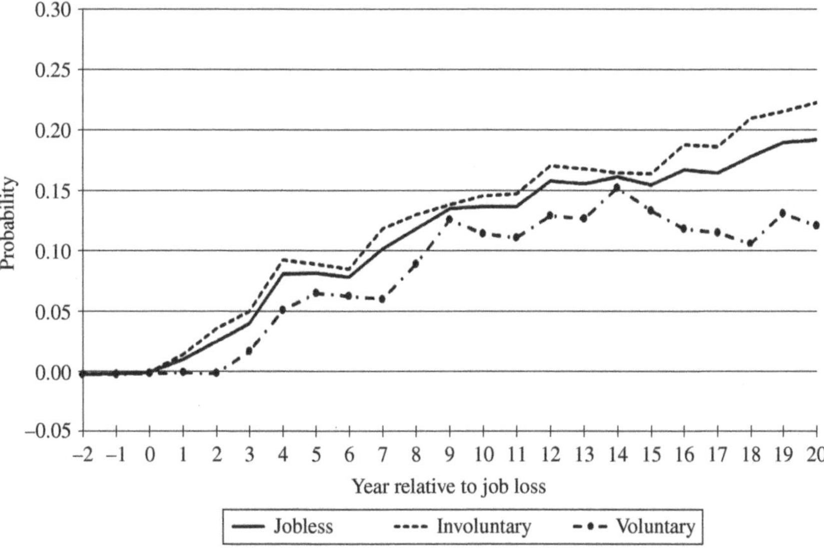

Fig. 5. Fixed-Effects Estimates of Disability Receipt (DI or SSI) for Jobless Men Prior to Age 65, Respondents with Pre-Existing Health Limitations Removed. *Notes*: Models control for age, age squared, and calendar year in each person-year. Standard errors are clustered at the individual level. Data use SIPP person weights adjusted for non-matches.

significant at the .10 level.[14] In the 20th year after job loss, the estimated increase in the probability of receipt of DI-SSI is 19 percentage points for all job leavers, 22 among the involuntarily unemployed, and 12 among voluntary separators.

In comparison to the sample that did not screen for pre-existing health conditions (Fig. 2 and the section "Receipt of DI-SSI Benefits for Full Sample"), the increased probability of having received DI-SSI 20 years after job loss is reduced from 25 to 19 percentage points. Among those who left employment voluntarily, the reduction is more substantive, from a 28 percentage point increase in the probability of receiving DI-SSI to 12 percentage points. This indicates that screening for pre-existing health conditions sharply reduces the impact on DI-SSI receipt for voluntary leavers relative to other groups. In contrast, there is no change in the increased probability of receiving DI-SSI following a period of involuntary unemployment from the unscreened (22 percent) to the screened

(22 percent) sample. Standard errors contained in Table A5 indicate the orderings across groups are likely within sampling error.

In sum, screening the samples to remove those with pre-existing health limitations has a sizeable impact on the average increase in the probability of receiving DI-SSI for all job leavers and those who separate from employment voluntarily. However, it does not fundamentally alter the conclusion that prolonged unemployment leads to substantial increases in the long-term likelihood of receiving DI or SSI benefits.

Again, we estimated a linear probability model for whether a person had ever received DI-SSI benefits conditional on being in one of the job loss groups. Those estimates can be found in Appendix B, Table B1, Panel B. There it can be seen that those models yield estimates similar, albeit slightly smaller, to those obtained from the fixed-effects models. The estimated increases in the probability of DI-SSI receipt across all, involuntary and voluntary job leavers are 17, 19, and 11 percentage points, respectively.

Mortality for Sample Screened for Pre-Existing Health Problems

Fig. 6 contains estimates of the association between extended unemployment and subsequent mortality using the sample that removes individuals with pre-existing health conditions shown in Panel B of Table 1. As can be seen in the figure, for all job leavers and those who separate from employment involuntarily, there is a steady rise in the probability a person dies after long-term unemployment. From the 11th year until the end of the observation period, all of the parameter estimates provided for the group of all leavers are statistically significant at the .05 level and at the .10 level among involuntary leavers.[15] After 20 years, the increased risk of having died is 9 percentage points for all job leavers and 10 percentage points for the involuntarily unemployed.

The estimated parameters for those who voluntarily leave employment plotted in Fig. 6 are statistically insignificant and the associated trend appears somewhat erratic. This result is due to the small number of voluntary leavers in this sample (52) combined with the relatively rare event of death in the analysis. This speculation is supported in part by considering the results in Figs. 3 and 6, which show that the increased probability of death is similar for all job leavers whether those with pre-existing conditions are included or not included in the sample. Similarly, among involuntary leavers, screening the sample to remove those with pre-existing health conditions does not alter the increased probability of dying within 20 years, which is estimated in both samples to be 10 percent. Thus, the insignificant

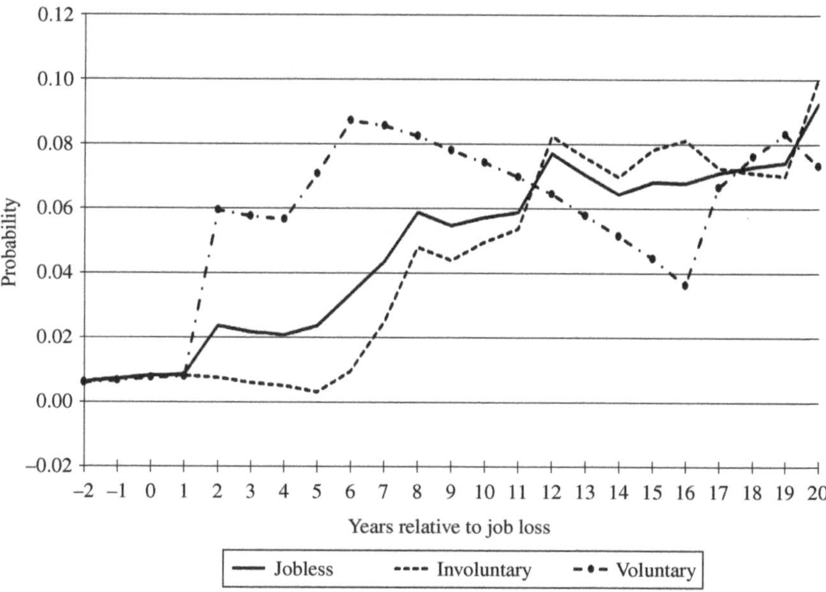

Fig. 6. Fixed-Effects Estimates of Mortality for Jobless Men, Respondents with Pre-Existing Health Limitations Removed. *Notes*: Models control for age, age squared, and calendar year in each person-year. Standard errors are clustered at the individual level. Data use SIPP person weights adjusted for non-matches.

and erratic results for the sample of voluntary leavers is most likely associated with the small sample available for that group.

Again, we estimated a linear probability model for the likelihood of dying within the first 20 years following job loss in our samples. Those estimates can be found in Appendix B, Table B2, Panel B. For all of the long-term unemployed, as well as the involuntary and voluntary separators, the estimated increases in the probability of dying are 6, 7, and 5 percentage points, respectively.

ROBUSTNESS CHECKS

The Impact of Differentiated Earnings and Health Paths

Paths of earnings and health are inter-related (Dustmann & Windmeijer, 2000) and likely to be differentiated by factors such as age, level of education, pre-existing health conditions, and initial level of earnings. To explore implications for our estimates, we conducted alternative estimates for Figs. 4 through 6 including additional interactions between age, age-squared, and year of the particular data observation with level of education. We also include interactions between age, age-squared, and whether the individual was above or below the median level of income in 1980. We provide estimates here for the sample which omits those with pre-existing health conditions to demonstrate that including the additional interaction terms does not substantially impact the original estimates. We also estimated the fixed-effects models with the relevant interactions with all observations while interacting age and age-squared with pre-existing health conditions and found similar results. For purpose of brevity, those additional results are not included in the paper.

Tables C1 through C3 contain the estimates of Eq. (1) that include the additional interaction terms. They can be compared to the fixed-effects estimates without the interactions in Tables A4 through A6. As can be seen by comparing Table C1 and Table A4, the estimates for the earnings outcome do not vary a great deal once these interactions are included. Earnings losses 20 years after leaving employment are estimated to be $7,257, $7,010, and $7,731 across all, the involuntarily, and the voluntarily unemployed. Comparable estimates without the additional interactions are reductions in average annual earnings for the average job loser of $8,410, and $8,952 and $7,196 for the typical involuntary and voluntary separator, respectively. Including the interaction terms, these reductions amount to 24, 22, and 29 percent of the annual earnings of the workers in 1980. All of the estimates of earnings losses remain statistically significant except for the one for the sample of voluntary leavers. We attribute that result to the very large number of interactions included in the model relative to the somewhat small number of voluntary leavers who remain in the sample once those with pre-existing health conditions are removed.

For the outcome of receipt of DI-SSI benefits, the estimates contained in Table C2 and Table A5 allow for a contrast between parameter estimates that include the additional interaction terms and parameter estimates that do not. Including the additional interaction terms, the estimated increase in DI-SSI receipt 20 years later are 17, 20, and 10 percent across all, the involuntary, and the voluntary job leavers. Comparable estimates across the three groups not including the interactions are 19, 22, and 12 percent. Again, the estimates for all job leavers and those involuntarily unemployed remain statistically significant while the estimate for those who voluntarily leave employment becomes insignificant. As before, we attribute the lack of significance to the large number of parameters estimated relative to the sample size for voluntary leavers. Including the additional interaction terms does not appear to greatly alter the results or the qualitative conclusions of the paper.

With respect to mortality, Tables C3 and A6 contain estimates that allow for a contrast between parameter estimates when the interactions are included or not. Including the additional interactions, the estimated relationship between job loss and mortality is estimated to be 8, 8, and 6 percent for the samples of all, involuntary, and voluntary job leavers, respectively. Comparable estimates from Table A6 that did not include the interactions were 9, 10, and 7 percent, respectively. As before, the parameter estimates for the involuntary and all job leavers remain statistically significant. In conclusion, while including these interactions slightly modifies the estimates obtained without them, it does not alter the qualitative conclusions drawn from the primary estimates of the paper.

Propensity Score Matching Estimates

As the individuals in the sample experience extended periods of unemployment, it is possible that the association between unemployment and the later outcomes is being driven by pre-existing health conditions. Here, we provide matching estimates following the nearest neighbor method with draws to break ties and kernel weighting as described in Becker and Ichino (2002). We focus on estimates of the association between unemployment and outcomes 20 years later. Tables of parameter estimates of the logistic regressions used to calculate propensity scores are available upon request from the authors. In all of those models, variables were included to reflect age, ethnicity, level of education, the position of the individual in the distribution of earnings, and pre-existing health limitations (where relevant). Standard balancing tests were conducted for each of the estimated models. The equal support condition for selecting observations to be included as possible matches was also imposed.

Appendix D contains the parameter estimates for the matching estimates of the relationship between unemployment and later earnings, receipt of DI-SSI, and mortality. Estimates are provided for the two samples used in providing the main estimates of the paper based on fixed-effects methods. With respect to the earnings outcomes, the estimates provided for both samples are generally as large as or larger than those based on the fixed-effects methods. All estimates conducted were statistically significant at the .05 level. Similarly, the estimates of the relationship between unemployment and later receipt of DI-SSI are of a similar order of magnitude to those obtained using fixed-effects methods while exhibiting a stronger pattern of statistical significance.

Finally, the propensity score estimates of the relationship between long-term unemployment and mortality indicate that for the sample of all leavers, the impact is somewhat smaller (6 percent) than what was found with the fixed-effects estimators, while remaining statistically significant at the .05 level. The long-term impact for voluntary leavers is also found to be significant at the .10 level using the kernel weighting method. In the smaller sample where those with pre-existing conditions are removed from the analysis, the association between unemployment and long-term mortality is reduced (5 percent) for all job leavers while remaining statistically significant at the .10 level using nearest neighbor matching.

As was the case with the fixed-effects methods, the association between long-term unemployment and mortality is not statistically significant 20 years later once those with pre-existing health conditions are removed from the sample. The one change observed here relative to the estimates based on the fixed-effects methods is the lack of a statistically significant relationship between the outcomes of involuntary job leavers and the comparison group, either in the full sample or when those with pre-existing health conditions are removed from the sample. For the voluntary leavers, as was the case with the fixed-effects estimates, the number of job losers is quite small so the insignificant result is understandable.

Additionally, in the matching models, the effective sample size is greatly reduced by the estimation procedure. In the nearest neighbor procedure, the largest sample (all leavers) is 336 observations (168 leavers and their matches). The lack of significance in the subsamples of voluntary and involuntary leavers is understandable since the number of observations used in the estimations would be even smaller. We would note that the kernel estimators construct a comparison for each job leaver by weighting across all observations. Thus, that procedure similarly reduces the effective sample size relative to the fixed-effects estimation. Although the propensity score estimators reveal weaker patterns of statistical significance due to the smaller effective sample sizes, the estimates do indicate that for the full sample of the long-term unemployed, there is a statistically significant relationship with later mortality.

CONCLUSION

This chapter examines the long-term economic and health outcomes of prime-aged workers who experienced prolonged joblessness lasting as long as 3 years around the time of the 1980–1982 recession. The analysis makes use of data from the 1984 SIPP linked to longitudinal earnings records and information on the receipt of disability benefits (DI-SSI) and mortality from the SSA. Estimates are provided of the association between prolonged joblessness initiated during a period of low aggregate demand and long-term earnings, the receipt of DI-SSI benefits, and mortality.

Our results indicate sizeable sustained losses of earnings for all of the unemployed workers examined. Sustained earnings impacts of 31 percent for those who experienced prolonged joblessness after an involuntary separation are larger than reports from prior studies that have examined the same period but focused on workers who were more quickly reemployed, as would be expected. The largest long-term earnings impacts (45 percent) are found for those who experienced prolonged joblessness after voluntarily separating from their prior employer. These earnings losses are consistent with estimates from the same period for displaced workers who were not reemployed quickly (Jacobson et al., 1993).

One concern with estimates of earnings losses among individuals who leave employment voluntarily and experience extended periods of unemployment is that health problems may drive both their departures from work and their subsequent earnings losses. In the analysis presented here, once individuals with health conditions that exist prior to job loss are removed from the estimation sample, those who voluntarily leave employment are found to have earnings losses 20 years later of 27 percent versus 45 percent when the health screen is not employed. In a sample of involuntary separators screened to remove those with pre-existing health conditions from the estimation sample, their earnings losses are altered from 31 percent to 27 percent. This demonstrates that prior health conditions play an important but not dominant role in determining long-term earnings outcomes among the long-term unemployed. This is particularly true for those who leave employment voluntarily.

While many economists have studied the impact of employment loss on earnings, this chapter provides the first look at the impact of prolonged joblessness for prime-aged workers on their receipt of DI-SSI benefits for the disabled non-elderly. In this dimension, we found that those who left employment around the time of the recession in the early 1980s and experienced a long-term spell of joblessness had significantly higher probabilities of receiving DI-SSI benefits. Our estimates show large increased probabilities of receiving DI-SSI benefits 20 years after separating from employment for both voluntary (28 percent) and involuntary leavers (22 percent). This illustrates how negative economic shocks can have a long-term association with the receipt of DI-SSI benefits and the underlying health conditions that are a condition of receipt.

Again a natural concern is that pre-existing health conditions both among those discharged from employment and those who leave work voluntarily might drive their subsequent receipt of DI-SSI benefits. In samples that removed people who reported health problems that existed prior to leaving employment, we found that the increased probability of receiving DI-SSI benefits was still 22 percent among involuntary leavers but fell to 12 percent among voluntary leavers. This confirms that among samples that voluntarily choose to leave employment, pre-existing health problems are likely to be associated with subsequent outcomes and that it is important to take this into account in the analysis.

In our examination of mortality, we found that there is a significant increase in the probability of death of 11 percentage points among all workers who experienced a spell of prolonged joblessness within the subsequent 20 years. The estimated risk is roughly similar among those who experienced a spell of sustained involuntary unemployment relative to voluntary leavers. Significantly elevated long-term probabilities of mortality among the involuntarily unemployed are consistent with prior studies.

We again used samples that removed individuals who reported health conditions that preceded their unemployment. The estimates indicate that for the average job leaver, the increased probability of dying in the first 20 years after a period of prolonged unemployment falls slightly to 9 percentage points. Similarly, the increased risk of mortality among those who separate from employment involuntarily is 10 percentage points in the sample excluding those with pre-existing health problems. These elevated risks of mortality are costly to society in terms of lost productivity and leave survivors at greater economic risk in their old age. Seeing significant increases in mortality among those who did not have pre-existing conditions indicates that declines in health may be induced by long-term joblessness among prime-aged workers.

Because of the concern that pre-existing health limitations might drive both the losses from employment and influence the severity of the outcomes examined, two sets of robustness checks were performed on the main results of the paper. First, fixed-effects models that allowed for different paths in earnings and health were estimated. Second, propensity score matching estimations were conducted based on nearest neighbor and kernel density approaches. For the outcomes of earnings losses and receipt of DI-SSI benefits, these alternative estimates did not suggest different qualitative conclusions of the paper. For the examination of mortality, in the primary sample, long-term unemployment was found to be significantly related to mortality, although the impact was reduced from 9 to 6 percent. Patterns of significance in sub-groups were equivocal as might be expected given the effective reduction in sample size when using the matching estimators. In sum, the robustness checks did not reveal extensive sensitivity to alternative estimation approaches.

Our findings provide useful evidence that the commonly reported pattern of long-term earnings losses among those who involuntarily separate from employment and are quickly re-employed is also found among those who experience sustained periods of joblessness; however, the long-term losses are much larger among those who experience long-term unemployment. Similarly, this study provides independent confirmation that the long-term probability of mortality is significantly higher among those who experience sustained periods of unemployment during a recession. Our results indicating a higher long-term probability of receiving DI-SSI follows in the wake of voluntary or involuntary unemployment that occurs during a recession provides new evidence on the linkage between joblessness and health. Together, these results suggest that the health conditions underlying the increased receipt of DI and SSI have functional and systemic impacts that ultimately raise mortality. Finally, the empirical demonstration of the association between long-term unemployment and subsequent earnings, receipt of DI-SSI benefits, and mortality are largely robust, even when individuals with pre-existing health conditions are removed from the sample. This is novel within the literature on the impacts of job loss among prime-aged workers.

NOTES

1. By focusing on workers who lose their jobs due to slack demand and are subsequently re-employed elsewhere, economists have sought to learn what portion of the skills that workers are paid for in one job are transportable to others. In the most basic theory of wage setting, the common component of a worker's skills that are rewarded across employers is considered general. The proportion of earnings that is lost as workers move across employers is considered to be specific.

2. Administrative records have been used in other countries to examine health outcomes of prime-aged workers. For example, Browning et al. (2006) use a ten percent sample of the Dutch population to examine hospitalizations due to stress related illness in the first four years following job displacement as well as the duration to first hospitalization for a stress related illness and find no impact for either outcome relative to the continuously employed using propensity score matching estimators. Two important differences in the U.S. context and that of many European countries not examined here are the impact of differences in the structure of unemployment insurance benefits as well as access to health care outside of the employment arrangement. As documented by Gruber and Madrian (1997), it is common for U.S. workers to lose access to health care following job displacement.

3. We have also estimated linear probability models for having ever received DI-SSI benefits or having died within our sample. Those models give the same patterns of effects and statistical significance as those shown in the text and can be found in Appendix B.

4. More specifically, we use the program PSCORE2 using Stata Version 12.1.

5. Wave 3 contains the Education and Work History and the Health and Disability topical modules.

6. The match rate between the SIPP and SSA administrative records is high. For the overall 1984 SIPP, the total match rate is around 90 percent.

7. We allow as many as four years of no earnings for several reasons. First, this allows those long-term unemployed to have up to the three years of no earnings consistent with their unemployment. Second, it allows for those who enter disability during the screening period to have associated non-earnings. Finally, we found that allowing more years of non-zero earnings led to unstable results while requiring additional positive observations produced qualitatively similar estimates.

8. We adjust the sample selection requirement of five positive years of earnings in the period from 1980 through 1988 for job leavers who die or start to receive DI or SSI benefits in the years 1984 through 1988 by allowing them to remain in the sample as long as they have no more than three years of non-earnings from 1980 through the year prior to death or receipt of benefits.

9. The share of workers covered by the Social Security system who have earnings over this threshold (the Social Security taxable maximum) has been approximately 6 percent since 1983 (SSA, 2011, Table 4B.1). For more information on the Social Security taxable maximum, see: http://www.socialsecurity.gov/OACT/COLA/cbb.html

10. The CPS used in conjunction with the Displaced Workers Supplement to study job displacement is one example where the available earnings information is censored at an upper limit. The SIPP also caps earnings.

11. SSI for the non-elderly is a means-tested disability program that requires restricted income and asset holdings to qualify. SSI disability recipients must meet the same medical requirements as Social Security DI insurance. Recipients who never receive Social Security Disability Insurance do not have the quarters of coverage for full and current insurance under the Social Security program. In contrast to Social Security disability, SSI disabled recipients are more likely to enter and exit the program over time. In this study, we measure the probability of ever receiving Social Security or SSI disability benefits. Among our jobless sample, the share

indicated as ever disabled by 2003 increases around 6 percentage points (25–31 percent) when SSI is included into our definition of disability.

12. Appendix A contains parameter estimates and standard errors for all of the figures presented in the paper.

13. All of the parameter estimates and standard errors for the points plotted in Fig. 4 can be found in Table A4.

14. All of the parameters shown in Fig. 5 and their associated standard errors can be found in Table A5.

15. The parameters graphed in Fig. 6 and their standard errors can be found in Table A6.

REFERENCES

Becker, S. O., & Ichino, A. (2002). Estimation of average treatment effects based on propensity scores. *The Stata Journal*, *2*(4), 358–377.

Browning, M., Dano, A. M., & Heinesen, E. (2006). Job displacement and stress related health outcomes. *Health Economics*, *15*(10), 1061–1075.

Chan, S., & Stevens, A. H. (2000). The effects of job loss on older workers: Employment, earnings and wealth. In P. P. Budetti, R. V. Burkhauser, J. M. Gregory, & H. Allan Hunt (Eds.), *Ensuring health and income security for an aging workforce*. W.E. Upjohn Institute, Kalamazoo, MI.

Couch, K. A. (1992). Late life job displacement. *The Gerontologist*, *38*(1), 7–17.

Couch, K. A., Jolly, N., & Placzek, D. (2011). Earnings losses of displaced workers and the business cycle. *Economics Letters*, *111*(1), 16–19.

Couch, K. A., & Placzek, D. (2010). Earnings losses of displaced workers revisited. *American Economic Review*, *100*(1), 572–589.

Deb, P., Gallo, W. T., Ayyagari, P., Fletcher, J. M., & Sindelar, J. L. (2011). The effect of job loss on overweight and drinking. *Journal of Health Economics*, *30*, 317–327.

Dustmann, C., & Windmeijer, F. (2000). *Wages and the demand for health: A lifecycle analysis.* IZA Discussion Paper No. 171. IZA, Bonn, Germany.

Farber, H. S. (2013). Job loss: Historical perspective from the Displaced Workers Survey, 1984–2010. In K. A. Couch, M. C. Daly, & J. M. Zissimopoulos (Eds.), *Lifecycle events and their consequences: Job loss, family change, and declines in health*. Stanford, CA: Stanford University Press.

Gallo, W. T., Bradley, E. H., Dubin, J. A., Jones, R. N., Falba, T. A., Teng, H.-M., & Kasl, S. V. (2006). The persistence of depressive symptoms in older workers who experience involuntary job loss: Results from the health and retirement survey. *Journal of Gerontology: Social Sciences*, *61B*(4), S221–S228.

Gallo, W. T., Bradley, E. H., Falba, T. A., Dubin, J. A., Cramer, L. D., Bogardus Jr., S. T., & Kasl, S. V. (2004). Involuntary job loss as a risk factor for subsequent myocardial infarction and stroke: Findings from the health and retirement survey. *American Journal of Industrial Medicine*, *45*, 408–416.

Gallo, W. T., Brand, J. E., Teng, H.-M., Leo-Summers, L., & Byers, A. L. (2009). Differential impact of involuntary job loss on physical disability among older workers: Does predisposition matter? *Research on Aging*, *31*(3), 345–360.

Gruber, J., & Madrian, B. C. (1997). Employment separation and health insurance coverage. *Journal of Public Economics*, *66*, 349–382.

Jacobson, L., LaLonde, R. J., & Sullivan, D. (1993). Earnings losses of displaced workers. *American Economic Review*, *82*(4), 685–709.

Kim, C. H., & Tamborini, C. R. (2012). Response error in earnings: An analysis of the Survey of Income and Program Participation matched with administrative data. *Sociological Methods & Research*. doi:10.1177/0049124112460371.

McNabb, J., Timmons, D., Song, J. G., & Puckett, C. (2009). Uses of administrative data at the social security administration. *Social Security Bulletin*, *69*, 75–84.

Rupp, K., & Davies, P. S. (2004). A long-term view of health status, disabilities, mortality, and participation in the DI and SSI disability programs. *Research in Labor Economics*, *23*, 119–183.

Salm, M. (2006). Does job loss cause Ill health? *Health Economics*, *18*(7), 1075–1089.

Siegel, M., Bradley, E. H., Gallo, W. T., & Kasl, S. (2003). Impact of husbands' involuntary job loss on wives' mental health, among older adults. *Journal of Gerontology: Social Sciences*, *58B*(1), S30–S37.

SSA. (2011). *Annual statistical supplement to the social security bulletin, 2010*. Washington, DC: SSA.

Stewart, J. (2001). The impact of health status on the duration of unemployment spells and the implications for studies of the impact of unemployment on health status. *Journal of Health Economics*, *20*(5), 781–796.

Sullivan, D., & Von Wachter, T. (2009a). Average earnings and long-term mortality: Evidence from administrative data. *American Economic Review Papers and Proceedings*, *99*(2), 133–138.

Sullivan, D., & Von Wachter, T. (2009b). Job displacement and mortality: An analysis using administrative data. *Quarterly Journal of Economics*, *124*(3), 1265–1306.

Tamborini, C. R., & Iams, H. M. (2011). Are generation X'ers different than late boomers? Family and earnings trends among recent cohorts of women at young adulthood. *Population Research and Policy Review*, *30*, 59–79.

Von Wachter, T., Song, J., & Manchester, J. (2009). Long-term earnings losses due to mass-layoffs during the 1982 recession: An analysis using U.S. administrative data from 1974 to 2004.

APPENDIX A

Table A1. Parameter Estimates for Fixed-Effects Model of Earnings Graphed in Fig. 1.

Variable			Jobless Sub-Samples			
	All Jobless		Involuntary		Voluntary	
	(1)		(2)		(3)	
	Coeff.	SE	Coeff.	SE	Coeff.	SE
Dependent Variable = Social Security Earnings						
Pre2	386	956	−203	1,203	1,288	1,559
Pre1	−2,094†	1,147	−2,491†	1,394	−1,487	1,946
0	−10,577***	1,146	−10,951***	1,560	−10,064***	1,613
Post1	−25,499***	1,329	−26,421***	1,742	−24,226***	2,018
Post2	−23,048***	1,491	−22,367***	1,973	−24,105***	2,218
Post3	−19,104***	1,591	−18,301***	1,965	−20,369***	2,639
Post4	−15,485***	1,674	−15,355***	2,142	−15,709***	2,646
Post5	−14,165***	1,736	−14,042***	2,207	−14,397***	2,763
Post6	−13,985***	1,704	−13,928***	2,273	−14,126***	2,477
Post7	−13,900***	1,701	−13,202***	2,246	−15,036***	2,508
Post8	−13,706***	1,694	−13,651***	2,227	−13,835***	2,538
Post9	−14,120***	1,706	−14,562***	2,222	−13,534***	2,601
Post10	−13,949***	1,708	−14,768***	2,117	−12,820***	2,785
Post11	−13,062***	1,861	−13,942***	2,285	−11,876***	3,058
Post12	−12,147***	1,888	−12,552***	2,498	−11,628***	2,820
Post13	−11,161***	1,884	−11,796***	2,494	−10,323***	2,800
Post14	−11,187***	1,931	−10,513***	2,494	−12,190***	2,945
Post15	−10,057***	1,954	−8,735***	2,426	−11,941***	3,105
Post16	−11,167***	2,048	−9,828***	2,636	−13,110***	3,098
Post17	−11,018***	2,112	−9,881***	2,702	−12,669***	3,235
Post18	−10,660***	2,326	−10,805***	2,976	−10,505**	3,614
Post19	−10,939***	2,433	−11,012***	3,155	−10,886**	3,709
Post20	−10,710***	2,550	−10,014**	3,229	−11,803**	4,004
Age	2,235***	196	2,244***	197	2,232***	198
Age, Squared	−42***	2	−42***	2	−42***	2
Constant	18,174**	5,554	18,579***	5,568	18,819***	5,603
Post Years Relative to Jobless Event	20		20		20	
N (person-years)	132,347		130,502		129,590	

Notes: Models also include dummies for calendar year, which are available upon request. All estimates are in 2008 dollars. Standard errors are clustered at the individual level. Weights adjusted for non-matches are applied.

†$p < .10$; *$p < .05$; **$p < .01$; ***$p < .001$.

Table A2. Parameter Estimates for Fixed-Effects Model of Disability Graphed in Fig. 2.

Variable	Jobless Sub-Samples					
	All Jobless		Involuntary		Voluntary	
	(1)		(2)		(3)	
	Coeff.	SE	Coeff.	SE	Coeff.	SE
Dependent Variable = Receipt of DI or SSI for disabled non-elderly						
Pre2	−0.006	0.008	−0.001	0.008	−0.012	0.017
Pre1	0.001	0.010	0.000	0.008	0.005	0.021
0	0.020	0.015	0.000	0.008	0.049	0.036
Post1	0.050*	0.020	0.013	0.014	0.107*	0.045
Post2	0.073***	0.021	0.041*	0.020	0.124**	0.046
Post3	0.103***	0.023	0.052*	0.022	0.182***	0.047
Post4	0.135***	0.026	0.095**	0.029	0.198***	0.048
Post5	0.135***	0.026	0.091**	0.029	0.202***	0.049
Post6	0.136***	0.026	0.087**	0.029	0.210***	0.049
Post7	0.154***	0.027	0.115***	0.031	0.213***	0.049
Post8	0.167***	0.029	0.125***	0.035	0.230***	0.050
Post9	0.175***	0.030	0.132***	0.037	0.240***	0.051
Post10	0.180***	0.030	0.137***	0.038	0.247***	0.053
Post11	0.193***	0.031	0.160***	0.039	0.242***	0.053
Post12	0.207***	0.032	0.180***	0.040	0.249***	0.053
Post13	0.221***	0.034	0.177***	0.042	0.288***	0.058
Post14	0.221***	0.034	0.169***	0.042	0.298***	0.059
Post15	0.215***	0.034	0.166***	0.042	0.287***	0.059
Post16	0.222***	0.035	0.186***	0.044	0.275***	0.059
Post17	0.223***	0.036	0.193***	0.045	0.269***	0.059
Post18	0.237***	0.036	0.210***	0.047	0.278***	0.060
Post19	0.249***	0.038	0.223***	0.048	0.290***	0.063
Post20	0.245***	0.038	0.223***	0.049	0.280***	0.063
Age	−0.016***	0.001	−0.016***	0.001	−0.016***	0.001
Age, Squared	0.000***	0.000	0.000***	0.000	0.000***	0.000
Constant	0.284***	0.019	0.280***	0.019	0.278***	0.019
Post Years Relative to Jobless Event	20		20		20	
N (person-years)	146,731		144,717		143,693	

Notes: Models also include dummies for calendar year, which are available upon request. All estimates are in 2008 dollars. Standard errors are clustered at the individual level. Weights adjusted for non-matches are applied.

$^{*}p <$ 05; $^{**}p < .01$; $^{***}p < .001$.

Table A3. Parameter Estimates for Fixed-Effects Models of Mortality Graphed in Fig. 3.

Variable	All Jobless		Jobless Sub-Samples: Involuntary		Jobless Sub-Samples: Voluntary	
	(1)		(2)		(3)	
	Coeff.	SE	Coeff.	SE	Coeff.	SE
Dependent Variable = Death of Respondent						
Pre2	−0.001	0.006	−0.005	0.008	0.005	0.008
Pre1	0.000	0.006	−0.005	0.008	0.006	0.008
0	0.001	0.006	−0.004	0.009	0.006	0.008
Post1	0.001	0.006	−0.003	0.009	0.006	0.009
Post2	0.017	0.014	−0.004	0.009	0.048	0.030
Post3	0.015	0.014	−0.006	0.009	0.046	0.030
Post4	0.027†	0.016	−0.008	0.009	0.080*	0.035
Post5	0.043**	0.016	0.008	0.010	0.097**	0.037
Post6	0.049**	0.017	0.013	0.013	0.104**	0.037
Post7	0.061**	0.019	0.026	0.017	0.113**	0.038
Post8	0.077***	0.022	0.055*	0.026	0.109**	0.038
Post9	0.072**	0.022	0.050†	0.026	0.105**	0.037
Post10	0.072**	0.022	0.054*	0.027	0.100**	0.037
Post11	0.082***	0.024	0.064*	0.029	0.109**	0.040
Post12	0.098***	0.025	0.087**	0.032	0.113**	0.040
Post13	0.091***	0.025	0.081*	0.032	0.106**	0.040
Post14	0.085***	0.025	0.075*	0.032	0.099*	0.040
Post15	0.086***	0.026	0.081*	0.033	0.092*	0.040
Post16	0.083**	0.026	0.082*	0.034	0.083*	0.040
Post17	0.082**	0.026	0.073*	0.034	0.096*	0.042
Post18	0.084**	0.027	0.070*	0.034	0.106*	0.043
Post19	0.090**	0.027	0.075*	0.035	0.112*	0.044
Post20	0.107***	0.030	0.098*	0.039	0.120**	0.045
Age	−0.017***	0.001	−0.017***	0.001	−0.017***	0.001
Age, Squared	0.000***	0.000	0.000***	0.000	0.000***	0.000
Constant	0.302***	0.016	0.297***	0.016	0.301***	0.016
Post Years Relative to Jobless Event	20		20		20	
N (person-years)	165,075		162,940		161,860	

Notes: Models also include dummies for calendar year, which are available upon request. All estimates are in 2008 dollars. Standard errors are clustered at the individual level. Weights adjusted for non-matches are applied.
†$p<.10$; *$p<.05$; **$p<.01$; ***$p<.001$.

Table A4. Parameter Estimates for Fixed-Effects Model of Earnings Graphed in Fig. 4.

Variable	All Jobless		Jobless Sub-Samples			
			Involuntary		Voluntary	
	(1)		(2)		(3)	
	Coeff.	SE	Coeff.	SE	Coeff.	SE
Dependent Variable = Social Security Earnings						
Pre2	460	1,086	181	1,338	1,089	1,800
Pre1	−2,499[†]	1,343	−2,604[†]	1,487	−2,319	2,796
0	−10,919***	1,385	−11,102***	1,689	−10,597***	2,328
Post1	−24,995***	1,577	−26,495***	1,883	−21,537***	2,786
Post2	−21,133***	1,770	−21,514***	2,157	−20,274***	3,018
Post3	−17,478***	1,779	−17,343***	2,132	−17,910***	3,176
Post4	−12,673***	1,874	−13,633***	2,373	−10,464***	2,762
Post5	−12,011***	1,966	−12,856***	2,440	−10,036	3,110
Post6	−11,821***	2,048	−12,659***	2,501	−9,865**	3,424
Post7	−11,975***	2,059	−11,989***	2,492	−12,038***	3,549
Post8	−11,965***	2,040	−12,942***	2,466	−9,750**	3,511
Post9	−12,576***	2,054	−14,007***	2,465	−9,354**	3,579
Post10	−12,309***	2,040	−14,117***	2,347	−8,176*	3,858
Post11	−11,462***	2,156	−13,840***	2,521	−6,161[†]	3,912
Post12	−10,217***	2,246	−11,624***	2,788	−7,150*	3,636
Post13	−9,703***	2,263	−11,298***	2,807	−6,248[†]	3,669
Post14	−9,047***	2,314	−9,415***	2,793	−8,145*	4,035
Post15	−8,270***	2,305	−7,995**	2,701	−8,660*	4,250
Post16	−9,816***	2,456	−9,142**	2,955	−11,007**	4,250
Post17	−9,908***	2,516	−9,090**	3,014	111,348**	4,398
Post18	−9,555***	2,773	−10,075**	3,344	−8,346[†]	4,830
Post19	−9,338**	2,946	−10,497**	3,530	−6,799	5,200
Post20	−8,410**	3,025	−8,952*	3,574	−7,196	5,445
Age	2,215***	201	2,217***	201	2,223***	202
Age, Squared	−41***	2	−42***	2	−42***	2
Constant	18,550**	5,653	18,823***	5,667	18,898***	5,697
Post Years Relative to Jobless Event	20		20		20	
N (person-years)	125,336		124,256		123,030	

Notes. Models also include dummies for calendar year, which are available upon request. All estimates are in 2008 dollars. Standard errors are clustered at the individual level. Weights adjusted for non-matches are applied.

[†]$p < .10$; $^{*}p < .05$; $^{**}p < .01$; $^{***}p < .001$.

Table A5. Parameter Estimates for Fixed-Effects Model of Disability Graphed in Fig. 5.

Variable	All Jobless		Jobless Sub-Samples			
			Involuntary		Voluntary	
	(1)		(2)		(3)	
	Coeff.	SE	Coeff.	SE	Coeff.	SE
Dependent Variable = Receipt of DI or SSI for disabled non-elderly						
Pre2	−0.003	0.007	−0.002	0.009	−0.003	0.009
Pre1	−0.002	0.007	−0.002	0.009	−0.002	0.009
0	−0.001	0.007	−0.001	0.009	−0.001	0.010
Post1	0.009	0.011	0.014	0.015	−0.001	0.010
Post2	0.024†	0.015	0.035†	0.020	−0.002	0.010
Post3	0.040*	0.017	0.050*	0.022	0.016	0.018
Post4	0.080***	0.024	0.092**	0.031	0.051†	0.031
Post5	0.081***	0.025	0.088**	0.031	0.064†	0.035
Post6	0.078***	0.025	0.085**	0.031	0.062†	0.035
Post7	0.101***	0.026	0.118***	0.034	0.059†	0.035
Post8	0.118***	0.030	0.130***	0.038	0.088*	0.042
Post9	0.134***	0.032	0.138***	0.040	0.125*	0.051
Post10	0.136***	0.033	0.145***	0.041	0.114*	0.050
Post11	0.136***	0.033	0.147***	0.041	0.110*	0.051
Post12	0.158***	0.035	0.170***	0.043	0.129*	0.054
Post13	0.155***	0.036	0.167***	0.045	0.126*	0.055
Post14	0.161***	0.036	0.164***	0.045	0.151*	0.059
Post15	0.154***	0.037	0.163***	0.046	0.133*	0.058
Post16	0.167***	0.038	0.187***	0.049	0.118*	0.058
Post17	0.164***	0.039	0.186***	0.049	0.114*	0.058
Post18	0.178***	0.040	0.209***	0.051	0.105†	0.059
Post19	0.189***	0.042	0.215***	0.053	0.130*	0.066
Post20	0.191***	0.043	0.223***	0.054	0.120†	0.066
Age	−0.014***	0.001	−0.014***	0.001	−0.014***	0.001
Age, Squared	0.000***	0.000	0.000***	0.000	0.000***	0.000
Constant	0.250***	0.019	0.249***	0.019	0.246***	0.019
Post Years Relative to Jobless Event	20		20		20	
N (person-years)	138,599		137,457		136,041	

Notes: Models also include dummies for calendar year, which are available upon request. All estimates are in 2008 dollars. Standard errors are clustered at the individual level. Weights adjusted for non-matches are applied.

†$p<.10$; *$p<.05$; **$p<.01$; ***$p<.001$.

Table A6. Parameter Estimates for Fixed-Effects Models of Mortality Graphed in Fig. 6.

Variable	Jobless Sub-Samples					
	All Jobless		Involuntary		Voluntary	
	(1)		(2)		(3)	
	Coeff.	SE	Coeff.	SE	Coeff.	SE
Dependent Variable = Death of Respondent						
Pre2	0.006	0.004	0.006	0.005	0.005	0.008
Pre1	0.007†	0.004	0.007	0.005	0.006	0.008
0	0.008†	0.004	0.008	0.005	0.007	0.008
Post1	0.008†	0.004	0.008	0.005	0.008	0.008
Post2	0.023†	0.014	0.007	0.005	0.059	0.042
Post3	0.022	0.014	0.006	0.006	0.057	0.042
Post4	0.020	0.014	0.005	0.006	0.056	0.042
Post5	0.024	0.015	0.003	0.006	0.071	0.045
Post6	0.033*	0.016	0.009	0.010	0.087†	0.046
Post7	0.043*	0.019	0.025	0.016	0.086†	0.046
Post8	0.059*	0.024	0.048†	0.028	0.082†	0.046
Post9	0.054*	0.024	0.044	0.028	0.078†	0.046
Post10	0.057*	0.025	0.049†	0.030	0.074	0.046
Post11	0.059*	0.026	0.054†	0.031	0.070	0.046
Post12	0.077**	0.028	0.082*	0.035	0.064	0.046
Post13	0.071*	0.028	0.076*	0.035	0.058	0.046
Post14	0.064*	0.028	0.070*	0.035	0.051	0.045
Post15	0.068*	0.029	0.078*	0.036	0.044	0.045
Post16	0.068*	0.030	0.081*	0.037	0.036	0.045
Post17	0.071*	0.030	0.073†	0.037	0.067	0.050
Post18	0.073*	0.031	0.071†	0.038	0.076	0.053
Post19	0.074*	0.031	0.070†	0.038	0.083	0.054
Post20	0.092**	0.034	0.100*	0.043	0.073	0.054
Age	-0.016***	0.001	-0.016***	0.001	-0.016***	0.001
Age, squared	0.000***	0.000	0.000***	0.000	0.000***	0.000
Constant	0.284***	0.016	0.282***	0.016	0.282***	0.016
Post years relative to jobless event	20		20		20	
N (person-years)	155,317		154,059		152,633	

Notes: Models also include dummies for calendar year, which are available upon request. All estimates are in 2008 dollars. Standard errors are clustered at the individual level. Weights adjusted for non-matches are applied.

$^{\dagger}p < .10$; $^{*}p < .05$; $^{**}p < .01$; $^{***}p < .001$.

APPENDIX B

Table B1. Linear Probability Regressions of Receipt of Disability Benefits between 1983–2003.

	(1) All		(2) Involuntary		(3) Voluntary	
	Coeff.	SE	Coeff.	SE	Coeff.	SE
Panel A: Full analysis sample						
Jobless (ref. group = employed)	0.228***	0.035	0.191***	0.043	0.282***	0.056
Age (in 1984)	0.034***	0.006	0.035***	0.005	0.034***	0.006
Age squared	0.000***	0.000	0.000***	0.000	0.000***	0.000
Nonwhite[a]	0.041**	0.015	0.040**	0.015	0.043**	0.015
Education (in 1984, ref. group = high school graduate)						
Bachelor's degree	−0.074***	0.008	−0.075***	0.008	−0.074***	0.008
Less than high school	0.111***	0.015	0.111***	0.015	0.111***	0.015
Constant	−0.674***	0.112	−0.676***	0.112	−0.671***	0.112
n =	6,040		5,955		5,913	
Panel B: Respondents with pre-existing health limitations removed						
Jobless (ref. group = employed)	0.165***	0.038	0.187***	0.047	0.112[†]	0.064
Age (in 1984)	0.034***	0.005	0.035***	0.005	0.036***	0.005
Age squared	0.000***	0.000	0.000***	0.000	0.000***	0.000
Nonwhite[a]	0.046**	0.015	0.045**	0.015	0.047**	0.015
Education (in 1984, ref. group = high school graduate)						
Bachelor's degree	−0.067***	0.008	−0.069***	0.008	−0.068***	0.008
Less than high school	0.106***	0.016	0.106***	0.016	0.104***	0.016
Constant	−0.666***	0.110	−0.676***	0.111	−0.692***	0.110
n =	5,690		5,643		5,583	

[†]$p < .10$; *$p < .05$; **$p < .01$; ***$p < .001$; (two-tailed).

Notes: Standard errors are robust. Data use SIPP person weights adjusted for non-matches. Individuals who never received disability benefits and who died before the end of the 20-year observation period were removed from the model.

[a]Nonwhite = Hispanic, Black, Asian, and Other.

Table B2. Linear Probability Regressions of Mortality between 1983–2003.

	(1) All		(2) Involuntary		(3) Voluntary	
	Coeff.	SE	Coeff.	SE	Coeff.	SE
Panel A: Full analysis sample						
Jobless (ref. group = employed)	0.079**	0.028	0.073*	0.037	0.088*	0.041
Age (in 1984)	−0.030***	0.005	−0.029***	0.005	−0.031***	0.005
Age squared	0.000***	0.000	0.000***	0.000	0.000***	0.000
Nonwhite[a]	0.034**	0.013	0.033**	0.013	0.034**	0.013
Education (in 1984, ref. group = high school graduate)						
Bachelor's degree	−0.041***	0.008	−0.042***	0.008	−0.041***	0.008
Less than high school	0.038**	0.013	0.038**	0.013	0.038**	0.013
Constant	0.521***	0.106	0.499***	0.106	0.537***	0.106
$n=$	6,607		6,520		6,476	
Panel B: Respondents with pre-existing health limitations removed						
Jobless (ref. group = employed)	0.060†	0.032	0.065†	0.040	0.047	0.050
Age (in 1984)	−0.030***	0.005	−0.030***	0.005	−0.030***	0.005
Age squared	0.000***	0.000	0.000***	0.000	0.000***	0.000
Nonwhite[a]	0.033**	0.013	0.032*	0.013	0.034**	0.013
Education (in 1984, ref. group = high school graduate)						
Bachelor's degree	−0.037***	0.008	−0.039***	0.008	−0.038***	0.008
Less than high school	0.039**	0.013	0.038**	0.013	0.036**	0.013
Constant	0.518***	0.108	0.516***	0.109	0.522***	0.109
$n=$	6,215		6,164		6,106	

†$p<.10$; *$p<.05$; **$p<.01$; ***$p<.001$; (two-tailed).

Notes: Standard errors are robust. Data use SIPP person weights adjusted for non-matches.

[a]Nonwhite = Hispanic, Black, Asian, and Other.

APPENDIX C

Table C1. Parameter Estimates for Fixed-Effects Model of Earnings (with Interactions) for Respondents with Pre-Existing Health Limitations Removed.

Variable	All Jobless		Jobless Sub-Samples			
			Involuntary		Voluntary	
	(1)		(2)		(3)	
	Coeff.	SE	Coeff.	SE	Coeff.	SE
Dependent Variable = Social Security Earnings						
Pre2	457	1,060	332	1,309	762	1,764
Pre1	−2241†	1,296	−2,108	1,437	−2,583	2,704
0	−10,422***	1,379	−10,312***	1,695	−10,754***	2,269
Post1	−24,396***	1,561	−25,588***	1,869	−21,629***	2,765
Post2	−20,434***	1,738	−20,506***	2,133	−20,286***	2,896
Post3	−16,648***	1,743	−16,163***	2,088	−17,881***	3,095
Post4	−11,764***	1,818	−12,362***	2,317	−10,383***	2,609
Post5	−11,133***	1,898	−11,615***	2,385	−10,020***	2,863
Post6	−10,941***	1,983	−11,397***	2,437	−9,898**	3,250
Post7	−10,957***	1,978	−10,511***	2,418	−12,105***	3,290
Post8	−10,832***	1,923	−11,312***	2,359	−9,775**	3,180
Post9	−11,386***	1,953	−12,288***	2,374	−9,401**	3,286
Post10	−11,070***	1,949	−12,335***	2,281	−8,209*	3,565
Post11	−10,206***	2,054	−12,018***	2,446	−6,212†	3,592
Post12	−9,091***	2,158	−9,928***	2,723	−7,318*	3,314
Post13	−8,751***	2,193	−9,799***	2,769	−6,544†	3,361
Post14	−8,178***	2,216	−7,946**	2,718	−8,618*	3,673
Post15	−7,346***	2,215	−6,431*	2,633	−9,154*	3,898
Post16	−8,675***	2,364	−7,333*	2,848	−11,313**	3,998
Post17	−8,720***	2,448	−7,238*	2,912	−11,585**	4,253
Post18	−8,454**	2,674	−8,268**	3,199	−8,746†	4,677
Post19	−8,230**	2,855	−8,641*	3,399	−7,323	5,076
Post20	−7,257*	2,945	−7,010*	3,403	−7,731	5,465
Age	1,353***	297	1,383***	298	1,295***	298
Age, squared	−40***	3	−41***	3	−40***	3
Constant	22,228***	5,609	22,393***	5,624	22,810***	5,649
N (person-years)	125,336		124,256		123,030	

Notes: Models also include dummies for calendar year, and interaction terms for age and age-squared interacted with level of education (Bachelor's Degree or not) and level of earnings (above or below median earnings), and year interacted with level of education. All estimates are in 2008 dollars. Standard errors are clustered at the individual level. Weights adjusted for non-matches are applied.

$^{\dagger}p<.10$; $^{*}p<.05$; $^{**}p<.01$; $^{***}p<.001$.

Table C2. Parameter Estimates for Fixed-Effects Model of Disability (with Interactions) for Respondents with Pre-Existing Health Limitations Removed.

Variable	Jobless Sub-Samples					
	All Jobless		Involuntary		Voluntary	
	(1)		(2)		(3)	
	Coeff.	SE	Coeff.	SE	Coeff.	SE
Dependent Variable = Receipt of DI or SSI for Disabled Non-elderly						
Pre2	−0.003	0.007	−0.002	0.008	−0.003	0.010
Pre1	−0.003	0.007	−0.002	0.009	−0.003	0.010
0	−0.002	0.007	−0.002	0.009	−0.002	0.010
Post1	0.008	0.011	0.013	0.015	−0.002	0.010
Post2	0.023	0.015	0.034†	0.020	−0.004	0.010
Post3	0.038*	0.017	0.048*	0.022	0.014	0.018
Post4	0.077**	0.024	0.089**	0.031	0.048	0.031
Post5	0.077**	0.024	0.084**	0.031	0.061†	0.035
Post6	0.073**	0.024	0.080**	0.030	0.058	0.036
Post7	0.095***	0.026	0.112***	0.033	0.054	0.036
Post8	0.111***	0.029	0.123***	0.037	0.082†	0.042
Post9	0.126***	0.032	0.130***	0.039	0.117*	0.051
Post10	0.126***	0.032	0.136***	0.040	0.104*	0.050
Post11	0.125***	0.032	0.136***	0.041	0.099*	0.050
Post12	0.145***	0.035	0.157***	0.043	0.115*	0.054
Post13	0.140***	0.035	0.153***	0.045	0.112*	0.055
Post14	0.145***	0.036	0.149***	0.045	0.135*	0.059
Post15	0.137***	0.036	0.146**	0.045	0.116*	0.059
Post16	0.148***	0.038	0.169***	0.048	0.100†	0.058
Post17	0.144***	0.039	0.166***	0.049	0.095	0.059
Post18	0.155***	0.040	0.186***	0.051	0.084	0.060
Post19	0.165***	0.042	0.190***	0.052	0.108	0.067
Post20	0.165***	0.043	0.196***	0.053	0.096	0.067
Age	−0.016***	0.002	−0.016***	0.002	−0.016***	0.002
Age, squared	0.000***	0.000	0.000***	0.000	0.000***	0.000
Constant	0.275***	0.019	0.274***	0.019	0.269***	0.019
N (person-years)	138,599		137,457		136,041	

Notes: Models also include dummies for calendar year, and interaction terms for age and age-squared interacted with level of education (Bachelor's Degree or not) and level of earnings (above or below median earnings), and year interacted with level of education. All estimates are in 2008 dollars. Standard errors are clustered at the individual level. Weights adjusted for non-matches are applied.

$^{\dagger}p < .10$; $^{*}p < .05$; $^{**}p < .01$; $^{***}p < .001$.

Table C3. Parameter Estimates for Fixed-Effects Model of Mortality (with Interactions) for Respondents with Pre-existing Health Limitations Removed.

Variable	Jobless Sub-Samples					
	All Jobless		Involuntary		Voluntary	
	(1)		(2)		(3)	
	Coeff.	SE	Coeff.	SE	Coeff.	SE
Dependent Variable = Death of Respondent						
Pre2	0.005	0.004	0.005	0.005	0.004	0.008
Pre1	0.006	0.004	0.006	0.005	0.005	0.008
0	0.007	0.004	0.007	0.005	0.006	0.008
Post1	0.007	0.004	0.008	0.005	0.005	0.008
Post2	0.022	0.014	0.007	0.005	0.057	0.042
Post3	0.020	0.014	0.005	0.006	0.055	0.042
Post4	0.019	0.014	0.004	0.006	0.053	0.042
Post5	0.022	0.015	0.002	0.007	0.067	0.045
Post6	0.031†	0.017	0.008	0.011	0.083†	0.046
Post7	0.041*	0.019	0.023	0.017	0.081†	0.046
Post8	0.056*	0.024	0.046	0.028	0.077†	0.046
Post9	0.051*	0.024	0.041	0.028	0.072	0.046
Post10	0.052*	0.025	0.046	0.030	0.067	0.046
Post11	0.053*	0.026	0.049	0.031	0.062	0.045
Post12	0.071*	0.028	0.077*	0.035	0.056	0.045
Post13	0.063*	0.028	0.069*	0.035	0.048	0.045
Post14	0.055†	0.028	0.061†	0.035	0.040	0.046
Post15	0.058*	0.029	0.069†	0.036	0.032	0.045
Post16	0.056†	0.030	0.071†	0.037	0.022	0.046
Post17	0.058†	0.030	0.060	0.037	0.052	0.050
Post18	0.059†	0.031	0.057	0.038	0.060	0.053
Post19	0.059†	0.031	0.055	0.038	0.066	0.054
Post20	0.076*	0.034	0.084*	0.043	0.055	0.054
Age	−0.018***	0.002	−0.018***	0.002	−0.018***	0.002
Age, Squared	0.000***	0.000	0.000***	0.000	0.000***	0.000
Constant	0.297***	0.016	0.295***	0.016	0.295***	0.016
N (person-years)	155,317		154,059		152,633	

Notes: Models also include dummies for calendar year, and interaction terms for age and age-squared interacted with level of education (Bachelor's Degree or not) and level of earnings (above or below median earnings), and year interacted with level of education. All estimates are in 2008 dollars. Standard errors are clustered at the individual level. Weights adjusted for non-matches are applied.

†$p<.10$; *$p<.05$; **$p<.01$; ***$p<.001$.

APPENDIX D

Table D1. Propensity Score Estimates of Earnings (in the 20th year post job loss), 1983–2003.

Method	All Jobless (1)		Jobless Sub-Samples: Involuntary (2)		Jobless Sub-Samples: Voluntary (3)	
	Coeff.	SE	Coeff.	SE	Coeff.	SE
Panel A: Full analysis sample						
Nearest neighbor	−10,500**	3,370	−11,900***	3,613	−14,600*	5,783
Kernel	−17,400***	2,713	−19,100***	3,753	−20,700***	3,925
N	3,147		3,099		3,077	
Panel B: Respondents with pre-existing health limitations removed						
Nearest neighbor	−11,200**	3,683	−10,100**	3,899	−12,800†	6,853
Kernel	−18,700***	3,164	−19,000***	4,220	−21,300***	6,173
N	3,014		2,983		2,955	

Notes: All estimates use bootstrap standard errors based on 200 replications.
†$p < .10$; *$p < .05$; **$p < .01$; ***$p < .001$; (two-tailed).

Table D2. Propensity Score Estimates of Receipt of Disability Benefits (in the 20th year post job loss), 1983–2003.

Method	All Jobless (1)		Jobless Sub-Samples: Involuntary (2)		Jobless Sub-Samples: Voluntary (3)	
	Coeff.	SE	Coeff.	SE	Coeff.	SE
Panel A: Full analysis sample						
Nearest Neighbor	0.175***	0.038	0.172***	0.047	0.179**	0.056
Kernel	0.212***	0.035	0.206***	0.045	0.250***	0.056
N	6,040		5,955		5,913	
Panel B: Respondents with pre-existing health limitations removed						
Nearest neighbor	0.173***	0.040	0.192***	0.051	0.128*	0.059
Kernel	0.175***	0.037	0.197***	0.048	0.125†	0.064
N	5,690		5,643		5,583	

Notes: All estimates use bootstrap standard errors based on 200 replications.
†$p < .10$; *$p < .05$; **$p < .01$; ***$p < .001$; (two-tailed).

Table D3. Propensity Score Estimates of Mortality (in the 20th year post job loss), 1983–2003.

Method			Jobless Sub-Samples			
	All Jobless		Involuntary		Voluntary	
	(1)		(2)		(3)	
	Coeff.	SE	Coeff.	SE	Coeff.	SE
Panel A: Full analysis sample						
Nearest neighbor	0.059*	0.030	0.055	0.037	0.066	0.043
Kernel	0.060*	0.027	0.055	0.035	0.082†	0.044
N	6,607		6,520		6,476	
Panel B: Respondents with preexisting health limitations removed						
Nearest neighbor	0.046†	0.028	0.050	0.035	0.038	0.047
Kernel	0.041	0.028	0.043	0.036	0.037	0.053
N	6,215		6,164		6,106	

Notes: All estimates use bootstrap standard errors based on 200 replications.
$^{\dagger}p < .10$; $^{*}p < .05$; $^{**}p < .01$; $^{***}p < .001$; (two-tailed).